WHY CHIEF JUDGE JOHN ROBERTS SWITCHED HIS VOTE ON OBAMA CARE

ISBN: 1484905164
ISBN 13: 9781484905166

TABLE OF CONTENTS

WHY Chief Judge John Roberts Switch His vote on Obamacare

FOREWORD

This is a true story that explains why the Chief Judge of the United States Supreme Court, John Roberts switched his vote and voted to make the Obamacare law, legal in June 2012.

In June of 2012 all eyes was on the United States Supreme Court, waiting for the Supreme Court to make a decision on the so called Obamacare bill that Congress had made law.

Legalizing Obamacare would change the face of America, forever, regarding health care. The country was locked in the biggest debate since abortion and civil rights, regarding social issues facing America.

America was expecting Judge Roberts to vote with the four (4) other conservatives' judges on the Supreme Court. America was abuzz that the five conservatives would vote down the Obama health care law, which Congress had approved in 2009.

The buzz by most scholars was that the Supreme Court would vote down the entire law or at least the provision that the Federal Government could force every America to obtain an insurance policy that covered them.

When the Supreme Court upheld the Obamacare law, the country was shocked by Judge Roberts' vote. Across America it was abuzz that Judge Roberts, who was appointed to the Supreme Court by President George W. Bush, would vote against Obamacare. It was taken for granted that Judge Roberts would vote with the other conservatives, as he had on all other issues before this law. The conservatives in America were sure they had the 5 votes.

Speculation was that Judge Roberts had originally told his staff to draft a document denying Obamacare as a law in part and then later he changed his mind, telling his staff to draft an opinion that said the Obamacare law met the constitution.

This book addresses why Judge Roberts changed his mind and the events that led up to the time, Judge Roberts had to vote.

The Supreme Court is more political than the Congress.

The Democrats in the United States Senate and President Obama were searching for a way to convince one of the Supreme Court five (5) conservative judges to vote to make "Obamacare" legal and the law of the land. The President knew the other four judges of the nine (9) members of the court were liberal and he knew he could count on them to make Obamacare legal.

Shortly before the vote was to become final, the President and Democrat Senate leaders had a gift from God fall into their laps.

This book is about that gift from God and the events that took place, which changed Judge Roberts's mind and thereby changed history. There were a series of events, that individually, didn't mean anything, but the series of events added up and the pressure built on Judge John Roberts.

The series of events include a number of lawsuits that worked their way to the Supreme Court of America. It also includes a number of letters to the judges on the Supreme Court and letters to Senators in Congress. Mitch McConnell, Senate minority leader of the Senate, played a big role in Judge Roberts changing his vote.

The news media and law scholars were speculating that if any conservative judge would vote in favor of the Obamacare law it would be Judge Anthony Kennedy, who at times was the swing vote between the conservatives' judges and the liberal judges on the court.

The news media and law scholars have speculated about all kind of theories, why Judge Roberts changed from his conservative roots. The news media, law scholars and conservatives have speculated that maybe Judge Roberts had really believed that it was best for America, or Judge Roberts was at odds with Judge Scalia, about who was going to run the Supreme Court.

Then a perfect storm formed. The book will explain why Judge Roberts switched his vote. The series of events that changed his vote started in 2007. This book will consist mostly of actual court documents, which were created throughout various lawsuits cases. It also will contain letters to various people.

I am going to try and put in simple terms how lawsuits are handled in Federal Courts, for the benefit of people who don't understand the courts system. Everything about how the courts system functions is done by Rules of the Courts, so everyone is equal, if the courts themselves adhere to them. I the author did not know any of the rules when I started.

I, the author of this book was pro, se in all of my lawsuits, which led up to the facts in this book. Pro, Se in legal terms means acting as one's own attorney. Being Pro, Se is tough because the courts make you compete with educated attorneys and this is impossible. In fact it is discrimination.

Supreme Court rulings made me realized that the justice system in America is neither fair nor honest. The justice system does not protect the average person in America. I will explain why the system stinks and why it is not the system our forefathers wanted or what they originally established.

I sent documents to the Senate of Congress about lawsuits and these documents in the end applied pressure, which created Judge Roberts's actions. These documents will show and prove why Judge Roberts switched his vote.

I will put in simple terms what was happening in the court system, after Congress had passed the Obamacare law, a couple of years before.

Some group filed a complaint (lawsuit) in a Federal District Court, complaining that Obamacare was not constitutional and asked a judge to throw out the law.

In federal lawsuits after a complaint is filed, a judge in District Court will decide what happens next in a case.

Regarding the issue of Obamacare, after the complaint was filed, the District court judge made a ruling and that ruling was appealed to a Court of Appeals. The losing party in the Court of Appeals then appealed that ruling to the Supreme Court.

At the Circuit Court of Appeals level, a panel of judges, will review the lower court ruling, they will also ask for more documents to be presented by both parties. After both party presented their case, the panel of judges make a decision on the case. After the ruling by the Court of Appeals, President Obama appealed to the Supreme Court. The Supreme Court was going to make a ruling, based on the constitutional of the law. The entire country was waiting on a ruling with bated breath.

When a lawsuit is appealed to the Supreme Court, the party that is appealing the case must file what is called a Petition for a writ of Certiorari. In Supreme Court language this means lawsuits that have made their way to the Supreme Court, for the court to review, for errors by judges or for wrong rulings by judges and the constitutionally of the subject matter.. A Petition for writ of Certiorari is heard by the nine members of the Supreme Court and they decide if they will obtain the complete file and review the complete case. If the court denies the petition then the lawsuit is over and the ruling of the Court of Appeals is final.

The book will contain a summary of each lawsuit that I filed in federal court and how those lawsuits became part of why Judge Roberts came to his decision on Obamacare.

Each lawsuit involved will also contain a copy of the actual Petition to the United States Supreme Court.

The lawsuits that I filed played a role in Judge Roberts's decision to switch his vote. The outcome of my cases caused me to take other actions. The action I took led to other action that led to Judge Roberts switching his vote. The Supreme Court denied Certiorari on all 14 of my lawsuits. If the Supreme Court had granted Certiorari in one of my cases this book would have never been written.

The court documents and letters are true and factual. The book will also contain the author's comments and in the end, readers will not only know why Judge Roberts switched his vote, but also how the America's justice system is crumbling and how Judge Roberts didn't want to face fixing the system.

Other Justices on the Supreme Court was aware of and blessed the decision made by Judge John Roberts to switch his vote on Obamacare.

I am sure that are some who will dispute my facts, but the facts speak for themselves. A deal was made behind the scenes, which no one will admit to.

WHY CHIEF JUDGE ROBERTS SWITCHED HIS VOTE ON OBAMACARE

CHAPTER 1

A TRUE STORY BASED ON ACTUAL COURT DOCUMENTS, LETTERS TO MEMBERS OF CONGRESS AND PRESSURE PUT ON JUDGE ROBERTS.

The author is 82 years old, has lived through the great depression and seen the horrible conditions that the great depression brought to people, who lived during that time. The author credits the depression with instilling the appreciation for truth and the appreciation of hard work and being neighborly with all mankind, in him. The author lived through World War II and all wars thereafter. He lived through the civil rights issue and all other changes America have gone through since.

The author has a high school education, He had number of careers in his life, such as manufacturing, sales, race horse industry, working for Kentucky State government, lobbying in General Assemblies and other things in between, but he never studied law.

In 2007 the author lived in a condo and ran for the board of directors of the condo. He ran because he was asked to by a number of owners to run. However he didn't win and became convinced that the election was flawed. He discovered that the current Board of Directors had switched ballots on him.

The Holy Spirit told him that God wanted him to file a lawsuit, because God wanted the Devil out of the condo building. The Holy Spirit told the author that he, the Holy Spirit would tell him how to write the court documents and what to say. The author

1

reluctantly agreed and filed the lawsuit. It was hard, but with the Holy Spirit's guidance he was able to file the lawsuit. The Holy Spirit guided him on how and where to look for his research.

The author discovered in 2006 he had cancer of the prostate and had an operation.

The author was sold an illegal drug by Target Corporation. The Holy Spirit told the author to file a lawsuit against Target Corporation in Federal Court. The Holy Spirit told him God would have other lawsuits and ask the author to promise to file them. God promised that the author no harm would come to him and in the end it would help God do his will.

The author had never written a book in his life, had terrible grammar and couldn't spell a lot of four letter words. The Holy Spirit promised that it would be hard, but he the Holy Spirit would get him through the ordeal.

The author agreed he would do it, provided God kept him healthy of body and healthy of mind. At the age of 77 he started working night and day doing God's will.

The readers will see where the author is PRO, SE in court documents. Pro, Se means representing yourself in court.

The author filed two lawsuits, one against a Condo Association and one against Target Corporation, at the same time; he also started writing a book titled **"Understand Jesus is Simple"**. The Target lawsuit was filed in Federal Court in Louisville, Kentucky. The Condo lawsuit was filed in Jefferson County Circuit Court in Louisville.

The author wrote a book about the lawsuit he filed against Target Corporation. The book told how the Federal and Supreme Courts turned their head and helped Target sell illegal drugs to customers. How the courts didn't care what the law said, they were going to do as they please. The title of the book is **"CORRUPT JUDGES"**

The author didn't win any of his lawsuits. He had always believed the court system was fair and honest. He believed that with the Holy Spirit helping him he would win his cases, but he didn't.

The court system is neither fair nor honest on any level, from the smallest state court, to the United States Supreme Court. The author has lost every case and the Holy Spirit still tells him to keep his promise to do God's will. The Holy Spirit had me do things that I never thought I would do. It was hard and depressing.

The readers of this book will learn that the author was able to compete with the best lawyers and was able to file fourteen (14) Petitions for Certiorari with the United States Supreme Court. These 14 cases will lead the readers, to the reason Judge Robert's changed his vote and switched on the health care (Obamacare) law.

The book is about fourteen (14) lawsuits that were appealed to the United States Supreme Court. Most of the 14 lawsuits were against Judges, but two was against the Governor of Kentucky, one was against Churchill Downs race track, one against the New York and NASDAQ stock exchanges, one against Target Corporation, and one was against MetLife Insurance Company, one was against Hewlett Packard Company, along with a number of the State of Kentucky officials.

The Supreme Court of the United States is not about to let any lawsuits filed against large companies be tried by a jury, they know that juries do not protect large Corporations who harm people. The majority of the Supreme Court judges protect large companies, they protect their friends, and they protect corrupt judges and also any issue that might expose to the people the way the public is being treated by the American court system.

Read the case about the Stock Market which is Chapter 8 in the book, to find out how the Supreme Courts refuses to let the truth be known. People, who lost money in the stock market, will be sick when they read how the Supreme Court protects those who manipulate the stock market. The stock market is manipulated.

The United States Supreme Court was not about to let me win a case, because I had sued eleven (11) judges. I sued large corporations and asked for a lot of money, but for charity. I created a headache for the Supreme Court judges; one in particular and it was not Judge Roberts. It's the one who thinks only he knows what the founding fathers wanted, for the people, but he refuses to judge by what the founding fathers wanted. The one who is a bigger politician that most members of Congress. The one who has a large ego.

The readers will learn how the court system in America works and how we don't have the legal system that our forefathers wanted.

The constitution and laws means nothing to judges, specially the Supreme Court of the United States of America. All of these facts played a role in Judge Roberts switching his vote

To help you understand a judge's role in law cases, Judge John Roberts, Chief Judge of the United States Supreme Court explained it best on what a judge's role is. At Judge Roberts's confirmation hearing in the United States Senate, a Senator asked him what was a judge's duty and role. He stated and I quote, **"Judges are like umpires. Umpires don't make the rules. They apply them. The role of an umpire and a judge is critical. They make sure everybody plays by the rules. But it is a limited role."** Chief Judge Roberts has refused to make the courts live up to the duty and their role, as he explained it. This issue played into the reason Judge Roberts went against his belief and switched his vote on Obamacare as you will see.

I will cite you a Supreme Court case that every Federal court in America cites and uses, to let judges off the hook, if you sue one. The Case is **Stump v Sparkman 435 U.S. 349, 357 (1978).** This case was ruled on by the United States Supreme Court in 1978.

To help explain this case I have inserted from Wikipedia, the free encyclopaedia, the following four paragraphs.

1)- *Stump v. Sparkman*, 435 U.S. 349 (1978), is the leading United States Supreme Court decision on judicial immunity. It involved an Indiana judge who was sued by a young woman

2)- Judge Stump signed the requested order ex parte the same day that he received the petition. The daughter had no notice of it. No guardian was appointed to represent her interest, and no hearing was held. Neither the petition nor the order was filed with the clerk of the circuit court, nor did the order cite any statutory authority for the action being taken.

3)- Addressing Judge Swygert's assertion that even if Judge Stump had jurisdiction he was deprived of immunity because of his failure to observe elementary principles of procedural due process, Justice White countered:

4)- A judge is absolutely immune from liability for his judicial acts even if his exercise of authority is flawed by the commission of grave procedural errors. The Court made this point clear in Bradley, 13 Wall., at 357, where it stated "[T]his erroneous matter in which [the court's] jurisdiction was exercised, however it may have affected the validity of the act, did not make it any less a judicial act; nor did it render the defendant liable to answer in damages for it at the suit of the plaintiff, as though the court had proceeded without having any jurisdiction whatever...."

I have taken **From Wikipedia; the free encyclopaedia** a summary of the Supreme Court's ruling on the case and facts the following summary of them for you. I cut and inserted them below.

"A judge will not be deprived of immunity because the action he took was in error, was done maliciously, or was in excess of his authority. He will be subject to liability, only when he has acted in the clear absence of all jurisdictions"

In 1978, Judge Harold D. Stump granted a mother's petition to have a tubal ligation performed on her 15-year-old daughter, whom the mother alleged was "somewhat retarded." The petition was granted the same day that it was filed. The judge did not hold a <u>hearing</u> to receive <u>evidence</u> or appoint a <u>lawyer</u> to protect the daughter's interests. The daughter underwent the <u>surgery</u> a week later; having been told that she was to have her <u>appendix</u> removed.

The daughter married two years later. Failing to become <u>pregnant</u>, she learned that she had been sterilized during the 1971 operation. The daughter and her husband sued the judge and others associated with the sterilization in <u>federal district court</u>.

The District Court found that Judge Stump was immune, legally from any responsible, from the suit. The Seventh Circuit <u>Court of Appeals</u> reversed the decision, holding that the Judge Stump had lost his immunity because he failed to observe "elementary principles of <u>due process</u>" when he ordered the sterilization.

Finally, in 1978, the U.S. Supreme Court, in a 5-3 decision, reversed the Court of Appeals, announcing a test for deciding when judicial immunity should apply and holding that the judge could not be sued. Their ruling was **"A judge will not be deprived of immunity because the action he took was in error, was done maliciously, or was in excess of his authority. He will be subject to liability only when he has acted in the clear absence of all jurisdictions"**

Think about what the Supreme Court of America said in their ruling above, in 1978. No matter how dumb or how crazy or how maliciously any judge wants to be or how many laws the judges breaks, or how in excess of their authority, judges cannot be sued and held accountable for actions, in a court of law, in America.

The Supreme Court by their decision in 1978 created many, many loose cannon judges across America and those loose cannons fire quickly and often every day and at their pleasure, in our courts. They don't even smile when they destroy a person.

The 1978 case ruling by the Supreme Court was a bigger assault on America's freedom that the 2011 bombing on the World Trade Center. But an even bigger tragedy is the current Supreme Court refusing to stop the assault.

Every person in America can be held accountable for their action except judges. The President of our country and members of Congress can be held liable in courts, but Judges cannot he held liable. This ruling came from the highest court we have in our country and in their ruling they granted immunity to every judges across America, including them. They have immunity from being sued. It was the Supreme Court taking care of themselves and their fellow judges. The Supreme Court of the United States and all other courts though out America cites this authority as law on every case that involves a judge that has been sued.

I am not talking about the decisions a judge made based on the evidence in a case. I am saying any judge in America can violate any Federal or any state law or court rule and still have immunity. Any judge who is not fair and honest in every decision they make, are corrupt.

I sued 11 judges for violating of court rules or state and federal laws. Every judge was given absolute immunity by the District court were I filed the lawsuits and by every federal court of appeals when I appealed. The Supreme Court hid behind the privilege they have when you appeal to them. They just refuse to hear the case.

If a judge can't obey laws and court rules, then they shouldn't be a judge. It is as simple as that. The Supreme Court is giving judges absolute immunity for violating laws and Court rules. Our forefathers were looking for true justice, equal justice and that is what the Constitution is about. The Supreme Court has carried it to extremes and they fail to rule by the Constitution of the United States or court rules. They make up new rules to fit their needs.

They Supreme Court changed the meaning of the judge's code of conduct by the actions they took in 1978. If a judge is not smart enough to know the laws and rules then they should not be a judge. If a judge doesn't care enough to follow the laws and rules then they should not be a judge.

Either way, Americans will never know true justice, unless judges can be held liable for their actions. But don't hold your breath. This subject played a role in Judge Roberts switching his vote.

Congress approved a law that I will now insert it for you – **"42 U.S.C. § 1985(3) permits recovery of damages upon proof of a conspiracy "for the purpose of depriving, either directly or indirectly, any person or class of persons of the equal protection of the laws, or of equal privileges and immunities under the laws."** This law to me says a person can sue a judge for damages. This led me to believe that if a judge violated laws and court rules he could be sued and again this played into why Judge Roberts switched his vote.

Target Company, the one I sued was granted Summary Judgment by the trial Judge. The judge refused to let me try the case by jury.

I want to show you a Federal Court rule on Summary Judgment, it is Rule 56 and I will now insert the rule-

Federal Rules of Civil Procedure

Rule 56. Summary Judgment

MOTION FOR SUMMARY JUDGMENT OR PARTIAL SUMMARY JUDGMENT. A party may move for summary judgment, identifying each claim or defense — or the part of each claim or defense — on which summary judgment is sought. **The court shall grant summary judgment if the movant shows that there is no genuine dispute as to any material fact** and the movant is entitled to judgment as a matter of law. The court should state on the record the reasons for granting or denying the motion.

This says that a judge cannot grant summary judgment if any part of the complaint contains evidence that a jury can hear and judge. My complaints, my briefs and my responses, all had evidence, that a jury could hear and judge. Our constitution and the court's rule above, said that Summary Judgment should not be granted, but corrupt judges grant summary judgment any way.

My complaint against Target Corporation had 46 different issues that a jury could and should have heard. Instead the judge dismissed the entire case. The Judge's mind was made up on who was going to win the case, before the case started. The question is why.

Target gave me pills in my third fill of a prescription that was from a different manufacturing company, than the first two fills. Neither the pills nor the company that produced them was ever approved by the FDA to make these pills. The pills contained 230% more drugs, than they should have. The pills also had 10 different non-active drugs in them, which were not in the prior pills they had given me. The pills harmed my body in a number of ways. I will explain in the book, the whole story about this case. The trial Judge, then later the Sixth Circuit Court of Appeals and then the United States Supreme Court, by their action, OK'd and blessed the **selling of illegal drugs by Target**.

The author will start at the beginning and will copy the part of the complaint he filed in each lawsuit. He will copy part of the court orders. He will copy parts of briefs filed in the case. However he will copy the entire Petition for Certiorari to the Supreme Court in each case. The Petition will explain to the reader the case the way that the Supreme Court seen the case. These lawsuits played a role in Judge Roberts's vote, along with Senator Mitch McConnell who is the Minority Leader in the Senator and other Senators who are Democrats.

I will explain each lawsuit, what it was about, what the judges did and what the Court of Appeals did and what the Supreme Court did. I will also insert my letters to Congress about some of these cases. The author will give his comments on each document that he inserts and explain them. Everything that I explain can be found in the court documents of the cases. The court files are in the courts for anyone to read. Only after the entire history and explanation of these letters will the reader understand why Judge Roberts switch his vote on Obamacare.

The author will explain each issue that happened in this matter. He will explain everything he did trying to find justice. He wrote letters to Chief Judge Roberts, to other Judges on the Supreme Court, and to Members of the United States Senate. Mitch McConnell, who is Minority leader of the Senate, played a major role in this matter.

When you are finished reading the book you will know two things. One, we don't have a fair and honest justice system in America and two, the reason Judge Roberts switched his vote on Obamacare. I promise you will be surprised by the reason that caused Judge Roberts to switch his vote on Obamacare.

You have to read the legal documents in this book to fully understand how the book ends. The legal lawsuits in the book caused the ending.

CHAPTER 2

EDWARD H. FLINT V TARGET CORPORATION LAWSUIT

I will insert the complaint that I filed against Target, so you will understand the issues. The complaint I am inserting is an amended complaint that the trial judge refused to let me file. The rules of the courts state that every person can amend their complaint one time without any questions asked. But the judge in this case refused to let me amend mine.

UNITED STATES DISTRICT COURT
WESTERN DISTRICT OF KENTUCKY
LOUISVILLE DIVISON

CASE NO <u>3:07CV600-R</u>

EDWARD H. FLINT   PLAINTIFF

VS

TARGET CORPORATION   DEFENDANT

AMENDED COMPLAINT

Comes the Plaintiff, Edward H. Flint Pro, and Se amending his original complaint to the following:

On or about November 15, 2006 plaintiff was operated on for prostate cancer, On November 16, 2006 plaintiff was given a prescription by his doctor, with 2 additional refills for a drug named Pyridium (Phenazopyridine). Plaintiff had the prescription filled later the same day at a Target Store located at 4174 Westport Road in Louisville,

Kentucky and was directed to take three (3) pills per day. Plaintiff took the prescription as directed and with no problem.

On November 26, 2006 Plaintiff had the prescription refilled at the same store, again with no problems.

On December 6, 2006 plaintiff had the same prescription refilled again. The pills given him December 6, 2006 were a different shape and size. The pills purchased on December caused the Plaintiff to break out with red spots (hives) that itched and caused his mouth to draw up inside with small bumps or ridges, causing his tongue to go numb and Plaintiff stopped tasting food, and developed other problems.

After taking 8 of the pills purchased on December 6, 2007 Plaintiff quit taking the pills, and called his doctor, who confirmed not taking them.

On December 11, 2006 the plaintiff went to the Target store where the pills was purchased and spoke with the pharmacist Mr. Rob Warford, who was the pharmacy manager, about his problems from the pills. Plaintiff was told by Mr. Warford that he was not given the wrong medicine, but the pills were from a different company. Mr. Warford said all he could do for the Plaintiff was refund his cost of the pills. After Plaintiff complained further, Mr. Warford stated that the problem should go away in several days after Plaintiff stopped taking the pills. Rob the manager stated, Plaintiff should call Defendant's customer services if the problem didn't start to clear up in a couple of days. Plaintiff asked for the phone number and Mr. Warford gave him a card with a customer service number.

Before calling Target's customer service, Plaintiff waited a few days, as Mr. Warford suggested, and after getting no relief, Plaintiff called the Target customer service phone number on December 20, 2006 and told the person answering the phone, what happen with the drug. The person took the complaint, asking questions about what transpired, and said they would put the complaint into the computer and send it to the right department, and someone from that department would call Plaintiff in four (4) days.

The Plaintiff waited and after not hearing from anyone at Target, called the customer service phone number again on January 10, 2007. The person answering Plaintiff's call this time told the Plaintiff that his complaint from December 20, 2006 was in the computer, but she would put it in again. Plaintiff asked if there was someone else he could talk with about his problem. The person then gave Plaintiff a phone number saying it was the department who was responsible for this type of complaint.

Plaintiff called the number of the responsible department and a person by the name of Jenny answered the phone, Jenny was pleasant and very concerned. Jenny stated she would make sure the complaint was put in the computer again and said the person who would handle this complaint in the future was a person named Cindy. Jenny went to fine find Cindy at that time. Jenny could not find Cindy. Jenny stated she would have Cindy call the Plaintiff the next morning. The next morning when Cindy did not call Plaintiff, the Plaintiff called Cindy's number, her voice mail answered the phone, and Plaintiff left word for her to call, stating it was urgent. At 3:00P.M. Cindy called the Plaintiff and was very rude. Plaintiff then asked to speak with Cindy's boss. She said he was in a meeting and she would give him a message and Plaintiff's phone number.

A Mr. Wright returned the call about two (2) hours later, stating he was Cindy's boss. The Plaintiff told Mr. Wright the problem he was having. Mr. Wright said he would have another person call. The next day a Mr. Paul Wirkkala called Plaintiff and stated he was now handling the case. Mr. Wirkkala told Plaintiff that Target could not do anything about this problem, Target was not responsible for the pills content, and that they only sold the pills that Plaintiff should contact the manufacture of the pills for relief. Plaintiff communicated with Mr. Wirkkala about this matter, a number of times after that conversation, by both phone and letters, attempting to find the answer to who the manufacture was and what was in the pills that made him lose his taste and caused his injury.

Defendant refused to help Plaintiff find the solution to his injury and put the burden on the Plaintiff to find the solution. Plaintiff was told by Target that the manufacture was responsible, not Target.

Plaintiff alleges that he had expected to receive the same medication on December 6, 2006 as he received on November 16, 2006 and November 26, 2006 and Target failed to deliver the same medication.

Plaintiff alleges that Target failed to live by its own policy by not notifying Plaintiff that it changed suppliers, regarding the pills Plaintiff received pills on December 6, 2006. The pills and type of drug dispended to Plaintiff on December 6, 2006 were from a different manufacture, than the first two fills of pills he received on November 16, 2006 and November 26, 2006. Target has a written policy that states, when it dispenses subsequent refills of prescriptions to quest that are manufactured by a different company than prior fills, Target notifies quests of the change by placing a green sticker on the bottle that states "This is the same medication you have been getting. Color, size or shape may appear different". Target did not place a green sticker on the bottle that contained the pills Plaintiff was given on December 6, 2006. The medication was not the same as in the first two fills.

Plaintiff alleges that with the pills Target dispensed to Plaintiff on December 6, 2007, Target also gave Plaintiff a "Patient Card", which stated the pills side effects would be Headaches and Belly Pain. The Patient Card never notified Plaintiff that the pills would cause hives. The dispended pills Plaintiff received on December 6, 2006 caused him to break out with hives over his body including his lips, tongue and mouth. The hives caused Plaintiff to lose his taste and other injuries to his body.

Plaintiff alleges that the thirty (30) pills he received on December 6, 2006 which contained one (1) active ingredient and fifteen (15) in-active ingredients, were defective. The pills compositions were different in types of materials, in weight of pill and in size of pill than the pills were from the two fills Plaintiff had received in November, 2006.

Plaintiff contents that Target cannot shrug off the blame for defective drugs and put the blame on the manufacture or on Plaintiff. It is clear that the system Target has set up on obtaining drugs has faults. Plaintiff did not and could not control the quality of drugs Target receives.

Plaintiff alleges that the pills sold to him on December 6, 2006 by Target were out of the Manufacture's Specification tolerance limit in weight; and these pills should have been rejected and never sold to any customers.

Plaintiff alleges that Target sent two pills from the batch, Plaintiff's pills came from to Breckenridge to be tested and Target refuses to give Plaintiff the test results.

Plaintiff alleges that Target was neglectful in their responsibility to Plaintiff.

Plaintiff alleges that the Defendant switched suppliers of drugs, with no consideration for the health of their customers.

Plaintiff alleges Target did not test the complete finished pills before or after receiving them from the manufacture, for safety, before selling to Plaintiff.

Plaintiff alleges that Target was more concern about their own profits than about customer's health.

Plaintiff alleges that Target had no control over the drugs they sold, from the time the drug was ordered, to the time the container from the supplier was opened at Target's Louisville store.

Plaintiff alleges that Target did not purchase the pills from a manufacture. Target contracted with a distributing company to purchase and keep Target's stores stock with drugs. Target didn't know who was manufactured the drugs they sold and told Plaintiff to take his injury problem to the manufacture and not to blame Target.

Plaintiff alleges that Target at no time had control and never attempted to have control over the quality of the pills they sold to Plaintiff. Target had no control over the raw materials that went in the pills or no control over the manufacturing process of the pills or even as much as an agreement with any supplier that the pills shipped to Target would be certified safe for human consumers. Target has failed to establish a safety program regarding drugs consumed by humans purchased from their stores.

Plaintiff alleges that Target has set up a supply system, starting at purchasing; all the way through to delivery to Targets stores, without any consideration for consumer's safety or any system that guarantees consumer's drug safety.

Plaintiff alleges that Target refused to hold their supplier responsible to identify the ingredient in the pill which caused plaintiff's problems.

Plaintiff alleges that Target refused to attempt to find a solution to clear up the Plaintiff's health problems, except to give Plaintiff at his request, some information about who manufactured the pills in question, the active and in-active materials contained in the pills. This information turned out to be wrong and misleading. Target themselves didn't know who the manufactures of the pills was.

Plaintiff alleges that Target has a Fiduciary Duty and Responsibility to their customers and failed to perform that Duty and Responsibility when selling the flawed pills to Plaintiff.

Plaintiff alleges that Target dispended drugs to Plaintiff over which they had no control over at any time and their lack of control, injured Plaintiff.

Plaintiff alleges that Target pushed Plaintiff's health to the side and refused to find the source of what caused Plaintiff's injury.

Plaintiff alleges that Target has never attempted to have their suppliers certify the in-active materials in prescriptions drugs as being safe for customers.

Plaintiff alleges that Target failed to take Plaintiff injury and complaint serious and failed to write up Plaintiff's injury and complaint as an incidence report, required by their own policies.

Plaintiff alleges that after he warned them, Target refused to take serious that other customers could be affected, by the pills, which harmed the Plaintiff.

Plaintiff alleges that Target knew that when applying for the right to do business in Kentucky, they took on the responsibility to supply safe drugs to their customers, they also knew they would have to take all steps to correct any harm done to their customers caused by their produces and Target failed to live to this responsibility.

Plaintiff alleges that Target broke the trust that the State of Kentucky granted them by granting them the right to do business in Kentucky. Target when applying for the right to do business in Kentucky, knew that with the right, there was a trust to sell safe products to consumers.

Plaintiff alleges that when Target applied for and received the right to do business in the State of Kentucky; they took on the responsibility and duty to deliver safe drugs to all Kentucky citizens. If the burden of such Responsibility and Duty was too heavy for Target to carry, Target should not have applied for or accepted the right to sell drugs in Kentucky.

Plaintiff alleges that Target has a duty to its customers to completely investigate serious health complaints and not tell customers that, they the customers must contact the manufactures for relief.

Plaintiff alleges that a trust exist between Doctor, Patient and Pharmacies, and Target breached that trust when they sold flawed pills to Plaintiff, Target had the responsibility to assure the pills was safe.

Plaintiff alleges that Target has failed to attempt to have Breckenridge or any other testing facilities to run test on all ingredients that were contained in the pills in question, to find out if foreign materials or overages was in the pills.

Plaintiff alleges Target has refused to demand that Breckenridge produce the test results, which Breckenridge stated they ran on the two pills, which had been sent to them by the Target store in Louisville. The two pills sent were from the same container as the pills that injured Plaintiff came from.

Plaintiff contends that Target may have broken other laws or regulations that have not come forward as of this time, that may before or during trial.

WHEREFORE, the Plaintiff demands the following relief

1- A trial by jury

2- If Defendant is found guilty of any allegation in this complaint, or found guilty of neglect on any other issue that was due to Plaintiff, or broke any law or regulation that may come forward during trial, then Plaintiff demands Defendant be held accountable by the demands in the following 5 paragraphs.

3- Defendant is ordered to use all efforts possible and to pay all cost necessary, to find the cause and cure for Plaintiff's health problems cause by the pills sold to Plaintiff on December 6, 2006

4- Plaintiff is award financial damages as determined by a jury, both compensatory and punitive damages.

5- Plaintiff also demands that this court orders the Defendants to develop a policy that states, "all in-active materials in prescription drugs that Target sells, are certified to contain no harmful materials" and hang a sign it their stores stating the policy.

6- For all cost of this suit.

7- For any other relief to which said plaintiff may appear entitled.

Respectfully submitted

Edward H. Flint Pro, Se

After the District Court refused to let me file the amended complaint, that I was entitled to, I filed another motion with the court asking for permission to amend the complaint and add two companies to the complaint, as defendants. The Court refuse to answer my motion and then the court granted summary Judgment for Target and against me. Summary Judgment means that Target wins and I don't get to try my case in front of a jury.

The motion I filed to add two companies follows.

UNITED STATES DISTRICT COURT
WESTERN DISTRICT OF KENTUCKY
LOUISVILLE DIVISON

CASE NO <u>3:07CV600-R</u>

EDWARD H. FLINT   **PLAINTIFF**

VS

TARGET CORPORATION   **DEFENDANT**

<u>PLAINTIFF'S MOTION FOR LEAVE TO JOIN TWO (2) OTHER PARTIES INTO THIS COMPLAINT AS DEFENDANTS</u>

Comes the Plaintiff Edward H. Flint Pro, Se, making a motion for leave to join two (2) other parties into this complaint as defendants and conspirators.

Breckenridge Pharmaceutical Inc.-1141 S. Rogers Circle, Suite 3-Boca Raton, FL 33487 and Contract Pharmacal- 135 Adams Avenue-Hauppauge NY 11788.

Contract Pharmacal was the manufacturer of the pills that injured Plaintiff.

Contract then sold the pills to Breckenridge Pharmaceutical who sold them to Target's suppler.

Plaintiff has been unable to take depositions from Breckenridge or Contract.

Breckenridge has twice refused to show for subpoenaed depositions and has also refused to produce subpoenaed documents.

Contract has failed to show for a subpoenaed deposition.

Plaintiff has not obtained enough discoveries to know what part McKesson Corporation played in his injury.

Therefore Plaintiff makes the following motion.

MOTION

Plaintiff moves that he be given leave to join Breckenridge Pharmaceutical and Contract Pharmacal into this suit as Defendants and Conspirators.

Respectfully submitted

Edward H. Flint Pro, Se

I appealed the District Court's order to the Sixth Circuit Court of Appeals and a copy of the brief I submitted starts here.

CASE NO. 09-5153
UNITED STATES COURT OF APPEALS
FOR THE SIXTH CIRCUIT

EDWARD H. FLINT,   Plaintiff – Appellant

v.

TARGET CORPORATION,   Defendant – Appellee

On Appeal from the United States District Court
For the Western District of Kentucky
Civil Case No. 3:07CV6000R

APPELLANT'S BRIEF

STATEMENT OF THE ISSUES PRESENTED FOR REVIEW

Did the trial court error by granting Defendant/Appellees Summary Judgment motion, prematurely.

1) Did the trial court error in not considering Plaintiff's/Appellant's evidence made in his allegations objecting to Appellees motion for summary judgment and **2)** did the court err in not letting a jury decide the merits of the case, instead of the trial court using only the Appellees evidence (which is little).

1) did the trial court error in interpreting the laws it used and if not, **2)** then are the laws unconstitutional? **3)** Has the Supreme Court recent ruling in Wyeth Pharmaceutical changed the landscape on who can be sued?

Did the court err- **1)** in not letting Appellant complete discoveries ---**2)** did the court err in not ruling on forty seven (47) motions of Appellant's for discoveries and other issues regarding this case ---**3)** did the court err in not compelling three persons who refused to show up for depositions, after being subpoenaed,--- **4)** did the court err in squashing the deposition of a very important witness to Appellant, for no reason,--- **5)** did the court err in not making Appellees compel on discoveries,---- **6)** did the court err in refusing to grant Appellant leave to file an amended complaint and by using the original complaint in the trial court consideration of Summary Judgment,--- **7)** did the court err in not granting Appellant leave to file an amended complaint that joined two (2) in not letting Defendants to the complaint and adding more allegation against Appellees in the complaint,---**8)** did the court err in refusing to grant Appellant's Motion to Compel a company that refused to honor a subpoena to produce documents ---**9)** did the court err in refusing to rule on Appellant motion asking that the Counsel's for Appellees be removed for conspiring with a company that was a adverse witness that Appellant had subpoenaed for deposition and who refused to show for deposition, and then hired Appellees Counsel to draft an agreement to sign for Appellant to sign. (which he would not), --- **10)** did the court err in not ruling on other motions regarding poor conduct by three (3) Counsels for Appellees, ---**11)** did the court err by not giving Appellant a fair and honest opportunity at a fair trial by not letting the discovery go forward.

STATEMENT OF FACTS IN THIS CASE

Edward Flint Appellant is 78 years and was operated by a surgeon for cancer of the prostate on November 15, 2006 and was given a prescription for the drug Pyridium (Phenazopyridine), when he left the hospital. Flint took the prescription to a Target Pharmacy to be filled. Flint was to take three (3) pills per day and after the first fill of the prescription ran out with no problems, again on November 26, 2006 Flint had Target refill the prescription and took them with no problems. On December 6, 2006 Flint had the drug refilled again for the third time. The pills he received from in the last refill were different in weight, shape, and size and content. The instructions and literature on the last fill package was the same as the first two. There were no markings on the container warning Flint that they were from a different company. After taking eight (8) pills of the last refill he broke out with hives in his mouth, on his tongue and in his groin area. Flint called his Doctor who told him to quit taking the pills and go ask Target if the different pills were given to him in error. Flint went to the Target store and was told that he had the right drug, but they were from a different company. Tests by an independent testing laboratory has measure the weigh both the last pills Flint had retained and pills like from the first refills, which Target sent to the lab. The test results showed that the last pill Mr. Flint was given weighed two-hundred (230%) and thirty percent more that the pills of first two fills. Test on last pills Appellant received from Target that caused the injury--Louisville Testing Laboratory weigh of 21 pills on samples received 2/29/08. The results shows every pill was over the norm which was .750 grams +or- 5% and six (6) pills which is 28.57% over the maximum allowed tolerance which was .7875 grams. Test on Five (5) pills that were shipped to Louisville Testing Laboratory by Target based on a court order and the weight of the 5 pills received on 6/20/08. The average weight was .342 grams. The normal weight different was to be .750 vs. .340 or 221%. The actual weight as measured was 230% different between the two pills, which means the last pills Appellant received was 230% heavier in weight that the first 2 fills he had, which means the content was 230% more in content of ingredients, or more than twice a regular dose.

Flint went to his family Doctor, who sent him to an allergy specialist, who ran test and stated in a letter and again in a deposition that it could have been cause by either the active or inactive materials in the pills.

Target Corporation has stated in discovery that they sell nothing but FDA approved drugs. Appellant was not allowed to prove to a jury that the pills he received, was not FDA approved and had never been approved by the FDA, in fact the manufacturer of the pills never applied to the FDA for approval. Target would not give an FDA approved certificate.

Appellant on July 8, 2008 took the deposition of a person Target designated, Mr. Will Greygor who is a pharmacist. On page 16 when asked if all of prescription drugs sold by Target FDA approved and he answered," yes" and he added it would be illegal for us to dispense any medication that wasn't approved by FDA. And on page 18 he answered 'Well FDA – approved medication is one that is safe and effective for use in the United States After examining data sheets that Target had given Appellant regarding the in-active ingredients in both the pills Mr. Flint had taken from the first two fills and the last fill that injured him, on page 84 Mr. Greygor testified that that both pills contained 15 in-active ingredients and only five (5) were the same in both and ten (10) were different. This means that the manufacturer of the last fill use 10 different ingredients in producing their pills. And on page 87 he testified to a question of "So if one medication got changed then it could affect a person regardless, right" " answer "if something changed they could have an adverse reaction to it, yeah. I mean, if there was an ingredient in one tablet versus an ingredient in another tablet that changed that they were allergic to yeah it could happen"

The injury caused to Flint was permanent and Flint still has the damage from the drugs he was given and Doctors believe that after this period of time, the injuries will be permanent. Some of the damage caused by the pills are 1-Flint has lost his taste 2- Flint's groin area has to be cleaned and have ointment put on it 2 to 3 times per day 3- Flint has hot flashes that occur at any time 4- Flint cannot sleep on his right side without his nose clogging up and he can't breathe and there are other injuries.

Flint asked for help from Target a number of times in both written communicate and verbal communication over the phone. Target refused to help and told Flint that he needed to talk with from the manufacture, that Target has no responsible for the pills they sell. Flint found out that the pills in question went through three (3) companies before reaching Target's store. After trying to get help with no luck then Flint file a complaint.

AGRUMENT

First, yes appellant is Pro, Se, but he has good common sense and understanding of the law or at least the intent of the law. Second this case lays at the feet this court, about what and who has a responsibility to consumers of prescriptions drugs. Prescription drugs are the most dangerous product sold in mass in the world today, and the one product everyone needs sometime in their lifetime and the one product a person has no control over. The trial court ruling will affect not only Target, but all pharmacies that dispense medications. The ruling this court now makes will have an effect on every person in America that will ever need prescription drugs. Appellant begs this court to read every pleading, document, order etc., in the files of this case before deciding their verdict.

The trial court ruled prematurely on issues that a jury should have rule on, the trial court issued an order without holding a hearing on the facts and in the trial court's Memorandum they relied on Appellees statements, but did take into account Appellants statements. The trial court based its ruling on facts that are either, not true or not the complete story. The court based its ruling on Kentucky laws that Appellants believe the court mis-interpreted or else the law is unconstitutional.

There are many separate issues involved. Does Target have a duty regardless of who the manufacture was, did Target have a duty beyond the duty as stated by the trial court? The trial court's rulings sounds like Target have no responsible except to delivery of the drugs to the patient regardless (which is what Target claims). Appellant raised the question and still does, did Target have a duty to investigate the manufacturing company to make sure the pills were FDA approved, to check the material specifications for the pills and including checking to see the FDA certificate of approval before ordering the pills.

Appellant was denied by the trial court the opportunity to fully investigate; Forty-seven (47) of Appellants Motions are still not ruled on. Appellees were allowed to lie, change answers without a court order, allowed to submit evidence that had the ends of documents covered before being copied, allowed not to produce documents required by CR, and to do everything to choke off Appellant efforts, including allowing the changing of answers previous given in request for documents and interrogatories. Appellant sent motions and documentation to the trial court about these actions and the trial court still let it happen. Appellant asked through motions to amend his original complaint, and the court refused to rule. Appellant then filed a motion to an amended his complaint that added the manufacturer and distributor of the pills in question to the complaint as defendants, the court refuses to rule. Appellant was not allowed to probe into Target's records. He was not allowed to have documents relating to McKesson (the fourth company involved in these pills). Target has testified that McKesson purchases the drugs, and until Appellant can obtain discovery per CR he doesn't know if McKesson should be made a Defendant or not. Appellant requested documents regarding contracts with McKesson showing the two companies' relationship and Target refused to product the documents, stating they would not produce any useful information, And now Target in their DISCLOUSE OF CORPORATE AFFILATIONS AND FINANCIAL INTEREST to this Court states and I quote **"McKesson Corporation will indemnify Target unless claim is due to the negligence of Target."** Appellant file a motion for Target to compel on this issue. The trial court refused to rule on the motion. Also Appellant was denied by the court to take the deposition of the President of Target, for no reason.   Also three (3) others company's personnel were allowed not to show up for a deposition for which subpoenas were issued. Companies on which a subpoena was served to produce documents failed to do so and the court would not compel after motions were filed to do so. Counsels for Appellee Target was allowed by the trial court to do as they wish, including talking with a witness who was not a Target witness, which Appellant had subpoenaed and then Appellees counsel conspired with the witness and the trial court turned their head after Appellant filed motion to compel and dismiss that Counsel. Appellees filed a motion for summary judgment and after Appellant responded, the trial court let Appellee file a second motion for summary judgment before asking for leave to do so and before asking to remand the first one. After appellant complained, the trial court then allowed the first motion to be remanded. There is nothing fair about the trial court granting Appellees anything they want and have refused to rule on Appellant 47 motions. Appellant submitted Exhibits with every pleading he filed, if one was required. Not lawyer could have done a better job with the facts that what Appellant has, except the legal language and the straight talk he used in telling the truth, which some don't like to hear. This case is a travesty, unless the courts believe that drugs retailers can substitute a different formula in place of one the FDA approved.

Appellant will now make his case for why this court should reverse the trial court's granting Appellees their motion for summary judgment.

1- All parties in a lawsuit by CR have a right to take depositions and the only way a witness can be excused is when the court is asked for a protective order and it is granted. All parties have a right to discovery for the producing of document and all parties have to produce when served, unless the court grants an order otherwise. All parties have a right to file motions and expect the court to rule within a reasonable length of time. The trial court issued an order on September 30, 2008 stating over fifty non disposition motions are pending and Appellant believes forty seven (47) of them are his. When these actions don't take place, then the legal system fails its mandate. Appellant was denied these rights many times in this case. In appellant Motion for leave filed on August 27, 2008 he made allegations that he believes the trial court overlooked in the decision. By the trial court not granting Appellant his motion, the court didn't look at his allegations, again Appellant made these same allegation in his responses to Appelees second motion for summary judgment and other pleadings, however if Appellant had been granted leave to amend his complaint and added more defendants and been granted more time for discovery as he asked for by motion, he is positive he would have produced lots more solid evidence. Not to allow Appellant to amend his complaint is against everything the court system is about. The rules clearly state leave should be given freely. To make this subject clear to this court, in May, 2008 appellant filed a motion to amend his original complaint. In an order dated June 10, 2008 the court denied the motion; because Appellant had not attached a proposed amended copy. However the court gave Mr. Flint ten days to renew his motion and attach a proposed amendment for the courts consideration. Appellant resubmitted his motion on June 13, 2008 with an attached amended complaint. The trial court has not ruled as of this date. Also Appellant decided that to find all guilty parties to his injury he had to join both the manufacture and distributor to the complaint. On August 27, 2008 Appellant filed the following motion **"Plaintiff moves this court, to grant Plaintiff leave to amend the original complaint with the attached complaint which also joins two (2(other) Defendants and if this motion is granted then Plaintiff asks for leave to remand the motion he filed on June 13, 2008 on which this court has not rule."** Appellant also filed another motion on the same day August 27, 2008 filed a motion **"for leave to join two other parties into this case as Defendants."** Appellant filed this motion attempting to cover all his bases. It is clear Appellant was attempting to join 2 others into the case, somehow.

Appellant on July 14, 2008 filed a motion **FOR JUDGMENT IN HIS FAVOR, DEFENDANT BE HELD IN CONTEMPT AND TARGET COUNSEL REMOVED FROM THIS CASE.** The trail court never ruled on this motion.

2-   The trial court stated and I quote, **"what is the specific duty of care owned by pharmacists to their customers"** The court then made the case those **pharmacists under similar circumstances- that are to dispense the correct medication in accordance with the prescribing physician's instructions.** However there is more to pharmacist's duties than just that just dispensing the correct drug. Target has a policy to notified customers when the dispense pills are from a different supplier. Target testified they had a policy, the Target exact language when they testified was and I quote **Target notifies quests of the change by placing a green sticker on the bottle that states "This is the same medication you have been getting. Color, size or shape may appear different".** (The court should note that the label doesn't say anything about being heavier or having different ingredients, which there were in the pills the appellant received that injured him) Appellant has sworn that there no label was on the bottle that contained the pills that injured him and therefore a matter for a jury to decide who is right.

The trial court based its ruling on the pharmacist's duties only, but the trial court forgot that Target Corporation itself is being sued and there are more Target personnel involved than pharmacists, in selling drugs to customers. Target hides behind the "middle" man law and don't worry about customer safety, because they believe they are protected from lawsuits. The question is can Target order or receive drugs from a company without checking to see if the drugs are FDA approved or can the just tell suppliers, send me some drugs and not worry about the customer. The question is, is Target obligated to check out the companies for quality control or do they just order and not worry about the quality of the drugs they sell. In other words, it's for this court to answer what responsibility the so called middle man has, if any on such a dangerous product.

Appellant was given a sheet that was a "**Patient Education**" page. He was given the same document for each fill of the drug regardless of the manufacture of the pills. The sheet is a document that Target gives when filling prescriptions. Appellant was given the same Patient Education document for all three fills. The first two fills did not affect Appellant however when Target gave Appellant pills from another manufacture, those pills broke Appellant out with hives. The Patient Education page stated and I quote" **POSSIBLE SIDE EFFECTS: SIDE EFFECTS that may go away during treatment, include headache, stomach upset or cramps, if they continue or are bothersome, check with your doctor".** Again it said nothing about hives. In addition Appellant also received a printed card called **PATIENT INFO CARD** with each fill of the pills and that card stated and I quote **"Patient Card," which stated the pills side effects could be Headaches and Belly Pain.** Should a customer should be able to rely on information that comes with their medicine? **Neither the Patient Education sheet nor the Patient Card given Appellant notified Appellant that the pills would cause hives, which it did.** The manufacture of the pills had nothing to do with the patient education sheet or card; Target designed and printed the card and sheets themselves to inform their customers, so Target had a direct responsibility to give Appellant Flint the right instructions. Why would a customer expect hives if the Card and sheet didn't say so?

Target has an obligation to fill all 3 fills called for on the prescription filled with the same ingredients. The first two fills of pills that Appellant received had 16 ingredients 1 active and the other 15 in-active. The last fill of pills Appellant received also had 16 total ingredients. However of the 15 in-active ingredients in the last fill, ten (10) of the ingredients, where different chemicals than the first two fills. Did the manufacturer make the changes or did Target have the responsibility to know before ordering what changes were going to be made. Whose responsibility was it to make sure the drugs were the same each time. Two Target employees Rob Warford and Will Greygor both pharmacist testified in their depositions that the inactive ingredients in the pills are all chemicals and all can be as harmful as the active ingredient. How would a consumer know who was at fault and who to sue? If the manufacturer only was sued, he could use the excuse that he delivered what Target ordered or he told Target what was going to be in the pills or he could say Target never asked about inactive ingredient. Appellant finally came to the conclusion that the only way to find who was responsible was to sue all involved and let a jury decide who was guilty and who was not guilty. The trial court should have ruled that Appellant could amend his original complaint and joined the manufacturer and the distributors in the suit.

Target refused to help Appellant find the solution to his injury and put the burden on the Plaintiff to find the solution. Appellant was told by Target that the manufacture was responsible, not Target. In this case ever Target didn't know who the manufacturer was, Target told Appellant that Breckenridge Pharmaceuticals was the manufacturer. Even the trial court in its opinion, states Breckenridge is the Manufacturer. As Appellant found out later the manufacturer of the pills in question was Contract Pharmacal. How can patients help themselves in such complicated issues? The pills in question went through four company's hands before Appellant received them. Drugs the most harmful produce that most people use, has to have some restriction or we are going to kill a lot of people and the only way to make businesses like Target take the responsibility is to hold them accountable in court. There are plenty of reasons Target can and should be tried in court for issues other than just dispensing the right drug. Other than the "middle man" theory the trial court used, there are plenty of issues the court should have considered and should not have granted summary judgment.

The court stated and I quote" **in Kentucky, there are two possible theories of recovery against pharmacists who dispense allegedly medication: negligence and product liability. In this matter, there exists no genuine issue of material fact that would permit plaintiff to proceed to trial against Target on either claim. Accordingly, for the reasons stated herein, the courts will grant Target's motion for summary judgment and dismiss this action.**" This trial court was saying 1) that Target does not have to notify customers when they change suppliers, Target's Patient's Cards or Patient Education sheets that they give customers about the effects of the drug, has no meaning, 2) that Target has no responsibly to make sure the drugs formula has been FDA approved, 3) that Target has not responsibly to check out companies to make sure they have quality control on each batch they purchase through certification of each shipment they receive, to assure customers they drugs are safe. 4) That Target has no responsibly to make sure the compound of in-active ingredients are the same as they had been dispensing to customers in like drugs. 5) That Target has no responsibly and can do as they please and they have protection. The trial court has thrown a blanket of security over Target and every business in America that dispenses drugs. Appellant believes a jury should decide these facts.

The trial court stated in its opinion memorandum and I quote **"the court has reviewed Target motion, Mr. Flint's response thereto, and the evidence of record in this case."** This cannot be so because Mr. Flint made allegations that he gave to the court and that he can prove to a jury and the court completely overlooked this record. The trial court took for granted that Appellant would not fine any other evidence, if he was given the opportunity, as he asked for in his motions, and if he was allowed to joined the other parties to the suit, If Appellees had been made to live by CR regarding discovery it would have made a big different. No court can look at the evidence and motions without drawing a different conclusion.

In the trial courts **II** it stated and I quote **"It is well known to all in the legal community by now, but because Mr. Flint is acting as his own counsel it bears repeating that summary judgment as a matter of law is proper only when there exists no genuine issue of material fact, Fed. R. Civ.P.56 (c) (emphasis added) in considering a motion for summary judgment, this court must construe the evidence and draw all reasonable inferences in favor of the non-moving party (in this case, Mr. Flint). Matsushita Elec. Indus. Co v. Zenith Radio Corp., 475 U.S. 574, 587 (1986) and determine "whether the evidence presents a sufficient disagreement to require submission to a jury or whether it is so one-sided that one party must prevail as a matter of law" Anderson v. Liberty Lobby, Inc., 477 U.S.242, 251-52 (1986).** Appellant stated and does so again that there is plenty of evidence to present to a jury and if the case is allowed to for forward and the trial courts rules on Appellant's motions there will be a lot more evidence to present to a jury, the trial court jump to the wrong conclusions.

To defeat Target motion for summary judgment, Mr. Flint must point to in record. Or proffer, actual evidence." Mr. Flint has pointed out a number of places in the record as well as Supra in this brief. There are many numbers of genuine issues that a jury should decide and summary judgment should not have been granted.

The trial court stated **"that Mr. Flint in his claim for Negligence must establish the following four elements of the chain that the court described in terms particular to Mr. Flint allegation.**

That Target owed Mr. Flint a duty of care

That Target breached that duty

That Mr., Flint suffered injury, and that the injury he allegedly suffered was direct or proximately cause by Target breach of its duty of care

The court continued and asked the question. What is the specific duty of care owed by pharmacists to their customers? In Kentucky, the care owed is the duty of care used by ordinarily skillful and prudent pharmacists under similar circumstances- that is to dispense correct medication in accordance with the prescribing physician's instructions." Once again the court has shifted the subject only to the store pharmacists and away from Target Corporation. The buying of the drugs and the specification of the drugs content and information given patients are Target Corporations duties. Pharmacists at the stores can only dispense drugs they are given and they have no control over purchasing of the drugs or who makes the drugs, or the control of the content of drugs.

In this case the Pharmacists did had a duty to put a label on the bottle warning Mr. Flint that the last fill was produced by another company and he failed to do that.

Target had a duty to deliver and breached that duty by not delivering to Mr. Flint a drug equal to the fills he had been given previously. Instead they delivered a pill that was two hundred and thirty (230%) percent heavier in weight, that the previous pills they had given Mr. Flint, a pill which ingredients contained ten (10) different chemicals than the other pills pervious given to Mr. Flint, a pill that was 28.5% where out of the manufactures specification tolerances for weight of pill. Not average weigh, but over the high side of the tolerance, which means the pills had more ingredients that they were intended to have.

Target had a duty to see that the Patient Education and Patient Card contained the correct information and in this case it did not. Target failed to notify customer with a green label that the manufacturer was different. This again proves that Target has no control over the drugs they sell in any way. Hiding behind the "middleman law" makes Target neglectful in every way.

Target breached their duty by not supplying FDA approved drugs. Target says it only sells FDA approved drugs and this was not correct in this case. Target cannot prove the compound in the pills Mr. Flint was given, were approved by the FDA.

Did Mr. Flint suffer an injury?

Appellant will cut and paste direct from the plaintiff's response to Appelees first motion for summary judgment the question and answer filed with the court, NO 10.

10- Defendant's Stat- In February, 2007, Mr. Flint consulted with Dr. Forrest Kuhn, an allergist, regarding his alleged allergic reaction to the pill as well as his history of other allergies. Dr. Kuhn testified that the Plaintiff complained of a reaction in the form of inflammation in the oral cavity after taking the third fill of the medication. He also complained of a loss of taste. See, Kuhn Deposition, p.5, Exhibit D.

Plaintiff's ANSWER: This statement is not true and is mis-leading. Dr. Kuhn's testimony was not as Defendant has stated. Dr. Kuhn testified that when Plaintiff seen him on February 5, 2007 and I quote" he came to see me because he had developed a suspected reaction to a medication, which included a reaction initially in the mouth, the oral cavity, the lips, which resulted in what we call a stomatitis or an inflammation, and also a loss of taste that was associated with this. He had developed a rash as well in the groin area, which has persisted." (See Plaintiff EXHIBIT 7 Dr. Kuhn d p10) Dr. Kuhn examined Plaintiff fully on February 5, 2008. Defendant is twisting words. Defendant has told this court a fact that is different, than what the true facts show. Only with Dr. Kuhn on a witness stand will the truth be known. Following is NO 11 cut and pasted from the same response to motion for summary judgment

11- Defendant's Stat- At the time of the appointment the inflammation in the Plaintiffs mouth had resolved, although the Plaintiff still complained of a loss of taste. Id at p. 11. Dr. Kuhn diagnosed the Plaintiff as having a "possible drug sensitivity related to either the specific drug Pyridium or the dyes and additive substances to that drug."

Plaintiff's ANSWER: Again this is not true and Defendant has again twisted and misquoted Dr. Kuhn testimony. a) The inflammation in the Plaintiff mouth had not resolved at the time of the first appointment. Dr. Kuhn on page 11 was speaking about a recent visit Plaintiff had with him and not about the first appointment. He stated and I quote from Page 11 of his testimony to Defendant

Q And do you know if Mr. Flint's condition, which was, I believe, the swelling of the tongue and lips, and the rash in the groin area, has that resolved?

A At the time of my visit, the ulceration and irritation to the mouth had resolved, but the loss of taste had persisted. And at the time of his evaluation, the rash in the groin was definitely persistent as I examined him.

As this court can read, Defendant question ended with the word" has that resolved" and the Defendant statement above left out the part about the groin area. Dr. Kuhn stated it had "definitely persistent"

b) Plaintiff agrees with statement about Dr. Kuhn's statement, because Plaintiff has maintained all along that there was something in the inactive materials that caused the injury. Dr. Kuhn words were "possible drug sensitivity related to either the specific drug Pyridium or the dyes and additive substances to that drug."

The Defendant is very loose with words attempting to paint a picture that is not there. Again Dr. Kuhn on a witness stand will paint a clear the picture

Doctor Forrest Kuhn is an allergy specialist and an expert witness for both parties, wrote a letter to Doctor W. Alan Currie, Mr. Flint's family doctor and also testified that stated that the reaction to Mr. Flint could have been caused by the Phenazopyridine the active ingredient **or** the 15 in-active ingredients. Following is a cut and paste direct from the same response to summary judgment.

12- DEFENDANT' Stat- See, Letter from Dr. Kuhn to Dr. Currie, Exhibit E. In his deposition, Dr. Kuhn also testified that he could not be absolutely certain that the drug Pyridium caused the allergic reaction that the Plaintiff complained of. See, Kuhn Deposition, p. 10, Exhibit D. Dr. Kuhn stated that an adverse drug reaction begins after a patient becomes sensitized to the drug, that is to say, it does not happen immediately but sometime after the body's first exposure to the drug.

PLAINTIFF'S ANSWER: Again Defendant is attempting to put words in Dr. Kuhn mouth. a) What Dr. Kuhn said was a number of things in the drug could have caused the Plaintiff injury. In EXHIBIT E Dr. Kuhn's letter to Dr. Currie he stated and I quote "Possible drug sensitivity related to either the specific drug Pyridium or the dyes and additive substances to the drug." B) Defendant also stated that "Dr. Kuhn stated that an adverse drug reaction begins after a patient becomes sensitized to the drug, that is to say, it does not happen immediately, but sometime after the body's first exposure to the drug." Plaintiff took 8 pills before he quit taking the pills, which was a period of two and a half days. Plaintiff was taking three (3) pills per day. Defendant statement sounds like they are attempting to say they know how long it takes to become sensitized. (See Plaintiff's EXHIBIT 4 Dr. Kuhn letter to Dr. Currie line marked)

The trial court also stated, that Doctor Kuhn testified that he recommended Mr. Flint consult a Doctor Fowler and there were no evidence Mr. Flint ever sough Dr. Fowlers assistance or consulted with any other specialist capable of opining with a reasonable degree of certainly about the cause of Mr. Flints symptoms. This statement is not true and the trial court took it out of the Appellees motion for summary judgment. In the Appellees first Motion for summary judgment Appellant answer this remarks about seeing Doctor Fowler and trying to find a doctor to find the cause for Mr. Flint injury. I will insert the remarks Appellees made in their first summary judgment and which the trail court agreed to read before deciding on summary judgment motion. The following insert is cut and pasted directly from the page.

13- Defendant Stat- He also testified that it was reasonable to advise the patient to stop taking the medication and to consult with his physician. Id at pp. 10-11. Dr. Kuhn recommended that the Plaintiff consult with another physician, Dr. Fowler, who specializes in contact sensitivity and may be able to conduct further tests to isolate the cause of the allergic reaction. Id at p.9; See also. Letter from Dr. Kuhn to Dr. Currie, Exhibit E. The Plaintiff has not yet consulted with Dr. Fowler. See, Kuhn Deposition, pp.9-10, Exhibit D.

Plaintiff's ANSWER: Again Defendant is twisting words and trying to testify for the Plaintiff. Plaintiff tried to see Dr. Flower. Plaintiff called Dr. Flower's office to make an appointment and was told that Dr. Flower only tested clothing dyes. Plaintiff then asked his Doctor, Dr. Currie to find a Doctor to test him for dyes. Dr. Currie responded later that he couldn't find anyone in the Louisville area to test him for the dyes. Plaintiff in a letter begged Paul Wirkkala of Target Customer Service to find a doctor to test for dyes and Mr. Wirkkala stated he couldn't do that, because Target does become involved with finding Doctors. The exact quote Plaintiff made in the letter to Paul Wirkkala was "As I was typing this letter my doctor just called and said he couldn't find any one in Louisville to test the dyes. I beg you to help get to the end of this problem." Plaintiff alleges that Target has a duty to help a customer that one of its drugs injury. Would Target let a dying person die because of a lack of a policy? (See EXHIBIT 8 letter to Wirkkala) Defendant is trying to paint a picture with a defective brush.

As this court can see from the above the trial court did not use any of Appellants answers and responses and other records in his response to motion for summary judgment, in reaching its decision. Mr. Flint has shown that he has met the four points above the court stated he had to meet. This also shows that there are much evidence that creates a great number of genuine issues and this case should go forward to trial and let a jury decide the where the truth lies.

Appellant was told by his contact at Breckenridge a Mr. Tony Malafronte that the pills had been tested. Breckinridge has admitted they had the test results and have given

Target copies of them, but refuse to given them to Appellant, unless Mr. Flint signed a contract holding them harmless. Appellant has twice serve subpoenas on Breckenridge for depositions and documents on June 18, 2008 and July 25, 2008 they refused to show for either of the depositions. Appellant also served a subpoena on Breckenridge July 11, 2008 to produce documents and they have refused to send those documents. Appellant has file motions with the trial court to compel and to hold them in contempt, but the court refuses to rule on these motions. Appellant served a subpoena on Aron Podell an employee of Contract Pharmacal on July 25, 2008 and he failed to show.

Plaintiff filed a motion on August 27, 2008 asking the court for leave to amend his complaint which would add Breckenridge and the manufacture Contract as defendants, but the trial court has refused to rule on the motion. Appellant served a subpoena on Mr. Gregg Steinhaffel who is President of Target on July 9, 2008 for a deposition and documents; On July 15, 2008 Appellees filed a motion to quash the deposition. Appellant filed a motion on July 18, 2008 objecting to the quash motion and asking the court to deny Appellees motion. Appellant also in a motion asked for a hearing on the matter. There were no hearings held and the trial court issued an order on July 23, 2008 quashing the subpoena for deposition.

Appellant serve a subpoena on June 18, 2008 on Breckenridge Pharmaceuticals to take a deposition and produce documents. On July 9, 2008 a Mr. Eugene Kim-General Counsel for Breckenridge wrote a letter to Appellant stating Breckenridge would not show for the deposition on July 15, 2008, and also that he had Mr. Noel Halpin who is one of the lawyers representing Target in this lawsuit, write an letter stating they had the test results of the testing on the pills Appellant had asked for many times and they refuse to give them to Appellant, Mr. Kim had given them to Target, but Target refuse to give them to Appellant. Mr. Halpin drafted a confidential document for Mr. Kim that they wanted Appellant to sign, along with a protective order, before sending Appellant the test results he was attempting to obtain. Appellant serve a subpoena for these documents, but Breckenridge refuse to honor the subpoena. Appellant put all facts in motion pleadings and the trial court refused to rule or take action.

Appellant begs this court to read the case file completely. As the saying goes, the devil is in the details. If the panel does read all documents it will learn what has happen in this case and will return the case back to the trial court for trial.

PRODUCT LIABILITY

The trial court misinterpreted **Ky. Rev. Stat. 411.340**. And the reading of it allows for unless wholesaler, distributor or retailer breached an express warranty or knew or should have known at the time of distribution or sale of such product that the product was in a defective condition, unreasonably, dangerous to the user or consumer. Appellant argues that Target had a duty to make sure the products they purchase are FDA approved, to make sure the product was the same that they was going to replace, had identical weight and ingredients and the manufacture and distributor had the right and capability to produce safe products for consumers, based on established criteria's and a method to assure each customer that they would stand behind their product. Appellant has been denied by Target and the trial court, records to discover the relationship between Target, Breckenridge and McKesson Corp. Appellant has from the beginning believed that a salesman walked into Target office, said I can sell you this drug for this price and that all there was to starting the relationship and an order for the pills was given. If these three (3) companies had done business the way it should be done when it comes to safe drugs, all three would open their records and obey CR. The trial court has protected Target by not granting Appellant the right to CR discovery. The trial court in its memorandum state and I quote **"Target identified Breckenridge Pharmaceutical as the manufacturer of the Phenazopyridine dispensed to Mr. Flint in his second refill of his prescription, and Mr. Flint has neither disputed this in his pleading, nor proffered evidence to the contrary."** This statement shows that the trial court has not read the record. Appellant has told the court in a number of pleadings that Contract Pharmacal is the manufacture of the pills and that Breckenridge is not the manufacture. Appellant so stated in his motion for leave to file an amended complaint on June 13, 2008. Item 17 of the purposed amended complaint is cut and pasted below.

Plaintiff has learned that the pills that injured him was manufactured by Contract Pharmacal, who the sold the pills to Breckenridge Pharmaceutical, who in turn sold them to McKesson Corporation, who then sold them to Target.

The record will show that this statement about Contract being the manufacturer was stated in at least 7 pleadings and even Breckenridge has so stated that Contract was the manufacturer.

Trial Court used **Ky, Rev. Stat. 454.210** discussing the circumstances under which company may be subject to the jurisdiction of this court. The court has misinterpreted the this law, (2) (a) states A court may exercise personal jurisdiction over a person who acts directly or by an agent, to a claim arising from the person's: There is nothing in this statue that prohibits Target from being held tried by courts The Kentucky Statute also states in (5) A court of this Commonwealth may exercise jurisdiction on any other basis authorized in the Kentucky Revised Statutes or by the rules of civil procedure, notwithstanding this section. Reading this statute does nothing, except says Target can be sued in Kentucky for breaching their duty and product. The Kentucky Supreme Court has stated that "the PLA applies to all damage claims arising from the use of products, regardless of the legal theory advanced." No matter what the legal theory a plaintiff advances, "the central purpose is the same: recovery of damages for injury or property damage caused by a product." In this case, the central purpose of Plaintiff's lawsuit is the recovery of damages for injury allegedly caused by the use of Pyridium (Phenazopyridine). Because Plaintiff's damage claims arise from the use of a product, Kentucky products liability law is applicable."

Time after time the trial court has based its opinion on store pharmacists and not on Target as a Corporation. The trial court keeps referring to the pharmacists the person who dispenses the drugs in order to take away the spotlight from the one who is sued, Target Corporation.

The trial court also used **Ky. Rev. Stat. 411-340**, to reach their opinion. The court has misconstrued this statue. Prescription drugs are the most dangerous product sold to consumers. The Federal Government recognized this fact and established the FDA, to control drugs and inform the public. All drugs sold by prescription must be approved by the FDA, and must take precedent over Kentucky statutes. In the drug industry there are those who have no scruples and pray on beating the FDA system by making cheaper, nonconforming drugs. The trial court didn't dig deep enough into the law. The law pertains to retailers that have no control over the content or specifications of the product, they sell. Target has not produced any evidence that they ever asked if the drugs were FDA approved. When it comes to drugs Target and other retailers have the duty to make sure drugs are FDA approved, before purchasing them. A shake of the head by the seller is not enough. Target can't rely on anybody but Target doing it right.

Prescription drugs do not fall into the same class, the statute contains. Target had or should have had input into the specification of what they purchased. Target could have asked if the product had been approved by the FDA, when talking with the manufacturer or distributor, who was attempting to sell the product to them and if the answer was yes, Target should have asked for a copy of the FDA approval document. Target should have asked if the specification would be the same regarding ingredients and weight as the pills they were replacing. No, instead Target found a company that had a cheaper price and that blinded them. To save pennies Target forgot about the consumer. Target forgot there are companies that have no scruples and will tell you anything you want to hear. Target fell for the save money routine and forgot about customer safety. In this case the trial court misconstrued the statute. If Target took someone's word that the pills were approved, then Target redress is with that company. The Kentucky middleman statute does not protect users of prescription drugs.

On the last part of this II of the trial court's memorandum it states and I quote, **"As for the third and last question, there simply is no evidence that the pills supplied by Breckenridge were in a defective, unreasonably dangerous condition. Rather the evidence presented indicated that they fell within manufacturing specifications."**

This again shows that the trial court did not read the records of the case. Appellant has submitted documentation from a testing facility, that the court has been given copies of more than once, that shows the 28.5% of the pills were outside of the manufacture's weight tolerance and the pills were 230% heavier that the first two fills he had, which means it contained 230% more chemicals and Targets own witness stated that the pills that injured Appellant contained ten (10) different ingredients than were in the pills that didn't injurer him. The appellant in its allegations stated a number thing that showed the pills was dangerous because of its content. To produce an FDA approved drug a company has to reproduce the approved formula. Target refused to produce a person for deposition that could testify about FDA approved drugs and the trial court refuse to rule on Appellants motion to compel Target to do so. Target has refused to produce an FDA approved document and cannot do so, because the manufacturer in not listed on the FDA approved list for this drug and has never applied to be approved.

Under the Hatch-Waxman Act, a generic manufacturer is permitted to file an abbreviated new drug application ("ANDA"), which allows the applicant to provide data showing that the generic drug is the same as a previously approved drug in terms of its use, active ingredients, dosage, and strength. 21 U.S.C. § 355(j). This allows the generic manufacturer to not perform safety and effectiveness studies if it can show that its drug is equivalent to a previously approved drug. The key words above, is the drug is the **same as a previously approved drug** and **equivalent to a previously drug**. **The pills that Appellant received had not been applied for ("ANDA"), were not the same as previously approved and were not the equivalent to a previously approved drugs and Target did not ask if they were approved.**

In its closing the trial Court stated and I quote, **"the court is also mindful that several pending discovery motions recently were remanded pending the Court's adjudication of Target's Motion for summary Judgment."** The court remanded in June, 2008 its own order regarding how bad Appelee had acted in not producing documents, Appellees asked for a hearing and the trial court for no reason, remanded its own order. At the hearing no evidence was presented to give the trial Court a reason to remand the order. The other order the court remanded was letting the Appellees have a second bite of the apple on submitting a second Motion for Summary Judgment. This actions show Appellant did not have a shot at a fair case. Giving Appellees a second bite was not fair.

Appellant has been denied the opportunity to uncover evidence to help his case and for the trail court to say that none of the discovery soughs in the remanded motion would have materially affected the courts determination, is saying the court's mind was made up long ago. How can a court make such a ruling when they refused to let Appellant add two (2) defendants to his complaint, one which was the manufacturer of the pills which the court is trying to say must be the one held liable?

The trial court stated and I quote, **"Not all injuries are capable of redress by the courts, even if plaintiff were permitted unlimited time and access to potential sources of proof. This is not always easy for a lay person to understand."** Appellant states that his injury is capable of redress and to deny him the opportunity to try is wrong. Appellant may be a lay person, but he understands what has happen to him and if he loses this appeal he will ask the Supreme Court to review the case. That is how important Appellant thinks this case is for the citizens of America. More people are killed each year by bad drugs, than any other product. These types of injuries occur because someone wanted to save a few pennies and this has to stop. Ill people have to have and need rights and protection. Companies like Target in America should not be permitted to continue harming people, because they can spend big bucks in courts and in Kentucky rely on the middleman statutes. This is not what the laws or America is about. When the injury first happen Target's customer service department told Appellant the manufacture was responsible for drug problem. Target trains their service people that the middle man law protects them and I am sure the purchase department has been told not to worry, we can't be held responsible, and save every penny you can. Like cancer it spreads and spreads and soon no one cares about safety. This court has an opportunity to straighten this theory out and make all companies buying prescription, drugs demand safe FDA approved drugs from suppliers.

The trial court closed with this quote. **"Courts are supposed to right wrongs and they do, but only when and to the extent the law permits."** If this is true, then the appeal court must reverse the trial court's order and let the case continue, because the law favors Appellant in this case.

LAW

Steelvest v. Scansteel, Ky. 807 S.W. 2nd 476, 483 (1991) states

"The proper function of summary judgment is to terminate litigant when as a matter of law, it appears that it would be impossible for the respondent to produce evidence at the trial wanting a judgment in his favor. We further declared that such a judgment is only proper where the movant shows that the adverse party could not prevail under any circumstances. Finally in that opinion we recognize that summary judgment is not a substitute for trial nor is it the functional equivalent of a motion for direct verdict. "

Kentucky standard, we conclude that the movant should not succeed unless his rights to judgment is shown with such clarify that there is no room left for controversy. Only when it appears impossible for the nonmoving party to produce

evidence at trial warranting a judgment in his favor should the motion for summary judgment be granted

Under Steelvest v. Scansteel, the Summary Judgment should not have been granted by the trial Court. It is not only possible for Appellant to prevail at trial; in fact, the evidence shows Appellant will prevail. **<u>Movant had not shown with such clarify that there is no room left for controversy</u>**.

Under Kentucky products liability law, a plaintiff may advance numerous theories of liability. <u>Clark v. Hauck Mfg. Co.</u>, **910 S.W.2d 247, 250, 42 12 Ky. L. Summary 28 (Ky. 247)**. Whatever products liability theory a plaintiff pursues, there are certain requirements that are found in all products liability cases. One such requirement is a defendant's product must have caused Plaintiff's injury to be liable under Kentucky products liability law. Appellant has proven that Target's product caused his injury and therefore Target is liable under Kentucky product law.

CONCLUSIONS

1- Kentucky Revised Statute **411-340**, so called middleman law does not protect consumers, but does the opposite, it protects con artist, those with no scrupled and those who pray on the ill. The law's intent was to protect retailers who had no input into the products. In this case the retailer must be held responsible for what and from whom it purchases drugs. If this is not so then the law is unconstitutional and the court should state that it is unconstitutional.

The trial court in its opinion kept hanging it opinion on the acts of the pharmacists at the store and not on Target Corporation which appellant has charged. The only wrong action Appellant has contributed to the pharmacists at the store, is not putting a green label on the bottle to warn that suppliers have been changed, which in its self is a serious mistake, but has nothing to do with his ability, but only his forgetfulness. In fact Target's headquarters wrongful actions make store pharmacists look bad. Target Corp. bears all of the other breaches of duty.

The case files will show, Appellees were allowed by the trial court 1)to lie, 2) to change interrogatories answers, 3) change answers to documents, 4) cover ends of documents to hide printing before coping 5) other things to impede Appellant's discovery search. The last true order issued in this case was by Judge Moyer on June 11, 2008.

The trial court refused to rule on a motion Appellant filed on July 14, 2008, **For Judgment in his favor, Defendant be held in contempt of Court and Target**

Counsel Removed from this Case. The caption alone, says a good look was needed and needed to be answered. Appellant was used.

Appellant should be granted his motion filed on August 27, 2008 for leave to file the amend complaint and remand the June 13, 2008 motion for leave and add in addition McKesson Corporation since Target has now stated McKesson is now going to indemnify Target, which means McKesson must think someone is guilty of something and now we know why Target withheld giving Appellant discovery regarding McKesson. By **Fed. Rule 19 (2)** the trial court should have joined Breckenridge, Contract and McKesson to the complaint.

Target breached their duty to their customers, by not using good business procedures of exploring and analyzing all potential purchases of drugs, which could affect the safety of customers. Although this procedure may not come easy or inexpensive, safety must come first and is paramount in dispensing of drugs for human consumption and anything less, is pure neglect. Target breached its duty by failing to order a drug that was FDA approved.

The trial court stated a number of times in its opinion, that Breckenridge Pharmaceutical was the manufacture of the pills in question. The trial court is confused; Contract Pharmacal was the manufacturer, not Breckenridge. The court could not correctly identify the manufacturer.

The trial court misinterpreted **KRS 454.210** and **KRS 411.340.** No person(s) should be protected from law that had an opportunity and obligation to protect consumers, but chose to make an extra penny instead. The Kentucky Supreme Court has stated that "the PLA applies to all damage claims arising from the use of products, regardless of the legal theory advanced." No matter what the legal theory a plaintiff advances, "the central purpose is the same: recovery of damages for injury or property damage caused by a product." In this case, the central purpose of Plaintiff's lawsuit is the recovery of damages for injury allegedly caused by the use of Pyridium (Phenazopyridine). Plaintiff's damage claims arise from the use of a product that was not FDA approved, Kentucky products liability law is applicable."

Target failed to warn Appellant about changing suppliers, by failing to put a green label on the bottle that contained the pills that injured him, an important safety procedure that management at Target designed and put into place as a safety measure policy.

The last fill of pills that Target supplied to Appellant did not contain the same ingredients and same amounts by weight, as the first two fill pills he had received; therefore could not possibly been FDA approved, therefore is neglect caused by greed for saving pennies.

The pills Appellant was given on the third fill did not conform to the side effects published on the "Patient Education" sheet and also the "Patient Card" that was attached to the bottle. Target failed of making sure Appellant's pills contained the same amounts by weight and same ingredients, as the language on the product was written for.

Target did not dispense Appellant FDA approved pills. This issue was both the easiest and most important step in drugs purchased by Target. All Target had to do in discussing the purchase of the drug with the supplier was to ask, a simple question "Is the drug FDA approved"? If the answer was "yes" then the buyer should have said give me a copy of the FDA approval and then we can continue discussing your product. If Target did not receive a copy of the FDA approval, then they should have forgotten about changing suppliers. Target cannot put this responsibility on another person or a supplier. Target has a duty to help people, not to harm them and when they registered to do business in Kentucky they knew or should have known what it has to do, to assure their customers safe FDA approved drugs. If Target had done their duty, Appellant would never have been injured.

The trial court denied Appellant a chance to develop his case by not compelling Breckenridge and Contract to compel on three subpoenaed depositions and producing subpoenaed documents, plus other motions. Why would anyone be denied a right to pursue their case?

The trial courts error in quashing a subpoena for a deposition served on Gregg Steinhaffel, President of Target. There was no reason for the trial court to quash the subpoena. Being president of a company does not give anyone a free ride, he would have more knowledgeable that any one at Target, to answer the questions Appellant wanted to explore. There was absolutely no reason to quash his deposition. The trial courts err.

The trial Court ruled wrongly by their interpretation of **Matsushita Elec. Indus. Co v. Zenith Radio Corp., 475 U.S. 574, 587 (1986)** Summary judgment is available under **Fed. R. Civ. P. 56(c)** if the moving party can establish that the "pleadings, depositions, answers to interrogatories, and admissions on file, together with the affidavits, if any, show that there is no genuine issue of material fact and that the moving party is entitled to judgment as a matter of law." In determining whether summary judgment is appropriate, a court must resolve all ambiguities and draw all reasonable inferences against the moving party. There are many genuine issues of material facts in this case and the court should have construed the evidence and drew all reasonable conclusions in favor of the Appellant. The evidence presents sufficient evidence, and the case requires submission to a jury for a jury to decide and it is not one sided that one party should prevail as a matter of law, **Anderson v. Liberty Lobby, Inc., 477 U.S.242, 251-52 (1986). There should be no question that a jury should decide**

this case." The test is whether the party bearing the burden of proof has presented a jury question as to each element in the case. **Hartsel v. Keys, 87 F.3d 795, 799 (6th Cir. 1996)**. The plaintiff has presented more than a mere scintilla of evidence in support of his positions; the plaintiff presented evidence on which the trier of fact could reasonably find for the plaintiff. *Anderson v. Liberty Lobby, Inc.*, **477 U.S. 242, 251-52, 106 S. Ct. 2505, 91 L. Ed. 2d 202 (1986)**

Appellant is bothered by the fact that the trial court let four (4) served subpoenas for depositions and document, be ignored by companies which could be part of the crime.

Continuing on the same theme, events happen that proves Appellant's theory. A hearing was held in court on June 9, 2008 regarding a number of issues and Judge Moyer on June 11, 2008 issued an order. In **II** of that order he stated facts, that were true, but not in favor of Appellees. The order contained some harsh language against the Appellees. The judge stated that **"Target's representation to the court and to Mr. Flint cause the court concern"** Appellees filed a motion for a hearing on reconsideration on June 13, 2008 and Appellant on June 16, 2008 responded, objecting to Appellees motion, stating "Plaintiff thought the court order was clear and Defendants actions were misleading." A hearing was held on July 1, 2008. Appellant secured a transcript of the hearing and the substance of what the Judge said in his June 11, 2008 order was not discussed at the hearing. On July 3, 2008 Judge Moyer issued an order that vacated the June 11, 2008 order. Why would a judge write such a strongly worded order on June 11, 2008 then vacate it twenty day later, without strong evidence that would be needed to change his mind. The facts Judge Moyer stated in his order still happened and nothing can change that. After the order was vacated, **none** of Appellant's motions was ruled on. Something happen in the trial court after Judge Moyer issued his order on June 11, 2008, because there were no rulings on Appellant's motions after that. Why?

Under the Hatch-Waxman Act, a generic manufacturer is permitted to file an abbreviated new drug application ("ANDA"), which allows the applicant to provide data showing that the generic drug is the same as a previously approved drug in terms of its use, active ingredients, dosage, and strength. 21 U.S.C. § 355(j). This allows the generic manufacturer to not perform safety and effectiveness studies if it can show that its drug is equivalent to a previously approved drug. The key words in above, is the drug is the **same as a previously approved drug** and **equivalent to a previously drug**. **Approval for the pills that Appellant received, had not been applied for ("ANDA"), nor were they the same as previously approved and were not the equivalent to the previously approved drugs.** For pennies, Target chose to buy from someone, who could only obtain orders by cutting the price of the drugs and to do that, they deviated from producing the drugs from an established formula and

Target didn't care, they saved money. Target has a duty to known if the drug was FDA approved before placing an order with a new company. Target found a loop hole in the middleman law and drove right through the hole. The FDA, made obtaining approval easy and still no one attempted to have the pills that were given to Appellant FDA approved. Target is so concerned about making pennies that they have turned their head on human's safety. The court must stop this now for all consumers' safety.

Appellant's doctor ordered one kind of drug, but Appellant received two kinds. The issue of how drugs are sold in America needs to be correctly and clearly defined and Appellant is willing to press all issues to see that they are defined, correctly and clearly.

There is no way in our society today that consumers injured by drugs can sue the manufacturers, even the trial court didn't know who the manufacturer was.

The Supreme Court recent ruling in the Wyeth Pharmaceutical case has changed the landscape. Both personal injury and FDA approval must take precedent over Kentucky's statutes concerning who can be sued regarding prescription drugs.

Only Prescription drugs which are pre-packaged and imprinted with the words FDA approved on the package can be applicable to Kentucky's middleman law, as the law is written.

If this court rules that Appellees cannot be sued in Kentucky based on Kentucky statues, then Appellant asks the court to rule on the constitutional of such statutes. When statutes are written, every circumstance cannot be taken into account and Courts have to determine goal.

Appellant respectfully asks this court 1) to read all documents, 2) consider the recent Supreme Court ruling against Wyeth Pharmaceutical, 3) keep an open mind on the consequence this court's ruling will have and 4) sent the case back for trial.

Respectfully submitted

Edward h. Flint

****My Brief to the Court of Appeals ends here*****

The court of Appeals upheld the District Court's ruling

I had 47 different facts of evidence to present to a jury and the judge refuse to let a jury hear them and the Court of Appeals agreed with the District Court.

A first year law student would know that Summary Judgment was not the proper ruling. The judge made up his mind, Target was going to win the case, before it started. This was as horrible ruling as a judge could make.

My Petition asking the Supreme Court for certiorari starts here

No._____

In The
Supreme Court of the United States

Edward H. Flint   Petitioner,

Versus

Target Corporation   Respondent

On Petition for Writ of Certiorari

PETITION FOR WRIT OF CERTIORARI

Edward H. Flint Pro, Se
Pro, SE, Counsel for Petitioner

QUESTIONS PRESENTED

1- Is KRS411.340 unconstitutional on its face?

2- Is KRS 411.340 unconstitutional when applied to prescription drugs, ordered by a Doctor?

3- Does KRS 411.340 pertain to Prescription drugs dispensed by a pharmacy?

4- Can KRS 411.340 relieve a pharmacy from the responsibility of supplying FDA approve prescriptions drugs to their customer?

5- Was Petitioner denied his due process when the trial court ignored the facts that Target had the responsibility to notified Petitioner that the drugs that injured him was manufacturer by a different company than the first two fills that did not injured him

6- Was Petitioner denied due process when the trial Court refused to grant Petitioner permission to submit an amended complaint adding new allegations, adding the Manufacturer and Distributor of the pills that injured Petitioner in?

7- Was Petitioner denied due process when the trial court ignored the facts that documents produced by Respondent, and given to Petitioner with the drugs that injured him, did not show the possibly of the injury Petitioner received.

The documents listed side effects as headaches and belly pain and Petitioner received hives.

PROCEDURAL HISTORY

This action arises out of a complaint filed on in Jefferson County Kentucky Circuit Court on October 10, 2007 case No. 07-CI-09987. Petitioner was Pro, Se and was 77 years old. Respondent on October 30, 2007 had the case removed to Western District Court of Kentucky, case No. 3:07-CV-600R. Respondent was granted Summary Judgment on January 13, 2009. Petitioner appealed the case to the Sixth Circuit Court on January 19, 2009. The Sixth Circuit Court on January 21, 2010 affirmed the district court ruling. Petitioner on January 27, 2010 filed a motion for a rehearing and on April 14, 2010 the appeals court denied the rehearing.

RELEVANT FACTS OF THE CASE

1- Petitioner Flint was operated on for prostate cancer in November of 2006 at the age of 76. When he was discharged his Doctor gave him a prescription for Pyridium a drug to keep down potential infection. The prescription had three fills for the drug. Petitioner took the prescription to Target, and ordered the first fill. When the first fill ran out Petitioner ordered the second fill, neither fill gave him any injury.

2- When the second fill ran out Petitioner ordered the last fill. The last pills Petitioner received was from a different supplier.

3- After Petitioner took three days' supply of the amount the Doctor prescribed of the last fill Flint broke out with hives in his mouth, tongue, and groin area. Flint's doctor told him to quit taking the pills and see his family doctor. Flint's family doctor sent him to a specialist, who confirmed he had hives.

4- Petitioner from the injury of the last pills has lost his taste, along with having hot flashes, he can't sleep on his right side of his body, he has dry mouth and chapped lips constantly, his groin area has to be cleaned and treated with ointment two to three times per day.

5- Flint discovered that the last pills dispensed to him from the new supplier were never approved by the FDA.

6- Petitioner discovered that the last pills each weight two hundred and thirty percent (230%) more than each of the pills he received in the first two fills.

7- Petitioner also discovered that there were ten (10) different in-active Ingredients in the last fill pills that were not in the first and second fill pills.

The in-active ingredients were chemicals which can be as harmful as the active ingredients.

8- The trial court quit ruling on Flint's motions after June 13, 2008 and left forty-seven motions that was never ruled on.

9- With the last fill Petitioner was given a sheet that was a "Patient Education" page. The sheet is a document that Target gives to customers when filling prescriptions. The Patient Education page stated and I quote" **POSSIBLE SIDE EFFECTS: SIDE EFFECTS that may go away during treatment include headache, stomach upset or cramps, if they continue or are bothersome, check with your doctor"**. Again it said nothing about hives.

10- In addition Petitioner also received a printed card called **PATIENT INFO CARD** with the last fill of the pills and that card stated **"side effects could be Headaches and Belly Pain.** A customer should be able to rely on information that comes with their medicine.

11- Neither the Patient Education sheet nor the Patient Card given Petitioner notified Petitioner that the pills would cause hives, which they did.

12- Neither the manufacture or distributor of the pills had anything to do with the wording in the patient Education Sheet or Patient Card.

13- Target designed and printed the information sheets to inform their customers about what side effects to expect.

14- Target had the direct responsibility to give Petitioner the right instructions. Why would a customer expect hives if the Card and sheet didn't say so?

15- Petitioner filed a motion with the trial court to amend his original complaint in May 2008. The amended complaint contained many new allegations.

16- The trial court issued an order dated June 10, 2008 denying the motion, because Petitioner forgot to attach a copy of the proposed amendment to the motion. However the court's order stated Petitioner could resubmit the motion with the proposed amended copy attached.

17- On June 13, 2008, three (3) days later Petitioner resubmitted his motion with a copy of the proposed amended complaint.

18- The trial Court refused to rule either way on Petitioners amended complaint motion.

19- In that complaint was were new allegations that Respondent alone was responsible for and wouldn't fall under KRS 411.340 under any reading of the statute.

20- When the case first started the trial judge issued on January 4, 2008 a scheduling order under Fed.R.Civ.P. 26. Discovery was to be completed by July 28, 2008. The trial Court never ruled on any motion regarding discovery after the June 10, 2008 order that was issued.

21- Respondent filed a motion for summary judgment on May 23, 2008.

22- Petitioner filed a motion for summary judgment on July 28, 2008 and the trial court never ruled on this motion.

23- On August 14, 2008 Respondent filed a motion requesting the remand of their motion for a summary judgment that had been filed on May 23, 2008 and the court on September 30, 2008 granted the motion.

24- August 27, 2008 over four months before Summary Judgment was granted to Target on January 13, 2008 by the trial court, Petitioner on filed the following motion **"Plaintiff moves this court, to grant Plaintiff leave to amend the original complaint with the attached complaint which also joins two (2) other) Defendants and if this motion is granted then Plaintiff asks for leave to remand the motion he filed on June 13, 2008 on which this court has not rule."**

This new motion added new allegations plus added the Manufacturer and Distributor of the pills that injured Flint, to the original complaint. <u>Petitioner never received a ruling of any type on this motion from the trial court.</u>

25- Petitioner also on the same day, August 27, 2008 <u>filed</u> another motion, asking for the following, **"for leave to join two other parties into this case as Defendants. And conspirators"** Petitioner was never granted leave nor received an answer of any type from the trial court on either of these two motions.

26- The trial court in its summary judgment opinion order stated and I quote, "what is the specific duty of care owned by pharmacists to their customers" The court then made the case that pharmacists are to dispense the correct medication in accordance with the prescribing physician's instructions. However there is more to pharmacist's duties than just that dispensing the correct drug. Target has a policy to notified customers when they dispense pills that is from a different supplier.

27- Target testified they had a policy on changing suppliers. The exact language they testified was and I quote,

"Target notifies quests of the change by placing a green sticker on the bottle that states "This is the same medication you have been getting. Color, size or shape may appear different".

28- The last fill that Petitioner received, did not have a sticker warning him that the pills were from a different supplier.

29- The trial court refused to rule on motions to compel on two persons who were served with subpoenas for depositions. From both the manufacture and distributor.

30- The trial Court quashed a subpoena Petitioner served on the President of Target and refused to let Petitioner take his deposition.

31- Target like most chain store pharmacies have no involvement in ordering or monitoring drugs they sell to customers. In the case of Petitioner the pills went through four hands before Flint received them.

REASONS FOR GRANTING THE WRIT

KRS 411.340:

KRS 411.340 is unconstitutional.

KRS 411.340 puts a burden pertaining to prescription drugs on the customer that is all most impossible for that person to know or discover in prescription drugs, since drugs are manufactured the world over and shipped to America. The language in KRS 411.340 put the burden of the customer rather than on the seller to sell high-quality products

In this case the pills and the container they came in did not meet the requirement of the statute. The statute requires the Manufacturer to be identified and subject to the jurisdiction of the court. The container the pills came in stated the manufacturer as Breckenridge, who was not the manufacture. Petitioner was misled by the respondent.

The Respondent in all discoveries, pleading, and brief stated the manufacture as Breckenridge. Until the Respondent in it response to Petitioner Brief in the Court of Appeals stated for the first time the real Manufacturer was Contract Pharmacal Corporation.

4- Prescription drugs sold as individual fills cannot meet the requirement of KRS 411.340 of being in its original condition or package when delivered to the customer. This statement eliminates prescription drugs

5- KRS 411.340 as written is broad and was meant for prepackage items or a product standing on its own that is not packaged like a lawn mower or a car or chair rather than drugs. KRS 411.340 is unconstitutional the way it is written because it tries to take in to account ever product made or sold.

6- The only way Prescription drugs could fall in to this statute is if a drug was prepackage, sealed, printed with the words FDA approved and contained the Manufacturer name.

7- There is no question that the product in question was defective, unreasonably dangerous to the user.

8- In America today with thousands of companies making generic drugs being shipped into America from all over the world, with over half of the population being on prescription drugs (mostly elder) any Pharmacy could sell anything to a consumer and hide behind this statute in Kentucky. A drug dealer could take a bad drug from one state and ship it to Kentucky, sell it and hide behind this law. It took Petitioner a long time to find out who the true manufacturer was, because Target told Petitioner the manufacturer was Breckenridge instead of Contract.

ANOTHER REASON FOR GRANTING WRIT

1- The trial court should have granted Petitioner leave to amend his original complaint, especially to add new allegations, to add the manufacturer of the drugs that harmed him and to add the distributor of the drugs in question. The Petitioner filed his motion for leave to amend the complaint over 4 months before the trial court granted Respondent summary judgment. What reason was there to hurry the summary judgment motion? Justice should come before anything else.

OTHER REASONS FOR GRANTING WRIT

1- The trial court error by granting all of Respondent's actions under KRS 411.340. Respondent actions of not warning Petitioner about changing suppliers of his drugs by putting a label on the container that contained the pills that supplier was changed, did not fall under KRS 411.340

2- Also Target was the only one responsible for the printed information on the sheet and card, which was in error. The education sheet and Patient information sheet failed to inform Petitioner the truth about what harm the drug could cause him.

3- The pills that Petitioner received was not FDA approved.

CONCLUSION

1- This court should rule on the Unconstitutional of KRS 411.340 on its face.

2- This Court should rule on the Unconstitutional of KRS 411.340 when prescription drugs are purchased.

3- The last fill of pills given to Petitioner was not FDA approved drugs.

4- Petitioner should have been allowed to amend his complaint and add the manufacturer and distributor along with all new allegations he discovered as he filed two motions to do.

5- Petitioner did not receive the due process he deserved by the constitution to a fair trial. Any fair mined judge would have allowed Petitioner sufficient time to get to the end of this case and would have treated all parties equal.

6- As shown above the summary judgment of the Trial Court was in error and the Appeal Court was in error and must be reversed.

7- This Court should grant certiorari and remand the case back to the trial court with instructions to grant leave to Petitioner on amending his complaint. 8-The trial court should rule on all motions that were not ruled on and the case should continue and a trial takes place.

9- KRS 411.340 fails to protect the consumers of Prescription drugs and puts a blanket over those who prey on the ill and elderly and those who put trust in our government.

10- Respondent should not been granted summary judgment on the issues that Target was answerable for, issues that the manufacturer and distributor had no connection to.

11- Every person deserves a fair and complete trial and it's impossible for the court to set a firm trial dated at the beginning of a case and not allow additional time when needed. Unless the court's mind is made up at the beginning.

11- The elderly of this country needs this issue ruled on by this court in order they will know what to except from the drug industry as they purchase prescription drugs.

12- This Petition is not the best worded, but it's the best a 80 year old man who is not trained in law and who does his own typing with one finger can do and he prays it is worded good enough to put his point across to this honorable body

Respectfully submitted,
s/ Edward H. Flint, Pro, Se.

***********The Supreme Court Petition ends here***********

"The Supreme Court refused to grant my Petition and refuse to do anything about the case, except let it drop.

It became clear that The Supreme Court didn't care that illegal drugs were being sold to consumers.

It also became clear that I was naive to believe that judges tried cases by the laws and rules of the Court system.

I found that the judges do as they want and no one can challenge them and win. Judges make up new rules to fit their rulings.

I realized that Judges can be bought by companies and attorneys and do as they please. I have lived a long time and never knew how corrupt the court system is.

I became angry and hurt and prayed to God, asking him to let me out of my promise to file and pursue all lawsuits he told me to file, through the Holy Spirit.

I have been taught all of my life that God works in strange ways, but I questioned why he would want me to lose, such a cut and dry case.

The Holy Spirit told me to honor my commitment and someday I would understand.

I wrote a Book titled "Corrupt Judges," about this lawsuit.

I sent copies of the book to each justice on the United States Supreme Court. Judge Sotomayor had an aide return the book with a note that she doesn't except gifts. Judge Thomas wrote me a thank you note. I never heard from the other judges.

I know that some of the judges read the book, because not long after I sent the book to them, something happened in the Louisville District Court.

The trial judge, Judge Thomas Russell, who had wanted badly for a long time to be named Chief Judge of the Louisville District Court, was named Chief Judge. Soon after I sent the book and after Judge Russell was made Chief Judge, Judge Russell was taken out as Chief Judge and he was put on senior status, which means he was made a part time judge. Chief Judge Roberts knew in his heart that my case against Target was judged wrong.

Every Judge on the Supreme Court read the book, but rather than do the right thing for me, they may have become mad at me, for publishing the book. I was never able to get the Supreme Court to review any of my cases.

If the Supreme had judged my cases by the law, I would not have been able to write this book. Don't ever believe that God doesn't work in strange way.

CHAPTER 3

LAWSUIT FLINT V. JUDGE JAMES SHAKE ET AL

I will insert part of my complaint for you to understand the lawsuit

UNITED STATES DISTRICT COURT
WESTERN DISTRICT OF KENTUCKY
LOUISVILLE DIVISON

CASE NO 3:09-CV-116-H

EDWARD H.FLINT   PLAINTIFF

VS

AMENDING ORIGINAL COMPLAINT
AND JOINING TWO (2) ADDITIOAL DEFENDANTS

JUDGE JAMES SHAKE   DEFENDANTS

Judicial Center 700 W. Jefferson Street
Louisville, KY 40202

Judge Audra Eckerle
Judicial Center-Room 816
700 W. Jefferson Street
Louisville, KY 40102

Judge Ann Shake O'Malley
Judicial Center 700 W. Jefferson Street
Louisville, KY 40202

Jane Does and John Does

AMENDED COMPLAINT

Comes now the Plaintiff, Edward H. Flint acting as his own counsel is amending the original complaint and joining two (2) new Defendants, Judge Ann O'Malley Shake and Judge Audra Eckerle to the complaint. Plaintiff is suing Defendant(s) for actions committed since March 2, 2008, that moved a case No. 07-CI-10558 from one judge to another judge for no reason and against the courts rules and for this cause of action, Plaintiff states as follows:

1- Plaintiff Edward H. Flint lives at

2· Plaintiff filed a civil lawsuit, case No. 07-CI-10558 in Jefferson County Kentucky Circuit Court on October 24, 2007, against other Defendants.

3- Defendant Judge James Shake was and still is Chief Judge of the Jefferson County Kentucky Circuit Court.

4- Plaintiff alleges Judge Shake Chief Judge signed an order that he knew or should have known violated the courts rules, which injured and impeded Plaintiff.

5- Plaintiff alleges that in April and or May case No. 07-CI-0558 was in Division 7 of Jefferson Circuit Court and one or more Defendants switched the case to Division 10 without notice and against rule 11 of the Thirtieth Judicial Jefferson Circuit Court rules. The action that was taken by Defendants harmed and impeded Plaintiff.

6- Plaintiff alleges that the case files in Jefferson Circuit Court does not contain records where a person can see why and who requested the change and for what reason in the case except the order signed by Judge Eckerle which states she signed it at the order of the Chief Judge.

7- Plaintiff alleges that Defendant(s) used the power of their position to persuade others to take actions that were unlawful that harmed and impeded Plaintiff.

8- Plaintiff alleges that Defendant(s) injured Plaintiff both mentally and physically.

9- Plaintiff alleges Defendant(s) broke rule 11 of the Thirtieth Judicial Jefferson Circuit Court and or Kentucky Supreme Court by their action.

10- Plaintiff alleges that Defendants action denied actions denied Plaintiff his judicial rights and discriminated against him by making these and other changes.

11- Plaintiff alleges that Defendant(s) fail to perform both their duty and ethical responsibility in the justice system and turned their head on unlawful activity in case No. 07-CI-10558.

12- Plaintiff alleges that Defendants actions were not in the interest of justice but was for personal gains.

13- Plaintiff alleges that Defendant's actions caused others connected with the justice system to break rules of the justice system.

14- Plaintiff believes other laws, rules and other action could have been broken and only discovery will tell and at that time will ask for leave to amend this complaint only.

Therefore Plaintiff demands that Defendant(s) be held liable for their actions in harming Plaintiff.

*****The complaint ends here*****

This is part of the Court's order showing that the court granted the judge immunity

MEMORANDUM OPINION AND ORDER

FILED: April 27, 2009

Judges are protected by absolute immunity for their judicial acts under both state law and in federal civil rights suits. In order to overcome a judicial immunity defense, Plaintiff must allege facts that would demonstrate that a judge's acts were not judicial in nature or that the judge acted "in clear absence of jurisdiction. *Stump v. Sparkman,* 435 U.S. 349, 357 (1978). Even assuming for the purpose of this motion that plaintiff's allegations were true, Plaintiff cannot meet this burden because he fails to set forth in his complaint or response to the pending motions any facts to support his argument that any of Defendants were without jurisdiction to act in their capacities as a judge.

A judge is immune, under Kentucky law, from personal liability for those acts undertaken while that judge has jurisdiction over a case. Even when jurisdiction is contrary to law, judicial immunity still applies.

The District Court stated that no matter what the three judges did, they are still granted Absolute Immunity. The court system doesn't care if a person get hurt by a judge violating court rules, a judge cannot be sued in any court, for any reason in America.

My Petition to the Supreme Court starts here

No._____

In The
Supreme Court of the United States

Edward H. Flint   Petitioner,

Versus

JAMES SHAKE, Judge-et al   Respondent

PETITION FOR WRIT OF CERTIORARI

Edward H. Flint Pro, Se

QUESTIONS PRESENTED

1- Can Judges be granted absolute judicial immunity after violating Kentucky Supreme Court Rules of Practice and Procedures to illegally gain control of a case for political campaign contributions and to injury a party?

2- Was Petitioner denied Due Process by Respondents judges who violated Kentucky Supreme Court Rules?

3- Does a judge have jurisdiction of a case that was illegally obtained by violating Supreme Court's rules?

4- If a judge violates Supreme Court Rules, are they entitled to absolute judicial immunity?

5- If a judge violates a law of a state are they entitled to absolute judicial immunity?

6- Is Stump v. Sparkman 435 U. S. 349, 356, 57 (1978) constitutional regarding immunity for judges?

STATEMENT OF THE CASE

PROCEDURAL HISTORY

This action arises out of a complaint filed in Jefferson County Kentucky Circuit Court on October 2007 case No. 07-CI-10558. Petitioner was Pro, Se and was 76 years old. The case was about a flawed election for officers at a Condo Association where Petitioner lived. Petitioner believed based on evidence he had seen the ballots had been substituted for and when the Board of Directors refuse to response to his letters asking that a meeting be called and the Petitioner filed a suit.

The case was assigned to Division 13 Judge Fred Cowan of the Jefferson County Circuit Court. The Petitioner after subpoenaing the President of the Association for a deposition received a letter from the Counsel for the Defendants stating his client would not appear for the deposition and the letter showed a copy was also sent to another attorney Mr. Brennan S. Cox who Petitioner had never heard of. Petitioner checked and found Mr. Cox was a law partner of Judge Cowan, who had the case in Circuit Court.

After Petitioner filed a motion to compel with the Division 13, Judge Cowan, the Judge said he wanted the case mediated. Petitioner asked Judge Cowan to recuse himself from the case and he did.

The case was assigned to Division 10 Judge Kathleen Voor Montano. After about four hearing in front of Judge Montano, on March 20, 2008 she recused herself, stating she discovered that

The case was then assigned to Division 7 Judge Audra Eckerle.

Counsel for the Defendants on April 8, 2008 filed for motion for summary judgment and the court by order stopped Petitioner from taking any more discovery.

Judge Audra Eckerle on April 16, 2008 wrote a letter to Defendants Counsel Mr. Dennis Stilger stating she had received his motion for summary judgment and she reminded Mr. Stilger she must receive an AOC 280 Notice of Submission form before she could rule.

Mr. Stilger mailed the required AOC form to Judge Eckerle and Petitioner Edward Flint on April 25, 2008, which was a Friday.

On Monday April 28, 2008 Judge Eckerle marked the AOC 280 form as overruled regarding the motion. The form was signed by Judge Eckerle's Secretary R. Combs and the form showed it was mailed to AOC of April 28, 2008.

Mr. Stilger clocked in a new AOC 280 form at the clerk's office on April 28, 2008.

This new form was marked issue decided granted on May 5, 2008 by Judge Ann Shake and shows mailed to AOC on May 7, 2008. Division 7 had been marked out and division 10 was put in place of seven.

An order signed by Judge Eckerle sending the case back to Division 10 appeared in the file. The order that Judge Eckerle signed stated "**In accordance with authorization set forth in the re-allotment order of the Chief Judge**"

Judge Montano the judge who had Petitioner's case till she disqualified herself on March 20, 2008, took ill and died on April 21, 2008.

Chief Judge Shake four days later on April 24, 2008 appointed his wife Judge Ann O'Malley Shake to set in for Judge Montana until the Governor appointed someone to take over Division ten.

Judge Ann Shake was not a full time judge but a retired judge only setting temporary.

OTHER RELEVANT FACTS OF THE CASE

Kentucky Supreme Court issued a set of rules for the Thirtieth Judicial Circuit of Jefferson County Circuit Court which was last approved on July 11, 2006.

Rule 11 of the Supreme Court rules contain the following text regarding civil cases 1101-1102-1103-

Rule- 11 ALLOCATION OF CASE DIQUALIFICATION OF JUDGES

1101 Method of Allotment

All cases shall be allotted equally and at random among the thirteen (13) divisions of the court. However the Chief Judge may receive a twenty-five percent (25%) reduction in criminal and civil cases assigned.

A.   Civil Cases. The automated case register in the Circuit Courts Clerk's Office assigns all District Court Appeals and all other civil cases to the various division of the Court. The register has been programmed by the AOC to ensure both the randomness of the assignments and equal distribution of cases.

1102   Refiled Cases.

A.   Civil Cases. Whenever a case has been dismissed without prejudice and is refiled, the parties shall, after allotment, have been transferred to that division from which it was dismissed. Whenever any Judge discovers the allotment to her division of a case so dismissed from another division, the Judge shall immediately transfer the case to the division from which it was dismissed.

1103-   Disqualification of Judge.

If a judge is disqualified pursuant to KRS 26A.015, the case shall be randomly reallotted to another member of the Jefferson Circuit Bench. If all judges of the

Jefferson Circuit Bench are disqualified, the Chief Regional Judge shall certify the need to assign a special judge.

Under the Kentucky Supreme Court Code of procedures rules the word "shall" means <u>must.</u>

The Jefferson Circuit Court Rule 11 is simple, fair and clear.

1- When a case is filed, in Jefferson Circuit, the Court Clerk by an automated register assigns the case to a Division. No judge can give up a case and no judge gets to choose any case.

2- The Case remains with the division it's assigned forever, unless a Judge is disqualified by reasons outlined in Kentucky Statute 26A.015

3- If a Judge is disqualified for any reason the Court Clerk by the automated register assigns the case to another division.

4- If a case was dismissed without prejudice and is refiled, it has to be assigned by the Court Clerk by the automated register and then it is to be transferred to the original division.

5- The Kentucky Supreme Court designed these rule years ago, to make sure all persons filing lawsuit received a fair shake, to make sure the same judge would hear the complete case and the Supreme Court by Rule 11 made sure that cases were distributed evenly to all Judges. There are 13 Divisions in the Jefferson County Circuit and if every judge was allowed to move cases at will, it would create confusion to no end. These rules supplement the Kentucky Rules of Civil Procedure

6- Under Supreme Court Rule 11 there is no way a case can be transferred to another judge by judges, for any reason.

7- Regardless of how a case is legally transferred it must be re-allotted by the automated register system.

8- There was no reason why the case in question should have been moved from division 7 to division 10 and under the Kentucky Supreme Court Rule 11 should not have been transferred.

9- Petitioner was denied due process of a fair trial of his case, a summary judgment decision that was found in Petitioner's favor <u>once</u> was changed, caused by the transferring of the case, by the three Respondents.

10- Chief Judge James Shake knew Rule 11 when he ordered Judge Audra Eckerle to re-allot the case to division 10 and he knew he knew it was wrong to do so.

As Chief Judge, he knows when cases are to be transferred and why, it his duty to see that Rule 11 is followed.

11- Judge Audra Eckerle knew Rule 11 and she knew she could not re-allot the case to another division regardless to what the Chief Judge orders.

12- Judge Ann O'Malley Shake knew Rule 11 and she knew not to accept the case from Judge Eckerle and should have notified the Court Administrator.

The three Respondents conspired to harm Petitioner and they succeed.

Petitioner does not know all of the facts; he was not allowed to take discovery before the trial court granted Summary judgment.

ARGUMENTS

A review of the Appeal Court's ruling entered on December 30, 2009 clearly shows that the court did not review or use the evidence materials that Petitioner has submitted with this petition.

It is also clear that the Appeal Court was protecting the Respondents because they are judges. The Appeals Court stated at the top of their order, "Not Recommended for full-text Publication"

The case in question should have never been moved out of Division seven (7). There was no reason by rule to transfer the case from Division 7 and Rule 11 prohibited it. Judge Eckerle made her decision regarding the summary judgment motion and she rejected the defendant's summary judgment motion.

The Kentucky Supreme Court rule 11 leaves no room regarding its meaning. It has a definite meaning and by the Supreme Court rules of procedures must be strictly inhered to. The rule was established to keep Judges in a large Court district from switching cases at will because the order entered on July 11, 2006 starts with these words, **"Upon recommendation of the Chief Judge of the Thirtieth Judicial Circuit and being otherwise sufficiently advised."**

Chief Judge James Shake had no juridical involvement of any type, at any time, in the case.

Judge James Shake knew that by ordering the case transferred he was violating Rule 11. Judge James Shake knew that ordering a Judge to give the case to another judge that wasn't assigned by Rule 11, was in violation of the Supreme Court Rules.

Judge Ann O'Malley Shake never at any time had any judicial involvement in the case and she knew she was violating Rule 11 if she asked for the case. She knew that accepting the case violated Rule 11.

Judge Audra Eckerle knew that it was her case and she knew she could not to give the case to another judge per rule 11. All cases must be reassigned by Rule 11. Judge Eckerle had no reason to give the case up, but if she had a reason, she knew how to disqualify herself. Regardless the case had to be randomly reallotted to another judge.

Judge James Shake was running for election as judge on the Kentucky Supreme Court and was soliciting donation for his election campaign.

Judge James Shake received and accepted a campaign donation from Defendants Counsel Mr. Dennis Stilger on May 19, 2008 and Judge James Shake's wife Judge Ann Shake sign the Defendant's Motion for Summary Judgment the next day May 20, 2008.

It is clear that besides breaking Kentucky Supreme Court rules Judge James Shake's and Judge Ann Shake's actions was in "clear absence of all jurisdictions."

Our county is exploding and in the process, falling apart, because of so many different. Petitioner is 80 years old and after being Pro, Se in a couple of other law cases he is convinced that the justice system is leading the way to the unrest in America.

The fourteenth amendment gave due process to justice and the court system has taken this right away.

The Courts protects judges by the court's new made law. A judge is protected by absolute immunity for any reason. I will quote from Stump v. Sparkman 435 U.S 349, 356, 57 (1978) **"a judge will not be deprived of immunity because the action he took was in error, was done maliciously, or was in excess of his authority: rather, he will be subject to liability only when he has acted in the clear absence of all jurisdiction."**

If Stump V, Sparkman is the standard then the Rules of The Supreme Court of Kentucky Code of Judicial Conduct SCR 4.300 which contain Cannon 1-2-3-4-5, (the judiciary commandments) has no meaning, let alone Due Process. Absolute Immunity is in clear conflict with both state's Supreme Court Codes and Rules and Due Process

Every court in America in both Federal and State Courts is now quoting and using the Stump V. Sparkman case to protect judges for any and all reasons. There-by the courts have taken away the due process from the people and the integrity that assured citizens a fair and honest trial. Some judge in America has become dictators because they know they are protected by the law. Any person that gets elected as a judge could dictate the future of every citizen who comes before them.

The court system gets all types of judges, smart ones, ones dumb, sincere ones, mean ones, honest ones, dishonest ones, etc., it doesn't matter, if every judge get immunity.

Judges have become God to dishonest attorneys. A Judge needs campaign financing to run for office and they have made slaves out of attorneys who must make a living. A judge with absolute immunity can control most attorneys, especially bad attorneys.

This honorable body should look at the harm done by granting absolute immunity to judges is doing to our county and the repercussions it has on the justice system.

Example, in a case that was filed to be tried by a jury the judge should not become involved except to shepherd the case to a trial. They should not use their position to see the case never gets to trial, such as granting summary judgment when there is no reason to. Some Judges don't care about the damage they cause, because they know that they are protected by absolute immunity. Eliminating absolute immunity would make honest judges out of dishonest judges.

Attorney are afraid to defend them self against the abuse they are receiving from judges, because the will lose their lively hood if they complain.

The ruling made in Stump V. Sparkman may have been a good ruling based on what happen at the time. The Courts have cited that case many times and it keeps getting extended in meaning every time it is cited. Judges today use it for everything a mind can think up.

This body owes it to America and to the future of our country to clarify the Due Process and immunity for judges' issues. This body has a chance to help put this country back to the way our founding fathers wanted it to be. Fair and equal treatment for all.

An honest and fair judge doesn't need immunity and this country existed for over 200 years before the Stump V. Sparkman ruling in 1978.

America is under attack from many sides. This Petitioner believes that America cannot survive the way we all want it to be, without a true and honest Due Process system, which must come first.

If this court believes in the jury system, then why is the system not good enough for judges? Why do judges need to be protected? Americans don't believe any one should be granted absolute immunity. If they did, it would have been put it in the constitution

What makes Judges different that the rest of the citizens of America? Are they better people? Are they indispensable? Why do they receive immunity?

This issue and the results that will come from it, is not a political issue, but an issue that will determine the future of our families, our children's, and neighbor's.

As Jesus said, we will be judged, on the thoughts that were in our mind and the deeds we did, not on the words we say.

REASONS FOR GRANTING THE WRIT

1- The Respondents violated The Kentucky Supreme Court's Rules of Practice and Procedure of the Thirtieth Judicial Circuit, Jefferson Circuit Court and absolute immunity should never   have been granted.

2- This court should not allow judges violating Court's rules and laws turn out to be the norm in America.

3- This court should review this case because the Court of Appeals had no intention of ruling against judges. The wording of their order states no evidence was presented and that is not so, as the files will show.

4- Covering up for offenses done by judges is the worst thing any court can do, if justice is to prevail in America.

5- This Court should review the Appeal Court's ruling order and plus all evidence materials previous submitted to the Trial Court and Appeal Court in this case. The Court of Appeals order shows they did not review all of the evidence and Petitioner is entitled to a full review of all evidence.

CONCLUSION

The Respondent judges violated the Kentucky Supreme Court Rules that injured Petitioner and did not deserve Absolute Immunity.

Judges cannot have jurisdiction in a case they obtained illegally.

This case should be returned to the trial court with instructions to hold a trial and let a jury judge the actions of the Respondents, based on the evidence.

Cannon 1 states and I quote, **"An independent and honorable judiciary is indispensable to justice in our society"** and further it states, **"And (judges) shall personally observe these standards so that the integrity and independence of the judiciary will be preserved"**

Cannon 2 states, **"A judge shall respect and comply with the law and shall act at all times in a manner that promotes public confidence in the integrity and impartiality of the judiciary"**

The Cannons are the commandments of the judiciary system and to give judge's immunity, goes against the writers of Cannons and kicks them in the teeth.

The future of America depends on this court to define a set of rules, based on the Constitution, to assure that every citizen receives the same Due Process and also, so state's Supreme Courts can write A Code of Judicial Conduct, to match this court's rules.

America is crying out for justice for all.

This Petition is not the best worded, but it's the best a 80 year old man who is not trained in law and who does his own typing with one finger can do and he prays it is worded good enough to put his point across to this honorable body

Respectfully submitted,

s/ Edward H. Flint, Pro, Se.

The Supreme Court refused to grant certiorari and refused to review the case. This means that the Supreme Court and all other courts in America will give judges immunity, if you sue one of them. Judges can make any ruling for any reason and nothing can be done to them. The Supreme Court says judges are God.

There is no other group of people in America that receives such immunity. Our service men and women don't receive immunity, our police and firemen don't receive immunity. Only judges can have absolute immunity against liability in America and the Supreme Court doesn't want to change that rule, because they are judges also. Judges are granted absolute immunity and even Congress can do nothing to stop them from receiving immunity. Example, Congress passed a law regarding a judge recusing themselves and the Supreme Court ignores it. Americans believe we live in a country with an unbiased court system and we don't.

The Supreme Court judges tell the public that they are guiding this county by the constitution of our country. Nowhere in the Constitution does it say judges are entitled to have immunity. And Congress never passed a law giving judges immunity.

When any person is given absolute immunity and a life time position at their job, as all Federal judges are, hell breaks loose. Judges cannot be fired and they become, self-righteous. I can't think of any group of people that wouldn't become self-righteous and corrupt if they were given a lifetime job with immunity for any

action they take. I know that this is against what our forefathers sought. Our forefathers sought a fair and honest justice system. We have let the Supreme Court create tyrants with every judge in America.

The immunity fact is not well known in America. Most attorneys are afraid to raise the issue or discuss the issue of suing a judge. The attorneys can't afford to lose every case they have in the courts, which is what happens when you file a lawsuit against a judge. The entire justice system rallies around and protects every judge.

Because I am Pro, Se I could get by with filing lawsuits and raising the absolute immunity issue and telling the truth. God had to have a helper who couldn't be hurt by the courts and he found me and used me.

The author was told by the Holy Spirit that he would be safe and so far he has been. You might ask why God would pick him, a person who has no education in law. The answer is simple. God wanted someone who was willing to fight for right, someone who is not afraid of the court system. By being Pro, Se, what else can the court do to me except rule against me in every case and make sure the Court of Appeals and all District Courts does the same? Although I admit there were times that I thought and was afraid, that judges might have me taken care of in some form.

God knew I have been fighting for right and against wrong all of my life. God knew that I prayed to him each night, that if he gave me something to do that would help him with his will, I would it. This is why he chose me.

God knew from my past that I would not be intimidated in front of judges, although I was scared at times. God knew that once I started suing judges that the entire court system would gang up on me and he told me through the Holy Spirit that he would give me the right words to use in court and tell me how to write court documents and he would point me to where I could find the rules that I needed.

Before you finish reading this book you will see a shocking and corrupt side of the court system. About how the judges, don't like to work hard and how they dismiss cases, in order to protect companies and their friends. Judges are dictators and bullies. You will see how every Federal judge in the Western District of Kentucky ganged up on me, along with the Sixth Circuit of Appeals judges." The judges in the Sixth Circuit Court of Appeals are nothing but yes men, for the District judges.

CHAPTER 4

LAWSUIT FLINT V. JUDGE KATIE KING

I will now insert my Complaint against Judge King

UNITED STATES DISTRICT COURT
WESTERN DISTRICT OF KENTUCKY
LOUISVILLE DIVISON

CASE NO 09-CV-779-S

EDWARD H. FLINT	**PLAINTIFF**
VS	
COMPLAINT	
JUDGE KATIE KING	**DEFENDANT**

COMPLAINT

Comes now the Plaintiff, Edward H. Flint acting as his own counsel against Defendant Judge Katie King for actions committed on July 17, 2009 and July 24, 2009 and for this cause of action, states as follows:

1- Plaintiff Edward H. Flint lives at

2- Plaintiff filed a civil lawsuit case No.-09-C-004506 in Jefferson County Kentucky District Court on May 1, 2009 against other Defendants.

3- Defendant Judge Katie King was and still is a Judge in Jefferson County District Court.

4- Plaintiff alleges Judge Katie King made Terroristic Threaten against him and terrified him.

5- Plaintiff alleges that Defendant had it in for Plaintiff from the start of the first hearing and was spiteful because Plaintiff had sued three (3) Jefferson County Circuit Judges.

6- Plaintiff alleges that Defendant actions denied Plaintiff his judicial rights and discriminated against him.

7- Plaintiff alleges that Defendant's actions denied Plaintiff his Constitutional civil rights.

8- Plaintiff alleges that the Defendant was bias against him and harassed him.

9- Plaintiff alleges that Defendant conspired with others against him.

10- Plaintiff alleges that Defendant's actions injured Plaintiff both mentally and physically.

11- Plaintiff alleges that Defendant didn't know the Civil Rules of the Kentucky Court System

12- Plaintiff alleges Plaintiff was put into a horrifying position by Defendant's actions. Defendant represented herself to the voting public that she was qualified to be a Judge and she was not qualified to be a Judge.

13- Plaintiff alleges that Defendant failed to perform both her duty and her ethical responsibility required by the Kentucky justice system and Kentucky Supreme Court.

14- Plaintiff alleges that Defendant actions were not in the interest of justice.

15- Plaintiff believes other laws, rules and/or other action may have been broken and only discovery will tell, and at that time Plaintiff will ask for leave to amend this complaint.

Therefore Plaintiff demands that Defendant be held liable for her actions in harming Plaintiff.

Respectfully submitted

Edward H. Flint Pro, Se

********The District Court Order starts here********

UNITED STATES DISTRICT COURT
WESTERN DISTRICT OF KENTUCKY AT LOUISVILLE

CIVIL ACTION NO.3:09CV-779-S

EDWARD H. Flint   PLAINTIFF

v.

KATIE KING   DEFENDANT

The judge gave Judge King Immunity by stating the following.

Judges are generally entitled to immunity from personal liability for actions taken on the bench. "A judge will not be deprived of immunity because the action he took was in error, was done maliciously, or was in excess of his authority, rather, he will be subject to liability only when he has acted in the 'clear absence of all jurisdictions." *Stump v. Sparkman*, 435 U.S. 349, 356-57 (1978) quoting Bradley V. Fisher, 80 U.S. (13.) 335, 3511 (1872.

I appealed to the Supreme Court and filed this Petition for Certiorari

No._____

In The Supreme Court of the United States

Edward H. Flint   Petitioner

v.

KATIE KING   Respondent

PETITION FOR WRIT OF CERTIORARI

Edward H. Flint Pro, Se
Pro, SE, Counsel for Petitioner

QUESTIONS PRESENTED

1- Does the ruling by the United States Supreme Court in **Stump v Sparkman 435 U.S. 349, 357 (1978)** eliminate the requirement that a judge has to obey all court rules, cannons and state laws

2- What are the limits and meanings of **"normal functions"** and **<u>"clear absence of all jurisdiction</u>** in granting immunity to a judge as used in the Judgment issued by the United State Supreme Court in **Stump v Sparkman 435 U.S. 349, 357 (1978)**?

3- Is violating of the Kentucky Supreme Court Rules, violating Kentucky Statutes, denying a party Due Process violating Kentucky's Code of Procedures Rules and Cannons considered to be a normal function for a judge as stated in **Stump v Sparkman 435 U.S. 349, 357 (1978)**?

4- Was the trial court correct that no cause of action exists against a judge for judicial actions except when the judge acts was in the clear absence of jurisdiction, even when the judge denied Petitioner a Due Process trial and the judge violated Kentucky Supreme Court Rules and state laws and cannons ?

5- Was the trial and appeal courts correct when they ruled, a judge has immunity on all decisions a judge makes, regardless of the circumstances, if court rules and state laws, has been violated.

6- Is Chief Judge Roberts correct when he stated **"Judges are like umpires. Umpires don't make the rules. They apply them. The role of an umpire and a judge is critical. The judge makes sure everybody plays by the rules**

STATEMENT OF THE CASE

PROCEDURAL HISTORY

This action arises out of a complaint filed in Jefferson County Kentucky Circuit Court on October 2007 case No. 07-CI-10558. Petitioner was Pro, Se and was 76 years old. The case was about a flawed election for officers at a Condo Association where Petitioner lived. Petitioner knew based on evidence he had seen, the ballots had been substituted for and when the Board of Directors refuse to response to his letters asking that a meeting be called for a reelection and the Petitioner filed a suit.

Petition was Pro, Se and three judges violated Kentucky Supreme Court's rule regarding the moving and reassigning of cases. The judges by Kentucky Supreme Court Rules could not move the case without a reason, which they didn't have.

Petitioner sued the three judges in Federal District Court. The District Court granted the three judges immunity and dismissed Petitioner case. Petitioner appealed to the Court of Appeals. The Court of Appeals upheld the District Court order dismissing the appeal. Petitioner appealed to this court for Writ of certiorari and this court denied Petitioner certiorari.

Petitioner filed a different case in Jefferson County District Court and the first judge, on the first hearing denied Petitioner everything he asked for and out of the blue for no reason,(as the tape of the hearing shows), the judge threaten to put Petitioner in jail.

The case was assigned to Judge King the respondent. Judge King refused to let Petitioner have any discovery. Judge King threatens to put Petitioner in jail, for no reason as the recorded audio CD shows. It became clear that Judge King had been talked to by other judges in the court system and no judge in Jefferson County was going to give Petitioner a fair and honest trial. Petitioner sued Judge King in Federal Court alleging her of violating his "civil rights" by "Terroristic threatening. "

Judge King would not grant Petitioner discovery. Petitioner asked Judge King to move the case out of Jefferson County and she refused. Petitioner gave the trial court an audio CD recordings and the trial court stated a judge is granted the power to declare a person in contempt and thereby to put him in jail. The trial court judge is saying that a judge can on its own declare a person in contempt, when the CD shows there was no reason for Judge King to do what she did, except that other judges had told her to get Flint, because he sued fellow judges.

Petitioner asked all four judges to let him move the case to another county and all four refused, because they did not want Flint to have a chance to win a case in any court, including Federal

Court. All four judges denied Petitioner discovery.

The Federal District Court has dismissed all four of Petitioners cases against the judges. The Court of Appeals has denied Petitioner any relief. On all cases where Petitioner has sued judges, the Federal District Court dismissed all cases based on the fact that regardless of the bases for the suit, stating judges have absolute immunity. Each Judge cited **Stump v Sparkman 435 U.S. 349, 357 (1978)**

The Court of Appeals upholds the District Courts and states that the Supreme Court 1978 ruling has not changed nor has the language in Stump v Sparkman been changed or clarified and therefore they have no choice but to grant immunity, regardless of how bad the actions by the judge was.

ARGUMENTS

Petitioner argues that the Sixth Circuit Court of Appeals hung it case based on the district court dismissal and stated that "Judges are generally entitled to immunity from personal liability for actions taken on the bench. :a judge will not be deprived of immunity because the actions he took was in error, was done maliciously or in excess of his authority; rather he will be subject to liability only when he has acted in the clear absence of all jurisdiction" *Stump v. Sparkman*, 435 U.S. 349, 356-57 (1978)

No court in Jefferson County has said one word about what rights Petitioner had to due process. Petitioner states that denying Due Process, violating Courts rules and state's laws cannot be judicial actions and therefore is non-judicial.

If this court doesn't clarify the *Stump v. Sparkman* ruling there will never again be an honest judge in America. All Judges in America sooner or later will harm someone and use this case as an excuse.

There is no way the court system in America can keep judges under control from abusing the system, except for the possibility that a judge could be sued by a jury. The judge in this case as the record will show violated every issue to see that Petitioner never received a fair trial. Judge King had pressure on her, because Petitioner trying to find justice, sued judges.

Recently the United State Senate removed a judge for violating rules and being on the take. If this court thinks the same thing is not going, then you are living in a make believe land in your mind.

This court has the future of the America justice system in their hands. By leaving the Stump v Sparkman case as is, will set off a fire storm in every court house across America to see which party has the most money to buy a judge in a case. You children, your grandchildren's future children depend on this court's action and the legend you want to leave.

Petitioner again will tell this court that there are many, many cases being handled today in our country by corrupt judges and congress cannot pass a law to stop it. The only change of having an honest justice system is by this court to write the rules on how a judge must conduct them self and allow judges to be sue if it can be proven they violated the rules. This court let the pendulum swing too far when they wrote Stump v. Sparkman and this court now has a chance to frame the future of justice in America, even more that the framers of our constitution. Does any member of this court believe that our fore fathers would have let judges do as they please?

Our forefathers could not see the future and see how judges can be so corrupt. If they could, maybe they would have set up a different justice system, because they wanted an honest system. Our country was founded by people who were running away from what is now taking place by judges. If the President of our country can be sued then why should anyone be exempt?

The appeals court in their ruling stated and I quote,

"Here Judge King engaged in conduct soundly within the scope of her judicial duties and within the court's jurisdiction. Contrary to Flint's argument, even if Judge King erred in finding him in contempt of court, her decision is still protected by judicial immunity because it was made within the scope of her official duties as a judge. See Stump, 435 U.S. at 356-57. Finally, although Flint argues that Stump is "bad law," it has not been overruled by the Supreme Court and we are bound by the precedent set forth therein

This court owes it to every America to frame the rules on which a judge can be sued or tell the people that a judge cannot be sued under any condition.

This court has an opportunity to leave its mark on America history forever.

REASONS FOR GRANTING THE WRIT

1- This honorable body should want to see that every citizen of America is granted Due Process.

2- This court should and needs to clarify the meaning of the wording of "Clear Absence of all Jurisdiction and normal functions" as used in *Stump v. Sparkman*.

3- Only by straightening out the question of immunity for judges, which has been raging ever since the ruling was made in 1978, will true confidence exist in the justice system in America that the justice system is working hard to make sure every American will receive justice in the entire court system, throughout America. Without total confidence in honest judges America cannot stand

4- Petitioner deserves an opportunity to try his case.

5- If all judges was honest this ruling would not be needed, but like all parts of our society, there are bad eggs in every group.

CONCLUSION

1- The language in *Stump v. Sparkman* is vague, open for different interpretations and all parties in the justice system need to know their simplified actual meanings.

2- America needs to know in order to remove any doubt. The decision was 5 to 3 with one dissenting vote when this court made its ruling in 1978.

3- Petitioner has been harmed by the lower courts interpreting. He has other cases that will come to this court unless he gets a clarification.

4- Petitioner asks this honorable body to move this issue forward with a clear interpretation.

5- Unless the court clarifies the meaning of Stump v Sparkman, immunity for judges, the issue will expand as to what a judge can do in their court. There has to be a limit of all judge's actions, at some point in law and this court needs to make sure that all decisions are a correct decision, so everyone is playing the same game, by the same rules.

6- A clear definition gives honest judges, lawyers and average persons a better shot at equal justice.

7- Every honest ethical judge in America would welcome a clarification of the meaning of Stump v. Sparkman.

8- The trial court and the court of appeals both are defending Judge King because they know Flint sued the judges. Neither court listened to the audio CD to search for the truth. The CD proves that Flint did nothing to cause Judge King to threaten to put Flint in jail. Judge King did not give Flint Due Process. The CD is what every judge should have listened to and none did. The Federal District court and the Sixth District Court of Appeals are not interested in justice but only interest in showing they have power and will use it to crucify any person who would dare to try to find justice after suing judges. Flint begs this court to listen to the CD.

Respectfully submitted,

s/ Edward H. Flint, Pro, Se.

*******My Petition to the Supreme Court ends here********

The Supreme Court refused to consider the case.

"As you can read, the issue of Absolute Immunity is ingrained in every judge in the Federal District Courts and in the Sixth Circuit Court of Appeals, plus the Supreme Court.

By this time, I became more determine that I had to find a way to find one judge that believed a judge cannot violate the court's rules and get by with it."

CHAPTER 5

LAWSUIT FLINT V. JUDGE DONALD ARMSTRONG

I will now insert the complaint I filed

UNITED STATES DISTRICT COURT
WESTERN DISTRICT OF KENTUCKY
LOUISVILLE DIVISON

CASE NO. 309-CV-878-H

EDWARD H. FLINT   **PLAINTIFF**

VS

COMPLAINT

JUDGE DONALD L. ARMSTRONG JR.   **DEFENDANT**

COMPLAINT

Comes now the Plaintiff, Edward H. Flint acting as his own counsel against Defendant Judge Donald Armstrong Jr. for actions committed by Defendant in case NO. 09-C-004506 in Jefferson County District Court and for this cause of action, states as follows:

1- Plaintiff Edward H. Flint lives at

2- Defendant Judge Armstrong was and still is a Judge in Jefferson County District Court.

3- Plaintiff alleges that Defendant's actions injured Plaintiff both mentally and physically.

4- Plaintiff alleges that Defendant's actions denied Plaintiff his US Civil Rights.

5- Plaintiff alleges that Defendant failed to perform his duty required by the Kentucky Justice System and Kentucky Supreme Court.

6- Plaintiff alleges that Defendant failed to perform his ethical responsibility required by the Kentucky Justice System and Kentucky Supreme Court.

7- Plaintiff filed a civil lawsuit case No.-09-C-004506 in Jefferson County Kentucky District Court and Judge Armstrong was assigned the case on August 14, 2009, after another judge recused themselves.

8- Plaintiff alleges that Defendant's actions were vindictive and harmful because Plaintiff had sued three (3) judges from the Jefferson County Circuit Court in Federal Court before Plaintiff filed case NO 09-C- 004506 in District Court.

9- Plaintiff alleges that Defendant's actions were vindictive and harmful after Plaintiff asked Judge King the original judge to recuse herself from case N0-09-C-004560, which she did on July 24, 2009 and Defendant was then assigned to be the judge starting August 14, 2009.

10- Plaintiff alleges that Defendant's actions were also vindictive and harmful after Plaintiff on September 25, 2009 sued the Judge King that recused herself on July 24, 2009.

11- Plaintiff alleges that Defendant actions denied Plaintiff his judicial rights and discriminated against him.

12- Plaintiff alleges that the Defendant was bias against him and harassed him.

13- Plaintiff alleges that Defendant conspired with others against him.

14- Plaintiff alleges that Defendant harmed him when Defendant did not abide by the Civil Rules of the Kentucky Court System

15- Plaintiff alleges Plaintiff was put into a horrifying position by Defendant's actions. Defendant told Plaintiff he was experienced and honest as a judge and Defendant failed to perform to those experiences.

16- Plaintiff alleges that Defendant actions were not in the interest of justice.

17- Plaintiff believes other laws, rules and/or other action may have been broken and only discovery will tell, and at that time Plaintiff will ask for leave to amend this complaint.

Therefore Plaintiff demands that Defendant be held liable for his actions in harming Plaintiff.

Respectfully submitted

Edward H. Flint Pro, Se

********The district court order starts here*********

UNITED STATES DISTRICT COURT
WESTERN DISTRICT OF KENTUCKY AT LOUISVILLE

CIVIL ACTION NO.3:09CV-878-H

EDWARD H. Flint   PLAINTIFF

v.

JUDGE DONALD E. AMSTRONG, JR.   DEFENDANT

The court granted immunity to Judge Armstrong

ORDER

Plaintiff has filed a lawsuit against Kentucky District Court Judge Donald E. Armstrong, in connection with his actions in a case involving Plaintiff. Defendant has moved to dismiss this complaint on numerous grounds including those of sovereign immunity and judicial immunity. The court has reviewed the pending motions and agree entirely with the basses for Defendant's request for dismiss.

Plaintiff is not alleging that Judge Armstrong did not have jurisdiction over his case. Quite the contrary, Plaintiff claims are based on the assertion that Judge Armstrong had jurisdiction over this case but failed to manage it in a proper manner. No cause of action exists against a judge for judicial actions except acts in the clear absence of jurisdiction. Here, Plaintiff claims against Judge Armstrong are barred by absolute judicial immunity and must be dismissed.

I appealed to the Supreme Court My Petition starts here.

No._____

_____

In The Supreme Court of the United States

Edward H. Flint   Petitioner

v.

Donald L. ARMSTRONG JR.   Respondent

On Petition for Writ of Certiorari
Court of Appeals for the Sixth Circuit.

PETITION FOR WRIT OF CERTIORARI

QUESTIONS PRESENTED

1- Does the ruling by the United States Supreme Court in **Stump v Sparkman 435 U.S. 349, 357 (1978)** eliminate the requirement that a judge has to obey all court rules, cannons and state laws

2- What are the limits and meanings of **"normal functions"** and **"clear absence of all jurisdiction** in granting immunity to a judge as used in the Judgment issued by the United State Supreme Court in **Stump v Sparkman 435 U.S. 349, 357 (1978)**?

3- Is violating of the Kentucky Supreme Court Rules, violating Kentucky Statutes, denying a party Due Process violating Kentucky's Code of Procedures Rules and Cannons considered to be a normal function for a judge as stated in **Stump v Sparkman 435 U.S. 349, 357 (1978)**?

4- Was the trial court correct that no cause of action exists against a judge for judicial actions except when the judge acts was in the clear absence of jurisdiction, even when the judge denied Petitioner a Due Process trial and the judge violated Kentucky Supreme Court Rules and state laws and cannons ?

5- Was the trial and appeal courts correct when they ruled, a judge has immunity on all decisions a judge makes regardless of the circumstances, if court rules and state laws, has been violated.

6- Is Chief Judge Roberts correct when he stated **"Judges are like umpires. Umpires don't make the rules. They apply them. The role of an umpire and a judge is critical. The judge makes sure everybody plays by the rules**

STATEMENT OF THE CASE

PROCEDURAL HISTORY

This action arises out of a complaint filed in Jefferson County Kentucky Circuit Court on October 2007 case No. 07-CI-10558. Petitioner was Pro, Se and was 76 years old. The case was about a flawed election for officers at a Condo Association where Petitioner lived. Petitioner knew based on evidence he had seen, the ballots had been substituted for and when the Board of Directors refuse to response to his letters asking that a meeting be called for a reelection and the Petitioner filed a suit.

Petition was Pro, Se and three judges violated Kentucky Supreme Court's rule regarding the moving and reassigning of cases. The judges by Kentucky Supreme Court Rules could not move the case without a reason, which they didn't have.

Petitioner sued the three judges in Federal District Court. The District Court granted the three judges immunity and dismissed Petitioner case. Petitioner appealed to the Court of Appeals. The Court of Appeals upheld the District Court order dismissing the appeal. Petitioner appealed to this court for Writ of certiorari and this court denied Petitioner certiorari.

Petitioner filed a different case in Jefferson County District Court and the first judge, on the first hearing denied Petitioner everything he asked for and out of the blue for no reason,(as the tape of the hearing shows), the judge threaten to put Petitioner in jail. Petitioner sued this judge in Federal Court for terrorist threatening.

Petitioner sued this judge in Federal Court for terrorist threatening.

The case was assigned to Judge Armstrong the respondent. Judge Armstrong refused to let Petitioner have any discovery. It became clear that no judge in Jefferson County was going to give Petitioner a fair and honest trial. Petitioner sued Judge Armstrong in Federal Court.

Petitioner then trying to find justice moved the case to Jefferson County Circuit Court. The first judge would not grant Petitioner discovery and Petitioner sued him in Federal Court.

The case was moved to a second judge in Circuit court. This judge refused to give Petition any discovery. Petitioner sued him in Federal court and then asked him to recuse himself from the case and he refused to recuse himself.

Petitioner asked all four judges to let him move the case to another county and all four refused.

Petitioner now has the case in the Kentucky Court of Appeals and the Kentucky Supreme Court, regarding the judge recusing him from the case.

The Federal District Court has dismissed all four of Petitioners cases against the judges. The Court of Appeals has denied Petitioner any relief. On all case where Petitioner has sued judges the District Court has dismiss all cases based on the fact that regardless of the bases for the suit, judges have absolute immunity. Each Judge cited **Stump v Sparkman 435 U.S. 349, 357 (1978)**

The Court of Appeals upholds the District Courts and states that the Supreme Court 1978 ruling has not has not changed nor has the language in Stump v Sparkman been changed or clarified and therefore they have no choice but to grant immunity, regardless of how bad the actions by the judge was.

ARGUMENTS

Petitioner argues that the Sixth Circuit Court of Appeals hung it case based on the district court dismissal that stated "Armstrong is entitled to absolute judicial immunity." The Appeals court stated "that a judge will not be deprived of immunity because the action he or she took was in error." The Appeal Court cited *Stump* v *Sparkman* 435 U.S. 349, 356-357 (1978). The court again quoted "immunity is overcome only when a judge engages in non-judicial actions." Petitioner states that denying Due Process, violating Courts rules and state's laws cannot be judicial actions and therefore is non-judicial.

If this court doesn't clarify the Stump v. Sparkman there will never again be an honest judge in America, someday. All Judges sooner or later will harm someone and use this case as excuses.

There is no way the court system in America can keep judges in control from abusing the system except for the possibility that a judge could be sued by a jury. The judge in this case as the record will show violated every issue to see that Petitioner never received a fair trial. Judge Armstrong had pressure on him, from other judges, to stop Flint.

Recently the United State Senate removed a judge for violating rules and being on the take. If this court thinks the same thing is not going on across, then you are living in a make believe land in your mind.

This court has the future of the America justice system in their hands. By leaving the Stump v Sparkman case as is, will set off a fire storm in every court house across America to see who has the most money to buy a judge in a case. You children, your grandchildren and all future children depends on this court's action.

Petitioner again will tell this court that there are many cases being handled today in our country by corrupt judges and congress cannot pass a law to stop it. The only chance of having an honest justice system is by this court writing the rules on how a judge must conduct them self and allow judges to be sue if it can be proven they violated the rules. This court in 1978 let the pendulum swing too far when they wrote Stump v. Sparkman and this court now has a chance to frame the future of justice in America, even more that the framers of our constitution. Does any member of this court believe that our fore fathers would have let judges do as they please?

Our fore fathers could not see the future and see how many judges can be so corrupt. If they could, maybe they would have set up a different justice system, because they wanted an honest system.

Our country was founded by people who were running away from what is now taking place by judges.

If the President of our country can be sued then why should anyone be exempt?

This court owes it to every America to frame the rules on which a judge can be sued or tell the people that a judge cannot be sued under any condition.

This court has a chance to leave its mark on America history forever.

REASONS FOR GRANTING THE WRIT

1- This honorable body should want to see that every citizen of America is granted Due Process.

2- This court should and needs to clarify the meaning of the wording of "Clear Absence of all Jurisdiction and normal functions" as used in Stump v. Sparkman.

3- Straightening out the question of immunity for judges, which has been raging ever since the ruling was made in 1978, will true confidence be in America, that the justice system is working hard to make sure every American alike will receive justice in the entire court system, throughout America.

4- Petition deserves an opportunity to try his case.

5- If all judges was honest this ruling would not be needed, but like all parts of our society, there are bad eggs in every group.

CONCLUSION

1- The language in Stump v. Sparkman is vague, open for different interpretations and all parties in the justice system needs to know their simplified actual meanings.

2- America needs to know what a justice is in order to remove any doubt. The decision was 5 to 3 with one dissenting vote when this court made its ruling in 1978. A clarification is good for America. When there is no doubt of a court's ruling, it's good for America and for justice.

3- Petitioner has been harmed by the lower courts interpreting. He has other cases that will come to this court unless he gets a clarification.

4- Petitioner asks this honorable body to move this issue forward with a clear interpretation.

5- Unless the court clarifies the meaning of Stump v Sparkman, immunity for judges, the issue will expand as to what a judge can do in their court. There has to be a limit of all judge's actions, at some point in law and this court needs to make sure that all decisions are correct decisions, so everyone is playing the same game, by the same rules.

6- A clear definition gives honest judges, lawyers and average persons a better shot at equal justice.

7- Every honest ethical judge in America would welcome a clarification of the meaning of Stump v. Sparkman.

Respectfully submitted,

s/ Edward H. Flint, Pro, Se.
Pro, Se, Counsel for Petitioner

The Supreme Court refused to review the case

CHAPTER 6

LAWSUIT FLINT V. JUDGE McKAY CHAUVIN

I will now insert the complaint I filed.

UNITED STATES DISTRICT COURT
WESTERN DISTRICT OF KENTUCKY
LOUISVILLE DIVISON

CASE NO. 3:10-CV-149-M

EDWARD H. FLINT   PLAINTIFF

VS

<u>COMPLAINT</u>

A.C. MCKAY CHAVIN- Judge   DEFENDANT

COMPLAINT

Comes now the Plaintiff, Edward H. Flint acting as his own counsel against Defendant Judge A.C. McKay Chauvin an individual for actions committed by Defendant in case NO. 09-CI-010478 as judge in Jefferson County Circuit Court and for this cause of action, states as follows:

1- Plaintiff Edward H. Flint lives at

2- Defendant Chauvin was and still is a Judge in Jefferson County Circuit Court.

3- Plaintiff filed a civil lawsuit, case No.-09-CI-010478 in Jefferson County Kentucky Circuit Court and Judge Chauvin was assigned the case about December 22, 2009, after another judge recused themselves.

4- Plaintiff alleges that Defendant's actions denied Plaintiff his US Civil Rights and his Constitution Rights.

5- Plaintiff alleges that Defendant's actions injured Plaintiff both mentally and physically.

6- Plaintiff alleges that Defendant failed to perform his duty required by the Kentucky Justice System, the Kentucky Supreme Court Rules and laws of the state of Kentucky.

7- Plaintiff alleges that Defendant failed to perform his ethical responsibility required by the Kentucky Justice System, The Kentucky Supreme Court Rules and laws of the state of Kentucky.

8- Plaintiff alleges that Defendant's actions were vindictive and harmful because Plaintiff had sued four (4) judges from the Jefferson County Circuit Court in Federal Court and two Judges from the Jefferson District Court before case NO 09-CI-010478 was filed in Circuit Court.

9- Plaintiff alleges that Defendant's actions were vindictive and harmful after the case was assigned to him

10- Plaintiff alleges that Defendant actions denied Plaintiff his judicial rights and discriminated against him.

11- Plaintiff alleges that the Defendant was bias against him.

12- Plaintiff alleges that Defendant conspired with others against him.

13- Plaintiff alleges that Defendant harmed him when Defendant did not correctly abide by the Civil Rules of the Kentucky Court System and the laws of the state of Kentucky.

14- Plaintiff alleges that Defendant actions were not in the interest of justice and denied the Plaintiff a fair and honest trial

15- Plaintiff believes other laws, rules and/or other action may have been broken and only discovery will tell, and at that time Plaintiff will ask for leave to amend this complaint.

This case is worth more than $75,000.00 as required by this court

Therefore Plaintiff demands that Defendant be held liable for his actions in the above allegations.

Respectfully submitted

Edward H. Flint Pro, Se

The court issued an order that stated,

''A judge will not be deprived of immunity because the action he took was in error, was done maliciously, or was in excess of his authority; rather, he will be subject to liability only when he has acted in the clear absence of all jurisdiction.'' *Stump o. Sparkman*435 U.S. 349, 356-57 (1978) *see also Baker v. Fletcher,* 204 S.w'3d 589, 595 (Ky. 2006). Because Flint's claim in this case is based on Judge Chauvin's rulings in the state court proceeding, and because there is no allegation of any facts suggesting that Judge Chauvin acted in clear absence of all jurisdiction, Defendant's motion to dismiss is GRANTED.

Defendant also requests sanctions in the form of attorney's fees and an order requiring pre-responsive-pleading judicial review of Plaintiff's future filings because "[t]his is the fifth suit against judges presiding over cases involving Mr. Flint. [and] enough is enough." (Defendant's Motion for Sanctions, P. 2). The Court agrees that enough is enough. However, as Judge Simpson recently noted in *Flint v. Edwards,* No. 3:09-cv-00956-CRS, *2 (W.D. Ky. May 4, 2010), an award of attorney's fees for defendants like Judge Chauvin would be an odd fit because they are represented by the Kentucky Attorney General's office and therefore have no attorney's fees. The Court also does not believe that an order requiring pre-screening of Plaintiff's future filings is warranted because what makes Flint's claims frivolous-the failure to plead anything that might overcome judicial immunity-also makes the responsive burden on the state very slight.

I appealed to the Supreme Court and my Petition starts here

No._____

In The Supreme Court of the United States

_____

Edward H. Flint   Petitioner,

Versus

A.C. MCKAY CHAUVIN   Respondent

PETITION FOR WRIT OF CERTIORARI

QUESTIONS PRESENTED

1- Does the ruling by the United States Supreme Court in **Stump v Sparkman 435 U.S. 349, 357 (1978)** eliminate the requirement that a judge has to obey all court rules and state laws, on decisions they make

2- What are the limits and meanings of **"normal functions"** and <u>**"clear absence of all jurisdiction**</u> in granting immunity to a judge as used in the Judgment issued by the United State Supreme Court in **Stump v Sparkman 435 U.S. 349, 357 (1978)**?

3- Is violating of the Kentucky Supreme Court Rules, violating Kentucky Statutes, denying a party Due Process and violating Kentucky's Code of Procedures Rules considered to be a normal function for a judge as stated in **Stump v Sparkman 435 U.S. 349, 357 (1978)**?

4- Was the trial court correct that Respondent was not in <u>**"clear absence of all jurisdictions"**</u> in its rulings, when he violated court rules and statute laws?

5- Was the trial and appeal courts correct when they ruled, a judge has immunity on all decisions a judge makes regardless of the circumstances, which means regardless if court rules and state laws, was violated.

6- Is Chief Judge Roberts correct or wrong when he told the United States Senate that a judge's role is as follows, **"Judges are like umpires. Umpires don't make the rules. They apply them. The role of an umpire and a judge is critical. The make sure everybody plays by the rules. But it is a limited role.**

STATEMENT OF THE CASE

PROCEDURAL HISTORY

This action arises out of a complaint filed in Jefferson County Kentucky Circuit Court on October 2007 case No. 07-CI-10558. Petitioner was Pro, Se and was 76 years old. The case was about a flawed election for officers at a Condo Association where Petitioner lived. Petitioner knew based on evidence he had seen, the ballots had been substituted for and when the Board of Directors refuse to response to his letters asking that a meeting be called for a reelection and the Petitioner filed a suit.

Petition was Pro, Se and three judges violated Kentucky Supreme Court's rule regarding the moving and reassigning of cases. The judges by Kentucky Supreme Court Rules could not move the case without a reason, which they didn't have.

Petitioner sued the three judges in Federal District Court. The District Court granted the three judges immunity and dismissed Petitioner case. Petitioner appealed to the Court of Appeals. The Court of Appeals upheld the District Court order dismissing the appeal. Petitioner appealed to this court for Writ of certiorari and this court denied Petitioner certiorari.

Petitioner filed a different case in Jefferson County District Court and the first judge, on the first hearing denied Petitioner everything he asked for and out of the blue for no reason,(as the tape of the Hearing shows), the judge threaten to put Petitioner in jail.

Petitioner requested that the judge recuse themselves from the case and the judge did.

Petitioner sued this judge in Federal Court for terrorist threatening.

The case was assigned to another judge and that judge refused to let Petitioner have any discovery. It became clear that no judge in Jefferson County was going to give Petitioner a fair and honest trial. Petitioner sued that judge in Federal Court.

Petitioner moved the case to Jefferson County Circuit Court. The first judge would not grant Petitioner discovery and Petitioner sued him in Federal Court.

The case was moved to a second judge in Circuit court. This judge refused to give Petition any discovery. Petitioner sued him in Federal court and then asked him to re-cuse himself from the case and he refused to recuse himself.

Petitioner asked all four judges to let him move the case to another county and all four refused.

Petitioner now has the case in the Kentucky Court of Appeals and the Kentucky Supreme Court, regarding the judge recusing him from the case.

The Federal District Court has dismissed all four of Petitioners cases against the judges. The Court of Appeals has the cases on appeal, except this case and one other that Petitioner is asking for a rehearing. On all case where Petitioner has sued judges the District Court has dismiss all cases based on the fact that regardless of the bases for the suit, judges have absolute immunity. Each judge cited **Stump v Sparkman 435 U.S. 349, 357 (1978)**

The Court of Appeals upholds the District Courts and states that the Supreme Court 1978 ruling has not has not changed nor has the language in Stump v Sparkman been changed or clarified and therefore they have no choice but to grant immunity, regardless of how bad the actions by the judge was.

ARGUMENTS

Petitioner argues that the Court of Appeals was not correct when it stated that "Although Flint has not expressly identified which improper actions the judge engaged in," and further stated that "It is clear that Flint challenges the judge's ruling in Flint lawsuit against the condominium." The appeals court is wrong in that statement. Flint gave the district court over an inch of pleadings with exhibits, which out lined the facts, where Judge Chauvin **denied Flint all discoveries he had requested, denied him a trial date, which he requested** and Judge Chauvin further stated, **"this case has a long way to go,"** Judge Chauvin **denied Flint the right to move the case to the next county, although there is a Kentucky law that says Flint was entitled to move the case".** The Appeals court failed to look at the records in the case.

The Appeals court is wrong in their statement that Flint questioned the Stump ruling. What Flint questioned was, does violating Court rules and state laws by a judge meet the ruling of Stump. This is the same question Flint is asking this Court. The Court of Appeals stated that their ruling was and I quote, **"Finally, although Flint takes issue with the holding in Stump, he does not allege that the case has been overruled by the Supreme Court, and this court is bound by the precedent set forth in that case. Hence, the district court properly concluded that judge Chauvin was entitled to judicial immunity."**

The courts have left no way for a judge to be sued, even if they violate rules and laws.

The reading of Stump v Sparkman shows it was meant by the Supreme Court for a judge to be sued under certain conditions and Petitioner is asking this honorable body to clarify the language in the Stump case, so all parties knows what those conditions are.

Petitioner will quote from Stump, **"a judge will not be deprived of immunity because the action he took was in error, was done maliciously, or was in excess of his authority: rather, he will be subject to liability only when he has acted in the clear absence of all jurisdictions."**

Petitioner's interpretation is in 1978 this court wanted to protect with immunity a judge who had made a ruling based up on their best judgment, excluding violating courts rules and laws. If this is the correct interpretation Petitioner believes it is a good ruling. But the court did not mean for it to extent to the point a judge can violate Court rules and laws. To do so take away a party's Due Process to a fair and honest trial.

However courts are interpreting the wording to mean it applies to everything a judge does regardless of what they do.

In Petitioner case the judge violated Kentucky Supreme Court Rules, violated the Due Process Amendment, violated Kentucky rules of civil Procedures and violated

Kentucky laws. In addition it is plain that judges across America believe they have immunity from each and everything they say or order or do.

Stump has two phases that should be clarified. The first being"**clear absence of all jurisdiction"** and the second being **"Normal Functions."**

Courts have taken a position that this language takes in everything a judge does or says and therefore a judge is granted immunity, regardless if the judges violated rules and laws.

Petitioner argues that no violation of court rules and any law can be in a judge's jurisdiction and such violations cannot be the normal function of a judge.

The interpretation by the lower courts is against Cannons Laws and all meanings of them. In really the court's rulings says that every judge in America can do as they please and be granted immunity. Only a clarification of the language in Stump v. Sparkman by this court can America be sure of when a judge steps out of bounds of his duty.

REASONS FOR GRANTING THE WRIT

1- This honorable body should want to see that every citizen of America is granted Due Process.

2- This court should and needs to clarify the meaning of the wording of "Clear Absence of all Jurisdiction and normal functions" as used in Stump v. Sparkman.

3- Only by clarifying Stump v Sparkman will true justice ever exist for everyone in America.

4- Straightening out the question of immunity for judges, which has been raging ever since the ruling was made in 1978, will true confidence be in America, that the justice system is working hard to make sure every American will receive justice in the entire court system, throughout America.

5- Petitioner deserves an opportunity to try his case.

6- If all judges was honest this ruling would not be needed, but like all parts of our society, there are bad eggs in every group.

CONCLUSION

1- The language in Stump v. Sparkman is vague, open for different interpretations and all parties in the justice system need to know their simplified actual meanings.

2- America needs to know in order to remove any doubt. The decision was 5 to 3 with one dissenting vote when this court made its ruling in 1978. A clarification is good for America. When there is no doubt of a court ruling, it's good for America and for justice.

3- Petition has been harmed by the lower courts interpreting. He has 3 other cases that will come to this court unless he gets a clarification.

4- Petitioner asks this honorable body to move this issue forward with a clear interpretation.

5- Unless the court clarifies the meaning of Stump v Sparkman, immunity for judges, the issue will expand as to what a judge can do in their court. There has to be a limit of all judge's actions, at some point in law and this court needs to make sure that all decisions are a correct decision, so everyone is playing the same game, by the same rules.

6- A clear definition gives honest judges, lawyers and average persons a better shot at equal justice.

7- Every honest ethical judge in America would welcome a clarification of the meaning of Stump v. Sparkman.

8- Petitioner deserves justice not heartaches. A clarification of the meaning of Stump v. Sparkman will make the details actual and leave no doubts.

Respectfully submitted,

s/ Edward H. Flint, Pro, Se.

The Supreme Court refused to look at the case

CHAPTER 7

LAWSUIT FLINT V. CHURCHILL DOWNS ET AL

***** I now insert the complaint I filed. ------

UNITED STATES DISTRICT COURT
WESTERN DISTRICT OF KENTUCKY
LOUISVILLE DIVISON

CASE NO 3:10-CV-202-H

EDWARD H. FLINT   PLAINTIFF

VS

COMPLAINT

CHURCHILL DOWNS INC.   DEFENDANT

Robert L. Evans-President and an individual

William C. Carstanjen-Chief Operating Officer and an individual

T. Kevin Flanery-President Churchill Downs Race Track and an individual

Rebecca "Becky" Reed- Secretary-Manager of Special Seating and an individual

John Does and Jane Does.

Comes the Plaintiff Edward H. Flint acting as his own counsel against Defendants as a corporation and as individuals for actions committed against and harmful to Plaintiff.

1. Plaintiff, Edward H. Flint lives at

2. Defendant Evans, Carstanjen, Flanery and Reed are employees of Churchill Downs Inc.

3. Defendant Churchill Downs Inc. Is a large corporation with headquarters in Louisville Kentucky with race tracks and gambling faculties throughout United States and are listed on the NASAQ Stock Exchange.

4. Plaintiff alleges that since the 1970's he was a major player in the Kentucky Horse Racing/ Legislation industry in Kentucky and has worked hard on behalf of Churchill Downs and other tracks in Kentucky to improve racing and the lives of people involved in racing and Churchill gained millions of dollars from his effort, which meant nothing to Defendants after Plaintiff wouldn't agree with Defendants on a public issue that would benefit Defendants now, so they decided to harm Plaintiff by not selling him the tickets.

5. Plaintiff had purchased the box seating for the Kentucky Derby and Kentucky Oaks plus other seating from Defendant for over thirty-seven (37) years seating for the same days and Defendant have refused to sell Plaintiff these same tickets the 2010 Derby and Oaks

6. Churchill Downs is a public traded company and the largest share of Churchill stock controls the employment of the individual Defendants, and has within the last Seven or Ten years has purchases hundreds of thousands of shares of Churchill Down's stock, anticipating the General Assembly of Kentucky would grant slot machines or full blown gambling at race tracks in Kentucky, their goal was either a casino or slot machines at their track.

7. The Governor of Kentucky in 2008 and 2009 backed a gambling, slot machine and or casino bill both in the General Assembly of Kentucky and publicly that that the Defendant's wanted, on the pretense it would save racing in Kentucky, however it would have made Defendants a lot of money.

8. Plaintiff reviewed the slot machine bill and openly told Kentucky that the bill was a dirty bill and or was a waste of money, because it would not save racing in Kentucky, but would make race tracks a lot of money, hundreds of million dollars per year.

9. Plaintiff alleges that Defendants for years of 2010 elected not to sell Plaintiff the same seating he had for over thirty-seven (37) years to the Kentucky Derby and Kentucky Oaks for the reason to be vindictive and harmful.

10. Plaintiff alleges that Defendant has been no bonafide reason to deny selling Plaintiff the same tickets as in the past, except to be hateful.

11. Plaintiff alleges that the only visible change in the relationship between the Plaintiff and Defendants since the 2009 Derby and Oaks and the invoicing of the 2010 tickets, is Plaintiff being outspoken against the slot machine legislation that the Defendant wanted and therefore Defendants decided to move Plaintiff out of the picture by harming him.

12. Plaintiff alleges that Defendants was upset with Plaintiff, because of the Plaintiff's public regarding the issue of the slot machine bill that the Governor and Defendants wanted passed, which was the Defendants' money making scheme. Defendant were mad at Plaintiff and the only they had to hurt Plaintiff was by denying him the tickets he had for over thirty seven years,

13. Plaintiff alleges that defendant had once promised they would sell Plaintiff the same tickets for life.

14. Plaintiff alleges that Defendants has a long history of being vindictive against Plaintiff when and if Plaintiff didn't do what the Defendants wanted.

15. Plaintiff alleges that Defendants gained nothing by denying Plaintiff purchasing the tickets the same as in the past, except to harm him to get even with him.

16. Plaintiff alleges that when Defendants didn't see eye to eye with Plaintiff, their reaction was to destroy Plaintiff.

17. Plaintiff alleges that Defendant discriminated against Plaintiff.

18. Plaintiff alleges that Defendants had a history of being spiteful to Plaintiff and found a reason to get even.

19. Plaintiff alleges that Defendants between themselves and with others conspired against Plaintiff to harm him by not selling him the tickets in question.

20. Plaintiff alleges that the only thing the Defendant had to gain by denying him the tickets in question was harming him.

21. Plaintiff alleges that the top management of Churchill Downs has changed a number of times over the last ten (10) years and no action was taken against Plaintiff's tickets, until Plaintiff wouldn't support their position on slot machines and opposes it, which they believe harmed them and blamed Plaintiff.

22. Plaintiff alleges that he worked hard to settle this complaint with Defendants and they refuse to make Plaintiff whole.

23. Plaintiff alleges that Defendants have a long history of being hateful when they don't get their way and they see the Kentucky Derby as a tool to use against

anyone who won't cow tail to them, just like they use the same tools to pay back those who helped them or could help them in the General Assembly.

24. Plaintiff alleges that within the last four or five years Defendants asked Plaintiff to come work for them to help get slot machines or casinos bills approved in the General Assembly and Plaintiff did not accept their offer, refused to help them and Defendants have held it against him.

25. Plaintiff alleges that the tickets in question were sold to friends of the Defendants, without consideration for Churchill Downs's shareholders to potential shareholders or the State of Kentucky or their obligation to Plaintiff.

26. The question is does the Kentucky Derby belong to the state of Kentucky or does it belong to a private organization that cam turn it policies on and off at will, like a water faucet.

27. Plaintiff alleges that Defendants tried to keep Plaintiff from filing this complaint by bribing/offering to sell him inferior seating.

28. Plaintiff alleges that Defendants based on prior year's history had no reason not to sell Plaintiff the tickets in question for the year 2010, except to harm him.

29. Plaintiff alleges that more than the cost of the tickets was involved in Defendants action of not selling Plaintiff the tickets this year.

30. Plaintiff alleges that if Plaintiff had agreed with Defendants on the issue of slot machines he would not have lost his tickets.

31. Plaintiff alleges that if he had attempted to help the Defendants obtain slot machines at race tracks he would have been allowed to keep his tickets.

32. Plaintiff alleges that the Kentucky Derby belongs to the people of Kentucky and proper management of the Derby is essential to maintain the renowned imagine of Kentucky and Defendants actions violated the trust that the people of Kentucky gave them.

33. Plaintiff alleges that all tickets to the Kentucky Derby and Kentucky Oaks was not sold out in the past five years and in the last weeks or so in those five years Defendants had to scramble and sell tickets to scalpers or friends to get rid of all of the Derby and Oaks tickets and therefore Defendants had no reason for taking away Plaintiff's tickets in 2010.

34. Plaintiff alleges that Defendants sold the tickets Plaintiff had bought for years, to someone else and Defendants had other tickets that they could have been sold

to that person instead, but chose to sell Plaintiff's tickets to that person, to hurt Plaintiff.

35. Plaintiff alleges that Defendants received no more money from the sale of the tickets in question, from another person, than what Plaintiff would have paid for them.

36. Plaintiff alleges that Defendants did not use good business practice in their selling of Kentucky Derby tickets and this action was not made in a way on which shareholders or possible shareholders or the state of Kentucky could rely.

37. Plaintiff alleges that Defendants violated his civil rights.

38. Plaintiff alleges that Defendants actions caused Plaintiff mental anguish and humiliation.

39. Plaintiff alleges that Defendants didn't have a reliable written policy on which a customer could depend on, but Defendants make up rules as they go along, to suit their likes and dislikes of a person and as a state regulated entity they had a duty to have a policy that their board of directors and the state of Kentucky had approved, one to be strictly enforced each year and Defendants failed to do so.

40. Plaintiff alleges that Defendants only cares about personal gains and have no concern for loyal fans, which is not in the best interest of Kentucky or potential shareholders.

41. Plaintiff alleges that the Kentucky Derby belongs to the people of Kentucky and proper management of the Derby is essential to maintain the renown imagine of the Kentucky Derby and Kentucky Oaks and Defendants actions violated the trust that the people of Kentucky gives them.

42. Plaintiff alleges that Defendants made personal gains by the way they handled the 2010 Kentucky Derby tickets, but not extra profit gains for the company and thereby had no reason to sell the tickets in question to another person, except to harm Plaintiff.

43. Plaintiff alleges that Defendants had other motives besides the duty expected of them by the shareholders, potential shareholders or their Board of Directors or Kentucky

44. Plaintiff alleges that Defendants actions were not performed to a board of directors approved company policy, but their actions were performed by their like or dislike of a person who they wanted to hurt for disagreeing with them.

45. Plaintiff alleges that Defendants never notified him about being denied his tickets.

46. Defendants claimed Plaintiff name was taken off of the list by a machine and Plaintiff alleges Defendant does not have a machine to randomly remove names off of their records, for a violation of something, but they use a who they like or dislike method, which violates civil rights, they acted as if people are slaves to do with as they please.

47. Plaintiff alleges that Defendants uses unknown tactics to get back at or get even with people they don't like and Plaintiff was one of those, thereby harming Plaintiff.

48. Plaintiff alleges that Defendants justification to defend their actions was not in the best interest of a public owned and public regulated company or the state of Kentucky.

49. Plaintiff alleges that Defendants had a duty to treat every person the same at all times and their actions regarding the tickets in question violated Plaintiff's rights.

50. Plaintiff alleges that Defendants harmed him because Defendant doesn't understand the horse racing industry, the complexity of the industry and they didn't take the time to learn the industry and the complexity of the industry before denying selling Plaintiff the tickets in question.

Plaintiff states that discovery could bring forth evidence that could cause more allegations to be added to the complaint.

Therefore for the reasons and allegations stated above, Plaintiff states that the Defendants must be held accountable for their actions, by a jury trial.

Respectfully submitted

Edward H. Flint Pro, Se

*******The Federal District Court's order starts here*********

UNITED STATES DISTRICT COURT

WESTERN DISTRICT OF KENTUCKY AT LOUISVILLE

_____

CIVIL ACTION NO.3:10-CV-202-H

_____

EDWARD H. Flint   PLAINTIFF

v.

CHURCHILL DOWNS INC. et al   DEFENDANT

MEMORANDUM AND ORDER

Plaintiff Edward H. Flint has filed a pro se complaint essentially alleging that Churchill Downs has discriminated against him and breached an oral agreement by failing to renew an offer of Derby tickets for the year 2010. Defendants, which comprise Churchill Downs and several of its officers, have moved to dismiss on the grounds that the complaint fails to allege any basis for jurisdiction in federal court.

The court has carefully reviewed Plaintiff's complaint. At best it can be said that it alleges the breach of some sort of oral contract between Plaintiff and Churchill Downs. In addition, it can be said that alleges that Churchill Downs discriminated against Plaintiff as compared to other long-time holders of Derby boxes. Plaintiff also asserts that the amount issued in the complaint exceeds $75,000.

Federal courts are constrained by a constitutional and statutory limit on their jurisdiction. Federal court do have jurisdiction over disputes between citizens of different states where over $75,000 is at issue, Plaintiff's complaint does not appear to meet these criteria as Plaintiff and Defendants in this case reside in the same state, that is Kentucky.

Federal courts also have jurisdiction over civil cases which involve federal statutes. Here, Plaintiff has not specifically alleged a cause of action under a federal statute. Normally, without a specific allegation of a cause of action or federal statute, federal courts will decline jurisdiction. This court has taken extra step of examining the complaint to determine whether it is possible to construe a federal claim under the facts alleged. To allege that Churchill Downs has discriminated against one long-time Derby box holder as compared to other Derby box holders does not allege a cause of action under any federal statute of which this Court is aware. Moreover, the fact that Churchill Downs is licensed and regulated by the state of Kentucky and offers itself as a public accommodation does not create a federal cause of actions under the facts alleged here.

Being otherwise sufficiently advised, It IS HEREBY ORDER that Defendants' motion to dismiss is SUSTAINED and Plaintiff's claims are DISMISSED WITH PREJUDICE.

This is a final order.

May 21, 2010   John G. Heyburn II, Judge

United States District Court

*************The district court's order ends here**************

****I appealed to the Court of Appeal and my Brief Starts here*****

CASE NO. 10-5663

UNITED STATES COURT OF APPEALS
FOR THE SIXTH CIRCUIT

EDWARD H. FLINT,   Plaintiff – Appellant

v.

CHURCHILL DOWNS et al   Defendant-Appellees

On Appeal from the United States District Court
For the Western District of Kentucky
Louisville Division

Honorable John G Heyburn II

Civil Case No. 3:10-CV-202-H

BRIEF FOR APPELLANT/ PLAINTIFF

STATEMENT OF FACTS

Appellant Flint is 79 years old and served as Director and President of both the Kentucky and National Horsemen Benevolence and Protective Associations (HBPA) for over 15 years throughout the 1970's and 1980's. The HBPA represented the owners and trainers of thoroughbred race horses, the grooms and hot walkers that cared for race horses. Flint got into racing in the 1960's as an owner and found that racing was in serious trouble and the backside workers was treated and lived like animals. All positions with the HBPA was voluntary, the Directors and President serve without pay. Plaintiff retired from his company and worked full time to improve Kentucky horse racing, with better purses for owners, backside living conditions, relationship with race tracks, Kentucky Racing Commission and other organizations involved in racing and laws pertaining to racing in the Kentucky General Assembly.

Besides the HBPA, the race tracks, the breeders, the jockeys and other organizations were involved in the dealings of the Kentucky General Assembly and between themselves. Each entity would have something to lose or to gain when changes was discussed or was made. There were many heated arguments and disagreement between the groups.

There were times when one group couldn't agree with the others and a lot of giving and taking was always taking place. Flint when he was in the manufacturing business had obtained the rights to two (2) Kentucky Derby boxes. Flint had no problems with Derby tickets until one year Churchill took Plaintiff's two boxes away from him. Important legislation that affected the racing industry was being considered in the Kentucky General Assembly. The Speaker of the House of Representatives told all parties that unless all sides agreed on a bill, no bill would pass the General Assembly that session. Churchill Downs wanting their way took the two boxes away from Plaintiff to be vindictive and to put pressure on Flint to see things their way.

Flint refused to give in to Churchill Downs and refused to discuss the legislation with any one that was so vindictive. The Kentucky Racing Commission and legislators became involved, trying to negotiation a settlement between the parties. A middle ground was purposed between Flint and the President of Churchill Downs, where Churchill Downs would keep one of the Derby boxes and Flint would keep the other one. For the good of racing Flint agreed to this, based upon two conditions. One, Flint got to pick which of the two he would keep and two, provided Churchill Downs would guarantee that they would never again take the box away from Flint, and he could purchase the box for as long as he lived and he wouldn't have to go through being harassed again over Derby tickets. The President of Churchill Downs agreed and the legislation was passed by the General Assembly.

The agreement has been honored every year until 2010, when Plaintiff openly opposed the legislation that was presented to the 2009 General Assembly regarding slot machines by the Governor of Kentucky that was good for the race tracks, but wasn't good for the owners and trainers and bringing fans back to the race tracks. Even when Churchill Downs changed Presidents throughout the years, the agreement has been honored.

The agreement between Churchill and Plaintiff has held every year until this year, 2010.

Flint loves racing and the people who make racing a success and based on his knowledge, the purposed bill regarding slot machines would have destroyed racing in Kentucky and Flint gave all who would listen his opinion.

Churchill Downs not only broke their agreement in 2010. They also discriminated against Flint, treating him different and unfairly, unlike other lifelong fan with Derby boxes. They took the Derby tickets away were to get even with Flint was because he spoke and distributed his opinion about the bill regarding horse racing and slot machines at race tracks in the Kentucky General Assembly. Flint's opinions were the opposite of the race tracks.

Churchill Downs knowing Flint was 79 years old took advantage of Flint and didn't figure Flint would file suit against them. If Flint had been forty years old, they would not have taken away his box.

The Kentucky Derby has become a world known event only because of the loyal fan base built throughout the years and without a loyal fan base the Derby would not exist. Fans must be treated fairly and with transparency and Derby boxes shouldn't be used to punish them. The Derby's fan based from the beginning of the Derby was built by Churchill having an equal policy regarding Derby tickets.

Appellant is Pro, Se and filed a lawsuit on March 29, 2010 against Churchill Downs and individuals for denying him of his civil rights, conspiring against him, harming him, reneging on a verbal contract and other issues. (See attached **EXHIBIT 1** which is a copy of the original complaint)

The trial court denied Appellant jurisdiction in the case, stating there were no Federal statutes involved. Appellant disagrees and therefore the reason for the appeal to this court.

Appellant claims that Defendants actions rose from Flint using his Freedom of Speech and disseminating his opinions regarding slot machine at race tracks legislation that had been filed and discussed in the Kentucky General Assembly in 2009 and would be refiled again. Appellant also believes that U.S. Code Title 28 #1391 Venues met the criteria for jurisdiction regardless.

In Appellant's complaint, exhibit 1, Appellant pointed out and so stated in paragraph 8 he **"openly told Kentucky that the bill was dirty and a waste of money and would make race tracks a lot of money, hundreds of million per year.** It is clear that Defendants actions were to shut up Appellant because he used his freedom of speech to express his opinion openly.

In paragraph 11 of the complaint Appellant pointed out and stated **"Plaintiff being outspoken against the slot machine legislation that the Defendants wanted and therefore Defendants decided to move Flint out of the picture by harming him."** Again it is clear that Defendants actions were because Appellant used his freedom of speech and told the people of Kentucky his opinion. Defendant's action of taking away Kentucky Derby tickets was to harm Appellant for speaking his opinion.

In paragraph 12 of the complaint Flint stated **"Defendants was upset with Plaintiff because of Plaintiff's public stand regarding the issue of the slot machine bill that Defendants wanted passed, which was Defendants' money making scheme.**

Defendants were mad at Plaintiff and the only way they had to harm Plaintiff was by denying him the tickets he had for over thirty seven years." Again it is clear that Defendants actions were because Appellant used his freedom of speech and told the people of Kentucky his opinion. Defendant's action of taking away Kentucky Derby tickets was to harm Appellant for speaking his opinion.

In paragraph 19 of the complaint Plaintiff alleged and stated, **"that Defendants between themselves and with other conspired against Plaintiff to harm him by not selling him the tickets in question."** U.S. Code 241 Conspiracy against rights- gives a person rights, if the conspirator's intent to prevent or hinder his free exercises or enjoyment of any right or privilege which includes freedom of speech. The defendants have conspired to deny Flint his right to speak out.

In paragraph 37 of the complaint it states, **"Plaintiff alleges that Defendants violated his civil rights."** U.S. Code #1983 Civil rights for deprivation of rights- states every person who under any color of any statutes shall be liable to the party injured in any suit for redress.

In paragraph 31 on the complaint states, **"Plaintiff alleges that if he had attempted to help the Defendants obtain slot machines at race tracks he would have been allowed to keep his tickets."** If Flint had spoken out for the slot machine bill the Defendants would have agree that Flint's Freedom of Speech in their favor was great.

BACKGROUND INFORMATION

Appellant has referred to him speaking out to citizens of Kentucky and Kentucky legislators and informing them of how bad the slot machine legislation was and how it would benefit the race track, but would not save racing in Kentucky. Flint talked to as many people he could and expressed his opinion.

Flint was asked by an organization of business people (Louisville Forum) to speak at one of their monthly meetings on the subject of slot machines at race tracks and the legislation that the governor of Kentucky and the race tracks was pushing for passage of in the General Assembly. The organization stated they wanted all sides of the slot machine legislation told and Flint had a view. The meeting was scheduled for July 8, 2009

Flint agreed to speak and explain his opinions, which was different that Churchill Downs and the Governor of Kentucky. Also on the dais to speak on the same subject were three (3) other speakers. One was the president of Churchill Downs (one of the Defendants); a second was a representative of the Governor and a third who represented the Breeders Cup, a horse racing organization. Each person gave their speech and answered question from the audience. The meeting was televised and copies of the speech were disseminated by Flint to members of the Kentucky General Assembly. (Attached is **EXHIBIT 2** a copy of the speech Flint gave at that July 8, 2009 meeting.

A lot of other people asked Flint, knowing his back ground, what was the answer to Kentucky racing problems, which was failing badly. Flint with his knowledge of the horse racing industry and based on his past experience, submitted an article to the Louisville Courier Journal newspaper explaining his position and reasoning. The Courier Journal printed the article on September 14, 2009, which was distributed throughout Kentucky. (Attached is **EXHIBIT 3** which is a copy of the September 14, 2009 article)

The Kentucky General Assembly went into session on January 2, 2010. The Governor of Kentucky made a number of public statements attempting to put pressure on getting the slot machine bill passed.

Flint wrote a letter to the editor of the Courier- Journal about the Governor's action and the newspaper published the letter on January 7, 2010, and it was distributed throughout Kentucky. (Attached is **EXHIBIT 4** which is a copy of the January 7, 2010 article printed in the Louisville Courier-Journal)

Flint has stated in his speech and writings that Racing in Kentucky must be re-vamped if it is to survive as we know it now. The Governor bill was not the savior of racing in Kentucky.

ARGUMENTS

As this court can see, there was nothing helpful in Exhibit 2 or exhibit 3 or exhibit 4 to the race tracks reaching their goal in Kentucky. In fact the content in the speech and published articles was damaging to the race tracks' goal of making a lot of money. Flint motive and goal was making the horse industry viable again in Kentucky and the slot machines bill that the race tracks wanted would not have done what Flint thought it would take for Kentucky to regain the fan base it once had but was losing.

The Kentucky General Assembly must have seen or read Flint's exhibits, because the slot machine legislation was not passed by the Kentucky General Assembly, in fact it never had a hearing doing the session..

Churchill Downs became upset over Flint's remarks and decided to pay Flint back for using Freedom of Speech to express his opinion, and the only way they had was denying Flint the Kentucky Derby tickets that they had agreed Flint could buy for life. Of course Churchill Downs had thoughts that if they took away Flint's tickets, he would not speak out against the slot machine bill in the future.

Maybe Flint by being Pro, Se didn't explain it to the trial court satisfactions in his Response to Defendants Motion to Dismiss, but he thought stated it quite well, when he stated the following in his response, **"Plaintiff has stated a claim for relief. Plaintiff in his complaint stated all that is required in a complaint and the complaint is not flawed. Plaintiff is entitled to relief for actions of Defendants."**

Paragraphs 8-11-12- 19 and 37 of the complaint clearly show Flint has been denied Freedom of Speech and how Defendants conspired to deny him Freedom of Speech.

Therefore the complaint clearly shows that the Freedom of speech in the 2d amendment, U.S. Code title 42 #1983 and U. S. Code Title 28 #241 are appropriate statues for this case to go forward in Federal Court.

Appellant filed the complaint in the proper venue and still believes he did. Flint also believes his complaint meets the criteria of U.S. Code Title 28 #1391 Venue.

CONCLUSION

Appellant has violated no rules and Federal statues show the case meets the criteria for Federal Court jurisdiction. The Appellant figured the trial court would know the Freedom of Speech, Code # 241, Code #1983 and Code # 1391 was statutes that prevailed, just by reading the complaint.

This Court should use the correct facts as Appellant stated above and below.

The trial court in its order stated "Federal Courts also have jurisdiction over civil cases which involve federal statutes." Appellant argues that 2nd Amendment to the Constitution- Freedom of Speech, - U.S. Code title 18> part 1chapter 13 # 241 - U. S. Code title 42 chapter 21 subchapter 1 # 1983 and U.S. Code Title 28 part IV chapter 87 # 1391 Venue, all meets the criteria needed to meet the courts statutes and rules.

Every party including defendants wants a Due Process fair and honest trial by statues and rules, so justice by using the proper statutes of the law is the thing to do. Appellant believes that even the Defendants wouldn't deny Flint the right of Freedom of Speech. Defendants would have encouraged Flint to speak out regarding the slot machine bill, if Flint had been for their bill instead of against the bill. Flint would be surprised if Defendants even responses to this brief since they use Freedom of Speech to tell their side of the slot machine issue all of the time.

Therefore, there is no reason the case should not be remanded back to the trial court and let a jury judge the case.

No judge can be against the Constitution Freedom of Speech amendment, which Appellant used when; he spoke out with his speech and writings. Even the trial court wanted to grant jurisdiction to Appellant, in trial court's order it stated, "This court has taken the extra step of examining the complaint to determine whether it is possible to construe a federal claim under the facts alleged." So the trial court will be pleased to know that there are a number of reasons in the complaint to grant Appellant jurisdiction. Appellant believes that the trial court just overlooked the facts in the complaint and he will be pleased to know that this court corrected his mistakes.

Appellant respectfully request this court to overrule the trial court's order granting the Defendants motion to dismiss and return the case back to the trial court for trial.

Respectfully submitted
Edward H. Flint Pro, Se

The Court of Appeals Order affirmed the District Court's Order

Accordingly, we affirm the district court's judgment. Rule 34(j)(2)(C), Rules of the Sixth Circuit.

I appealed to the Supreme Court and filed a Petition for Certiorari here

No._____

In The

Supreme Court of the United States

Edward H. Flint   Petitioner,

Versus

Churchill Downs Inc., et al.,   Respondent

PETITION FOR WRIT OF CERTIORARI

QUESTIONS PRESENTED

1- Are Pro, Se's held to the same standards in lawsuits as an educated lawyers and if yes how does the court system believe a pro, se, can compete with a trained lawyer?

2- Did the trial judge discriminate against Petition who is Pro, Se when the judge stated petitioner did not specific allegations of a cause of action or a federal statute, which was not true and the motion before the trial court made by defendant was for dismissal for failure to state a claim?

3- Is dismissing a civil complaint after Petitioner told both the trial court and Appeals Court that he used his Freedom Speech to speak out against slot machines at race tracks and the Race Track retaliated against Petitioner for using his Freedom of Speech?

4- Should a judge have disqualified himself from a case under 28 U.S.C #455 when the judge has both accepted favors from Defendants and Petitioner Flint had dismissed the judge's former law pardoner twice from being counsel for two associations the Petitioner was President of?

5- Why would an honest judge dismiss a case **WITH PREJUDICE** when no hearing has been held, except the judge was prejudice?

7- Why would a trial judge and appeal court dismiss a complaint that contained sufficient factual matter that stated a claim on different alleged items and one was freed of speech?

STATEMENT OF THE CASE

PROCEDURAL HISTORY

Flint would like to start by saying that when a Pro, Se is involved, a court should overlook some of the presentation by a Pro, Se and arrive at the truth by other means, regardless of what it takes. No fair minded judge or the framers of the constitution would expect a non-educated in law person to complete with a person who has been educated and trained for a number of years. There is nothing in the United States Constitution that says that the Court's Rule of Civil procedures must be adhered to by Pro, Se's. Nothing can supersede the 14th amendment to the constitution giving everyone Due Process, to a fair and honest trial.

Therefore any misstatement made or lack of presenting the proper federal law or rule in pleadings to a court, should not be held against a Pro, Se. If any court holds in their rulings that a Pro, Se didn't adhere to the rules of civil procedures or cite the right authority, then the court is giving the educated lawyer an unfair advantage over the pro, se, and denying the Pro, Se a Due Process fair trial. The court its self would be discriminating against a Pro, Se. Court's Rules of Civil Procedure are court drafted rules and are not constitution mandated for a due process fair trial. The 14th Amendment gives every person the right to protect their property and that is what Flint was doing in this complaint when he filed with the trial court. Pro, se's under all circumstances must be protected by this court, from harassing done by anyone, in not conforming to the courts rules on discovery, if any exits. A Pro, Se person have a right to explain their case the best they can and a court must take the time to get to the truth, even if everything is not done by the Courts rules.

A court's duty is to get the truth in any case, regardless of anything else or a pro se cannot win. Courts function is truth.

This action arises out of Complaint filed in Western District Federal Court by Petitioner Flint against Churchill Downs on March 29, 2010. The case NO.3:10-CV-202-H was assigned to Judge Simpson. Judge Simpson recused himself from the case the day after it was filed, against local rules and gave no reason in the interest of justice as required by local rules why he recused himself. He by order assigned the case to Judge Heyburn rather than by the assignment of court's rules

Churchill Downs on April 28, 2010 file a motion to dismiss for failure to state a claim. Flint responded telling the court that a bill to put slots machines at race tracks was filed in the Kentucky General Assembly. Flint told in all pleading that he was against the slot machines bill and told state legislators he knew it was a bad and dirty bill. In addition Flint wrote an Op-Ed article that was printed in the Louisville Courier – Journal, Flint in addition gave a speech at the Louisville Forum against the bill and the speech was televised and shown throughout Kentucky.

Flint as an individual was given the right to purchase 2 boxes at Churchill Downs for the Kentucky Derby and Kentucky Oaks in 1970 and did purchase them each year. In 1977 Flint was elected to be the President of the Kentucky Division of the HBPA, which represented all thoroughbred race horse owners and trainers in Kentucky and in addition he drafted bills and lobbied the General Assembly for laws for horsemen.

In 1984 Flint and Churchill Downs was in a disagreement over a bill and Churchill Downs by way of letter took away Flint's right to buy the two boxes he had been buying. The legislators would not move the bill until both sides agreed. Legislators finally mediated an agreement where Churchill would keep one box and Flint would have a right to purchase the second box, for life, at cost. Flint retired from the HBPA in 1986. And purchased the box each year until 2009, when Churchill refused to sell it to him.

In 2009 Churchill Downs was pushing a bill in the General Assembly that would have allowed slot machines at Kentucky Race Tracks. Flint as an individual spoke out against the slot machine at race tracks, Flint stated slot machines where bad for racing. Flint spoke to legislators, at meetings, in print by an op-ed article and across Kentucky via TV. Churchill Downs became vindictive and refused to sell Flint the tickets he had been purchasing for over 37 years.

Trial Judge Heyburn was a partner in a law firm in Louisville Kentucky before he was appointed to the District Court. The firm's name was Brown Todd and Heyburn. Another partner in the firm was a Mr. Ned Bonnie. Since 1972 Flint knew and did business with Bonnie and others in the firm.

Mr. Bonnie was Counsel for an organization by the name of HBPA which stood for Horsemen Benevolence and Protective Association, which represented 70,000 Owners and Trainers of Thoroughbred race horses in America. The group was a National origination with 27 divisions. Mr. Bonnie was Counsel for both the National and the Kentucky Division. Mr. Bonnie as Counsel for the HBPA was the largest or one of largest contributors of income to the Brown Todd and Heyburn law firm. Mr. Bonnie also made contact with and had relationships with all race tracks throughout America, including Churchill Downs and other horsemen's groups' thorough America.

In 1977 Flint was elected to be the President of the Kentucky Division of the HBPA. After becoming President, Flint and Bonnie parted company, as far as the Kentucky Division, when Flint hired another attorney, not connected with the Brown Todd and Heyburn firm.

Later, in early the early 1980's, Flint was also elected President of the National HBPA. Soon after Flint became President of the National HBPA, Flint and Bonnie again parted company and Flint hired a different Counsel. Flint's action had a large financial effect on Judge Heyburn and his law firm at the time.

When Flint, who is not a lawyer, filed his first lawsuit, Judge Heyburn should have recused himself in that case and every case filed by Flint that was assigned to him there-after. But instead Judge Heyburn kept the cases in his court to get even with Flint for parting company with their law firm. Judge Heyburn controlled every case that came before him regarding Flint and his actions harmed Flint badly. He either dismissed the case **WITH PREJUDICE** or Rule against Flint and made it a Final Order **WITH PREJUDICE**

By 28 U.S.C. #455 Judge Heyburn should have disqualify himself **The Supreme Court has held that a violation of section 455(a) takes place even if the judge is unaware of the circumstance that created the appearance of im-propriety.** In *Liljeberg* v. *Health Services Acquisition Corp., 486 U.S. 847, 860 n.8 (1988)* the trial judge was a member of the board of trustees of a university that had a financial interest in the litigation, but he was unaware of the financial inter-est when he conducted a bench trial and ruled in the case. The court of appeals nevertheless vacated the judgment under Fed. R. Civ. P 60(b) because the judge failed to recuse himself pursuant to section 455(a) and **the Supreme Court agreed. Noting that the purpose of section 455(a) is to promote public con-fidence in the integrity of the judicial process, the Court observed that such confidence "does not depend upon whether or not the judge actually knew of facts creating an appearance of impropriety, so long as the public might reasonably believe that he or she knew."'**

Judge Heyburn, by not recusing himself, knew what he was doing. Judge Heyburn wanted to make sure Flint couldn't win this case; he dismissed the case **WITH PREJUDICE.** He wanted to make sure Flint couldn't take it to another court. Flint appealed the case to the Sixth Circuit Court on January 21, 2011

The Appeals court affirmed the district court ruling. Petitioner on January 27, 2011 filed a motion for a rehearing and on April 14, 2011 the appeals court denied the rehearing.

RELEVANT FACTS OF THE CASE AND ARGUMENTS

1- Judge Heyburn judged this complaint without any evidence being presented and judged the meaning of each item alleged by Flint, incorrectly. Evidence a jury should decide.

2- Judge Heyburn should have disqualified himself from the case under 28 U.S.C #455 and not ruled

3- Flint was denied his right to Freedom of Speech per 1st Amendment of the constitution. Churchill Downs reneged on their agreement made to Legislators that Flint could purchase the Boxes for life, because Flint spoke against the slot machine bill Churchill Downs wanted passed. The slot machine bill was not passed by the legislators after Flint told the public of Kentucky that the bill was a dirty bill and would not save the race tracks.

Flint in his complaint stated in Paragraph 8. **Plaintiff reviewed the slot machine bill and openly told Kentucky that the bill was a dirty bill and or was a waste of money, because it would not save racing in Kentucky, but would make race tracks a lot of money, hundreds of million dollars per year.**

Flint in Paragraph 11 of his complaint stated **Plaintiff alleges that the only visible change in the relationship between the Plaintiff and Defendants, since the 2009 Derby and Oaks and invoicing of the 2010 tickets, is Plaintiff being outspoken against the slot machine legislation that the Defendant wanted and therefore Defendants decided to move Plaintiff out of the picture by harming him.**

Flint in Paragraph 12 of his complaint stated **Plaintiff alleges that Defendants was upset with Plaintiff, because of the Plaintiff's public regarding the issue of the slot machine bill that the Governor and Defendants wanted passed, which was the Defendants,' money making scheme. Defendants were mad at Plaintiff and the only way they had to hurt Plaintiff was by denying him the tickets he had for over thirty seven years.**

Flint in Paragraph 21 of his complaint stated **21- Plaintiff alleges that the top management of Churchill Downs has changed a number of times over the last ten (10) years and no action was taken against Plaintiff's tickets, until Plaintiff wouldn't support their position on slot machines and opposes it, which they believe harmed them and blamed Plaintiff.**

Flint in paragraph 37 of his complaint stated, **37- Plaintiff alleges that Defendants violated his civil rights.**

4- Judge Heyburn was vindictive and prejudice against Flint when he dismissed the case **WITH PREJUDICE.**

5- Judge Heyburn didn't want this case to go forward and took advantage of Flint and discriminated against Flint, thereby denying Flint his civil rights because Flint was an old man 81 years old who is Pro, Se,

6- The Defendants ask by motion that the case be dismissed for failure to state a claim. Flint's complaint had a total of over forty (40) allegations and it met criteria of. *Bell Atlantic Corp v. Trombly 550 U.S. 544, 563 (2007).* The complaint will survive a motion to dismiss if it "contain(s) sufficient factual matter; accept as true, to state a claim of relief that is plausible on its face. Ashcroft Lqbal 129 U.S. Ct. 1937, 1949 (2009) (quoting Twomby, 550 U.S. at 750. *See Benzon v. Morgan Distrub., Ins., 420 F3d 598, 605 (6th Cir 2005)* in considering a motion to dismiss under rule 12(b)(6) the court must accept all well pleaded factual allegations of the complaint as true and construe the complaint in the light most favorable to the plaintiff. Therefore Judge Heyburn was wrong in dismissing this case.

7- The trial judge in his order dismissing the case stated Flint had not specifically alleged a cause of action under a federal statute. Flint told the court his action was freedom of speech to the 1st amendment he was discriminate against, he loses his civil rights, when Churchill Downs retaliation was for Flint using his Freedom of Speech and the court ignored it.

Flint also told the court the following paragraphs in his complaint,

13-Plaintiff alleges that Defendants had once promised they would sell Plaintiff the same tickets for life.

Flint in Para 15 of the complaint stated,**15-Plaintiff alleges that Defendants gained nothing by denying Plaintiff purchasing the tickets the same as in the past, except to harm him to get even with him.**

Flint in Para. 17 of the complaint stated, **17-Plaintiff alleges that Defendant discriminated against Plaintiff.**

Flint in Para 19 of the complaint stated, **19- Plaintiff alleges that Defendants between themselves and with others conspired against Plaintiff to harm him by not selling him the tickets in question.**

Flint in Para 24 of the complaint stated, **24- Plaintiff alleges that within the last four or five years Defendants asked Plaintiff to come work for them to help get slot machines or casinos bills approved in the General Assembly and Plaintiff did not accept their offer, refused to help them and Defendants have held it against him.**

Flint in Para 37 of his complaint stated, **37- "Plaintiff alleges that Defendants violated his civil rights."** U.S. Code #1983 Civil rights for deprivation

Flint in Para 38 of his complaint stated, **38- Plaintiff alleges that Defendant actions caused Plaintiff mental anguish and humiliation.**

REASONS FOR GRANTING THE WRIT

1- The Court of Appeals focused their attention on one issue 42 U.S.C. #1983 in the case and there were many more issues in Flint's complaint. The Appeals court erred in interpretation of some of the authority they cited, some was very old cases. It looks like the Court of Appeals was protecting the trial court judge who should not have ruled in the case because of bias.

2- The trial court should not have dismissed the case, because Flint had plenty of factual matter in his complaint, to try the case and the complaint complied with Fed C R 12(b)(6) under *Bell Atlantic Corp v. Trombly 550 U.S. 544, 563 (2007).* "The complaint will survive a motion to dismiss if it "contain(s) sufficient factual matter; accept as true, to state a claim of relief that is plausible on its face."

1- Judge Heyburn was bias against Flint and showed it when he dismissed the case **WITH** PREJUDICE. And was bias against Flint because Flint was responsible for Heyburn's law firm losing a big client when Flint and Bonnie parted as counsel and client.

2- Judge Heyburn should have disqualified himself under 28 U.S. Code #455 (a) (b)(1)(2)(3)(4)(5)(iii) (c)

5- 18 U.S. C #241 Conspiracy against rights, gives a person rights, if the conspirator's intent to prevent or hinder his free exercises or enjoyment of any right or privilege which includes freedom of speech. The defendants have conspired to deny Flint his right to speak out, by harming him.

6- U.S. Code #1983 covers civil rights that Flint alleged in Para 37 of his complaint **"Plaintiff alleges that Defendants violated his civil rights."**

7- In paragraph 31 of Flint's complaint, he stated, **"Plaintiff alleges that if he had attempted to help the Defendants obtain slot machines at race tracks he would have been allowed to keep his tickets."** If Flint had spoken out in favor of the slot machine bill the Defendants would have agree that Flint's Freedom of Speech in their favor, was great.

8- After Churchill Downs retaliated and took away the two boxes Flint had for years, because Flint wouldn't agree to their terms of a bill. The legislators told Churchill Downs that taking away the two boxes was not the way to get a bill passed. The legislators said the bill would not move until Churchill Downs reached an agreement with Flint. Flint not wanting the hassle over Derby boxes again in his future, sat down with Churchill Downs they reach an agreement based on Flint would be able to purchase for life one box of his choice between the two boxes and Churchill Downs would tell the legislators what the agreement was. Churchill Downs told the legislators, Flint picked which box he wanted and the bill was passed.

9- The Court of Appeals stated that a pro se must be held to "less stringent standard than formal pleadings drafter by lawyers." But then the court says Flint failed to state a basis for federal jurisdiction over his claim. Flint argues that If Pro se are held to less stringent standard then failing to state a basis for a federal jurisdiction would fall into the same reasoning, a pro se doesn't understand those neither. But regardless Flint submitted a number of bases for a federal jurisdiction, such as freedom of speech, violations of his civil rights, discrimination, or others, Flint as pro se doesn't know about. The trial court didn't try and help a pro se but used a technically to harm him that had nothing to do with the truth. This isn't what justice is about.

10- The District Court and Court of Appeals has held Flint a Pro, Se to the same standard as a trained educated lawyer by stating Flint did not state a basis for jurisdiction by Federal code or Federal civil rues of procedures, but then they said that under 42 U.S.C. #1983 a plaintiff must alleged that he was deprived of a right secured by the constitution or laws of the United States. Flint told the court and they acknowledge that Flint told them about his freedom of speech being violated and was what caused Churchill Downs to do what they did to Flint. Only a trial could prove different. Also Flint in his complaint showed the court that Churchill Downs fall under the color al the state. Flint in his complaint stated Churchill Downs is license and regulated by the State of Kentucky to conduct horse racing which includes the Kentucky Derby and Kentucky Oaks and all laws pertaining to horse racing in Kentucky is established by the Kentucky General Assembly.

11- The District Court and Court of Appeals has held Flint a Pro, Se to the same standard as a trained lawyer by stating Flint did not state a basis for jurisdiction by Federal code of federal civil rules of procedures, but Flint told both courts in his complaint that he was denied his civil rights, he was discriminated against, he was conspired against, he was harmed by mental anguish and humiliation, he was lied to. Flint is being penalized against because he is not educated in law. This is discrimination against a non-educated in law person and a violation of his civil rights.

12- Flint contends that his complaint contained sufficient matter to meet the requirements of 28 U. S. C. #1391 venues generally. Under #1391(a)(1) (2) (3) (b) (1) (2) (c) and the case should not been dismissed

13- Drafter of the constitution meant for all persons to be given a fair and honest trial. The court system has developed a system to bring order to the system, however the court system have left out the person who represents them self. No Pro, Se person can compete with an educated attorney. Flint in his complaint lay out; he had been harmed, by who harmed him and why they harmed him. The court system can do what they want to a Pro, Se, use any excuse to continue harming the Pro, Se. Flint told his side of the truth and the other side should be able to tell their side, to a jury. But to deny Flint on a technically is against the constitution of our country.

CONCLUSION

Flint has laid out his case the best he can as a pro, se and there is no reason to deny him a chance to try his case. Flint's complaint met all of the cited cases See *Benzon v. Morgan Distrub., Ins.*, 420 F3d 598, 605 (6th Cir 2005) in considering a motion to dismiss under rule 12(b)(6) the court must accept all well pleaded factual allegations of the complaint as true and construe the complaint in the light most favorable to the plaintiff. Flint's complaint met criteria of. *Bell Atlantic Corp v. Trombly 550 U.S. 544, 563 (2007).* The complaint will survive a motion to dismiss if it "contain(s) sufficient factual matter; accept as true, to state a claim of relief that is plausible on its face. Ashcroft Lqbal 129 U.S. Ct. Flint's complaint was sufficient to meet the requirements of 28 U. S. C. #1391 venue generally. Under #1391(a)(1) (2) (3) (b) (1) (2) (c) and the case should not been dismissed Therefore Judge Heyburn was wrong in dismissing this case.

Petitioner claims that Churchill Downs gave him the rights to the box for life in return for his agreement to help pass the bill that Churchill Downs wanted from the

Kentucky General Assembly. Flint claims he owned the box, by verbal agreement for life and was to pay yearly. Churchill Downs retaliated by refusing to honor his right to Free Speech, his right to speak out against something that he believed was harmful to Kentucky.

Since the tickets are printed yearly Flint could only pay for them yearly. Churchill Downs was mad at Flint and wanted to force him to change his mind about the slot-machines. Churchill Downs took away Flint's civil rights and discriminated against him for no reason except to harm Flint. The sold the tickets to another person for the same amount they would have charged Flint.

Churchill Downs is license and regulated by the State of Kentucky to conduct horse racing, this includes the Kentucky Derby and Kentucky Oaks. All laws pertaining to horse racing in Kentucky is established by the Kentucky General Assembly. Therefore Churchill Down falls under the color of the state law. Flint in Para. 33 of his complaint stated, **33-Plaintiff alleges that the Kentucky Derby belongs to the people of Kentucky and proper management of the Derby is essential to maintain the renowned imagine of Kentucky and Defendants actions violated the trust that the people of Kentucky gave them.**

Petitioner asks this court to overrule the trial court and return the case to the trial court in the name of justice, for a jury trial.

Respectfully submitted,
s/ Edward H. Flint, Pro, Se.

The Supreme Court denied reviewing the case. It became clear that the District Court, the Court of Appeal and the Supreme Court of the United States were never going to even consider any of my cases.

In the justice system, truth and law carries very little weight. They had it in for me because I sued judges and I questioned the Federal Court system. There are other reasons, bigger that justice involved in this decision by the courts.

Judge Heyburn who ruled against me in District Court will appear again in a number of Chapters of the book. Judge Heyburn had been taking favours from Churchill Downs for years and he knew I could prove it and therefore wouldn't let me take discovery. Judge Heyburn the trial court judge, was the personal attorney and friend of Mitch McConnell who is the Minority Leader in the United States Senate.

Judge Heyburn has high hopes of being appointed someday to the United States Supreme Court.

At this point in my life I knew that I would never win a case because of suing judges and telling the courts how corrupt they were.

The courts ignored my freedom of speech constitution rights.

Churchill Downs must have given Judge Heyburn or Senator McConnell something in return for their help. They didn't want me taking discovery and seeing the history of what transpired in the past between, the race track and Judge Heyburn and Senator McConnell, in the past.

I would have liked to quit filing lawsuits, but the Holy Spirit refused to let me. They knew I would never break my promise to God. The Holy Spirit and God seen other issues that they wanted me to sue over. The cases become more intense from here. So I continued.

CHAPTER 8

LAWSUIT FLINT V. NEW YOUR STOCK EXCHANGE ET AL

I will now insert the amended complaint I filed.

UNITED STATES DISTRICT COURT
WESTERN DISTRICT OF KENTUCKY
LOUISVILLE DIVISON

CASE NO. 3:10-CV-00626-M

EDWARD H. FLINT   PLAINTIFF

VS

<u>COMPLAINT</u>

NEW YORK STOCK EXCHANGE   DEFENDANTS

NYSE
11 Wall Street
New York, New York 10005
NASDAQ STOCK MARKET
NASDAQ Stock Market
One Liberty Plaza
165 Broadway.
New York, New York 10006
FINANCIAL INDUSTRY REGULATORY AUTHORITY
Finra
1735 K Street
Washington D.C. 20006
JANE DOES and JOHN DOES

COMPLAINT

Comes now the Plaintiff, Edward H. Flint Pro, Se, acting as his own counsel against Defendants New York Stock Exchange, Nasdaq Stock Market, Finra, other unknown Companies, Corporations, Brokers, Market Makers, Regulators, and other unknown Jane Does and John Does and for this cause of action, states as follows:

1- Plaintiff Edward H. Flint lives at

2- New York Stock Exchange Headquarters is locator at 11 Wall Street, New York, New York

3- Nasdaq Stock Market Headquarters is locator at One Liberty Plaza, 105 Broadway, New York, New York.

4- Finra is locator at 1735 K Street Washington D.C.

5- The other Jane Does and John Does address is unknown at this time.

6- Plaintiff is part of the public at large that trades stocks in the stock market of buying and selling shares of companies stock and the Defendants control the movement of the trading of such stocks and have a monopoly on trading stocks. The Plaintiff and public at large expects, depend on, must have, and demands, honesty in every movement of those handling or controlling such trading.

7- Plaintiff alleges that the sale price of stocks and or the amount of stocks traded daily is being manipulated by Defendants or by others who they are responsible for controlling.

8- Plaintiff alleges that Defendants relying on computers and the honesty of those involved in the trading of stocks is not enough and Defendants has a duty to make sure that honesty and truthfulness prevailed at all times, regardless of the cost or effort needed.

9- Plaintiff alleges that the Defendants knew or should have known about the manipulation of the sale of stock that is traded in and or by their organization.

10- Plaintiff alleges that the Defendants knows or should have known that the stock sold and bought by or through their facility was manipulated by themselves or by others connected in some way with their organization.

11- Plaintiff alleges that Defendant's actions injured Plaintiff, financially, mentally and physically.

12- Plaintiff alleges that Defendant's actions denied Plaintiff and the public at large his U.S. Civil Rights.

13- Plaintiff alleges that Defendants failed to perform their duty as required by The Congress, the Government of the United States and the rules and laws of trading stocks throughout America.

14- Plaintiff alleges that Defendants failed to perform their ethical responsibility required by the Laws and rules of the United States Government and other entities.

15- Plaintiff alleges that Defendant's actions were harmful to him, because Plaintiff relied on the Defendants to look out for the welfare and well-being of Plaintiff, which is part of the public at large.

16- Plaintiff alleges that Defendants didn't take all actions necessary to guarantee Plaintiff and the public at large that all information and all true and honest facts were disseminated by the minute, hourly, daily and at all times to Plaintiff and the public at large.

17- Plaintiff alleges that Defendant's actions of manipulating the trading, selling or buying stock was done for selfish reasons.

18- Plaintiff alleges that the manipulation of stock cost may have the United States Treasury tax revenue.

19- Plaintiff alleges that Defendant's actions were done to control the price of stocks, to control the stock market, and to keep the stock market problems hidden, from the Plaintiff and from the public at large.

20- Plaintiff alleges that Defendants actions are a con game, done in a way to control the mind, the thoughts and the actions of Plaintiff and the public at large.

21- Plaintiff alleges that Defendant's actions discriminated against him.

22- Plaintiff alleges that the Defendants hid important facts from Plaintiff and the public at large.

23- Plaintiff alleges that Defendants conspired with others against him and the public at large

24- Plaintiff alleges that the Defendants action deceived Plaintiff and they knew it was happening.

25- Plaintiff alleges that Defendants harmed him when they hid important information regarding the trading of stocks from Plaintiff and the public at large.

26- Plaintiff alleges Plaintiff was put into a horrifying position of losing money by the actions of the Defendants.

27- Plaintiff alleges that Defendant's actions were not in the interest of honesty and fairness to the Plaintiff, the public, and the United States.

28- Plaintiff alleges that Defendants used their position, to manipulate or to allow the manipulation of, the price of stocks and or the perception of the health of the stock market to the public.

29- Plaintiff alleges that Defendants made money off of their manipulation of stocks, the image of the stock market and the future of the stock market.

30- Plaintiff alleges that Defendants family or friends or others made money off of the manipulation of stocks and the manipulation of the perception of the image of the stock market.

31- Plaintiff alleges that Defendants knew or suspected that stocks and stock market were being manipulated and took no actins to correct the problem, or to protect Plaintiff and the public at large.

32- Plaintiff alleges that Defendants had an hourly and daily duty to check the possibility of manipulation of the trading of stocks and failed to do so.

33- Plaintiff believes other laws, rules and/or other action may have been broken and only discovery will tell, and at that time Plaintiff will ask for leave to amend this complaint.

Therefore Plaintiff demands that Defendant be held liable for their actions in harming and deceiving Plaintiff.

DEMANDS

Plaintiff makes the following demands

1- A trial by jury.

2- On any allegations in this complaint that a jury finds any of the Defendants guilty, Plaintiff is awarded both compensatory and punitive damages from each defendant found guilty in the amount determined by a jury.

3- If any defendant is found guilty on any of the alleged issues, the one(s) found guilty be disbarred for life from employment in any industry connected in any form, to the stock market.

4- All party found guilty of any allegation in this complaint be turned over to the Federal Government for prosecution.

All cost of this complaint by Plaintiff

5- For any other relief to which said plaintiff may appear entitled.

Respectfully submitted
Edward H. Flint Pro, Se

******The Federal District Court's order start here******

UNITED STATES DISTRICT COURT
WESTERN DISTRICT OF KENTUCKY AT LOUISVILLE

CIVIL ACTION NO.3:10-CV-00626-JHM

EDWARD H. Flint   PLAINTIFF

v.

NEW YORK EXCHANGE, et al   DEFENDANT

ORDER

This matter is before the Court upon Defendants' motion to dismiss. The matter has been briefed and is ripe for decision.

Plaintiff's complaint alleges stock market manipulation and a failure on the part of Defendants to regulate and administer the market and its participants to prevent such manipulation. Defendants' motion claims absolute immunity for the Defendants, all self-regulatory organizations (SRO) under the supervisory authority of the Securities and Exchange Commission (SEC). The Defendants motion is well taken. The complaint alleges a failure by the Defendants to properly perform its regulatory duties in administering the stock markets. Congress decided to allow private SRO's to conduct the day to day regulation and administration of the stock market, under the supervision of the SEC. when engaged in these functions, the SRO's "are engage[d] in conduct consistent with the quasi-governmental powers delegated to [them] pursuant to the Exchange Act and the regulations and rules promulgated. D' Alessio v. NYSE, 258 F.3d 93, 106 (2nd Cir. 2001) As such, they are entitled to the same immunity as that of the Sec. As noted in the Defendants' memorandum, the absolute immunity afforded to the Defendant SROs turns "on whether specific acts and forbearances were incident to the exercise of regulatory power, and not on the propriety of these actions or inactions." In re NYSE Specialists Sec. Litig., 503 F.3d at 98.

Based on the foregoing, the Court does hereby **grant** the Defendants' motion and the Plaintiff's complaint against the NYSE, NASDAQ and FINRA is dismissed.

So ordered

May 21, 2010   Joseph H. McKinley, Jr., Judge

United States District Court

*************The district court's order ends here**************

*** I appealed to the Sixth Circuit Court of Appeals submitted the following brief***

On Appeal from the United States District Court
For the Western District of Kentucky
Louisville Division

Honorable, Joseph H. McKinley Jr.

Civil Case No. 3:10-CV-000626-JHM

APPELLANT BRIEF

Respectfully submitted
Edward H. Flint Pro, Se

STATEMENT OF THE ISSUES PRESENTED FOR REVIEW

1- Appellant's rights of the 14th amendment of the Constitution due process of law, of defending his right not to be deprived of his property, by laws that do not and can grant fraud. Does the law granting immunity to the Defendants supersede the 14th amendment?

2- Is fraudulent manipulation of stocks being traded (brought and sold), by the actions of the people who buy and sell stocks from the Defendants, (hereafter called brokers or executors,) immunize from fraudulent manipulation and is defendants themselves immunize from fraud.

3- What is the duty of the defendants regarding investors?

4- Is fraud a wrongful act regardless of any authority given by Congress?

3- Are the three Defendants granted immunity regardless, if they are profit making entity. Are the three defendants granted immunity under all circumstances?

4- Is the law clear that an entity contracted for by the Security Exchange Commission is given the same rights that Congress gave to the SEC. and if this court says yes they are, then how far down the line to employees and contractors are they allowed to pass immunity? Are all brokers that trade stocks granted immunity?

5- The trial court cited law cases that took place before since Congress passed new laws in 2007 that affected SEC and those who rely on the SEC immunity law.

6- Can Congress through their actions pass law what gives any entity the right to manipulate any business, which harms a citizen of America?

7- Does Defendants have complete control over the brokers in every respect, which affect the investor?

8- Will this court say that even if the defendants don't do it duty properly, no investor has any rights to sue them?

STATEMENT OF FACTS IN THIS CASE

Appellant in his complaint listed Jane Does and John Does as defendants in this case and the Appellant believe that there are others people who will need to be named in place of John and Jane Does. Dismissing the case takes away the Appellants rights

Appellant has alleged that the defendants have helped manipulate the stocks reported traded. By their involvement they either don't have the correct programs to stop the brokers from manipulating the market or they are turning their heads and letting it happen, for their own benefit.

Appellant invested in the market with both his and his wife's money, and lost over four hundred thousand dollars in 2010. Appellant has alleged that in 2010 the defendants changed way of reporting the total and amount of stocks traded. The brokers changed their system of trading, stating the amount of stocks they traded and reporting their system of trading. Appellant stated his allegations in his complaint and in his response to Appellee motion to dismiss. Appellant figured out how and why the market changed so rapidly and charged. Defendants are letting the manipulation of traded stocks take place by brokers. The trial court granted Defendants absolute immunity from being tried on charges of manipulation of stocks

AGRUEMENT

During the early part of 2010, investors were getting out of the investment market. The talk and worry was about fear of a double dip recession, which create near panic in this country. The stock market was losing its investors. Entities involved had to find a way of stopping the out flow of money that was invested in the stock market. The stock market was in trouble like the automobile industry.

There were wide swings in the Dow Jones on the NYSE and other measurements such as NASDAQ, from day to day with mostly down rather than up. All of a sudden, regardless of the news of the day that affects the stock market and most of it bad, the Dow and other exchanges their stocks started climbing up in value, going up on bad news the same as good news. This move was made to make the investor that was getting out or thinking about getting out, stop, and also to get those investors that had gotten out, getting back in.

Appellant alleges that the allegation he is making against the defendants was set up a long time ago, when Defendants stopped giving investors the stock certificate number of the company that they had brought.

From the time when the stock market first started, the buyer of stocks had always received the certificate number of stocks they brought. These certificates showed up on their stock records everywhere. Sometimes investor even had the stock certificates in their possession. The defendants stop issuing stock certificates numbers in transactions to consumers. This was the way that the companies kept track of how much stock was sold and who owned it and now there is no way except the integrity of the brokers and defendants.

This bring us back to where we are now and that is no person or computer able to keep track of all legitimate trades and or the money going to or from brokers and defendants takes advantage of the situation and let brokers manipulate the trades.

Appellant is saying that the system is set up so that the defendants or no one else has the capability that they can check each hour or each day or each week to see if all stock that is reported as traded was actual legitimate trades.

Appellant is saying as an example that if a broker reports they traded a hundred thousand shares and they only list the high and low values they traded, defendants do not verify the trades or the money for the trades. Because defendants cannot verify actual trades, a broker can buy or sell stocks to his own self, raising or lowering the price of stock as he see fit, thereby manipulating the stock and therefore no one, including the defendants, honestly verifies what trades are being made each day. The brokers only report a number of trades and that's all Defendants want. Appellant alleges that brokers are reporting more shares of stocks traded than are actually legitimately traded between legitimate people buying and selling stocks. Defendants know this and to protect their own positions in the industry, let it go rather that report it to the Sec or other government officials. Brokers therefore can report any amount of trades and prices, because no one is checking the broker's trades.

Appellant is alleges that the defendants don't have the capability to check and confirm that each trade is a legitimate transactions, but report what they are told by brokers and defendants trust the brokers. The Brokers are buying and selling stocks to themselves or other brokers to manipulate the investors, in order to make consumers believe that the stock market is healthy again, but no money is trading hands.

When the concern of the recession happened in early 2010 the defendants either let brokers get by with this by turning their head or they joined in with the brokers, in order to convince legitimate customer into believing the economy was improving. Every person employed in the stock market in some form has a duty not to let that happen to investors.

The brokers are manipulating which stocks go up and which stocks go down daily, weekly, monthly. Who gets hurt are the investor who owned the stock that the brokers determined would go down and investors in the stock market who sells stocks short. The defendants are part of the manipulating of stocks. What the defendant is doing is in a sense a ponzi scheme. In fact Bernie Madoff's scheme, (who was the head man for one of the Defendants,) was similar to what the Defendants are doing. If every investor took their money out of the stock market at the same time the market would crash worse that the 1929 crash. This is what happened in the crash of 2008, 2009.

Because Defendants through brokers have been manipulating the amount of stocks sold and also the prices of the stock sold each day and because Defendant does not verify and cannot verify the number of shares reported traded each hour or day, the Government of the United States is losing billions of tax dollars because no tax money is being paid on the unreported dollars if all trades are legitimate.

Brokers' trade shares of stock with each other or with themselves, but no money changes hands and the Defendants cannot and do not verify as legitimate the trades that brokers report. Broker "A" can sell Broker "B" a million shares of various stocks a day and all they report is the number of shares traded and the final closing price, however the Defendants are not checking to assure that the trades are legitimate. They control the number of shares traded and the prices up or down. Shares are being called as trades but no money is changing hands. The public only see that a certain amount stocks was traded and the stocks was either up or down, based on how the brokers reported them. So therefore the Investor is at the mercy of being lucky or losing their money, in a game of chance. This manipulation cost some investors' money. Those in the know make lots of money from knowing. This manipulation of trades also puts a better view of the health of the stock market for the once was buyers of stocks and those who was thinking about getting out. Not only did this manipulation of stock paint a rosy picture for the public, but it let the insides make a lot of money. However for every dollar someone makes, someone has to lose a dollar. The dollar an investor makes has to come from some other investor plus someone has to pay for salary and bonus of those employed in the stock market.

Appellant alleges that Defendant knows that manipulation is going on and they are participating and or turning their heads, either way is fraud on the public.

The stock market was started and meant to be the buying of selling stocks of a company based on the judgment of what an investor thought or maybe knew how a company would perform in the future. By brokers manipulating the trades each day, the market has become a game of chance.

The only way to save the stock market is to bring truth to it and the only way to bring truth to it is take away immunity. Honest and caring people don't need or want immunity, only manipulators and crooks needs immunity. Immunity is the thing that gives crooks their power.

The stock market is the back bone of America's investments and without truth at every stage; someday the market will become, extinct. Because people will never trust in it again. Congress or nobody is capable of writing laws that will be fool proof. The only system that is close to being fool proof is one that is run by truth and is free of immunity. Immunity creates and protects crooks.

When defendants let the brokers manipulate stocks, only those on the inside know how to make money. Every crook has a family and friends and those are the only people being told, where the stock market is going from hour to hour or day to day or month to month. The hard working people of America are the ones losing money. Those that have been granted immunity, get rich.

There is no money being made by in the stock market by selling a product. The stock market has to have corrections to compensate for the raising of the market. If everyone invested in the stock market cashed their stocks in today, there in not enough money to pay everyone off, therefore the market has to crash and go down and then everyone in the market loses except those who sold first and the defendants in the know. The stock market exists because investors pay for it existence. The stock market will fail unless integrity is built into it. Integrity is based on fear of being caught. Granting immunity creates manipulators, and those manipulators salaries and bonus are paid for by the average person who does not know. Investors have no immunity from loses.

Appellant has a right, by the 14th amendment to the constitution to a due process trial to defend and preserve his property, through the legal system. Appellant is asking this court reverse the trial courts order and grant him the right to try his case

Congress gave immunity to the SEC for the protection of investors and nowhere in that law is the SEC given immunity for fraud. They are only given immunity for protecting investors, not harming them. Someone is manipulating the trading of stocks and that responsibility lies at the feet of the Defendants.

Manipulation of stocks is fraud. Fraud cannot be anything but a wrongful criminal act and Congress does not give any entity immunity for a criminal act of fraud. So therefore no entity can be granted immunity, for fraud. Granting immunity to any entity for criminal fraud could do great harm to every person and every business in America.

Defendants have a Fiduciary duty to protect every trade, protect every dollar of investor's money at all times and when any one does otherwise, they are committing fraud.

Appellant alleges that Defendants does not control over every movement of the brokers who conducts the trades for them, even though defendants are obligated to control them and all other activities connected with the trading of stocks. There is manipulation and it is because Defendants let it happen.

The trial court cited cases in its order, but none cited, confront the issues Appellant has alleged, this is new allegations never before tried.

The law is not clear on what rights given to defendants can be passed on to their contractors. If an employee who is not a broker violated a SEC rule would that person be granted immunity, the answer is no. What makes the Defendants special?

The trial court cited NYSE Specialists Sec. Litig., 503 F.3d at 98. The cited case question the rights of brokers being regulated by SEC. Appellant agrees that Congress gave SEC the right and immunity to regulate the brokers. Appellant is alleging that the Defendants are manipulating the trades and SEC cannot or does not verify each day trades and defendants know this to be true and take advantage of these known facts, and use the loophole to manipulate stocks.

Are all three defendants immune from all duties they perform or they only immune from the duties that protect investors. Are all contractors and employees immune from all duties they perform on behalf of the defendants?

Appellant alleges that the defendants doesn't have the necessary tools to check defendant's daily trades from beginning to finish and therefore cannot certify every trade is a legitimate trade. Crooked brokers have found the loop hole in trading stocks and unless the hole is plugged, the manipulation will continue. The way to close the loop-hole is not to grant immunity.

The defendants rely on the integrity of the broker, which is not good enough for the protection of investors. Investors must be guaranteed that their money is being handled in the right way to protect them from losses. If investors lose money it should only come from investors making bad judgments in their trading of stocks, not what defendants do or don't do. Integrity is only as good as the penalty one may incur if they don't have integrity. The fear of penalties is what gives humans integrity. Without penalties America couldn't exist. What is the different between Bernie Madoff and brokers and defendants?

Appellant questions how FINRA one of the defendants, who is an independent entity, whose chief role is to protect investors by maintaining the fairness of the U.S. capitol market, can be given immunity as they are not part of SEC. Below is an article that explains FINA,

---

"FINRA is a private corporation that acts as a <u>self-regulatory organization</u> (SRO). FINRA is the successor to the **National Association of Securities Dealers, Inc. (NASD)**. Though sometimes mistaken for a government agency, it is a non-governmental organization that performs financial regulation of member brokerage firms and exchange markets.

FINRA is an association that regulates its members through the adoption and enforcement of rules and regulations governing business conduct of member firms. It often provides advice to the <u>U.S. Securities and Exchange Commission</u>, a U.S. government agency legally tasked with governing this conduct. According to the <u>Project on Government Oversight</u> (POGO), FINRA has an "abysmal record of protecting the investing public", incestuous ties to the very industry it is supposed to be overseeing, "was asleep at the wheel for most of the major securities industry scandals dating back to the 1980's," and "took a hands-off approach to regulating many of the larger firms that" collapsed, engendering "the financial crisis, including Bear Stearns, Lehman Brothers, and Merrill Lynch" ... and also failed to detect Bernie Madoff's US$65 billion Ponzi scheme. "Yet despite its countless regulatory failures leading up to the financial meltdown, FINRAS's board has repeatedly approved outrageous seven-figure compensation packages for its top executives." [1] FINRA also provides the binding arbitration service which investors (customers of Wall Street firms) are forced to agree to (through <u>contracts of adhesion</u>), rather than being able to bring their disputes against Wall Street firms and stock brokers, for example, into the federal court system for a judge or jury to rule upon. While arbitration cases are frequent, cases are brought and often permitted to go forward in courts as well, where binding arbitration contracts are sometimes rejected, typically after being ruled unconscionable.

FINRA has regulatory oversight over all securities firms that do business with the public, plus those offering professional training, testing and licensing of registered persons, arbitration and mediation, market regulation by contract for the New York Stock Exchange, the NASDAQ Stock Market, Inc., the American Stock Exchange LLC, and the International Securities Exchange, LLC; and industry utilities, such as Trade Reporting Facilities and other over-the-counter operations.

**** I also attached the first 6 pages of the book to the email.****

How can any court give immunity to this organization? It is the fox controlling the hen house. Appellant asks this court to put a stop to all of these self-servings' entities. Immunity for the Defendants is destroying America. Appellant deserves a chance to prove to this court and a jury that fraud manipulation is taking place every day in America and the average citizen is paying dearly. This court cannot let this fraud continue. It is time for this court to stand up for the average person. This case cries for a jury it hear it.

Will this court say that if defendants don't do their duty of protecting investors, that an investor cannot sue them?

CONCLUSIONS

1- **The trial court should not have dismissed this case.**

2- **Appellant has the right to protect his property under the 14th amendment to the Constitution of the United States, by a Due Process trial and this right supersedes any laws passed by Congress and the only way to protect his property is through the court system.**

1- **Defendants cannot be granted immunity for fraud a criminal act.**

2- **Defendant knows or should know that brokers are manipulating the trades they report each day.**

3- **Defendants' first and most important duty is to protect investors and they have not fulfilled that duty.**

4- **Defendants do not check and verify all trades reported by brokers, to make sure they are legitimate trades.**

5- **One of the Defendants FINRA cannot be granted immunity, under any circumstances.**

6- Immunity cannot be granted to any entity for fraud.

7- Congress's laws do not allow immunity to be passed to all contracted entities, if there is fraud.

8- The investing public (including Appellant) must be given the truth and told the truth, at all times and the defendants have not done so.

9- If immunity is granted to those who manipulate the stock market, then how do the investors receive protection?

10- Unless this court is willing to say, that there is absolute no manipulating of stocks taking place by any one, then this court must let Appellant go forward with his lawsuit. Which side is it better to error on?

11- By this court saying that anyone connected to the SEC has absolute immunity and can transfer that immunity on to employees and contractors, leaves investors with no place to go or no way to protect their property and gives defendants the right to do whatever they chose to investors.

12- Case NYSE specialists Sec. Litig., F.3d at 98 that the trial court cited is a different lawsuit, than this lawsuit.

Appellant closes by asking this court based on the information above to reverse the trial court's order and sent the case back for trial.

Respectfully submitted
Edward H. Flint Pro, Se

*****The New York Stock exchange responded to my brief and I responded to their response with another brief which starts now****

CASE NO. 10--6506

UNITED STATES COURT OF APPEALS
FOR THE SIXTH CIRCUIT

EDWARD H. FLINT,   Plaintiff – Appellant

v.

NEW YORK STOCK EXCHANGE ET AL   Defendant – Appellee

On Appeal from the United States District Court
For the Western District of Kentucky
Louisville Division

Honorable, Joseph H. McKinley Jr.

Civil Case No. 3:10-CV-000626-JHM

APPELLANT'S RESPONSE TO APPELLEE'S BRIEF

Respectfully submitted
Edward H. Flint Pro, Se

APPELLANT'S STATEMENT AGAINST THE ISSUE AS PRESEENTED FOR REVIEW BY APPELLEE

The Defendants has tried to make this a simple issue for this court to review. Appellant states that the issue is more that than what the Defendants have stated, they stated "did the court err in holding that an individual's claims are barred by well- established doctrine of absolute immunity for SROs." As the Defendants has stated. There is an issue of denying Appellant the right to protect his property under the 14th amendment to the Constitution of the United States, by a Due Process trial and does this right supersede any laws passed by Congress. The only way Appellant has to protect his property, is through the court system, with a trial.

APPELLANT REBUTIAL TO DEFENDANT'S STATEMENT OF THE CASE

Defendant's has stated that "NYSE and NASDAQ each operate a stock market on which millions of thousands of different companies are list." That statement it self makes a need why the lawsuit should go forward. With all of the money changing hands there are is a lot of people trying each day to find a way to keep some of it for themselves, which proves Appellant point.

Defendants also stated that "has been afforded absolute immunity from private suit relating to the performance functions." This case is about if the immunity Congress gave the SEC" Appellant asks this court that if that immunity can be handed down and to whom and how far down can the immunity can be handed down, does the janitor who works for a company that does business with the SEC receive immunity.

APPELLANT'S REBUTIAL TO DEFENDANT'S COUNTERSTATEMENT OF FACTS

Defendant's stated that "the three defendants play crucial roles in the regulation of the securities. Absolute immunity from private parties is necessary to maintain that comprehensive system." Defendants are saying that if any defendant does any wrong that harms a person who invests their money, they should still not be sued. Defendants are saying that the stock market is a perfect world and no one should question them or have to worry about them, every person who works for them are honest and none would want to harm a person. Therefore immunity is important to maintain the system, and there are no thieves in the selling of stocks. We all know that in all segments of our society that there are thieves looking for a way to get the money for themselves, but the larger the amount involved the more thieves there are thinking up ways, especially if they have immunity.

The Defendants cited a number of cases, however none is about the issue Appellant has raised.

The Defendants rattle on about how honest the SROs are and how Appellant should not be allowed to disrupt the current system. Defendant's last statement in their brief tells what is really on in the minds of the Defendants and I quote, "If left stand, claims like Mr., Flint's would cripple the regulatory system established by Congress and open the floodgates to investor lawsuits against SROs."

Appellant counters with this statement. If there is fraud going on then should the Federal court system keep turning their head and not get involved and let the thieves get rich at the expense of the investor. Defendants are saying that a smooth running regulatory system is more important that an honest regulatory system. This country went through this, in 2008 and 2009 and is still paying for it now. The citizens of this great country are demanding that the system be made fair and honest, in order that it doesn't happen again. The SROs have not learned from the experience and in fact are doing things worse today than then, so they get back what they lost (but not investors) through their blunder in the years that let up to the events of 2008 and 2009. If a poll could be taken among investors, asking do they want an honest system or a smooth running system, Appellant believes they would say both and why can't they have both. The only way that you can have both is by trying in a court of law those who violate the rules and the intent of an honest system. Congress did establish a system, but surely they meant for the system to be honest and for every action to see the light of the sun, not the darkness of night. Surely Congress meant for it to be keep honest and fair.

CONCLUSION

This court must decide 1) - if Congress meant for the immunity granted by the Congress to the SEC also meant for immunity be granted to each and every person involved with the SEC, and 2) - does the 14th amendment to the constitution that gives a citizen the right to protect their property and a Due Process trial, also mean that Congress take away those rights, by granting immunity to anyone.

An honest regulatory system must exist, regardless of the cost or disruption. A flawed system, just to have a system that runs smooth is no system; it is an excuse for thieves to exist. In fact a system where the participants can be sued will run smoother that a flawed system.

Today we don't have an honest regulatory system, but instead we have a con game.

Therefore Appellant asks this court to overturn the District order and sent the case back to the court for a trial.

Respectfully submitted
Edward H. Flint Pro, Se

***** My Brief ends here****

**** The Court of Appeal order starts hers*****

UNITED STATES COURT OF APPEALS
FOR THE SIXTH CIRCUIT

NO. 10-6506

EDWARD H. FLINT,   Plaintiff-Appellant

v.

NEW YOUR STOCK EXCHANGE et al   Defendant-Appellee

On Appeal from the United States District
Court for the Western District of Kentucky

FILED AUGUST 26, 2011

ORDER

Before: Boggs, Gibbons, and Cook, Circuit Judges

Edward H. Flint, a pro se Kentucky resident, Appeals a District court order dismissing his civil action asserting securities fraud. This case has been referred to a panel of the court pursuant to Rule 34(j)(1), of the Sixth Circuit. Upon examination, this panel unanimously agrees that an oral argument is not needed. Fed. R. App. P. 34(a)

Seeking monetary relief, Flint sued the New Your stock Exchange (NYSE), the NASDAQ Stock Market, The Financial Regulatory Authority (FINRA), Jane Does and John Does. Flint alleges that the defendants have a monopoly on the trading of stocks. He alleged that the defendants manipulated the sale price and volume of stocks on a daily basis and that the defendants are aware of this manipulation. Flint alleged that this manipulation caused him financial, mental and physical injuries.

Flint Claimed that the defendants failed to comply with their legal responsibilities. The defendants allegedly manipulation stock price for selfish reasons, which resulted in significant losses in tax revenues. The defendants, according to Flint, engaged in a "con game" and mind control, hiding stock-market problems from him and the public at large. The defendants moved to dismiss the complaint pursuant to Federal Rules of Civil Produce 12(b)(1) and 12 (b)(6). The district court subsequently dismissed Flint's complaint, fining that the defendant as quasi-governmental organizations were entitled to the same immunity to which the Securities and Exchange Commission (SEC) would have been entitled.

In his timely appeal, Flint argues that the defendants are not entitled to immunity and that the immunity cannot supersede the Due Process Clause of the Constitution. Flint complains about the stock-market crash of 2008 and blames it on stock manipulation. Flint states that he and his wife invested in the stock market and lost over $400,000. He blames the loss on the alleged manipulation of the market by stock brokers. Flint states that the immunity does not apply to claims of fraud.

The district court did not state whether it dismissed the complaint pursuant to Rule 12(b)(1) or Rule 12(b)(6). In either instance, the order is reviewed *de novo*. Bassett v. NCAA, 528 F, 3d 426,430 (6th Cir. 2008 (rule 12(b)(6); Bd of trs, of Painesville Twp. V. City of Painesville, Ohio, 200 F3d 396, 398 (6th Cir. 1999)(Rule 12(b)(1). In Bell Atlantic Corp. v. Twombly, 550 U.S. 544 (2007), the court explained that the factual allegations must "raise a right to relief above the speculative level." Id. At 555. A complaint must contain facts sufficient to claim relief that is plausible on its face." Id. At 750

Under 15 U.S.C. 33 78a-78oo, (the Securities Exchange Act of (1934), Congress created self-regulatory organizations(SRO's) to conduct the daily regulation of the United States stock markets under the supervision of the SEC. See 15 U.S.C. ## 78c(a)0(26), 78o-3(b), 78s(b), 78s(d); Sec v. Mohn, 465 F,3d 647,650 (6th Cir. 2006); D'Alessio v. N. Y. Stock Exch. Inc., 258 F3d 93, 105 (2d Cir. 2001). The SEC exercises supervisory authority over SROs. See, e.g., 15 U.S.C. #78s. The Sec approves all rules, policies, practices and interpretations of the SROs before thee implemented. See 15 U.S.C. 3 78s(b)(1); Merrill Lynch, Pierce, Fenner &Smith, Inc. v. Nat'l Assn. of Sec. Dealers, Inc., 616 F2d 1363, 1367 (5th Cir. (1980); see also Roney & C0. v. Goren, 875 F2d 1218, 122 (6th Cir. 1989). NYSE, NASDAQ and FINRA are SROs, subject to the authority of the SEC. Barber v. N.Y. Stock Exch., Inc. 99 F3d 49,51 (2d Cir, 1996) (NYSE; DL Capital Grp., LLC v. NASDAQ Stock Market., 409 F3d 93, 94, (2d Cir. (2005) (NASDAQ: Sacks v. SEC, 635 F3d 1121, 1122 (9th Cir. 2011) (FINRA)

As a result of this regulatory scheme, SROs are entitled to immunity from suit for conduct falling within the scope and general oversight responsibilities of the SRO. D'Alessio, 258 F3d at 105: Barbara, 99F.3d at 51, 59: Austin Mun, Sec. Inc. v. Nat'l Assn. of Sec. Dealers, Inc., 757 F2d 676, 690-91 (5th Cir. 1985; see also Inre Series 7 Brokers Qualification Exam. Scoring Litig., 548 F3f 110, 114 (D.C. Cir. 2008). The immunity applies where the Exchange Act or as a common-law tort or contract claim. In re Series 7 brokers Qualification Exam Scorning Litig., 548 F3d at 114; Sparta Surgical Corp. v. Nat'l Assn. of Sec. Dealers, Inc., 159 F3d 1209, 1215 (9th Cir. 1998).

In his complaint, Flint asserted that the defendants "failed to perform their duties] as required by [T]he Congress, the Government of the United States and the rules and laws of trading stocks throughout America." Because Flint's complaint is based on the very regulatory conduct to which immunity applies, the district court properly dismissed Flint's complaint/

Accordingly, we affirm the district court's order. Rule 34(j) (2) (c), Rules of the Sixth Circuit.   Enter by Order of the Court--s/Leonard Green- clerk

******* The Court of Appeals order ends here*******

*******My Petition to the Supreme Court starts here*********

No._____

In The
Supreme Court of the United States

Edward H. Flint   Petitioner,

Versus

New York Stock Exchange, NYSE; NASDAQ Stock Market;
Financial Industry Regulatory Authority,
Finra; Jane Does: John Does,   Respondents

On Petition for Writ of Certiorari
Court of Appeals for the Sixth Circuit.

PETITION FOR WRIT OF CERTIORARI

Edward H. Flint Pro, Se
Pro, SE, Counsel for Petitioner

QUESTIONS PRESENTED

1- Can the Congress of the United States grant absolute immunity to the Security and Exchange Commission (SEC) and all entities connected to it, which deprives a citizen their rights of Due Process of law as granted by the Constitution to protect his property?

2- Did Congress also grant absolute immunity to all self-regulatory organizations (SRO) under the supervisory of the SEC, regardless of the action taken by them or just certain items?

3- Does the immunity granted by Congress to the SEC and SROs also extend beyond the stock exchanges, to its employees or contractures and to the Brokers, (Market Makers) who sell the stocks and sets the price of the stock and therefore are they extended the same immunity?

4- If Brokers manipulates the sale of stocks on exchanges would that be fraud and if it was fraud, would absolute immunity still apply?

5- Is it possible that Congress has written a perfect law and there are no cheaters involved in selling or reporting the sale of stocks?

STATEMENT OF THE CASE

PROCEDURAL HISTORY

Flint would like to start by saying that when a Pro, Se is involved, a court should overlook some of the presentation by a Pro, Se and arrive at the truth by other means, regardless of what it takes. No fair minded judge or the framers of the constitution would expect a non-educated in law person to complete with a person who has been educated and trained for a number of years. There is nothing in the United States Constitution that says that the Court's Rule of Civil procedures must be adhered to by Pro, Se's. Nothing can supersede the 14th amendment to the constitution giving everyone Due Process, to a fair and honest trial.

Therefore any misstatement made or lack of presenting the proper federal law or rule in pleadings to a court, should not be held against a Pro, Se. If any court holds in their rulings that a Pro, Se didn't adhere to the rules of civil procedures or cite the right authority, then the court is giving the educated lawyer an unfair advantage over the pro, se, and denying the Pro, Se a Due Process fair trial. The court its self would be discriminating against a Pro, Se.

This action arises out of Complaint filed in Western District of Kentucky Federal Court by Petitioner Flint against New Your Stock Exchange et al, on October 4, 2010.

The Petitioner in his complaint alleged that Brokers who sell the stock for the Respondents was manipulating the selling of stocks, to each other and or reporting sales that never took place. Thereby fooling the public with an image that is false and such action lets brokers set the price of stock and the brokers salary, or pay is based on the number of orders they sell not number of shares at a time and knowing they can do this they are able to control the price of the stocks, for themselves of or friends.

The District Court dismissed the case based on Congress decided to allow private SRO's to conduct the day to day regulation and administration of the stock market, under the supervision of the SEC.

The District Court stated that as such they are entitled to the same immunity as that of the SEC.

The Sixth Circuit Court of Appeals upheld the ruling of the District Circuit; however neither the District Court nor the Sixth Circuit cites any authority from the United States Supreme Court. All authorities cite was from Circuit Courts rulings

The Sixth Circuit stated that because Flint's complaint is based on the very regulatory conduct to which immunity applies, therefore the dismissal by the district court properly dismissed Flint's complaint.

ARGUMENT

Appellant alleges that Defendants does not control over every movement of the brokers who conducts the trades for them, even though defendants are obligated to control them and all other activities connected with the trading of stocks. There is manipulation and it is because Defendants let it happen.

Brokers' trade shares of stock with each other or even with themselves, but no money changes hands and the Defendants cannot and do not verify as legitimate the trades that brokers report. Broker "A" can sell Broker "B" a million shares of various stocks a day and all they report is the number of shares traded and the final closing price, however the Defendants are not checking to assure that the trades are legitimate. They control the number of shares traded and the prices up or down. Shares are being reported as trades, but no money is changing hands. The public only see that a certain amount stocks was traded and the stocks was either up or down, based on how the brokers reported them. So therefore the Investor is at the mercy of being lucky or losing their money, in a game of chance. This manipulation cost investors' money. Those in the know make lots of money from knowing. This manipulation of trades also puts a better view of the health of the stock market for those who was once buyers of stocks to get them back into the market and to stop those who those who was considering about getting out. Not only does manipulation of stock paint a rosy picture for the public, but it let the insiders make a lot of money. However for every dollar someone makes, someone has to lose a dollar.

The dollar an investor makes has to come from some other investor plus someone has to pay for salary and bonus of those employed in the stock market.

Appellant alleges that Defendants knows that manipulation is going on and they are participating and or turning their heads, either way is fraud on the public. The market must crash at times because it's a manipulated ponzi scheme.

The stock market was started and meant to be the buying of selling stocks of a company based on the judgment of what an investor thought or maybe knew how a company would perform in the future. By brokers manipulating the trades each day, the market has become a game of chance.

The only way to save the stock market is to bring truth to it and the only way to bring truth to it is take away immunity. Honest and caring people don't need or want immunity, only manipulators and crooks needs immunity. Immunity is the thing that gives crooks their power.

The stock market is the back bone of America's investments industry and without truth at every stage; someday the market will become, extinct, because people will never trust in it again. Congress or nobody is capable of writing laws that will be fool proof. The only system that is close to being fool proof is one that is run by truth and is free of immunity. Immunity creates and protects crooks.

When defendants let the brokers manipulate stocks, only those on the inside know how to make money. Every crook has a family and friends and those are the only people being told, where the stock market is going from hour to hour or day to day or month to month. The hard working people of America are the ones losing money. Those that have been granted immunity, get rich.

There is no money being made by in the stock market by selling a product. The stock market has to have corrections to compensate for the raising of the market. If everyone invested in the stock market cashed their stocks in the same day, there in not enough money to pay everyone off at once, therefore the market has to crash and go down and then everyone in the market loses except those who sold first and the defendants in the know. The stock market exists because investors pay for it existence. The stock market will fail unless integrity is built into it. Integrity is based on fear of being caught. Granting immunity creates manipulators, and those manipulators salaries and bonus are paid for by the average person who does not know. Investors have no immunity from loses.

Appellant has a right, by the 14th amendment of the constitution to a Due Process trial in order he can defend and preserve his property, through the legal system. Appellant is asking this court reverse the trial courts order and grant him the right to try his case

Congress gave immunity to the SEC for the protection of investors and nowhere in that law is the SEC given immunity for fraud. Congress gave immunity to protect investors, not harm them. Someone is manipulating the trading of stocks and that responsibility lies at the feet of the Defendants.

Manipulation of stocks is fraud. Fraud cannot be anything but a wrongful criminal act and Congress does not give any entity immunity for a criminal act of fraud. So therefore no entity can be granted immunity, for fraud. Granting immunity to any entity for criminal fraud could do great harm to every person and every business in America.

Respondents have a Fiduciary duty to protect every trade, protect every dollar of investor's money at all times and when any one does otherwise, they are committing fraud.

Appellant is alleging that the Defendants are manipulating the trades and SEC cannot or does not verify each day trades and defendants know this to be true and take advantage of these known facts, and use the loophole to manipulate stocks.

Are all three defendants immune from all duties they perform or they only immune from the duties that protect investors. Are all contractors and employees immune from all duties they perform on behalf of the defendants?

Appellant alleges that the defendants doesn't have the necessary ability to check defendant's brokers daily trades from beginning to finish and therefore cannot certify every trade is a legitimate trade. Crooked brokers have found the loop hole in trading stocks and unless the hole is plugged, the manipulation will continue. The way to close the loophole is not to grant immunity.

The defendants rely on the integrity of the broker, which is not good enough for the protection of investors. Investors must be guaranteed that their money is being handled in the right way to protect them from losses. If investors lose money in the stock market it should only come from investors making bad judgments in their trading of stocks, not what defendants do or don't do.

Integrity is only as good as the penalty one may incur if they don't have integrity. The fear of penalties is what gives humans integrity. Without penalties America couldn't exist. What is the different between Bernie Madoff and brokers and defendants, none?

Appellant questions how FINRA one of the defendants, who is an independent entity, whose chief role is to protect investors by maintaining the fairness of the U.S. capitol market, can be given immunity as they are not part of SEC. Below is an article that explains FINA,

FINRA is a private corporation that acts as a <u>self-regulatory organization</u> (SRO). FINRA is the successor to the **National Association of Securities Dealers, Inc. (NASD)**. Though sometimes mistaken for a government agency, it is a non-governmental organization that performs financial regulation of member brokerage firms and exchange markets.

FINRA is an association that regulates its members through the adoption and enforcement of rules and regulations governing business conduct of member firms. It often provides advice to the <u>U.S. Securities and Exchange Commission,</u> a U.S. government agency legally tasked with governing this conduct. According to the <u>Project on Government Oversight</u> (POGO), FINRA has an "abysmal record of protecting the investing public", incestuous ties to the very industry it is supposed to be overseeing, "was asleep at the wheel for most of the major securities industry scandals dating back to the 1980's," and "took a hands-off approach to regulating many of the larger firms that" collapsed, engendering "the financial crisis, including Bear Stearns, Lehman Brothers, and Merrill Lynch" ... and also failed to detect Bernie Madoff's $65 billion Ponzi scheme. "Yet despite its countless regulatory failures leading up to the financial meltdown, FINRAS's board has repeatedly approved outrageous seven-figure compensation packages for its top executives." [1] FINRA also provides the binding arbitration service which investors (customers of Wall Street firms) are forced to agree to (through <u>contracts of adhesion</u>), rather than being able to bring their disputes against Wall Street firms and stock brokers, for example, into the federal court system for a judge or jury to rule upon. While arbitration cases are frequent, cases are brought and often permitted to go forward in courts as well, where binding arbitration contracts are sometimes rejected, typically after being ruled unconscionable.

FINRA has regulatory oversight over all securities firms that do business with the public, plus those offering professional training, testing and licensing of registered persons, arbitration and mediation, market regulation by contract for the <u>New York Stock Exchange</u>, the <u>NASDAQ</u> Stock Market, Inc., the <u>American Stock Exchange</u> LLC, and the <u>International Securities Exchange</u>, LLC; and industry utilities, such as Trade Reporting Facilities and other over-the-counter operations.

How can any court give immunity to this organization? It is the fox controlling the hen house. Appellant asks this court to put a stop to all of these self-servings' entities. Immunity for the Defendants is destroying America. Appellant deserves a chance to prove to this court and a jury that fraud manipulation is taking place every day in America and the average citizen is paying dearly. This court cannot let this fraud continue. It is time for this court to stand up for the average person. This case cries for a jury it hear it.

Will this court say that if defendants don't do their duty of protecting investors, that an investor cannot sue them?

REASONS FOR GRANTING THE WRIT

1- Neither court cited any ruling by the United States Supreme Court on the subject of immunity to brokers and other people involved in the sale of stocks.

2- There is a question of did Congress mean to give immunity to the complete chain of all who is involved with SEC.

3- There is a constitution questions regarding Congress taking away a person rights to Due Process.

4- How far down the chain does immunity go? If a worker for SEC robbed a person on the floor of an exchange is that person granted immunity

5- If Brokers have found a way of beating the system by selling to each other, but no money change hands, do they have immunity

6- If Brokers have found a way to report sales of stock to manipulate the price of the stock, without the SEC having knowledge of such sales, do they have immunity.

7- According to the ruling of the Sixth Circuit the SEC cannot do any wrong, because

8- There is no room to sue people who work for or under the SEC.

9- With so many people invested in the stock market the truth must be known for sure.

10- The Sixth Circuit in their order used the reason that the SEC approves all rules, policies, practices and interpretation of the SRO's before they are implemented, but this reasoning does not mean that crooks have not found a way to get around the System. Beating systems has been done since man has existed.

11- Electronic trading of stocks has open up a whole new ball game and it is easier to cheat now than before when Congress passed the Securities Exchange Act of 1934.

12- If Congress granted by statute to a correction agency, would all of the guards that was employed by that agency be automatically be grant absolute immunity

CONCLUSION

The question is, can Congress grant absolute immunity to any agency that takes away a person's right to Due Process of a trial to protect his property.

Did Congress grant absolute immunity to all sub-contractors of the SEC agency that Congress granted immunity to?

If Flint is correct in his allegations, then the actions by the respondents are fraud and no fraud act can be blessed with absolute immunity

Petitioner asks this court to overrule the trial court and return the case to the trial court in the name of justice, for a jury trial.

Respectfully submitted,
s/ Edward H. Flint, Pro, Se.

***********My Petition to the Supreme Court ends here*************

John Heyburn was the judge in this case and I will tie him into this story as being part of what influence Judge Roberts switching his vote on Obamacare.

The Supreme Court refused to consider this case.

There are billions of dollars invested each day in the stock market. Thousands of people lost a lot of money in the market in 2008 and 2009. They were affected by the way the markets do business. I can prove that the market is manipulated every day.

The Supreme Court refuses to let any trial take place that involves the stock market. They have interpreted the law that Congress wrote and passed. The law doesn't say what the Supreme Court has ruled it says.

Sure this would upset the stock market, but if the markets are being manipulated the people of America needs to know. Now the only investors who are guarantee to make money, is the person who is in the know.

The courts have said that no matter what takes place, no one can sue the people who are involved in the stock market; the Supreme Court ruled they all have immunity regardless of what they do.

This is not the way America was intended to operate. In America the people should come first in being protected from corruption.

If I am right about the market being manipulated, the public needs to know the truth.

If I am right about whom Congress gave immunity too, then the people of America needs to know.

If Congress didn't give immunity to the people I sued, then the Supreme Court is covering up for the corrupt people. A devil named corruption is controlling the people who invest money in the stock market.

If Congress gave immunity to the people I accused of manipulating the market, then it should be out in the open.

Investors needs to know that the people they are trusting, has immunity from fraud and corruption.

If Congress is not aware that the Supreme Court says the owners of the Stock Market have immunity, they need to know.

Congress needs to either change the law to what is best for investors or they need to tell the public that they gave immunity to all who controls the stock markets. Americans need to know the truth, openly.

The people of America needs to be told that everybody connected to the stock market has immunity and those who have immunity can do anything they please and get by with it.

Investors need to know the truth and after being told the truth, then its investor beware.

I cannot imagine any issue in America that needs to be cleared up more than this issue does. But the Supreme Court just swept it under the table. Unless the Supreme Court lets a case be tried, the issue will never be settled. Not settling the issue gives people the right to manipulate right to keep manipulate the markets.

Thousands of people are getting rich each year from the stock market. The question is are those people getting rich, because they are smart or are they connected to those who have immunity?

The Supreme Court should have let me pursue the case with a trial and let the facts come out.

By the Supreme Court denying me the right to forward with this case, is a cover up. If I am right about what takes place in the stock market, this means that only those who in the know, are getting rich off of poor hard working people, who blindly invest their money in the stock market.

I knew by now that I had no chance of winning a case with the court system in America, I was wasting my time. But I had promised God. And God wanted me to continue filing lawsuits. I was fighting for ways to continue doing God's will and trying to win the truth for America.

I started getting messages from the Holy Spirit to broaden my fight. So I continued. I will further in this book show you what steps I took to try and win and to expose, corrupt judges and corrupt companies.

CHAPTER 9

LAWSUIT FLINT V. JUDGE JOHN HEYBURN

This is the same Judge who was the judge in the Stock Market case, the Churchill Downs case and most of the others cases

****** **THE COMPLAINT STARTS HERE********

UNITED STATES DISTRICT COURT
WESTERN DISTRICT OF KENTUCKY
LOUISVILLE DIVISON

CASE NO. 3:11-CV-258-S

EDWARD H. FLINT   PLAINTIFF

VS

COMPLAINT

JOHN G. HEYBURN II – Judge   DEFENDANT

Comes the Plaintiff Edward H. Flint acting as his own counsel against Defendant as a judge in Federal Court in Louisville, KY.

1- Plaintiff, Edward H. Flint lives at

2- Defendant John G. Heyburn II an individual who is a judge in Western District Court

3- Plaintiff alleges that Defendant Heyburn is bias against him.

4- Plaintiff alleges that Defendant Heyburn has been bias against him ever since Plaintiff filed lawsuits against three Jefferson Country Circuit judges in 2009.

5- Plaintiff alleges that Defendant Heyburn has been bias against him in every lawsuit that was assigned to the Defendant's court ever since.

6- Plaintiff alleges that Defendant Heyburn refused to excuse himself in FEDERAL CASE 3:11-CV-54-H in which he had a conflict of interest.

7- Plaintiff alleges that Defendant Heyburn should have recused himself from case Federal case 3:10-CV-202-H because he had a conflict of interest.

8- Plaintiff alleges that Defendant Heyburn has been given favorers from parties whom he would later judge and the Defendant refused to recuse himself from those cases.

9- Plaintiff alleges that Defendant Heyburn violated a court rule, but denies he violated the rules but stated another Judge named Charles Simpson as the one who violated the court's rule in the Churchill Downs case.

10- Plaintiff alleges that Defendant actions harmed Plaintiff, physically.

11- Plaintiff alleges that Defendant actions harmed Plaintiff mentally

12- Plaintiff alleges that Defendant actions have stopped Plaintiff from receiving Due Process fair and honest trial under the 14th amendment to the constitution in each case that came before Defendant.

13- Plaintiff alleges that Defendant Heyburn in his order dated April 26, 2011 lied to try and throw an inexperience old man off tracks in order that this order would make the Defendant look good.

14- Plaintiff alleges that Defendant has denied Plaintiff his civil rights in each case

15- Plaintiff alleges that Defendant has been prejudice against Plaintiff in his rulings

16- Plaintiff alleges that Defendant has not conducted himself the way a judge should, on cases before him involving Plaintiff.

17- Plaintiff alleges that Defendant has violated the court of conduct rules that all judges must adhere to.

18- Plaintiff alleges Defendant has become a judge who makes rulings that fit his own wants. Pulling the justice system down with him

19- Plaintiff alleges that Defendant Heyburn in his actions took advantage of Plaintiff's inexperience and did not judge by Cannons conduct ethics.

20- Plaintiff alleges that Defendant violated court rules to get the Churchill Downs case FEDERAL CASE 3:11-CV-54- that wasn't assigned to him, but he wanted to be the judge in that case, thereby causing other judges to violating court rules and laws, but who Defendant Heyburn blames other for violating the court's rules not himself.

21- Plaintiff alleges that Defendant refused to recuse himself from case a FEDERAL CASE 3:11-CV-54-H, which he should have never been a judge on, according to court rules and court ethic.

22- Plaintiff alleges that Defendant was out to get Plaintiff because Plaintiff had sued parties; that he the Defendant Heyburn didn't want sued.

23- Plaintiff alleges that Defendant Heyburn violated court rules to make sure he was in control of the case and therefore he could control the court against Plaintiff.

Respectfully submitted
Edward H. Flint Pro, Se

****** THE COMPLAINT ENDS HERE******

*****The District Court order starts here****

UNITED STATES DISTRICT COURT
WESTERN DISTRICT OF KENTUCKY AT LOUISVILLE

CIVIL ACTION NO.3:11-CV-258-S

EDWARD H. Flint   PLAINTIFF

v.

JOHN G. HEYBURN II   DEFENDANT

ORDER

Upon review, the court concludes that sua sponte dismissal under Apple v. Glenn is appropriate because it is "no longer open to discussion" that Plaintiff's claims are devoid of all legal merit. See Metzenbaum v. Nugent, 55 F. App'x729 (6th cir 2003) (upholding district court's sua sponte dismissal of a complaint under Apple v. Glenn because the named defendant, a judge, was entitled to absolute judicial immunity): Forbush v. Zaleski, 20 F. App'x 481 (6th Cir. 2001) (same).

Accordingly, the court will enter a separate Order if Dismissal.

Date:

May 3, 2011   Charles R. Simpson III, Judge

United States District Court

The reader should take note of the judge's name; it will surface many times in this book. This is Judge Simpson, judging his friend Judge Heyburn. Both of these judges worked for Senator Mitch McConnell for 7 years and practiced law with him.

Please note what the judge said in his order. He said Judge Heyburn had absolute immunity and he dismissed my case. The judge stated the case was no longer open to discussions. His name will appear further into the book.

****I appealed to the Court of Appeal *****

The Court of Appeals Order stated that they affirmed the district courts order

Accordingly, we affirm the district court's order. Rule 34(j)(2)(C), Rules of the Six Circuit.

ENTERED BY ORDER OF THE COURT

Leonard Green, Clerk

******* I appealed and My Petition to the Supreme Court starts here*********

IN THE SUPREME COURT OF THE UNITED STATES

NO._____

Edward H. Flint,   Petitioner,

v.

JOHN G. HEYBURN, JUDGE,   Respondent

On Petition for a Writ of Certiorari to the
United States Court of Appeals for the Sixth Circuit

QUESTIONS PRESENTED

1- Does Judges have to abide by and honor 28 U.S. Code #455 which pertains to when a judge must disqualify themselves?

2- Did the 1988 United States Supreme get it right in their ruling in Liljeberg v. Health Servs. Acquisition Corp., 486 U.S. 847, 860 n.8 (1988).

3- Does a Judge have to abide by District Court Rules and not manipulate the judges in the case?

4- Should a judge have disqualified himself from a case under 28 U.S.C #455 when the Petitioner alleged, he the judge, has accepted favors from Defendants in the case for himself and others?

5- Should a judge have disqualified himself when Petitioner had once dismissed the judge's former law pardoner, twice from being counsel for two associations the Petitioner was President of and thereby caused loss of the two large producing money accounts, that was harmful to the law firm when the judge was a partner of the firm?

6- Why would a nonbiased judge dismiss a case **WITH PREJUDICE** when no hearing had been held in the case, unless the judge was prejudice?

7- Does the United States Constitution grant judges immunity when they have violated court rules and laws of the United States in their handing of a case.

STATEMENT OF THE CASE

PROCEDURAL HISTORY

Flint would like to start by saying that he is an 81 year old Pro, Se and he deserves a review on his Petition the same as any attorney. This Court has refused to hear a case by Petitioner even though he has showed this court how judges are violating laws and rules in Jefferson County, KY and this court has turned a dumb ear to his pleadings. Petitioner is concern about our country. This court is destroying America because they don't control the judges from violating rules and laws. Everyone knows that if the judges can be corrupt and get by with it, others they think its ok to be corrupt also.

This case involves a judge who is one of the best friends of Minority Leader Mitch McConnell of the United States Senate in Congress. They were best friends before Senator McConnell ever ran for public office. When Senator McConnell was elected a County Judge of Jefferson County, KY, The Respondent was Counsel for him. Judge Heyburn has plans to be appointed someday if a Republican President is elected of the

WHY CHIEF JUDGE JOHN ROBERTS SWITCHED HIS VOTE ON OBAMA CARE

United States to either the Court of Appeals or to the United States Supreme Court. Chief Judge John Roberts has appointed Respondent Judge Heyburn to serve on a committee of this court. For this reason, this court must judge this case based on the merits and law and not because he is a judge and friends with Mitch McConnell.

Petitioner filed a complaint against Judge Heyburn as an individual, alleging that Judge Heyburn was bias, among other things. Petitioner's complaint stated the following.

Comes the Plaintiff Edward H. Flint acting as his own counsel against Defendant as a judge in Federal Court in Louisville, KY.

1. **Plaintiff, Edward H. Flint lives at 5800 Coach Gate Wynde #293-Louisville Kentucky-40207**

2. **Defendant John G. Heyburn II an individual who is a judge in Western District Court**

3. **Plaintiff alleges that Defendant Heyburn is bias against him.**

4. **Plaintiff alleges that Defendant Heyburn has been bias against him ever since Plaintiff filed lawsuits against three Jefferson Country Circuit judges in 2009.**

5. **Plaintiff alleges that Defendant Heyburn has been bias against him in every lawsuit that was assigned to the Defendant's court ever since.**

6. **Plaintiff alleges that Defendant Heyburn refused to excuse himself in FEDERAL CASE 3:11-CV-54-H in which he had a conflict of interest.**

7. **Plaintiff alleges that Defendant Heyburn should have recused himself from case Federal case 3:10-CV-202-H because he had a conflict of interest.**

8. **Plaintiff alleges that Defendant Heyburn has been given favorers from parties whom he would later judge and the Defendant refused to recuse himself from those cases.**

9. **Plaintiff alleges that Defendant Heyburn violated a court rule, but denies he violated the rules but stated another Judge named Charles Simpson as the one who violated the court's rule in the Churchill Downs case.**

10. **Plaintiff alleges that Defendant actions harmed Plaintiff, physically.**

11. **Plaintiff alleges that Defendant actions harmed Plaintiff mentally**

12. **Plaintiff alleges that Defendant actions have stopped Plaintiff from receiving Due Process fair and honest trial under the 14th amendment to the constitution in each case that came before Defendant.**

13- **Plaintiff alleges that Defendant Heyburn in his order dated April 26, 2011 lied to try and throw an inexperience old man off tracks in order that this order would make the Defendant look good.**

14- **Plaintiff alleges that Defendant has denied Plaintiff his civil rights in each case**

15- **Plaintiff alleges that Defendant has been prejudice against Plaintiff in his rulings**

16- **Plaintiff alleges that Defendant has not conducted himself the way a judge should, on cases before him involving Plaintiff.**

17- **Plaintiff alleges that Defendant has violated the court of conduct rules that all judges must adhere to.**

18- **Plaintiff alleges Defendant has become a judge who makes rulings that fit his own wants. Pulling the justice system down with him**

19- **Plaintiff alleges that Defendant Heyburn in his actions took advantage of Plaintiff's inexperience and did not judge by Cannons conduct ethics.**

20- **Plaintiff alleges that Defendant violated court rules to get the Churchill Downs case FEDERAL CASE 3:11-CV-54- that wasn't assigned to him, but he wanted to be the judge in that case, thereby causing other judges to violating court rules and laws, but who Defendant Heyburn blames other for violating the court's rules not himself.**

21- **Plaintiff alleges that Defendant refused to recuse himself from case a FEDERAL CASE 3:11-CV-54-H, which he should have never been a judge on according to court rules and court ethic.**

22- **Plaintiff alleges that Defendant was out to get Plaintiff because Plaintiff had sued parties; that he the Defendant Heyburn didn't want sued.**

23- **Plaintiff alleges that Defendant Heyburn violated court rules to make sure he was in control of the case and therefore he could control the court against Plaintiff.**

Petitioner filed with the Court of Appeals in his brief the following.

Appellant as pro, se has filed a number of lawsuits in Western District Court a number of lawsuits and every case that was assigned to Appellee Judge Heyburn was dismissed WITH PREJUDICE. Heyburn by his own words has admitted he is prejudice against Flint. There was never a reason to dismiss any of the lawsuits WITH PREJUDICE Flint filed, the cases had just started and before any discovery were taken, except the first motion was made by the opposing party to dismiss and then dismissal WITH PREJUDICE was granted against Flint by Judge Heyburn. Dismissing a case WITH PREJUDICE takes a lot of facts or a judge that doesn't want the case refiled in another court for personal reasons; a personal reason are not in a judge's jurisdiction and is not normally performed by judges.

In 2009 Flint filed a lawsuit against three (3) Jefferson County Circuit Judges, case 3:09-CV-116-H for violating Kentucky Supreme Court Rules. Heyburn in his ruling order stated "judges routinely accept cases transferred to them from another division with in a circuit court" This statement was not true and the Kentucky Supreme Court rules states that all cases must be assigned by lot and cannot be transferred. Heyburn was given a copy of the rule with Appellant's brief and he completely ignored it, but dismissed the case WITH PREJUDICE. Judge Heyburn was given **Rule 11** of **Thirtieth Judicial Jefferson Circuit Court** which stated how the Jefferson County Circuit Court was supposed to function and Judge Heyburn ignored it, because he was going to rule against Flint and needed to justify his actions in his mind to take away his guilt feelings.

Flint filed other lawsuits that Judge Heyburn dismissed WITH PREJUDICE for no reason. In 2009 Flint filed a lawsuit against a Judge Armstrong in Jefferson District Court case No. 3:09-CV-878-H, which Heyburn dismissed WITH PREJUDICE without a reason on December 29, 2009.

Judge Hepburn has violated his sworn duty to be a fair and honest judge in all cases that became before him and has not lived up to his duty regarding Appellant.

The District Judge in his order in this case used as authority Apple v. Glenn 183 F. 3d 477 (6th Cir 1999) which doesn't exists. Appellant has searched the entire system and could not find the case cited. Appellant searched Pacer and the U.S. National Archives and can find no record of the case. Pl.

Flint filed this complaint on May 2, 2011and the Court issued an order dismissing the case on the next day May 3, 2011. The trial court did not give Appellant time to submit any pleadings or to amend his complaint.

In addition Judge Heyburn has violated another local court rule in another case when he violated the court rule, a rule that he wrote and approved when he was the Chief Judge of the Federal District Court, where he presides. Judge Heyburn should have given Appellant Flint a Due Process fair and honest trial in every case that came before him. Judge Heyburn but didn't, because of a personal bias against Appellant.

Judge Heyburn was a partner in a law firm in Louisville Kentucky before he was appointed to the District Court. The firm's name was Brown Todd and Heyburn. Another partner in the firm was a Mr. Ned Bonnie. Appellant knew and did business with Mr. Bonnie and others in the firm since 1972.

Mr. Bonnie was Counsel for an organization by the name of HBPA which stool for Horsemen Benevolence and Protective Association, which represented 70,000 Owners and Trainers of Thoroughbred race horses in America. The group was a National origination with 27 divisions. Mr. Bonnie was Counsel for both the National and the Kentucky Division. Mr. Bonnie was well known throughout America as an expert on laws pertaining to racing horses. Mr. Bonnie as Counsel for the HBPA was the largest or one of largest contributors of income to the Brown Todd and Heyburn law firm. Mr. Bonnie also made contact and had relationships with all race tracks throughout America, including Churchill Downs and other horsemen's groups' thorough America.

In 1977 Flint was elected to be the President of the Kentucky Division of the HBPA. After becoming President, Flint and Bonnie parted company as far as the Kentucky Division, because they saw the future of the division differently. Later, in early the early 1980's, Flint was elected President of the National HBPA. Soon after Flint became President of the National HBPA, Flint and Bonnie again parted company and Flint hired a different Counsel. Flint's action had a large financial effect on Judge Heyburn and his law firm at the time.

When Flint, who is not a lawyer, filed his first lawsuit, Judge Heyburn should have recused himself in that case and every case filed by Flint that was assigned to him thereafter. But instead Judge Heyburn kept the cases in his court to get even with Flint for parting company with their law firm. Judge Heyburn controlled every case that came before him regarding Flint and his actions harmed Flint.

Mr. Bonnie was one of the largest fund raiser for a candidate for the office of Governor of Kentucky in 2007. Mr. Bonnie's candidate, Mr. Steven Beshear won in 2007 and he appointed Mr. Bonnie appointed to the Kentucky State Racing Commission. Governor Beshear is running this year 2011 for reelection and Flint has sued him and others. The case was assigned to Judge Heyburn who dismissed the lawsuit. Mr. Bonnie and Judge Heyburn have had close ties, since at least the early 1970's. Judge Heyburn was a law partner with Mr. Bonnie until Judge Heyburn was appointed as a Federal District Judge. Judge Heyburn should have disqualified himself from all of Flint's cases.

Flint sued Churchill Downs a company connected with horse racing, and the case was assigned to Judge Charles Simpson. But the next day, Judge Simpson assigned it to Judge Heyburn, which was in violation of a local court rule, which Judge Heyburn wrote and put into effect when he was Chief Judge of his court. Judge Heyburn not only wanted the case in his court, he broke civil and local rules to get it. Judge Heyburn has

receives from Churchill Downs, Kentucky Derby tickets and tickets to other events for himself and other judges and friends and has been for years.

Every case that has been filed in Western District Court that pertains to Churchill Downs winds up in Judge Heyburn court, regardless if it was originally assigned to him or not. Judge Heyburn by his actions of violating court's rule, has also violated Flint's rights to Due Process, and in doing so has violated Flint Civil Rights.

On March 30, 2010 Flint filed the lawsuit against Churchill Downs Inc. Case No. 3:10-CV-00202-S. And the case was assigned to Judge Charles R. Simpson. Two days later on April 1, 2010 Judge Simpson without a reason, recused himself from the case. On the same day that Judge Simpson recused himself from the case, he assigned the case to Judge Heyburn, for no reason and again against the court's rules. Kentucky Western District has a local rule that states a judge cannot recuse himself without a reason and it's in the best interest of justice. (See **EXHIBIT 1** LR 40.1 "Assignment of Cases Among Judges And Calendaring.) Judge Simpson made no motion, gave no reason why him recusing himself was in the best interest of justice. There was absolute no legal reason for this recusal. Judge Heyburn who wrote the rule, Exhibit 1, should not have accepted the case, Judge Heyburn is the one who requested the case, asking Judge Simpson to violate the court rule **EXHIBIT 1- 40.1**(b) states that **"A case may be reassigned to another judge within the district upon the court's own motion, in the interest of justice, for reason stated in an order reassignment" "The court will determine a motion to reassignment on the basis of whether reassignment is in the interest of justice."**

Judge Simpson in his order did not state a reason, except he cited 28 U.S. Code #455, (see **EXHIBIT 2**-attached). Judge Simpson failed to quote what part of the code he recused himself for and failed to report why he recused himself and never said it was in the best interest of justice. (See **EXHIBIT 3**- attached, Judge Simpson's order recusing himself from the case.) Heyburn should have never accepted the case because it had not gone through process as stated in **Exhibit 1**. Appellant did not know this was taking place; he was never notified of the actions until he received a copy of the order and never had a chance to respond.

On May 21, 2010 Heyburn dismiss the Churchill Downs case WITH PREJUDICE. On the other hand Judge Heyburn failed in this case and the other cases above, to recuse himself under 28 U.S. Code #455 (a) (b)(1)(2)(3)(4)(5)(iii) (c) .**Exhibit 2** Under U.S. Code #455 Judge Heyburn should have disqualified his self from every case that Flint filed that was assigned to him.

In 2011 Flint filed a lawsuit against Kentucky Governor Beshear and in the complaint Flint said he had proof that Governor Beshear had given actuaries on long term insurance, a $340,000 no bid contract. In addition Flint in his complaint accused Governor Beshear of giving approvable to MetLife Insurance for a 36.2% premium increase on long term care insurance that affects many old people, without holding a hearing. Judge Heyburn dismissed the case. He should have recused himself when the case was first filed, but his friend Bonnie did not want the lawsuit dismissed because he wants Governor Beshear reelected, to remain on the Kentucky Racing Commission and Bonnie is raising money for the reelection of the Governor as this is being typed. Judge Heyburn should have disqualified himself from this case as well as all of the other cases, when filed.

Petitioner has discovered since filing his brief and his petition for a rehearing, two additional cases in the Western District of Kentucky where Churchill Downs was sued and both of those case was randomly assigned to a Judge Simpson. Judge Simpson recused himself from both cases and they were assigned by Chief Judge John G. Heyburn, the Respondent Judge John G. Heyburn. One case was filed in 2006 and the second was filed in 2008. Judge Heyburn controls what cases he wants and protects the company that gives him favors. This case shows and proves that Federal judges do as they want, because the Supreme Court rules that they can be granted immunity for violating laws and rules. This court must take the blame for America's spinning out of control. The court may turn its head and let it happen, but the courts children and future grandchildren will pay the price for ever. This court by its ruling in Stump v. Sparkman in 1978 started the snowball down the hill and it is still rolling and will continue to roll until the court decides to stop the movement and make rules that are fair to every citizen.

Petitioner complaint was dismissed for authority under Apple v. Glenn 183 F.3d 477 (6th cir 1999). The District court stated that "where a complaint is totally implausible, attenuated, unsubstantial, frivolous, void of merit or no long open to discussion" the court need not afford the plaintiff an opportunity to amend the complaint. One can look at the complaint and see that no matter what Petitioner said the court was not going to let Petitioner's complaint he heard that the court was going to protect the judge at all cost.

By 28 U.S.C. #455 Judge Heyburn should have disqualify himself. In *Liljeberg* v. *Health Services Acquisition Corp., 486 U.S. 847, 860 n.8 (1988)* **the Supreme Court noted that the purpose of section 455(a) is to promote public confidence in the integrity of the judicial process, the Court observed that such confidence "does not depend upon whether or not the judge actually knew of facts creating an appearance of impropriety, so long as the public might reasonably believe that he or she knew."**

Judge Heyburn, by not recusing himself, knew what he was doing. Judge Heyburn knew that with his connection to Mitch McConnell the courts would protect him.

Judge Heyburn controlled every case that came before him regarding Flint and his actions harmed Flint badly. He either dismissed the case **WITH PREJUDICE** or Rule against Flint and made it a Final Order **WITH PREJUDICE**

The Defendants ask by motion that the case be dismissed for failure to state a claim. Flint's complaint had over twenty (20) allegations and it met criteria of *Bell Atlantic Corp v. Trombly 550 U.S. 544, 563 (2007).* The complaint will survive a motion to dismiss if it "contain(s) sufficient factual matter; accept as true, to state a claim of relief that is plausible on its face. Ashcroft Lqbal 129 U.S. Ct. 1937, 1949 (2009) (quoting Twomby, 550 U.S. at 750. all well pleaded factual allegations of the complaint as true and construe the complaint in the light most favorable to the plaintiff.

Therefore Judge Heyburn was wrong in dismissing this case and dismissed it foe personal bias reasons.

REASONS FOR GRANTING THE WRIT

1- Congress knew what they were doing when the passed U.S. Code 28 #455 and this court should uphold the law.

2- This country has major problems and they will continue to grow unless this court fixes the justice system. Someone has to lead this country out of its problems and as long as this court fights to gets its way, the public will do just what the court does. And that is fight for their belief instead of doing what is right for America. Each side in America is fighting for their belief because the Supreme Court does it.

3- No honest open minded judge can say that Judge Heyburn has not violated U. S. Code 28 #455.

4- This court can turn its head and ignore this case and not grant certiorari, but this court knows that what Judge Heyburn did is not what our forefather wanted for the people and this court knows that it is happening in every court in America, and this court knows that the same thing is happening in every Court of Appeals Circuit Court. Does getting your way and showing the other side you have power and can stop almost anything before it, lead America?

5- The actions by this court in this case will tell Petitioner that this court doesn't really care about justice that this court only cares about their selfish selves.

6- Justice can only be assured only by obeying the law.

7- Dismissing the case "with prejudice" showed bias by Judge Heyburn

CONCLUSION

1- This court knows that Judge Heyburn was wrong   in violating court rules.

2- This Court knows Judge Heyburn should have disqualified himself.

3- This court knows Judge Heyburn should have been tried for taking favors from companies

4- This court knows that Judge Heyburn was bias when he ruled against Flint and stated "With Prejudice"

5- This Court knows the Petitioner has a good complaint and the court should have never dismissed the case based on that reason.

6- This Court knows that Judge Heyburn's actions do not meet the criteria to be granted immunity as outlined in Stump v. Sparkman.

7- This court cannot believe what judges in district courts and appeals courts are doing. Judges don't care about justice they only care about doing it their way. They know they are protected for life; however this court in years has made it to where judges don't even think about justice. They only think about whom they want the winner to be to winner. Percentage wise there are more crooks serving as judges that there are inmates in prisons. The judges on this court were lucky to be appointed to the court, just like all Federal judges. Is this the type of justice you want to leave for your future family?

8- Petitioner knows that some members of this court will be upset at Petitioner for saying what he has said about this court, but the truth is what it is and it can't be changed.

9- Petitioner knows that some members on this court have such a high opinion of themselves that they don't care about justice, they only about having their way, but he hopes and prays that five (5) of judges do care about justice and will vote to grant certiorari.

10- This court has an opportunity to correct the   American Justice system from the harm done by Stump v. Sparkman in 1978, by holding judges responsible for violating laws and rules of the court. If this court took away the immunity clause for violations of court rules and laws, ninety (90) percentages of the problems of the court system would go away. The fathers of our country did not put judges on a higher plateau than the people, but the Supreme Court made kings out of the judges and in doing so America is being destroyed.

11- This court is responsible for interpreting the constitution and should interpret if the constitution causes for Judges have immunity for violating courts rules and laws of our count.

Petitioner prays that at least five (5) member of this court cares about true justice and will grant certiorari and review this case. Petitioner also asks this court to interpret the constitution regarding immunity for judges and put America back the way it was once. This court should leave an honest and fair court system to their family and to America.

Respectfully submitted,

s/ Edward H. Flint, Pro, Se.

The Supreme Court refused to consider the case.

CHAPTER 10

LAWSUIT FLINT V. JUDGE CHARLES SIMPSON III

****** THE COMPLAINT STARTS HERE******

UNITED STATES DISTRICT COURT
WESTERN DISTRICT OF KENTUCKY
LOUISVILLE DIVISON

CASE NO 3:11-CV- 275-H

EDWARD H. FLINT   PLAINTIFF

VS

COMPLAINT

CHARLES R. SIMPSON, Judge -   DEFENDANT

Comes the Plaintiff Edward H. Flint acting as his own counsel against Defendant as a judge in Federal Court in Louisville, KY.

1- **Plaintiff, Edward H. Flint lives at**

2- **Defendant Charles R. Simpson is being sued as an individual who is a judge in the Federal District Court Western District of Kentucky**

3- **Plaintiff alleges that Defendant Simpson is bias against him.**

4- **Plaintiff alleges that Defendant Simpson has been bias against him ever since Plaintiff filed lawsuits against other Jefferson Country Circuit judges in 2009 and 2011.**

5- Plaintiff alleges that Defendant Simpson was assigned Federal lawsuit 3:10-CV-202-S, Flint v. Churchill Downs and for no reason, one day later, recused himself from the case and assigned it to another judge, which violated the courts rules. Such actions were a violation by both judges of the court's rules   .

6- Plaintiff alleges that Defendant Simpson has been given favorers from Churchill Downs, either directly or through another judge, who obtained them from Churchill Downs. The two judges decided it was best that this case be handled through Judge Heyburn rather that Defendant Judge Simpson, so therefore Judge Simpson recused himself and assigned it to Judge Heyburn, all against court rules.

7- Plaintiff alleges that Defendant actions harmed Plaintiff, physically.

8- Plaintiff alleges that Defendant actions harmed Plaintiff mentally

9- Plaintiff alleges that Defendant's actions stopped Plaintiff from receiving Due Process fair and honest trial under the 14th amendment to the constitution.

10- Plaintiff alleges that Defendant Simpson action has denied Plaintiff his civil rights.

11- Plaintiff alleges that Defendant has been prejudice against Plaintiff in his rulings

12- Plaintiff alleges that Defendant has not conducted himself the way a judge should, on cases before him, involving Plaintiff.

13- Plaintiff alleges that Defendant has violated the court conduct rules that all judges must adhere to.

14- Plaintiff alleges Defendant has become a judge who makes rulings that fit his own wants. Pulling the justice system down with him

15- Plaintiff alleges that Defendant Simpson in his actions took advantage of Plaintiff's inexperience and did not judge by Cannons conduct ethics.

16- Plaintiff alleges that Defendant should have recused himself from case FEDERAL CASE 3:11-CV-597-S, when it was assigned to him, but he kept it to make sure Plaintiff didn't win the case.

17- Plaintiff alleges that Defendant Simpson was out to get Plaintiff because Plaintiff had sued parties; that he the Defendant Simpson didn't want sued.

Respectfully submitted
Edward H. Flint Pro, Se

****** THE COMPLAINT ENDS *************

This judge was asked in number of cases to disqualify himself and he refused

*************The District Court order Starts here**************

UNITED STATES DISTRICT COURT
WESTERN DISTRICT OF KENTUCKY AT LOUISVILLE

CIVIL ACTION NO. 3:11-CV-275-S

EDWARD H. FLINT   PLAINTIFF

v.

JUDGE CHARLES R. SIMPSON, III   DEFENDANT

ORDER

For the reasons set forth in the memorandum opinion entered this date, and the court being otherwise sufficiently advised, **IT IS ORDERED** that the plaintiff's claims are **DISMISSED** pursuant to this court's authority under Apple v. Glenn, 183 F.3D 477 (6th Cir. 1999), because it is "no longer open to discussion" that his claims are devoid of legal merit under the doctrine of absolute judicial immunity.

There being no just reason for delay in its entry, this is a **final order**.

The clerk of court is directed to mail a copy of this order and the accompanying memorandum opinion to the pro se plaintiff and the defendant.

Signed on May 10, 2011

Jennifer B. Coffman
United States District Court

The judge stated that the judge had absolute immunity and that the case was no long open for discussion.

**** I appealed- to The Sixth Circuit Court of Appeals and their order stated *****

Accordingly, we affirm the district court's orders. Rule 34(j)(2)(C), Rules of the Sixth Circuit.

The Court of Appeals order said they agreed with the District Court

I appealed and my petition to Supreme Court starts here

N0._____

In The
Supreme Court of the United States

_____

Edward H. Flint   Petitioner,

Versus

CHARLES R. SIMPSON, III, Judge   Respondents

On Petition for Writ of Certiorari
Court of Appeals for the Sixth Circuit.

PETITION FOR WRIT OF CERTIORARI

_____

Edward H. Flint Pro, Se

QUESTIONS PRESENTED

1- Was this court's rulings, constitutional, that was made when this court granted judges absolute judicial immunity from liability in Stump v. Sparkman, 435 U. S, 349, 356 (1978)?

2- Does the United States Constitution give this Supreme Court the right to protect judges against liabilities by giving them absolute judicial immunity, and especially when such immunity to judges, denies United States citizens the right to due process and the right to protect their property?

3- Is Apple v. Glenn, 183, Fd 477 (6th cir. 1999) constitutional, as used in this case by both district and appeals courts in dismissing cases by granting judges immunity and denying plaintiffs a due process trial?

4- Must all judges comply and honor, a congress law, that this court has stated, **"that the purpose of section 455(a) is to promote public confidence in the integrity of the judicial process," the Court also observed that "such confidence "does not depend upon whether or not the judge actually knew of facts creating an appearance of impropriety, so long as the public might reasonably believe that he or she knew."?**

5- Which branch of government has the authority by the constitution to establish penalties for judges who violate federal laws and Courts Rules?

6- If a judge disqualifies his self under title 28 U.S.C. #455, in a Plaintiff's case, isn't he disqualified on all cases Plaintiff files in his court, after that?

7- Does absolute immunity given to a judge, supersede rights granted by the constitution?

STATEMENT OF THE CASE

PROCEDURAL HISTORY

Flint would like to start by saying that he is an 81 year old Pro, Se and he deserves a review on his Petition the same as any attorney. This Court has refused to hear a number of cases by Petitioner even though he has showed this court how judges are violating laws and rules in Jefferson County, KY and this court has turned a deaf ear to his pleadings. Petitioner is concern about our country. This court is destroying America because they don't or can't control judges across America from violating rules and laws. This court should know that if one judge can be corrupt and get by with it, others judge will follow, believing its ok to be corrupt.

This case involves Charles R. Simpson who is a federal district court judge in the Western District of Kentucky at Louisville.

Flint filed a complaint against Judge Simpson and the complaint was as follows.

COMPLAINT

Comes the Plaintiff Edward H. Flint acting as his own counsel against Defendant as a judge in Federal Court in Louisville, KY.

1- Plaintiff, Edward H. Flint lives at

2- Defendant Charles R. Simpson is being sued as an individual who is a judge in the Federal District Court Western District of Kentucky

3- Plaintiff alleges that Defendant Simpson is bias against him.

4- Plaintiff alleges that Defendant Simpson has been bias against him ever since Plaintiff filed lawsuits against other Jefferson Country Circuit judges in 2009 and 2011.

5- Plaintiff alleges that Defendant Simpson was assigned Federal lawsuit 3:10-CV-202-S, Flint v. Churchill Downs and for no reason, just one day later, recused himself from the case and assigned it to another judge, which violated the courts rules. Such actions were a violation by both judges of the court's rules.

6- Plaintiff alleges that Defendant Simpson has been given favorers from Churchill Downs, either directly or through another judge, who obtained them from Churchill Downs. The two judges decided it was best that this case be handled through Judge Heyburn rather that Defendant Judge Simpson, so therefore Judge Simpson recused himself and assigned it to Judge Heyburn, all against court rules.

7- Plaintiff alleges that Defendant actions harmed Plaintiff, physically.

8- Plaintiff alleges that Defendant actions harmed Plaintiff mentally

9- Plaintiff alleges that Defendant's actions stopped Plaintiff from receiving Due Process fair and honest trial under the 14th amendment to the constitution.

10- Plaintiff alleges that Defendant Simpson action has denied Plaintiff his civil rights.

11- Plaintiff alleges that Defendant has been prejudice against Plaintiff in his rulings

12- Plaintiff alleges that Defendant has not conducted himself the way a judge should, on cases before him, involving Plaintiff.

13- Plaintiff alleges that Defendant has violated the court conduct rules that all judges must adhere to.

14- Plaintiff alleges Defendant has become a judge who makes rulings that fit his own wants. Pulling the justice system down with him

15- Plaintiff alleges that Defendant Simpson in his actions took advantage of Plaintiff's inexperience and did not judge by Cannons conduct ethics.

16- Plaintiff alleges that Defendant should have recused himself from case FEDERAL CASE 3:11-CV-597-S, when it was assigned to him, but he kept it to make sure Plaintiff didn't win the case.

17- Plaintiff alleges that Defendant Simpson was out to get Plaintiff because Plaintiff had sued parties; that he the Defendant Simpson didn't want sued.

Judge Simpson dismissed himself from the Churchill Downs case against Flint and in his order he cited 28 U.S. Code #455 as the reason. If Simpson's words are true as he stated, then that would make him bias against Flint.

Judge Heyburn states, **"This judge did not request Judge Simpson to recuse the Churchill Downs case. Moreover, Judge Simpson did not select this judge for transfer. After Judge Simpson recused, this judge was selected for transfer by random selection among the remaining judges who take case of the Louisville docket."** The records show Judge Simpson assigned the case by his order to Judge Heyburn and not by random selection.

On March 30, 2010 Flint filed the lawsuit against Churchill Downs Inc. Case No. 3:10-CV-00202-S. And the case was assigned to Judge Charles R. Simpson. Two days later on April 1, 2010 Judge Simpson without a reason except he stated 28 U.C. Code #455 to recuse himself, Kentucky Western District Court has a local rule that states a judge cannot recuse himself from a case without a reason and it's in the best interest of justice. Judge Simpson gave no other reason in his order why he was recusing himself and didn't state it was in the best interest of justice. **40.1**(b) of the local rules states that **"A case may be reassigned to another judge within the district upon the court's own motion, in the interest of justice, for reason stated in an order reassignment"** **"The court will determine a motion to reassignment on the basis of whether reassignment is in the interest of justice."**

Judge Simpson violated the local rule, in his order except as he stated; he cited 28 U.S. Code #455, which is a reason if a judge is bias.

Judge Simpson by citing 28 U.S.C. #455 in the Churchill Downs case to recuse himself should have disqualified his self from every case that Flint filed after that, which was assigned to him, because he was bias in every case.

Judge Heyburn for years has accepted favors or favors and money from Churchill Downs in the way of Kentucky Derby tickets and tickets to other events, for himself, for his friends, and or for other judges and Judge Simpson and Judge Heyburn was determine that Flint was not going to take discovery and have those facts about favors, which Flint has stated along with other truths that would come out.

Judge Simpson and Judge Heyburn took advantage of Flint being Pro, Se and inexperience, to keep Flint from finding out the complete truth in the Churchill Downs case, in order Flint couldn't discover how deep or much the take from Churchill Downs really was.

Judge Simpson should have disqualified himself from all cases that Flint filed in the Western District Court, under 28 U.S. Code #455 but he has refused to. Flint filed a case against Hewlett Packard Company, 3:11-CV-597-S, it was assigned to Judge Simpson and Flint has asked Judge Simpson nine (9) times to recuse himself from that case and he is still refusing.

Flint's case should have never been dismissed because the complaint Flint filed contained factual allegations, under Benzon v. Morgan Stanley Distrub. Is., 420 F 3d 598, 605 (6th Cir. 2005). In considering a motion to dismiss under Fed rule 12(b) (6) a court "must except all well-pleaded factual allegations of the complaint as true and construe the complaint in the light most favorable to the Plaintiff." Benzon, 420 F3d at 605 (citing Inge v. Rock Din. Corp., 281 Fd 613, 619 (6th Cir. 2005), [O]a claim has been stated adequately, it may be supported by showing any set of facts consistent with the allegations in the complaint." Bell Atlantic Corp v. Twomby, 550 750 U.S. 544, 563 (2007) "the complaint will survive a motion to dismiss if it "contains(s) sufficient factual matter; accept as true, to state a claim of relief that is plausible on its face." Ashcroft v. Iqbal, 129 U.S. CT. 1937, 1949 (2009) quoting Twombly, 550 U.S. at 750. Flint's complaint has sufficient factual matter. Judge Simpson and Judge Heyburn did not want Flint taking Churchill Downs discovery to show what Flint has stated about the past and favors. They did what no judge should do and that is to treat a Plaintiff Pro, Se as equal to an educated attorney. Both judges should have did everything he could, to be fair and honest to a Pro, Se.

Judge Simpson figured he could count on his fellow judges in the Appeals courts and Supreme Court to protect him.

Flint claims that if Judge Simpson's actions of not disqualifying himself under 28 U.S. Code #455 in the Hewlett Packard case is wrong after he admitted in the Churchill Downs case, he was bias.

REASONS FOR GRANTING THE WRIT

1- Congress knew what they were doing when they passed U.S. Code 28 #455 and the Supreme Court in 1988 knew how important it was to have a fair unbiased judge handling every case. This court should uphold that law.

2- Judge Simpson under 28 U.S.C. #455 recused himself from the Churchill Downs case for being bias and then refused to recuse himself from the Hewlett Packard case. He knew instantly in the Churchill case he was bias, because he recused himself two (2) day after being assigned the case.

3- Judge Simpson violated the local court rule by assigning the case to Judge Heyburn and not by random selection.

4- Judge Simpson should not have ruled in the Hewlett Packard case after being asked nine (9) by Flint to recuse himself.

5- This case stinks as far as justice being served by a federal judge, which denies Flint his due process and civil rights.

6- Judge Simpson is not entitled to immunity

CONCLUSION

1- This Court knows what 28 U.S.C. #455 means and what its purpose was, honest judges.

2- Immunity granted under Apple v. Glenn is false because the complaint Flint filed was a good complaint with factual issues and therefore immunity should have not been granted.

3- This Court knows Petitioner has a good complaint and should not been dismissed.

4- This court should know that the movements in this country like Occupy Wall Street are only the beginning. Those people know there something wrong in this country, they just don't know what the problems are, that they are protesting about, but they don't want to continue living it, like it is now, but any smart judge should know that they want only what our forefathers came for, a fair and honest justice system, freedom of speech and freedom of religion. Only by everyone receiving these will this country survive.

5- This court knows what is being done by judges in district courts and appeals courts. Judges don't care about justice; they only care about getting their way. They know they are protected for life; however this court's ruling in years gone by has made it to where judges don't even think about justice. Is this the type of justice you want to leave for your family's future?

6- Petitioner knows that some members on this court have a high opinion of themselves as Scholars and hopefully these scholars will recognize that judges must obey 28 U.S.C. #455 Petitioner hopes and prays that five (5) of this court judges do care about justice and will vote to grant certiorari.

7- This Courts duty is to protect the all citizens of this country and not just judges.

8- The Judges in the Western District of Kentucky has become dictator not judges. Framers of the constitution did everything in their power to   keep this type of justice from happening in   America. The Mayflower people came to get away from Kings and Dictators and this court must use every muscle in it brain to keep this from happening in America.

9- If Judge Simpson was bias in the Churchill Downs case he was bias in all other cases after.

Petitioner knows that some members of this court have large egos and take great pride, when it comes to other judges, but fair and honest justice for all, is why this great county was founded. Justice means for everyone, not just a few, which corrupt themselves.

Petitioner prays that at least five (5) members of this court cares about true and fair justice and will grant certiorari and review this case and do justice in this case, the Churchill Downs case and the Hewlett Packard case .

Respectfully submitted,
s/ Edward H. Flint, Pro, Se.

The Supreme Court refused to consider the case

I had promise the Holy Spirit that I would continue filing lawsuits. However I didn't just file lawsuits to be filing lawsuits, but I did continue. I filed lawsuits that the Holy Spirit told me to file.

Every lawsuit that I filed was either against judges that had violate, court's rules, or judges that had violated the courts code of conduct or judges who had violated laws of a state or Federal laws. Or against large companies that either made terrible products and sold them to poor innocent people or entities that was conning consumers to make a profit off of the consumers.

I need to tell you about the last two lawsuits, which are Chapters 9 and 10 of the book. These two lawsuits played a big role in writing this book and a bigger role in why I could not win a lawsuit in Federal courts. And why Judge Roberts switched his vote.

The two suits were filed against Judge Heyburn and Judge Simpson. Both of these judges were judges in the Federal District Court in Louisville Kentucky.

If you look at all of the lawsuits I filed in Federal Court, you will see that most of them were assigned to either Judge Heyburn or Judge Simpson to judge. These two judges controlled the Western Division of Kentucky, Federal Court.

Both judges were appointed to the Federal Court by Republican Presidents. Both had practiced law with Mitch McConnell, who is the Minority Leader of the Senate in Congress. Senator McConnell had both of them appointed as Federal judges. Judge Heyburn was Senator McConnell's Special Counsel when the Senator was Judge Executive in Jefferson County, Kentucky, before he first ran to be elected a Senator. Judge Simpson had practiced law with Senator McConnell and was an assistance Counsel to Judge Heyburn when Judge Heyburn worked for Senator McConnell when he was judge-executive of Jefferson County.

Senator McConnell can in my opinion control every case that is filed in the Western District of Kentucky Court, by anyone.

Senator Mitch McConnell hasn't like me, since I dismissed one of his friends as counsel from an association in Louisville. If you read Chapter 9 about Judge Heyburn, you will read the name of the person I dismissed and why, it's in my Petition to the Supreme Court. Senator McConnell has never liked me since the early 1980's.

As minority leader of the United States Senate Senator McConnell has power in every federal court in America. Most Federal courts now have a majority of judges that were appointed by a Republican President. I believe that Senator McConnell will go to all ends to get his way, on any and every subject.

I have known Senator McConnell for thirty years and he has never like what I stand for and that is helping people who need help, without wanting something in return. Even when he attended high school in Louisville, Kentucky Senator McConnell was determined to be powerful, and in control. I know personal issues about Senator McConnell that I won't print in this book.

It is my belief that I can't win a case in any Federal Court, including the Court of Appeals and the Supreme Court of the United States, under any circumstances, because Senator McConnell has a hold on me.

I knew after my lawsuit against Target Corporation, that I was in trouble, but I didn't know why at the time. I hope every reader will careful read what each of my cases, were about. I was right on the issue in every lawsuit I filed. I never filed a bad lawsuit. Look at how my cases were handled by the judges. If an honest and fair judge had handled my cases I would have won everyone.

It is my belief now, that God wanted these lawsuits filed, so this book about why Judge Roberts switched his vote would be written.

When I first started filing these lawsuits I didn't think about this as being a reason for losing the lawsuits.

After losing the Lawsuit against Churchill Downs, (Chapter7) I knew why I was in trouble in the courts. Senator McConnell had always been a friend to Churchill Downs and always a friend of all companies, particular large ones. Senator McConnell still has the same outlook in the Senate and he will do whatever it takes to reach his goal.

I now believed regarding the Target lawsuit, that Judge Russell had instruction to make sure I didn't win the lawsuit, against Target Corporation. I believe that the judges on the Sixth Circuit Court of Appeals and the Supreme Court were told to never let me win any lawsuit.

The courts are more political than Congress and as I bring out more documents, you will know why God wanted the book published, based on the facts that took place.

The Senate is holding up President Obama's appointments to Federal Court judges. The reason why they are being held is because most all of the Federal Courts in America are now controlled by the Republicans, since most of the current judges are appointees of Presidents Regan or Bush.

The Republican will do anything to keep President Obama's appointments from taking office.

The Louisville Federal Court is understaffed and doesn't have enough judges and instead of the President appointments being approved, they hire Magistrate judges and assign them to judge cases.

This is happening across America. A magistrate judge is at the mercy of the appointed judges of that District. This means that the appointed Republican judges control the Magistrate judges' actions.

The Supreme Court Federal rules state that only appointed judges can hire and fire Magistrate judges, which means the appointed judges control the cases the way they want then controlled. It is possible that one judge could control a whole Federal District Court, where there are normally 5 or 6 appointed judges.

This way the Republican controls any issue that would help the Democrats in an election. It seems the Democrats in Congress are too stupid to see this. But this is how Senator McConnell does things and he uses his own party to do his bidding. He does not tell them what he is doing. He uses the fight Obama theme.

I hope when this book gets out to the public, someone who has the time and money, will look up how much money, the people I have sued, have given to Senator McConnell's campaigns, over the years, since he ran the first time. I know Churchill Downs has given him tons of money to his campaigns. I will bet that all of the large Companies have also.

CHAPTER 11

Lawsuit Flint v. MetLife Insurance and Governor of Kentucky et al

****** THE COMPLAINT STARTS HERE******

UNITED STATES DISTRICT COURT
WESTERN DISTRICT OF KENTUCKY
LOUISVILLE DIVISON

CASE NO;3:11-CV-54-H

EDWARD H. FLINT   PLAINTIFF

VS

COMPLAINT

METLIFE INSURANCE COMPANY OF
CONNECTICTICUT   DEFENDANTS

MILLIMAN INC.
STEVE BESHEAR- INDIVIDUAL- GOVERNOR OF KENTUCKY
ROBERT VANCE- INDIVIDUAL- SECRETARY OF

KENTUCKY PUBLIC PROTECTION CABINET
SHARON CLARK –INDIVIDUAL- COMMISSIONER OF
INSURANCE

KENTUCKY DEPARTMENT OF INSURANCE
WILLIAM J. NOLD- INDIVIDUAL- DIRECTOR OF HEALTH AND
LIFE DIVISION

KENTUCKY DEPARTMENT OF INSURANCE
SHARRON S. BURTON-INDIVIDUAL- COUNSEL KENTUCKY
DEPARTMENT OF INSURANCE

Jane Does and John Does

COMPLAINT

Comes now the Plaintiff, Edward H. Flint acting as his own counsel against Defendants.

Plaintiff is now eighty years old and in 1996 when he was 66 years old purchased a long term care insurance policy from Travelers Insurance. Travelers sold Plaintiff's policy to MetLife in 2006.

The Plaintiff and Defendants are as follows:

1- Plaintiff lives at

2- Defendant MetLife is an insurance company, is the current holder of the long term insurance policy that was sold to Plaintiff

3- Defendant Milliman Inc. is a company that MetLife hired to obtain a rate increase for them from the State of Kentucky. Milliman's office is Minneapolis, MN.

4- Defendant Steve Beshear an individual who is Governor of the State of Kentucky.

5- Defendant Robert Vance an individual is Secretary of the Public Protection Cabinet of Kentucky

6- Defendant Sharon Clark an individual is Commission of Insurance for the Kentucky Department of Insurance.

7- Defendant William Nold an individual is Director of the Health and Life Division of Kentucky Department Insurance.

8- Defendant Sharron S. Burton an individual is General Counsel for the Kentucky Department of Insurance.

9- Defendants Jane and John Does are persons unknown at this time, but if one or more appears, they will be added to the complaint by their real name.

Plaintiff's Complaint is as follows.

1- Plaintiff alleges that Travelers-MetLife has been over charging Plaintiff on his premium since 2005, against the terms of the policy, and has refused to refund the overcharged money and also refuses to lower the premium to the amount of the policy as originally called for. Plaintiff has attempted to have the over charge refunded and change the rate of the premium, but MetLife refuses to do so.

2- Plaintiff alleges that MetLife has forged documents to keep Plaintiff from knowing the truth.

3- Plaintiff alleges that Travelers-MetLife never had proper approval from the state of Kentucky to increase his rates or no other citizens of Kentucky rates, when they were raised in 2005 through 2010.

4- Plaintiff alleges that MetLife has committed fraud by their actions in Long Term Health insurance.

5- Plaintiff alleges that Travelers-MetLife actions has harmed him

6- Plaintiff alleges that MetLife has applied for and received the approval from the state of Kentucky to increase premiums for long term care policies again in 2010 or 2011 and their actions were not to Kentucky's rules and statutes and their actions harmed Plaintiff and other Kentucky citizens.

7- Plaintiff alleges that MetLife applied for and received the approval from the State of Kentucky for the years of 2005, 2006, 2007, 2008, 2009, 2010 for long term insurance premium and their actions where not to Kentucky rules and statutes, their presentation to Kentucky was not proper, but was misleading and their actions harmed Plaintiff and Kentucky citizens,

8- Plaintiff alleges that MetLife is not registered with the Kentucky Secretary of State to do business in Kentucky.

9- Plaintiff alleges that Defendant Milliman Inc. who is an agent for MetLife has on behalf of MetLife has given the state of Kentucky wrong information and has mislead the state of Kentucky and has not obeyed all Kentucky's rules and statutes and their action has harmed Plaintiff and the citizens of Kentucky. Plaintiff also alleges that there may be personal reasons in their actions.

10- Plaintiff alleges that Defendant Steve Beshear as Governor has not lived up to his Fiduciary Responsibility and Fiduciary Duty to Plaintiff and to the citizens of Kentucky. He has not performed his duties to the citizens of Kentucky as called for. That since he was elected Governor the State of Kentucky has given single bid contracts for actuaries services not needed, including in 2010 has given a

$340,000 and his reason may be personal. His actions have hurt the citizens of Kentucky which includes the Plaintiff.

11- Plaintiff alleges that Defendant Robert Vance as Secretary of the Public Protection Cabinet has not lived up to his Fiduciary Responsibility and Fiduciary Duty to Plaintiff and to the citizens of Kentucky. Has not performed the duties of his office. Plaintiff also alleges he knew about or should have known about the single bid contracts. His actions have harmed the people of Kentucky, including Plaintiff.

12- Plaintiff alleges that Defendant Sharon Clark as Kentucky Commissioner of Insurance did not preformed her duties as commissioner of insurance, in granting MetLife a thirty six point 2 percent (36.2%) average rate increase on long term care insurance in 2010 and has not performed her Fiduciary Responsibility and Fiduciary Duty to Plaintiff and to the citizens of Kentucky. She has not properly performed the duties of her office and has harmed the citizens of Kentucky including Plaintiff.

13- Plaintiff alleges that Defendant William Nold as Director of the Health and Life Division of the Kentucky Department of Insurance has not properly performed his duty as Director in granting MetLife a thirty six point two percent (36.2%) average rate increase on long term care insurance in 2010 and has not performed his Fiduciary Responsibility and Fiduciary Duty to Plaintiff and the citizens of Kentucky.

14- Plaintiff alleges that Sharron Burton as General Counsel of the Kentucky Department of Insurance has not properly performed her duties to citizens of Kentucky, including Fiduciary Responsibilities and Fiduciary Duties and has cause harm to Plaintiff and the citizens of Kentucky. Including not allowing Plaintiff his rights as citizen of Kentucky by having a security detail watch his every move and intimidate him when he was reviewing records at the Kentucky Insurance Department. In addition Defendant Burton would not give Plaintiff the public records he requested to review.

15- Plaintiff had requested that he be allowed to attend and speak at any hearing held regarding rate increases for long term care, but was never notified by any defendants including Clark and or Nold or Burton.

16- Plaintiff alleges that some actions in the granting of rate increases by defendants may be personal to some or all defendants.

17- Plaintiff alleges he has been harmed by the actions of all of the defendants.

18- Plaintiff is alleging that MetLife is charging Plaintiff too high rate for his long term care insurance and Plaintiff has been since 2005, the year Travelers/MetLife raised Plaintiff's rates thirty percent (30%) Plaintiff demands MetLife to charge the rate that the policy called for when he purchased the policy in 1996. Plaintiff has now been informed that his rates will be raised again in 2011 by another seven percent (7%).

19- Plaintiff is alleging that the Defendants connected with the State of Kentucky Government did not properly approved the rates increase for MetLife and did so for personal reasons when they approved the rate increases.

20- Plaintiff alleges that MetLife does not want to sell insurance as we know it, but they want a guarantee to make money on each and every policy they sell each and every year. After they sell a policy and so much premium is paid into it base on a set rate, they come to the Kentucky Department of Insurance and obtain rate increases each year, with a goal of making the people who bought the insurance drop the policy, because it has become more than they can afford, in order that Met Life doesn't have to pay out any money, but have made enormous profits on what they have collected.

21- Plaintiff alleges that MetLife actions are a rip off scheme perpetrated on the citizens of Kentucky.

22- Plaintiff alleges that MetLife deceived the Kentucky citizens by their actions and presentations to the Kentucky department of Insurance.

23- Plaintiff is alleging that the Kentucky Department of Insurance in 2010 has signed a single bid contract in the amount of Three hundred and forty thousand ($340,000) dollars against Kentucky Statutes, which was not in the best interest of Kentucky citizens.

24- In addition to the years 2010 the Kentucky Department of Insurance has signed single bid contracts for additional years. The facts are unknown at this time because the Department of insurance has refused to produce the records.

25- Plaintiff alleges that each Defendant who is connected with the State of Kentucky knew of the contracts and knew the contracts are in violation of Kentucky Statutes.

26- Plaintiff alleges that the State of Kentucky has employees who could have done the work that the contractor did and the defendants should have used those employees instead of spending enormous amount of the Kentucky tax payer's money.

In addition there may be more allegations and if other allegations come up in discoveries, Plaintiff will ask the court to grant Plaintiff leave to amend the complaint

DEMANDS

Plaintiff makes the following demands

1- **A trial by jury.**

2- **Plaintiff be rewarded all monies he was overcharged by MetLife plus 12% annual interest.**

3- **On any allegations in this complaint which a jury finds any Party guilty, Plaintiff is awarded both compensatory and punitive damages from each party found guilty in the amount determined by a jury.**

4- **If MetLife is found guilty on any allegations in this complaint, defendant is ordered to place full page ads in the top 10 newspaper across Kentucky, apologizing, for the way MetLife has treated its Kentucky citizen's policy holders. Also if MetLife is found guilty on any allegation, they are not allowed to do business in Kentucky for 10 years.**

5- **If MetLife is found guilty by a jury of committing fraud, they be fined fifty million (50,000,000) dollars, which Plaintiff must give to charities that are approved by this court.**

6- **Any Defendant that is now connected to the State of Kentucky government, in any way, that is found guilty of violating Kentucky's Rules and or statutes, be removed from having any association with the State Of Kentucky's government, at once and never be allowed to have association with the State Of Kentucky again.**

7- **All cost of this complaint by Plaintiff**

8- **For any other relief to which said Plaintiff may appear entitled.**

Respectfully submitted
Edward H. Flint Pro, Se

****** THE COMPLAINT ENDS HERE******

The Case was assigned to Judge John Heyburn

The District Court's Memorandum and order stated that the case was dismissed, it states,

IT IS HEREBY ORDERED that Defendants' motions to dismiss are SUSTAINED and Plaintiff claims are DISMISSED.

This is a final order.

April 26, 2011

John G. Heyburn II, Judge

United States District Court

Judge Heyburn dismissed my case

****I appealed to the Court of Appeals and my Brief starts here****

CASE NO. 11-5572/11-5573

UNITED STATES COURT OF APPEALS
FOR THE SIXTH CIRCUIT

EDWARD H. FLINT,   Plaintiff – Appellant

v.

On Appeal from the United States District Court
For the Western District of Kentucky
Louisville Division

Civil Case No. 3:11-CV-00054-H

METLIFE INSURANCE COMPANY
OF CONNECTICUT, et al   Defendant-Appellee

_____

BRIEF FOR APPELLANT/ PLAINTIFF

_____

Respectfully submitted
Edward H. Flint Pro, Se

STATEMENT OF FACTS AND BACK GROUND INFORMATION REGARDING THIS CASE

Appellant Flint is 81 years old and is Pro, Se, states he has lived his live believing that Judges was the most respected people along with Doctors in America. However Flint has discovered that some judges like to use their power to show parties before them, that they don't care how people perceive them and they think that this will get them in Heaven, just like the religious leaders did with Jesus, but how wrong they were. Flint believes in truth and it doing the right thing if life. He has seen and lived World War II, Hitler and everything that has come after that. Flint believes in Jesus and in God. Jesus said that Satan was the father of lies and Flint can't believe that some Judges doesn't care about justice that they only care about using their power and they believe in protecting other judges from everything a judge does corrupt. Judges like everyone will someday become equal to all others when they get old and on judgment day. **Jesus said on judgment day, we will all be judge by the thoughts we had in our mind and by the deeds we did, not by the words we said**.

Appellant Flint filed on April 26, 2011 a pleading with the trial court a heading **"PLAINTIFF"S RESPONSE TO AND OBJECTION TO DEFENDANT METLIFE'S REPLY MEMORANDUM TO SUPPORT ITS MOTION TO DISMISS** that had on its certification the month March, that Flint, who does his own typing forgot to change to the month to April. The Court docket will show it was received on April 27, 2011. In Flint's Response pleading he stated and I will cut and paste the first page and it is as follows:

Comes now the Plaintiff, Edward H. Flint Pro, Se, acting as his own counsel.

Plaintiff is responding to and objecting to the Defendant MetLife reply memorandum in support of its motion to dismiss.

The Plaintiff states that leniency granted to Pro, Se petitioner must be boundless to the point that truth must be found by a court, regardless of what it takes.

Plaintiff states that in consideration to dismiss a suit for failure to state a claim upon which relief may be granted, See *Benzon v. Morgan Stanley Distrub.,Ins.,* 420 F3d 598, 605 (6th Cir.2005). In considering a motion to dismiss under Rule 12(b)(6), the court "must accept all well-pleaded factual allegations of the complaint as true and construe the complaint in the light most favorable to the plaintiff." *Benzon*, 420 F.3d at605 (citing *Inge v. Rock Fin. Corp.,* 281 F.3d 613,619 (6th Cir. 2005). [O] a claim has been stated adequately, it may be supported by showing any set of facts consistent with the allegations in the complaint." *Bell Atlantic Corp v. Twombly*, 550 550 U.S. 544,563 (2007). The complaint will survive a motion to dismiss if it "contain(s) sufficient factual matter; accept as true, to state a claim of relief that is plausible on its face. Plaintiff has stated a number of factual allegations and this court has a duty to search for the truth, not fancy words to take advantage of a pro, se inexperience. There is no reason to dismiss this case except to let crooks off of the hook. The Defendants wanted to take advantage of Kentucky citizens and when they got caught, they look for past ruling in other cases that have nothing to do with this case.

Plaintiff complaint contained enough information to meet the requirements necessary to go forward and let discovery go forward and let a jury decide the facts given to them.

As this court can read, Flint stated that leniency granted to Pro, Se petitioner must be bound to the point that truth must be found by a court, regardless of what it takes. The trial court in its dismissing the case not only didn't search for the truth, but ignored it completely. In the next Paragraph Flint quoted a number of authorities on failure to state a claim and the trial judge completely ignored that. The trial court based its dismissal order on the fact that it didn't want Flint to have justice under any circumstances; the judge wants his friends to win this case. Flint prays that the panel reviewing this case believes in true and honest justice and will judge accordingly. Flint hopes the panel will read the entire pleading with Plaintiff's Response that the above was taken from. Flint has been beat to a pulp by judges in the last 3 years, who like to beat up on Pro, Se's and by judges who ignore the law, which means they put themselves above the law and if this panel chooses to defend Judge Heyburn, Flint will lose this case. Judges should remember that when they take sides they harm another side. The only winners in the justice system are the judges who judge by the law. Judge Heyburn harmed thousands of Kentucky citizens by dismissing this case; those harmed are worrying about health care when they get old.

Judge Heyburn wants to help a Governor win reelection so the Governor can keep running a corrupt office against the state's citizens, giving the states money away at the same time he is laying employees off and he can keep giving insurance companies premium increases to help his reelection. Flint prays that this panel cares more about people and justice than about helping a judge who did wrong.

Flint also states that; there is a constitutional question in this case that this court must address. Flint is entitled to a Due Process fair and honest trial as called for in the Constitution. Flint wants to also remind this court that the court duty by the constitution is to find the truth, over and above anything else. No person who is Pro,Se can possible know the Federal rules of civil procedures and cite laws like educated in law attorneys and for any court to expect a Pro, SE to follow all of the rules and cite laws is in violation of granting a person a Due Process trial. The Court's rules of civil procedures only exist to keep order among trained lawyers and are not the only way to determine the truth.

When a Pro, Se is involved, a court has to overlook some of the presentation by a Pro, Se and arrive at the truth by other means, regardless of what it takes. The framers of our constitution or a fair minded judge or would expect a non-educated person to complete with a person who has been educated and trained for a number of years. There is nothing in the United States Constitution that says that the Court's Rule of Civil procedures must be adhered to by Pro, Se's. Nothing can supersede the 14th amendment to the constitution giving everyone Due Process, to a fair and honest trial.

Therefore any misstatement made or lack of presenting the proper federal law or rule in pleadings to a court, should be held against a Pro, Se. If any court holds in their mind or in rulings that a Pro, Se didn't adhere to the rules of civil procedures or cite the right authority, then the court is giving the educated lawyer an unfair advantage over the pro, se, and denying the Pro, Se a Due Process fair trial. The court its self would be discriminating against a Pro, Se.

Court's Rules of Civil Procedure are court drafted rules and are not constitution mandated for a due process fair trial. Example, when a Plaintiff says he has been harmed by a defendant action and doesn't spell out which Federal law or civil rule should be used, doesn't mean that Plaintiff's case should be thrown out,. The truth which a court must find is was Plaintiff harmed by any method, whether it is physical or civil rights or property. The 14th Amendment gives every person the right to protect their property and that is what Flint was doing in this complaint he filed with the trial court. Pro, se's under all circumstances must be protected by this court, from the harassing done by any Defendant, in not conforming to the courts rules on discovery, if any exits. A Pro, Se person have a right to explain their case the best they can and a court must take the time to get to the truth, even if everything is not done by the Courts rules.

A courts duty is to get the truth in the case, regardless of anything else and regardless of what time and effort it takes the court to find the truth.

Chief Judge of the United States Supreme Court John Roberts stated at his confirmation hearing with the United States Senate replied when asked what a judge's duty was, and I quote,

"Judges are like umpires. Umpires don't make the rules. They apply them. The role of an umpire and a judge is critical. The make sure everybody plays by the rules. But it is a limited role. Nobody ever went to a ball game to see the umpires." His jurisprudence would be characterized by "modesty and humility"

No one can disagree with John Roberts's statements. The constitution gives every person Due Process of a fair and honest trial, regardless of what it takes and this court must see that Flint receives a Due Process fair and honest trial, especially if hot shots attorneys or judges try to take advantage of a Pro, Se's lack of experience. When a judge makes up their own rules or ignores and expands the court's rules and or legal laws, or judges by their personal feelings, the Justice System breaks down and fails. When the Justice system fails, social order fails.

Judge Heyburn issued two memorandums and orders dated April 26, 2011 regarding Flint's motions for reconsideration for Judge Heyburn to recuse himself and the other dismissing this case. Judge Heyburn by his answers in his memorandum of refusing to disqualify himself has taken advantage of Appellant Flint because Flint is Pro, Se. Judge Heyburn stated in his order **"that for a judge to rule against a litigant is not sufficient reason to require recusal of a judge, The dismissal "With Prejudice" indicates only that the case can be appealed, not the judge held bias." Plaintiff could also have attempted to refile his case in state court, where jurisdiction (though not successful) was certain."** Flint states Judge Heyburn and every judge knows that if Flint tried to file a case dismissed "With Prejudice" in any court Federal or State that the court would turn it down because Judge Heyburn had dismissed the case WITH PREJUDICE. There is no reason to dismiss a case WITH PREJUDICE unless it is to stop someone from processing with a case the judge don't want to be tried. Judge Heyburn also stated that "with prejudice" meant Flint could appeal the case. Every Judge in America marks cases as final and appealable, if that is what they mean.

Judge Heyburn meant what he stated WITH PREJUDICE, he meant he had a bias or he would not have wrote "with prejudice" He meant to take advantage of Flint and stop him.

Judge Heyburn also in his order stated **"That a judge would own a season box at Churchill Downs or have the right to purchase a Kentucky Derby tickets would not present a reason from a case involving Churchill Downs. Receiving free or discounted ticked would present a different question. In an event, this judge has done of the above. Regardless, the question is irrelevant here because Churchill Downs is not a part to his case."** Flint might agrees provided, however only if Heyburn paid for the ticket and any other "gift", provided he never received any free or he never asked for tickets for other judges or asked for tickets for other people, and or was given nothing of value by them and then that would be a conflict. Judge Heyburn actions have stopped Flint from pursuing this allegation in the Churchill Downs case and Heyburn stated that **"the question is irrelevant here because Churchill Downs is not a party to this case."** Heyburn forgets that he dismissed the Churchill Downs case against Flint and if Flint's allegations are true then it would be bias against Flint. Heyburn should have recused himself, under U.S. Code #455 (a) (b)(1)(2)(3)(4)(5)(iii) (c) but he knew what he was doing; he did not want to give Flint a chance to prove the allegations.

Heyburn states, **"This judge did not request Judge Simpson to recuse the Churchill Downs case. Moreover, Judge Simpson did not select this judge for transfer. After Judge Simpson recused, this judge was selected for transfer by random selection among the remaining judges who take case of the Louisville docket."** Judge Simpson assigned the case to Judge Heyburn. Judge Heyburn asked for the case or he is saying that Judge Simpson if the one who violated the court's rule, not him. Flint alleges that Heyburn should have not accepted the case because it was not done properly by rule and was a violation of the rules and Heyburn did not present a computer printout from the case docket showing how he was selected to that case. Judges can say or do anything if they don't have to prove it. Flint will outline the complete allegation against Heyburn and his conflict of interest, later down the pages. Heyburn did not want Flint involved in any case and took advantage of Flint being Pro, Se by denying him cases. Heyburn actions in dismissing this case were at the expense of the older citizens of Kentucky.

Judge Heyburn refused to recuse himself from this case when there is bias. Appellant as pro, se has filed a number of lawsuits in Western District Court a number of lawsuits and every case that was assigned to Appellee Judge Heyburn was dismissed WITH PREJUDICE. Heyburn by his own words has admitted he is prejudice against Flint. There was never a reason to dismiss any of the lawsuits WITH PREJUDICE Flint filed, the cases had just started and before any discovery were taken, except the first motion was made by the opposing party to dismiss and then dismissal WITH PREJUDICE was granted against Flint by Judge Heyburn. Dismissing a case WITH PREJUDICE takes factual reasons or a judge that doesn't want the case refiled in another court for personal reasons; a personal reason are not in a judge's jurisdiction and is not normally performed by judges.

In 2009 Flint filed a lawsuit against three (3) Jefferson County Circuit Judges, case 3:09-CV-116-H for violating Kentucky Supreme Court Rules. Heyburn in his ruling order stated **"judges routinely accept cases transferred to them from another division with in a circuit court"** This statement was not true. The Kentucky Supreme Court rules states that all cases must be assigned by random and cannot be transferred. Heyburn was given a copy of the rule with Appellant's brief and he completely ignored it, but dismissed the case WITH PREJUDICE. Judge Heyburn was given **Rule 11 of Thirtieth Judicial Jefferson Circuit Court** which stated how the Jefferson County Circuit Court was supposed to function and Judge Heyburn ignored it, because he was going to rule against Flint and needed to justify his actions in his mind to take away his guilt feelings.

Flint filed other lawsuits that Judge Heyburn dismissed WITH PREJUDICE for no reason. In 2009 Flint filed a lawsuit against a Judge Armstrong in Jefferson District Court case No. 3:09-CV-878-H, which Heyburn dismissed WITH PREJUDICE without a reason on December 29, 2009, by ignoring facts submitted

Judge Hepburn has violated his sworn duty to be a fair and honest judge in all cases that becomes before him and has not lived up to his duty regarding Appellant, but he dismissed them for personal reason.

In addition Judge Heyburn has violated another local court rule in the Churchill Downs case when he violated a court rule, a rule that he wrote and approved when he was the Chief Judge of the Federal District Court, where he presides. Judge Heyburn should have given Appellant Flint a Due Process fair and honest trial in every case that came before him. Judge Heyburn but didn't, because of a personal bias against Appellant, which Flint will explain.

Judge Heyburn was a partner in a law firm in Louisville Kentucky before he was appointed to the Federal District Court. The firm's name was Brown Todd and Heyburn. Another partner in the firm was a Mr. Ned Bonnie. Appellant knew and did business with Mr. Bonnie and others in the firm since 1972.

Mr. Bonnie was Counsel for an organization by the name of HBPA which stool for Horsemen Benevolence and Protective Association, which represented 70,000 Owners and Trainers of Thoroughbred race horses in America. The group was a National origination with 27 divisions. Mr. Bonnie was Counsel for both the National and the Kentucky Division. Mr. Bonnie was well known throughout America as an expert on laws pertaining to racing horses. Mr. Bonnie as Counsel for the HBPA was the largest or one of largest contributors of financial income to the Brown Todd and Heyburn law firm. Mr. Bonnie also made contact and had relationships with all race tracks throughout America, including Churchill Downs and other horsemen's groups' thorough America.

In 1977 Flint was elected to be the President of the Kentucky Division of the HBPA, by the owner of horses. After becoming President, Flint and Bonnie parted company as far as the Kentucky Division, because they saw the future of the division differently. Mr. Bonnie wanted to have the Kentucky Division ran his way. Later, in early the early 1980's Flint was also elected President of the National HBPA, by the 27 Presidents of the divisions. Soon after Flint became President of the National HBPA, Flint and Bonnie again parted company and Flint hired a different Counsel. Flint's action had a large financial effect on Judge Heyburn and his law firm at the time.

When Flint, who is not a lawyer, filed his first lawsuit, Judge Heyburn should have recused himself in that case and every case filed by Flint that was assigned to him thereafter. But instead Judge Heyburn kept the cases in his court to get even with Flint for parting company with their law firm and cutting the firms income. Judge Heyburn controlled every case that came before him regarding Flint and his actions harmed Flint.

In 2007 Mr. Bonnie was one of the largest fund raiser for a candidate for the office of Governor of Kentucky. Mr. Bonnie's candidate, Mr. Steven Beshear won in 2007 and he appointed Mr. Bonnie to the Kentucky State Racing Commission, his lifetime dream. Governor Beshear is running again this year, 2011, for reelection and Flint sued Governor Beshear and others in this case. Flint's case was assigned to Judge Heyburn who dismissed the lawsuit WITH PREJUDICE. Mr. Bonnie and Judge Heyburn have had close ties, since at least the early 1970's. Judge Heyburn was a law partner with Mr. Bonnie until Judge Heyburn was appointed as a Federal District Judge. Judge Heyburn should have disqualified himself from all of Flint's cases.

Flint sued Churchill Downs a company connected with horse racing, because of a bad bill Governor Beshear tried to get passed in the Kentucky General Assembly regarding slot machines. Flint was outspoken against the bill and Churchill Down took away Derby tickets that Flint had for over 37 years and tickets that Churchill Downs had promised the Kentucky General Assembly that Flint could buy till he died. The case was assigned to Judge Charles Simpson. But the next day, Judge Simpson recused himself and assigned it to Judge Heyburn, which was in violation of a local court rule, which Judge Heyburn wrote and put into effect when he was Chief Judge of his court. Judge Heyburn not only wanted Flint's case in his court, he broke civil and local rules to get it. Judge Heyburn has receives from Churchill Downs, Kentucky Derby tickets and tickets to other events for himself and other judges and friends and has been for years.

Every case that has been filed in Western District Court that pertains to Churchill Downs winds up in Judge Heyburn court, regardless if it was originally assigned to him or not. Judge Heyburn by his actions of violating court's rule, has also violated Flint's rights to Due Process, and in doing so has violated Flint Civil Rights.

On March 30, 2010 Flint filed the lawsuit against Churchill Downs Inc. Case No. 3:10-CV-00202-S. And the case was assigned to Judge Charles R. Simpson. Two days later on April 1, 2010 Judge Simpson without a reason, recused himself from the case. On the same day that Judge Simpson recused himself from the case, he assigned the case to Judge Heyburn, for no reason and again against the court's rules. Kentucky Western District has a local rule that states a judge cannot recuse himself without a reason and it's in the best interest of justice. (See **EXHIBIT 1** LR 40.1 "Assignment of Cases Among Judges And Calendaring.) Judge Simpson made no motion, gave no reason why him recusing himself and didn't state it was in the best interest of justice. There was absolute no legal reason for this recusal. Judge Heyburn who wrote the rule, **Exhibit 1**, should not have accepted the case, Judge Heyburn is the one who requested the case, asking Judge Simpson to violate the court rule. **EXHIBIT 1- 40.1**(b) states that **"A case may be reassigned to another judge within the district upon the court's own motion, in the interest of justice, for reason stated in an order reassignment" "The court will determine a motion to reassignment on the basis of whether reassignment is in the interest of justice."**

Judge Simpson violated a local rule, in his order did not state a reason, except he cited 28 U.S. Code #455. Judge Simpson failed to quote what part of the code he recused himself for and failed to report why he recused himself and never said it was in the best interest of justice. (See **EXHIBIT 2**- attached, Judge Simpson's order recusing himself from the case.) Heyburn should have never accepted the case because it had not gone through process as stated in **Exhibit 1**. Appellant Flint did not know this was taking place; he was never notified of the actions until he received a copy of the order and never had a chance to respond.

On May 21, 2010 Heyburn dismiss the Churchill Downs case WITH PREJUDICE. On the other hand Judge Heyburn failed in this case and the other cases above, to recuse himself under 28 U.S. Code #455 (a) (b)(1)(2)(3)(4)(5)(iii) (c).Under U.S. Code #455 Judge Heyburn should have disqualified his self from every case that Flint filed that was assigned to him. The two orders Judge Heyburn issued on April 26, 2011 should have never been considered or issued.

In 2011 Flint filed this case against Kentucky Governor Beshear and in the complaint Flint said he had proof that Governor Beshear had given actuaries on long term insurance, a $340,000 (668,000) no- bid contract. In addition Flint in his complaint accused Governor Beshear and other Kentucky employees violated their fiduciary duty by giving approvable to MetLife Insurance for a 36.2% premium increase on long term care insurance, which affects many old people, and without holding a hearing. Judge Heyburn dismissed the case. He should have recused himself when the case was first filed, but his friend Bonnie did not want the lawsuit dismissed because he wants Governor Beshear reelected, so to remain on the Kentucky Racing Commission. Bonnie is raising money for the reelection of the Governor as this is being typed. Judge Heyburn should have disqualified himself from this case as well as all of the other cases, when filed because he was bias and had conflict of interests.

Heyburn set out to get even with Flint on behalf of his friend Mr. Bonnie and to take care one of his friendly company and Heyburn's action harmed to Flint, mentally monitory and physical.

Judge Heyburn has intentionally set out from the first case filed by Flint to be assigned to him, to see that Flint would never get a fair and honest trial in Federal court that Flint has to file in. Judge Heyburn has persuaded other judges to rule against Flint in other cases.

Heyburn for years has accepted favors or favors and money from Churchill Downs in the way of Kentucky Derby tickets and tickets to other events, for himself, for his friends, and or for other judges and Judge Heyburn was determine that Flint was not going to take discovery and prove the facts Flint has stated, along with other truths that would come out.

Judge Heyburn knew it was against the local rules for him to accept the Churchill Downs case from Judge Simpson, because Judge Heyburn wrote the **Exhibit 1** rule in 2007.

Judge Heyburn took advantage of Flint being Pro, Se and inexperience, to keep Flint from finding out the complete truth in the Churchill Downs case, in order Flint couldn't discover how deep or much the take from Churchill Downs really was. It is not normal for judges to take advantage of parties and it is certainly not in their jurisdiction.

Heyburn should have disqualified himself from all cases that Flint filed in the Western District Court, under 28 U.S. Code #455 (a) (b)(1)(2)(3)(4)(5)(iii) (c)

Judge Heyburn dismissed Flint's lawsuit against Churchill Downs case No. 3:10-CV-202-S by granting Churchill Downs motion for dismissal on the grounds that Plaintiff failed to state a claim and in addition to dismiss it WITH PREJUDICE. Flint's complaint met not being dismissed under Benzon v. Morgan Stanley Distrub. Is., 420 F 3d 598, 605 (6th Cir. 2005. In considering a motion to dismiss under Fed rule 12(b) (6) a court "must except all well-pleaded factual allegations of the complaint as true and construe the complaint in the light most favorable to the Plaintiff." Benzon, 420 F3d at 605 (citing Inge v. Rock Din. Corp., 281 Fd 613, 619 (6th Cir. 2005), [O]a claim has been stated adequately, it may be supported by showing any set of facts consistent with the allegations in the complaint." Bell Atlantic Corp v. Twomby, 550 750 U.S. 544, 563 (2007) "the complaint will survive a motion to dismiss if it "contains(s) sufficient factual matter; accept as true, to state a claim of relief that is plausible on its face." Ashcroft v. Iqbal, 129 U.S. CT. 1937, 1949 (2009) quoting Twombly, 550 U.S. at 750. Flint's complaint has sufficient factual matter. Judge Heyburn wanted to get even with Flint for the past actions done to Heyburn's law firm, and his friend Mr. Bonnie and he did not care what the law says. Judge Heyburn did not want Flint taking Churchill Downs discovery to prove what Flint has stated about the past and favors. Judge Heyburn did what no judge should do and that is to treat a Plaintiff Pro, Se as equal to an educated attorney. Judge Heyburn should have did everything he could, to be fair and honest to a Pro, Se. Flint complaint stated a number of claims against Churchill Downs and Judge Heyburn ignored the complaint and came up with anything he could to keep Flint from trying the case, in his court or any other court. Judge Heyburn figured he could count on his fellow judges in the Court of Appeals to protect him. Judge Heyburn didn't care if he was making corrupt judges out of his fellow judges; it was no skin off his nose if they were gullible enough to corrupt themselves.

Judge Heyburn knew, like every Federal Court judges knows, that a motion to dismiss for failure to state a claim must not be granted. Under Benzon v. Morgan Stanley Distrub. Is., 420 F 3d 598, 605 (6th Cir. 2005. In considering a motion to dismiss under Fed rule 12(b) (6) a court "must except all well-pleaded factual allegations of the complaint as true and construe the complaint in the light most favorable to the Plaintiff." Benzon, 420 F3d at 605 (citing Inge v. Rock Din. Corp., 281 Fd 613, 619 (6th Cir. 2005), [O]a claim has been stated adequately, it may be supported by showing any set of facts consistent with the allegations in the complaint." Bell Atlantic Corp v. Twomby, 550 750 U.S. 544, 563 (2007) "the complaint will survive a motion to dismiss if it "contains(s) sufficient factual matter; accept as true, to state a claim of relief that is plausible on its face." Ashcroft v. Iqbal, 129 U.S. CT. 1937, 1949 (2009) quoting Twombly, 550 U.S. at 750.

Flint's complaint has sufficient factual matter. So Judge Heyburn wrote the opinion memorandum to make it look like that the evidence was confusing and non-existence. He must have believed that this panel would just take his word. Judge Heyburn wanted to get even with Flint for the past actions done to Heyburn's law firm, and his friend Mr. Bonnie and he didn't care what the law said. Judge Heyburn did not want Flint taking Churchill Downs discovery to prove what Flint has stated about the past and favors.

Appellant claims are that Judge Heyburn actions of not disqualifying himself under 28 U.S. Code #455 (a) (b)(1)(2)(3)(4)(5)(iii) (c) are violations of the Federal Civil Code of Procedures and Cannons law. Judge Heyburn admitted he was prejudice when he dismissed cases WITH PREJUCE and such action is not within the judge's jurisdiction and therefore was not in his jurisdiction. Judge Heyburn violating local Court rules is not part of his jurisdiction. Accepting favors from a party before him is not within his jurisdiction and in addition he dismissed the Churchill Downs case by using the wrong authority and not using Benzon v. Morgan Stanley Distrub. Is, 420 F 3d 598, 605 (6th Cir. 2005. In considering a motion to dismiss under Fed rule 12(b) (6) a court "must except all well-pleaded factual allegations of the complaint as true and construe the complaint in the light most favorable to the Plaintiff."

Appellant claims that Judge Heyburn actions denied him Due Process. Judge Heyburn was vindictive and selfish in his actions and his actions were in violation of court's rules.

Flint alleges that Judge Heyburn has violated Flint right to a Due Process trial. The fourteenth amendment gives a party the right to due process, a fair and honest trial. Such violation is not a normal function performed by a judge

Judge Heyburn's actions have denied Flint his Civil Rights. This is not a normal function performed by a judge.

Judge Heyburn put the blame on the violation of the local rule Exhibit 1 on his fellow judge rather than accepting the blame himself. To save his self-Judge Heyburn does not care about his fellow judge who helped him.

ARGUMENTS ON THE DISMISSAL OF THIS CASE BY THE DISTRICT COURT

Judge Heyburn should have never dismissed this case. There was not legal reason to dismiss the case. Judge Heyburn knew, like every Federal Court judges knows, a court "must except all well-pleaded factual allegations of the complaint as true and construe the complaint in the light most favorable to the Plaintiff." Benzon v. Morgan Stanley Distrub. Is., 420 F 3d 598, 605 (6ᵗʰ Cir. 2005. in considering a motion to dismiss under rule 12(b) (6) the court "must accept all well-pleaded factual allegations of the complaint as true and construe the complaint in the light most favorable to the plaintiff." Benzon, 420 F3d at 605 (citing Inge v. Rock Din. Corp. 281 Fd 613, 619 (6ᵗʰ Cir. 2005), [O]a claim has been stated adequately, it may be supported by showing any set of facts consistent with the allegations in the complaint." Bell Atlantic Corp v. Twomby, 550 750 U.S. 544, 563 (2007) "the complaint will survive a motion to dismiss if it "contains(s) sufficient factual matter; accept as true, to state a claim of relief that is plausible on its face." Ashcroft v. Iqbal, 129 U.S. CT. 1937, 1949 (2009) quoting Twombly, 550 U.S. at 750.

Flint's complaint has sufficient factual matter and there were no reason by law to dismiss the case except Judge Heyburn personal vindictiveness against Flint. (See **EXHIBIT 3** -Copy of Flint's complaint.)

Judge Heyburn wanted to get even with Flint for the past actions done to Heyburn's law firm, and his friend Mr. Bonnie and he did not care what the law says. Judge Heyburn wanted to protect the Governor of Kentucky and the other Kentucky employee's defendants, to protect the Governor in his reelection bid, for Mr. Bonnie.

Judge Heyburn was going to violate court rules for his friends and then get his friends in the Court of Appeals to protect him. He would ask them to violate rules and laws to protect him and didn't care if he jeopardized their position as judges in doing so.

Appellant Flint will now argue the facts Judge Heyburn used in his Memorandum opinion and order that dismissed the case dated April 26, 2011.

Courts Order I,

Judge Heyburn never held a hearing on this case and in this section he draws conclusion based on facts only submitted by the Defendant in their Brief, on motion to dismiss. Judge Heyburn took the word of all defendants, and did his own interpretation of their facts and said Flint was wrong and MetLife and the defendants were right. Judge Heyburn was not a neutral judge. Flint asked for a jury trial and not a trial by a judge. The facts Judge Heyburn used are wrong and self-serving. Example, Flint alleged MetLife has never applied correctly for the rate increases that MetLife is charging. No properly hearing was held before Kentucky approved the rates. Most of the facts stated by Judge Heyburn are wrong.

The actuary that gave the figures to Kentucky Department of Insurance was hired on a $340,000 (667,000) no-bid contact and never broke down the different long term care types of policies. He lumped all types of policies together and gave Kentucky the same rate for all policies. There are many different types of long term care policies. Some policies have a set amount of money only to use, and other have different variations, some have a number of days, some have weeks or some have both.

The facts in this case will show that the amount of dollars in insurance would remain the same for Flint if he used the policy. In 1996 when Plaintiff signed up for his policy he purchased $273,750.00 coverage, not so many days or so many weeks, but a set dollar amount His coverage has remained the same $273,000.00 and will never change, but his premiums have now been increased 37%. MetLife contends Flint policy could be increased every year, even though the pay out money to Flint will never change. In Flint's Response to MetLife's motion to dismiss Flint told the judge the following about his policy and what it said about his policy and the trial judge completely ignored the facts. Flint statement to the trial judge was as follows as cut from the original statement.

GUARANTEED RENEWABLE FOR LIFE

"As long as the premium is paid when due, we cannot change any provision of this policy or cancel it during your, life time. **PREMIUMS MAY BE CHANGED ON A CLASS BASIS ONLY"**

MetLife is saying that when they receive a premium increase of any kind on long term care from the State of Kentucky that it is a blanket increase and they can use the increase to raise the premium on all policies regardless of the type of policies or the structure of the policies.

Plaintiff states that the record shows that his type of policy has never been evaluated by Kentucky as a separate type of policy. Plaintiff is stating that insurance companies write all type of policies in long term care and they write policies some policies that are based on paying so much per week for a person care, and not a set dollar amount. Plaintiff policy had a specific dollar amount, not so many days or weeks and when that dollar amount runs out MetLife has no more responsibilities. Flint's type of policy has no more cost to MetLife now than it did in 1996; $273,750.00 is still the total payout. Flint still has $273,750.00 worth of insurance. The cost of other types of policy can cost the insurance company more each year because of inflation or cost of the medical field. Flint's policy will only buy him about forty percent (40%) of health care now of what it would have in 1996 when he took out the policy, but he is paying 37% more and MetLife is reaping the profits.

MetLife has a scheme to keep raising premiums each year and then the cost becomes so high that a person can't afford to carry the policy, then the policy holder drops the policy, MetLife then keeps the entire premium paid in and have no expense, which makes a big profit for MetLife. Travelers never once attempted to raise the premium, but when MetLife took them over they are raising premiums every year. The records will show that the Kentucky Insurance Department never evaluated the premiums cost on long term care policies; they let outside companies with close ties to one of the Defendants Milliman Inc. do the analyzing of the policies and they did it as an entire group and didn't break down the different types of policies. The Kentucky Department of Insurance never questioned them, but accepted their figures as being the truth.

Courts Order II

Heyburn stated **"Flint claims against MetLife fail for the following reason. First the filed rate doctrine operates as a complete bar to Flints claims for damages. Pursuant to this doctrine and as recognized by the Kentucky Court of Appeals and numerous federal and state courts around the country, insurance rates filed with state regulators are per, se, reasonable and are not subject to collateral attack."** Judge Heyburn submitted no authority to back up his claim and Flint claims Judge Heyburn's words are nothing but double talk, trying to throw an old man who's Pro,Se, off and is supposed to scare Flint and Flint is supposed to believe him. Can this court image what would happen if all states said to all insurance company "just send your rates in and we will accept them and won't let anyone attack your rates?" Judge Heyburn had no reason to dismiss this case and he made up stuff like this and he wants this panel to protect him. All states have statutes and regulations and a duty to protect their citizens and make sure the rate increase are justified. For judge Heyburn to claim that rate increase submitted by insurance company is not subject to collateral attack is laughable. Judge Heyburn in his statement showed he has no feelings for Kentucky citizens, and he only cares about helping his friends and he wants this panel of judges to back him up by jeopardizing their judgeship and integrity.

Heyburn stated MetLife properly filed the premium increase at issue with the Kentucky DOI pursuant to Kentucky's comprehensive insurance statutory and regulatory scheme and these rates were duly approved prior to their implementation.

Judge Heyburn did not know what he was talking about used his friendly Defendant's pleadings and Judge Heyburn never gave Flint a forum to present different facts. Flint has alleged that the rates were not properly approved. The Kentucky Insurance Department employees that Flint sued never approved the rates in official records and they never held hearings on the rate increase according to requirements of Kentucky statutes and regulations. Flint has claimed in his complaint that MetLife breached his contract. Again Judge Heyburn judged what he wanted to and failed to give Flint a fair and honest trial by jury.

COURT ORDER III

1. Heyburn stated Flint has sued state officials apparently for actions taken in their official capacities, the Eleventh Amendment of the United States Constitution bars suits brought in federal courts against the state or its agencies or its employees acting in their official capacities unless the state has waived its sovereign immunity or otherwise consented to be sued in federal court. Flint states that he sued the Kentucky employees as individuals who violated laws and regulations and further states that in their efforts they did not live up to their Fiduciary Duty. The constitution only protects those who does not violate their duty and who does not violate Kentucky rules regulations or laws. Many Kentucky employees have been sued for violation of laws, regulations and duty, and as individuals.

2. **Baker v. Fletcher, 204 S.W. 589 (Ky. 2006) pertains to the Governor of Kentucky, who is charged under section 81 of the Kentucky Constitution, with the responsibility to "take care, that the laws be faithfully executed." And then they would be granted absolute immunity for official acts why in office. The key is the "Laws Be Faithfully Executed." and if the laws of Kentucky were not faithfully executed, then the Governor is not granted immunity.**

Kentucky employees are sued regularly in courts for violating Kentucky rules regulations or laws. Every employee hired by the state of Kentucky owes and has a fiduciary duty to ever citizen of Kentucky.

Again Judge Heyburn has judged the case before facts are presented; he used in his opinion only the facts from Defendants pleadings and not Flint's. Judge Heyburn didn't understand the facts of the case and this is why a jury trial is required. Flint's complaint (**Exhibit 3)** is very clear on what he has alleged against the employees of Kentucky. Flint complaint meets under the previous stated authority, a court "Benzon v. Morgan Stanley Distrub. Is., 420 F 3d 598, 605 (6th Cir. 2005. in considering a motion to dismiss under rule 12(b) (6) the court "must accept all well-pleaded factual allegations of the complaint as true and construe the complaint in the light most favorable to the plaintiff." Benzon, 420 F3d at 605 (citing Inge v. Rock Din. Corp., 281 Fd 613, 619 (6th Cir. 2005), [O]a claim has been stated adequately, it may be supported by showing any set of facts consistent with the allegations in the complaint." Bell Atlantic Corp v. Twomby, 550 750 U.S. 544, 563 (2007) "the complaint will survive a motion to dismiss if it "contains(s) sufficient factual matter; accept as true, to state a claim of relief that is plausible on its face." Ashcroft v. Iqbal, 129 U.S. CT. 1937, 1949 (2009) quoting Twombly, 550 U.S. at 750.

Flint's complaint has sufficient factual matter and there were no reason by law to dismiss the case except Judge Heyburn personal vindictiveness against Flint. (See **EXHIBIT 3** Copy of Flint's complaint.)

COURT ORDER IV

Judge Heyburn says it is difficult to know the precise nature of Flint claim against Milliman. If he didn't know then he should not put it in the memorandum, Plaintiff always gets the benefit of doubts. Flint states his complaint is very clear and I quote directly from the complaint as follows.

Plaintiff alleges that Defendant Milliman Inc. who is an agent for MetLife has on behalf of MetLife has given the state of Kentucky wrong information and has mislead the state of Kentucky and has not obeyed all Kentucky's rules and statutes and their action has harmed Plaintiff and the citizens of Kentucky. Plaintiff also alleges that there may be personal reasons in their actions

---

Document exhibits for the record regarding some of the allegations in the complaint.

1- EXHIBIT-4-a letter dated July 19 from Flint to Bradley Nelson at the Kentucky Department Insurance showing correspondence regarding the issue of increasing Flint premiums and the meaning of Flint's policy.

2- EXHIBIT-5-a letter date February 19, 2010 from Milliman to Sharon Clark Commissioner of Insurance Kentucky Department of Insurance regarding Premium rates regarding long term care. This letter contains what MetLife is seeking in premiums increases. This letter shows that no Kentucky employee name is on the approval. The only approval given was by Mr. Burkhart the actuary.

3- EXHIBIT-6- an email from Ed Flint to Sharron Burton the General Counsel for the Kentucky Insurance Department, showing that she didn't want to cooperate on giving Flint the records on the non-bid contract and was trying to stop Flint. Kentucky Department of Insurance would not give Flint the records he asked for under the open records law and would go to any means to stop Flint.

4- EXHIBIT-7- a document dated 4/6/2010 regarding Solicitation # 1000000378. This document shows that only one company bit for the contract.

5- EXHIBIT-8- a 4 page document dated August 03, 2010. These documents were given to Flint by Sharron Burton the General Counsel for Kentucky Insurance Department as the documents Flint asked for in his request. The first page is a letter informing Wakely Consulting Group being awarded a Personal Service Contract. By the Kentucky Insurance company. The other 3 pages are first pages from the contract. Flint in his complaint stated that Kentucky had given a non-bid contract for $340,000; however after coping these 3 exhibits pages for this brief and studying them further, the 3 pages show the contract is for a total of $668,000, as the contract is for 2 years, the years 2011 and 2012.

There are a number of other alleged issues that Judge Heyburn did not confront in his memorandum opinion and order and all allegations must be put before a jury to determine guilt. Some allegations Judge Heyburn didn't confront are as follows

1- MetLife has been selling insurance in Kentucky without being registered and license with the Secretary of the State.

2- Kentucky employees did not proper authorize the increase in premiums to MetLife in the best interest of Kentucky citizens

3- Kentucky statutes and regulations and their duty was not followed by all employees listed as defendants and there may be more defendants from the John Doe list, still to be added as defendants

4- MetLife forged and intentionally misrepresent to Flint what his policy was.

5- The interpretation of the words "PREMIUMS MAY BE CHANGED ON A CLASS BASIS ONLY" in Flints policy must be determine by a jury as the two parties disagree to the meaning.

6- Flint alleges that Fraud was committed by defendants in the actions taken regarding the premiums increase and other actions taken.

7- Flint alleges that MetLife hired Milliman to represent them in Kentucky and Milliman did not properly fulfill their duty and their actions harmed Flint and others.

8- Flint alleges that employees of the State of Kentucky violated Kentucky their Fiduciary Duty to the citizens of Kentucky.

9- This court like the trial court owes Flint and the citizens of Kentucky the right to prove the allegations made in this complaint.

10- Flint has alleged the actions by MetLife are a rip off scheme.

11- Flint alleged that approving a $340, 000 (668,000) no bid contract by Kentucky employees was a violation of Kentucky statues and regulations.

12- Flint alleges that the 36.2 % increase in premiums done not properly issued and MetLife has charge customers a higher premium than they should have.

CONCLUSIONS

1- Flint has been denied a Due Process trial as called for in the 14th amendment to the constitution

2- Flint has asked for a jury trial as given by the constitution on all issues and there is no reason why a judge should judge this case on Flint's allegation.

3- Flint has been harmed by the trial court's actions, mentally, physical and monetary.

4- Judge Heyburn's actions have denied Flint his civil rights.

5- Judge Heyburn's action was bias against Flint

6- Judge Heyburn should have disqualified himself under 28 U.S. Code #455 (a) (b)(1)(2)(3)(4)(5)(iii) (c)

7- Judge Heyburn's opinion was based on facts that were presented by the defendants only and he also ignored Flint's facts and the case must be heard and judged by a jury.

8- The case should not have been dismissed and should have been tried under authority of Benzon v. Morgan Stanley Distrub. Is., 420 F 3d 598, 605 (6th Cir. 2005. in considering a motion to dismiss under rule 12(b) (6) the court "must accept all well-pleaded factual allegations of the complaint as true and construe the complaint in the light most favorable to the plaintiff." Benzon, 420 F3d at 605 (citing Inge v. Rock Din. Corp., 281 Fd 613, 619 (6th Cir. 2005), [O]a claim has been stated adequately, it may be supported by showing any set of facts consistent with the allegations in the complaint." Bell Atlantic Corp v. Twomby, 550 750 U.S. 544, 563 (2007) "the complaint will survive a motion to dismiss if it "contains(s) sufficient factual matter; accept as true, to state a claim of relief that is plausible on its face." Ashcroft v. Iqbal, 129 U.S. CT. 1937, 1949 (2009) quoting Twombly, 550 U.S. at 750.

9- The $340,000 (667,000) no-bid contract approved by the Governor of Kentucky and other Kentucky employees was not in the best interest of its citizens.

10- MetLife is charging customers higher premiums and doesn't have an official approval from Kentucky.

11- MetLife has been selling insurance in Kentucky without being registered and licensed with the Secretary of the State.

12- There is an issue between Flint and MetLife regarding the meaning of "premiums may be changed on a class basis only" and must be decided by a jury.

13- The 36.2% increase in premiums MetLife is charging policy holders was not properly approved by the State of Kentucky.

14- The allegations against Milliman must be presented to a jury.

15- The allegations against all Kentucky employees, must be presented to a jury

16- The allegations against the Governor of Kentucky must be presented to a jury.

17- Kentucky personnel did not proper authorize the increase in premiums to MetLife

18- Kentucky statutes, regulations and fiduciary duty was not followed by all personnel listed as defendants and there may be more defendants from the John Doe list, still to be added as defendants

19- MetLife forged and intentionally misrepresented to Flint what his policy was.

20- The allegation that Fraud was in the actions taken regarding the premiums increases, must be presented to a jury.

21- All allegations made in Flint's complaint (**Exhibit 3**) and in his response to all of Defendant's motions to dismiss, must be presented to a jury for trial.

22- The allegations made against Governor Beshear and the other state employees regarding all of the years that Governor Beshear has been Governor, regarding no-bid contracts and approval of premium increases to MetLife must, be pursued and presented to a jury.

This case should not be about politics, or friendship, It should be judged about the type of government Kentucky's should have, about people buying insurance for retirement and knowing that when you get old and after you have paid thousands of dollars for the policy, someone in not going to get you to give it up because you can no long afford the higher premiums or else you will have to pay higher premiums with money from your retirement funds that you work for all your life. This type of scheme by insurance companies could spread to every state. This type of treatment to old people is like conning or robbing them, because they are easy prey. What would each member of this panel do if a person was in front of them that had robbed an old person? Would you try the crook or would you dismiss charges against the crook?

Flint and the citizens of Kentucky needs and deserves to know the truth about their government, their employees, and their suppliers of products and the circumstances of no-bid contracts and premium increases to MetLife. The guilty must be investigated and held accountable.

There is no legal reason for this case to be dismissed and there is no legal reason why it cannot precede to trial, unless this panel believes that insurance companies should be given the right to rape old people and government turns its head.

Therefore Appellant asks that this court to consider their fellow citizens, reverse the trial court's order and return the case back to the trial court for trial.

Respectfully submitted
Edward H. Flint Pro, Se

The Court of Appeal order stated they agreed with Judge Heyburn's order by stating the following

Accordingly, we affirm the district court's orders. Rule 34(j)(2)(C), Rules of the Sixth Circuit.

Enter by order of the Court
S/Leonard Green- Clerk

I appealed and filed a Petition with the Supreme Court which starts here.

In The
Supreme Court of the United States

Edward H. Flint   Petitioner,

Versus

METLIFE INSURANCE COMPANY et al   Respondents

PETITION FOR WRIT OF CERTIORARI

Edward H. Flint Pro, Se

QUESTIONS PRESENTED

1- Is the so called "filed rate doctrine" that the district and appeals court used to dismiss this case constitutional?

2- Does the so called "filed rate doctrine" apply to insurance companies and all other companies that must file for an increase in rates through a state or does it just pertain to trucking industry only?

3- Is title 28 U.S. Code #455 a law that all judges must comply with to at all times, although the appeals court refused to consider the issue, after this court has stated **that the purpose of section 455(a) is to promote public confidence in the integrity of the judicial process, the Court also observed that such confidence "does not depend upon whether or not the judge actually knew of facts creating an appearance of impropriety, so long as the public might reasonably believe that he or she knew.'"**?

4- Is employees of a state that violates state laws and regulations, including the Governor of the state entitled to sovereign immunity under the Eleventh Amendment of the Constitution?

5- Can a court dismiss an allegation by saying the Plaintiff didn't present evidence, when the Plaintiff claimed a company wasn't registered with the Secretary of the State to do business in the state as required by law, because there was none on file.

PROCEDURAL HISTORY

Flint would like to start by saying that he is an 81 year old Pro, Se and he deserves a review on his Petition the same as any attorney. This Court has refused to hear a number of cases by Petitioner even though he has showed this court how judges are violating laws and rules in Jefferson County, KY and this court has turned a deaf ear to his pleadings. Petitioner is concern about our country. This court is destroying America because they don't or can't control judges across America from violating rules and laws. They should know that if one judge can be corrupt and get by with it, others judge will know its ok to be corrupt also.

This case involves MetLife insurance Company, a company hired by MetLife and five employees of the state of Kentucky. Petitioner sued the Defendants in January 28, 2011. When Flint learned that Judge Heyburn had been assigned the case, he filed on February 5, 2011 a motion asking Judge Heyburn to recuse himself from this case, because he was bias against Flint in another case. Flint after not hearing from Judge Heyburn, Flint filed another motion on February 26, 2011 asking Judge Heyburn to rule on Plaintiff's motion to recuse himself from the case, with Flint pointing out reasons why Judge Heyburn should recuse himself, which was based on Judge Heyburn actions in case 3:10-CV-202-H against Churchill Downs. Judge Heyburn issued an order on March 9, 2011 denying Flint's motion to recuse himself. Judge Heyburn's March 9, 2011 order mis-stated facts and he flat out lied based on the facts Flint had put in his February 5 and February 26, 2011 motions on why he should recuse himself.

Flint then filed a motion on March 11, 2011 asking Judge Heyburn to reconsider his March 9, 2011 order and asking him not to make any rulings on the case until he recused himself,. Flint gave him in the four (4) page motion the reasons he should recuse himself. On April 26, 2011 Judge Heyburn issued an order again denying recusing himself and in his memorandum he omitted the facts Flint gave him and the judge in his Memorandum lied again. He twisted the facts that Flint stated in the motion.

Flint appealed the April 26, 2011 order to the Court of Appeals and the case was combined with another appeal and assigned case No.11-5572/115573, because Flint filed another appeal in the same case on the same day, May 2, 2011. One appeal was for "Denial Plaintiff's motion to Judge Reconsideration Recuse Himself" and the second appeal was for order by Judge Heyburn Dated April 26, 2011 for "Plaintiff claims are dismissed"

Petition Flint in his brief to the Court of Appeals pointed out the reasons that judge Heyburn should have recused himself. Flint will now copy the part of his brief to the Court of Appeals that pertained to Judge Heyburn recusing himself.

Judge Heyburn by his answers in his memorandum of refusing to disqualify himself has taken advantage of Appellant Flint because Flint is Pro, Se. Judge Heyburn stated in his order **"that for a judge to rule against a litigant is not sufficient reason to require recusal of a judge, The dismissal "With Prejudice" indicates only that the case can be appealed, not the judge held bias." Plaintiff could also have attempted to refile his case in state court, where jurisdiction (though not successful) was certain."** Flint states Judge Heyburn and every judge knows that if Flint tried to file a case dismissed "With Prejudice" in any court Federal or State that the court would turn it down because Judge Heyburn had dismissed the case WITH PREJUDICE. There is no reason to dismiss a case WITH PREJUDICE unless it is to stop someone from processing with a case the judge don't want to be tried. Judge Heyburn also stated that "with prejudice" meant Flint could appeal the case. Every Judge in America marks cases as final and appealable, if that is what they mean.

Judge Heyburn meant what he stated WITH PREJUDICE, he meant he had a bias or he would not have wrote "with prejudice" He meant to take advantage of Flint and stop him.

Judge Heyburn also in his order stated **"That a judge would own a season box at Churchill Downs or have the right to purchase a Kentucky Derby tickets would not present a reason from a case involving Churchill Downs. Receiving free or discounted ticked would present a different question. In an event, this judge has done none of the above. Regardless, the question is irrelevant here because Churchill Downs is not a part to his case."** Flint might agrees provided, however only if Heyburn paid for the ticket and any other "gift", provided he never received any free or he never asked for tickets for other judges or asked for tickets for other people, and or was given nothing of value by them and then that would be a conflict. Judge Heyburn actions stopped Flint from pursuing this allegation in the Churchill Downs case and Heyburn stated that **"the question is irrelevant here because Churchill Downs is not a party to this case."** Heyburn forgets that he dismissed the Churchill Downs case against Flint and if Flint's allegations are true then it would be bias against Flint. Heyburn should have recused himself, under U.S. Code #455 (a) (b)(1)(2)(3)(4)(5)(iii) (c), but he knew what he was doing, he did not want to give Flint even a faint of a chance to prove the allegations.

Heyburn states, **"This judge did not request Judge Simpson to recuse the Churchill Downs case. Moreover, Judge Simpson did not select this judge for transfer. After Judge Simpson recused, this judge was selected for transfer by random selection among the remaining judges who take case of the Louisville docket."** The records show Judge Simpson assigned the case to Judge Heyburn. Judge Heyburn asked for the case or he is saying that Judge Simpson is the one who violated the court's rule, not him. Flint alleges that Heyburn should have not accepted the case because it was not done properly by rule and was a violation of the rules and Heyburn did not present a computer printout from the case docket nor does the court records show he was random selected in that case. Judges can say or do anything if they don't have to prove it.

Heyburn did not want Flint involved in any case and took advantage of Flint being Pro, Se by denying him cases. Heyburn actions in dismissing this case were at the expense of the older citizens of Kentucky.

Judge Heyburn refused to recuse himself from this case when there is bias. Appellant as pro, se has filed a number of lawsuits in Western District Court a number of lawsuits and every case that was assigned to Appellee Judge Heyburn was dismissed WITH PREJUDICE. Heyburn by his own words has admitted he is prejudice against Flint. There was never a reason to dismiss any of the lawsuits WITH PREJUDICE that Flint filed, the cases had just started and before any discovery were taken, except the first motion was made by the opposing party to dismiss and then dismissal WITH PREJUDICE was granted against Flint by Judge Heyburn for no reason given. Dismissing a case

WITH PREJUDICE takes factual reasons or a judge that doesn't want the case refiled in another court for personal reasons.

In 2009 Flint filed a lawsuit against three (3) Jefferson County Circuit Judges, case 3:09-CV-116-H for violating Kentucky Supreme Court Rules. Heyburn in his ruling order stated **"judges routinely accept cases transferred to them from another division with in a circuit court"** This statement was not true. The Kentucky Supreme Court rules states that all cases must be assigned by random and cannot be transferred. Heyburn was given a copy of the rule with Flint's brief and he completely ignored it, but dismissed the case WITH PREJUDICE. Judge Heyburn was given **Rule 11 of Thirtieth Judicial Jefferson Circuit Court** which stated how the Jefferson County Circuit Court was supposed to function and Judge Heyburn ignored it, because he was going to rule against Flint and didn't want Flint to file the case in another court.

Flint filed other lawsuits that Judge Heyburn dismissed WITH PREJUDICE for no reason. In 2009 Flint filed a lawsuit against a Judge Armstrong in Jefferson District Court case No. 3:09-CV-878-H, which Heyburn dismissed WITH PREJUDICE without a reason on December 29, 2009, by ignoring facts submitted

Judge Hepburn has violated his sworn duty to be a fair and honest judge in all cases that becomes before him and has not lived up to his duty regarding Flint, but he dismissed them for personal reason.

In addition Judge Heyburn has violated another local court rule in the Churchill Downs case when he violated a court rule, a rule that he wrote and approved when he was the Chief Judge of the Federal District Court, where he presides. Judge Heyburn should have given Flint a Due Process fair and honest trial in every case that came before him but Judge Heyburn but didn't, because of a personal bias against Flint, which Flint will now explain.

Judge Heyburn was a partner in a law firm in Louisville Kentucky before he was appointed to the Federal District Court. The firm's name was Brown Todd and Heyburn. Another partner in the firm was a Mr. Ned Bonnie. Flint knew and did business with Mr. Bonnie and others in the firm since 1972.

Mr. Bonnie was Counsel for an organization by the name of HBPA which stands for, Horsemen Benevolence and Protective Association, which represented 70,000 Owners and Trainers of Thoroughbred race horses in America. The group was a National origination with 27 divisions. Mr. Bonnie was Counsel for both the National and the Kentucky Division. Mr. Bonnie was well known throughout America as an expert on laws pertaining to racing horses. Mr. Bonnie as Counsel for the HBPA was the largest or one of largest contributors of financial income to the Brown Todd and Heyburn law firm. Mr. Bonnie also made contact and had relationships with all race tracks throughout America, including Churchill Downs and other horsemen's groups' thorough America.

In 1977 Flint was elected to be the President of the Kentucky Division of the HBPA, by the owner of horses. After becoming President, Flint and Bonnie parted company as far as the Kentucky Division, because they saw the future differently. Mr. Bonnie wanted to have the Kentucky Division ran his way. Later, in the early 1980's Flint was also elected President of the National HBPA, by the 27 Presidents of the divisions. Soon after Flint became President of the National HBPA, Flint and Bonnie again parted company and Flint hired a different Counsel. Flint's action had a large financial effect on Judge Heyburn and his law firm at the time.

When Flint, who is not a lawyer, filed his first lawsuit, Judge Heyburn should have recused himself in that case and every case filed by Flint thereafter that was assigned to him, under, 28 U.S.C #455. But instead Judge Heyburn kept the cases in his court to get even with Flint for parting company with their law firm and cutting the firms income. Judge Heyburn controlled every case that came before him regarding Flint and his actions harmed Flint.

In 2007 Mr. Bonnie was one of the largest fund raiser for a candidate for the office of Governor of Kentucky. Mr. Bonnie's candidate, Mr. Steven Beshear won in 2007 and Mr. Bonnie was appointed to the Kentucky State Racing Commission, his lifetime dream. Governor Beshear is running again this year, 2011, for reelection and Flint sued Governor Beshear and others in this case. Judge Heyburn was a law partner with Mr. Bonnie until Judge Heyburn was appointed as a Federal District Judge. Judge Heyburn should have disqualified himself from all of Flint's cases.

Flint sued Churchill Downs a company connected with horse racing, because of a bad bill Governor Beshear tried to get passed in the Kentucky General Assembly regarding slot machines. Flint was outspoken against the bill and Churchill Down took away Derby tickets that Flint had for over 37 years and tickets that Churchill Downs had promised the Kentucky General Assembly years ago that Flint could buy the tickets till he died. The case was assigned to Judge Charles Simpson. But the next day, Judge Simpson recused himself and assigned it to Judge Heyburn, which was in violation of a local court rule, which Judge Heyburn wrote and put into effect when he was Chief Judge of his court. Judge Heyburn not only wanted Flint's case in his court, he broke civil and local rules to get it. Judge Heyburn has receives favors from Churchill Downs, Kentucky Derby tickets and tickets to other events for himself and other judges and friends and has been for years.

The courts records show that every case that has been filed in Western District Court that pertains to Churchill Downs winds up in Judge Heyburn court, regardless if it was originally assigned to him or not. Judge Heyburn by his actions of violating court's rule, has also violated Flint's rights to Due Process, and in doing so has violated Flint Civil Rights.

On March 30, 2010 Flint filed the lawsuit against Churchill Downs Inc. Case No. 3:10-CV-00202-S. And the case was assigned to Judge Charles R. Simpson. Two days later on April 1, 2010 Judge Simpson without a reason, recused himself from the case. On the same day that Judge Simpson recused himself from the case, he assigned the case to Judge Heyburn, for no reason and again, against the court's rules. Kentucky Western District has a local rule that states a judge cannot recuse himself without a reason and it's in the best interest of justice. Judge Simpson made no motion, gave no reason why he was recusing himself and didn't state it was in the best interest of justice. There was absolute no legal reason for this recusal. Judge Heyburn who wrote the rule, he, should not have accepted the case, Judge Heyburn is the one who requested the case, asking Judge Simpson to violate the court rule. **40.1**(b) states that **"A case may be reassigned to another judge within the district upon the court's own motion, in the interest of justice, for reason stated in an order reassignment" "The court will determine a motion to reassignment on the basis of whether reassignment is in the interest of justice."**

Judge Simpson violated a local rule, in his order did not state a reason, except he cited 28 U.S. Code #455. Judge Simpson failed to quote what part of the code he recused himself for and failed to report why he recused himself and never said it was in the best interest of justice. Heyburn should have never accepted the case because it had not gone through process as stated in the local rule. Flint did not know this was taking place; he was never notified of the actions until he received a copy of an order and never had a chance to respond.

On May 21, 2010 Heyburn dismiss the Churchill Downs case WITH PREJUDICE. On the other hand Judge Heyburn failed in this case and the other cases above, to recuse himself under 28 U.S. Code #455 (a) (b)(1)(2)(3)(4)(5)(iii) (c).Under U.S. Code #455 Judge Heyburn should have disqualified his self from every case that Flint filed that was assigned to him. The orders Judge Heyburn issued on April 26, 2011 should have never been considered or issued.

The Court of Appeals ignored the facts Flint stated above and upheld the ruling of the District Court.

In the other order part of the appeal, Judge Heyburn didn't understand the complaint and ruled to what he wanted it be and used his facts and not the real facts. Flint broke down Judge Heyburn order of April 26, 2011 dismissing the complaint and will copy parts of the brief to the Court of Appeals as follows.

In 2011 Flint filed this case against Kentucky Governor Beshear and in the complaint Flint said he had proof that Governor Beshear had given actuaries on long term insurance, a $340,000 ($668,000) no- bid contract. In addition Flint in his complaint accused Governor Beshear and other Kentucky employees violated their fiduciary duty by giving approval to MetLife Insurance for a 36.2% premium increase on long term care insurance, which affects many old people, and without holding a hearing. Judge Heyburn dismissed the case. He should have recused himself when the case was first filed, but his friend Bonnie did not want the lawsuit dismissed because he wanted Governor Beshear reelected, so to remain on the Kentucky Racing Commission. Bonnie is raising money for the reelection of the Governor as this is being typed. Judge Heyburn should have disqualified himself from this case as well as all of the other cases, when filed, because he was bias and had conflict of interests.

Heyburn set out to get even with Flint on behalf of his friend Mr. Bonnie and to take care one of the company that hired him and his action harmed Flint, mentally, monitory and physical.

Judge Heyburn has intentionally set out from the first case filed by Flint to be assigned to him, to see that Flint would never get a fair and honest trial in Federal court that Flint has to file in. Judge Heyburn has persuaded other judges to rule against Flint in other cases.

Heyburn for years has accepted favors or favors and money from Churchill Downs in the way of Kentucky Derby tickets and tickets to other events, for himself, for his friends, and or for other judges and Judge Heyburn was determine that Flint was not going to take discovery and have those facts Flint has stated, along with other truths that would come out.

Judge Heyburn took advantage of Flint being Pro, Se and inexperience, to keep Flint from finding out the complete truth in the Churchill Downs case, in order Flint couldn't discover how deep or much the take from Churchill Downs really was.

Heyburn should have disqualified himself from all cases that Flint filed in the Western District Court, under 28 U.S. Code #455 (a) (b)(1)(2)(3)(4)(5)(iii) (c)

Judge Heyburn dismissed Flint's lawsuit against Churchill Downs case No. 3:10-CV-202-S by granting Churchill Downs motion for dismissal on the grounds that Plaintiff failed to state a claim and in addition to dismiss it WITH PREJUDICE. Flint's complaint met the criteria for not being dismissed, under Benzon v. Morgan Stanley Distrub. Is., 420 F 3d 598, 605 (6th Cir. 2005). In considering a motion to dismiss under Fed rule 12(b)(6) a court "must except all well-pleaded factual allegations of the complaint as true and construe the complaint in the light most favorable to the Plaintiff." Benzon, 420 F3d at 605 (citing Inge v. Rock Din. Corp., 281 Fd 613, 619 (6th Cir. 2005), [O]a claim has been stated adequately, it may be supported by showing any set of facts consistent with the allegations in the complaint." Bell Atlantic Corp v. Twomby, 550 750 U.S. 544, 563 (2007) "the complaint will survive a motion to dismiss if it "contains(s) sufficient factual matter; accept as true, to state a claim of relief that is plausible on its face." Ashcroft v. Iqbal, 129 U.S. CT. 1937, 1949 (2009) quoting Twombly, 550 U.S. at 750. Flint's complaint has sufficient factual matter. Judge Heyburn wanted to get even with Flint for the past actions done to Heyburn's law firm, and his friend Mr. Bonnie and he did not care what the law says. Judge Heyburn did not want Flint taking Churchill Downs discovery to show what Flint has stated about the past and favors. Judge Heyburn did what no judge should do and that is to treat a Plaintiff Pro, Se as equal to an educated attorney. Judge Heyburn should have did everything he could, to be fair and honest to a Pro, Se. Flint complaint stated a number of claims against Churchill Downs and Judge Heyburn ignored the complaint and came up with anything he could to keep Flint from trying the case, in his court or any other court. Judge Heyburn figured he could count on his fellow judges in the Appeals courts to protect him.

Flint filed the following complaint on January 28, 2011. This is the complaint that Judge Heyburn dismissed.

COMPLAINT

Comes the Plaintiff, Edward H. Flint acting as his own counsel, against Defendants.

Plaintiff is now eighty years old and in 1996 when he was 66 years old purchased a long term care insurance policy from Travelers Insurance. Travelers sold Plaintiff's policy to MetLife in 2006.

The Plaintiff and Defendants are as follows:

1- Plaintiff lives at 5800 Coach Gate Wynde #293- Louisville, KY, 40207 and is retired

2- Defendant MetLife is an insurance company, is the current holder of the long term insurance policy that was sold to Plaintiff

3- Defendant Milliman Inc. is a company that MetLife hired to obtain a rate increase for them from the State of Kentucky. Milliman's office is Minneapolis, MN.

4- Defendant Steve Beshear an individual who is Governor of the State of Kentucky.

5- Defendant Robert Vance an individual is Secretary of the Public Protection Cabinet of Kentucky

6- Defendant Sharon Clark an individual is Commission of Insurance for the Kentucky Department of Insurance.

7- Defendant William Nold an individual is Director of the Health and Life Division of Kentucky Department Insurance.

8- Defendant Sharron S. Burton an individual is General Counsel for the Kentucky Department of Insurance.

9- Defendants Jane and John Does are persons unknown at this time, but if one or more appears, they will be added to the complaint by their real name.

Plaintiff's Complaint is as follows.

1) Plaintiff alleges that Travelers-MetLife has been over charging Plaintiff on his premium since 2005, against the terms of the policy, and has refused to refund the overcharged money and also refuses to lower the premium to the amount of the policy as originally called for. Plaintiff has attempted to have the over charge refunded and change the rate of the premium, but MetLife refuses to do so.

2) Plaintiff alleges that MetLife has forged documents to keep Plaintiff from knowing the truth.

3) Plaintiff alleges that Travelers-MetLife never had proper approval from the state of Kentucky to increase his rates or no other citizens of Kentucky rates, when they were raised in 2005 through 2010.

4) Plaintiff alleges that MetLife has committed fraud by their actions in Long Term Health insurance.

5) Plaintiff alleges that Travelers-MetLife actions has harmed him

6) Plaintiff alleges that MetLife has applied for and received the approval from the state of Kentucky to increase premiums for long term care policies again in 2010 or 2011 and their actions were not to Kentucky's rules and statutes and their actions harmed Plaintiff and other Kentucky citizens.

7) Plaintiff alleges that MetLife applied for and received the approval from the State of Kentucky for the years of 2005, 2006, 2007, 2008, 2009, 2010 for long term insurance premium and their actions where not to Kentucky rules and statutes, their presentation to Kentucky was not proper, but was misleading and their actions harmed Plaintiff and Kentucky citizens,

8) Plaintiff alleges that MetLife is not registered with the Kentucky Secretary of State to do business in Kentucky.

9) Plaintiff alleges that Defendant Milliman Inc. who is an agent for MetLife has on behalf of MetLife has given the state of Kentucky wrong information and has mislead the state of Kentucky and has not obeyed all Kentucky's rules and statutes and their action has harmed Plaintiff and the citizens of Kentucky. Plaintiff also alleges that there may be personal reasons in their actions.

10) Plaintiff alleges that Defendant Steve Beshear as Governor has not lived up to his Fiduciary Responsibility and Fiduciary Duty to Plaintiff and to the citizens of Kentucky. He has not performed his duties to the citizens of Kentucky as called for. That since he was elected Governor the State of Kentucky has given single bid contracts for actuaries services not needed, including in 2010 has given a $340,000 and his reason may be personal. His actions have hurt the citizens of Kentucky which includes the Plaintiff.

11) Plaintiff alleges that Defendant Robert Vance as Secretary of the Public Protection Cabinet has not lived up to his Fiduciary Responsibility and Fiduciary Duty to Plaintiff and to the citizens of Kentucky. He has not performed the duties of his office. Plaintiff also alleges he knew about or should have known about the single bid contracts. His actions have harmed the people of Kentucky, including Plaintiff.

12) Plaintiff alleges that Defendant Sharon Clark as Kentucky Commissioner of Insurance did not preformed her duties as commissioner of insurance, in granting MetLife a thirty six point 2 percent (36.2%) average rate increase on long term care insurance in 2010 and has not performed her Fiduciary Responsibility and Fiduciary Duty to Plaintiff and to the citizens of Kentucky. She has not properly performed the duties of her office and has harmed the citizens of Kentucky including Plaintiff.

13) Plaintiff alleges that Defendant William Nold as Director of the Health and Life Division of the Kentucky Department of Insurance has not properly performed his duty as Director in granting MetLife a thirty six point two percent (36.2%) average rate increase on long term care insurance in 2010 and has not performed his Fiduciary Responsibility and Fiduciary Duty to Plaintiff and the citizens of Kentucky.

14) Plaintiff alleges that Sharron Burton as General Counsel of the Kentucky Department of Insurance has not properly performed her duties to citizens of Kentucky, including Fiduciary Responsibilities and Fiduciary Duties and has cause harm to Plaintiff and the citizens of Kentucky. Including not allowing Plaintiff his rights as citizen of Kentucky by having a security detail watch his

every move and intimidate him when he was reviewing records at the Kentucky Insurance Department. In addition Defendant Burton would not give Plaintiff the public records he requested to review.

15) Plaintiff had requested that he be allowed to attend and speak at any hearing held regarding rate increases for long term care, but was never notified by any defendants including Clark and or Nold or Burton.

16) Plaintiff alleges that some actions in the granting of rate increases by defendants may be personal to some or all defendants.

17) Plaintiff alleges he has been harmed by the actions of all of the defendants.

18) Plaintiff is alleging that MetLife is charging Plaintiff too high rate for his long term care insurance and Plaintiff has been since 2005, the year Travelers/MetLife raised Plaintiff's rates thirty percent (30%) Plaintiff demands MetLife to charge the rate that the policy called for when he purchased the policy in 1996. Plaintiff has now been informed that his rates will be raised again in 2011 by another seven percent (7%).

19) Plaintiff is alleging that the Defendants connected with the State of Kentucky Government did not properly approved the rates increase for MetLife and did so for personal reasons when they approved the rate increases.

20) Plaintiff alleges that MetLife does not want to sell insurance as we know it, but they want a guarantee to make money on each and every policy they sell each and every year. After they sell a policy and so much premium is paid into it base on a set rate, they come to the Kentucky Department of Insurance and obtain rate increases each year, with a goal of making the people who bought the insurance drop the policy, because it has become more than they can afford, in order that Met Life doesn't have to pay out any money, but have made enormous profits on what they have collected.

21) Plaintiff alleges that MetLife actions are a rip off scheme perpetrated on the citizens of Kentucky.

22) Plaintiff alleges that MetLife deceived the Kentucky citizens by their actions and presentations to the Kentucky department of Insurance.

23) Plaintiff is alleging that the Kentucky Department of Insurance in 2010 has signed a single bid contract in the amount of Three hundred and forty thousand ($340,000) dollars against Kentucky Statutes, which was not in the best interest of Kentucky citizens.

24) In addition to the years 2010 the Kentucky Department of Insurance has signed single bid contracts for additional years. The facts are unknown at this time because the Department of insurance has refused to produce the records.

25) Plaintiff alleges that each Defendant who is connected with the State of Kentucky knew of the contracts and knew the contracts are in violation of Kentucky Statutes.

26) Plaintiff alleges that the State of Kentucky has employees who could have done the work that the contractor did and the defendants should have used those employees instead of spending enormous amount of the Kentucky tax payer's money.

In addition there may be more allegations and if other allegations come up in discoveries, Plaintiff will ask the court to grant Plaintiff leave to amend the complaint

Flint's complaint has sufficient factual matter. Judge Heyburn wrote the opinion memorandum to make it look like that the evidence was confusing and non-existence.

Flint's complaint has sufficient factual matter and there were no reason by law to dismiss the case except Judge Heyburn personal vindictiveness against Flint.

Flint, claims that Judge Heyburn actions of not disqualifying himself under 28 U.S. Code #455 (a) (b)(1)(2)(3)(4)(5)(iii) (c) are also violations of the Federal Civil Code of Procedures and Cannons law.

Judge Heyburn wanted to get even with Flint for the past actions done to Heyburn's law firm, and his friend Mr. Bonnie and he did not care what the law says. Judge Heyburn wanted to protect the Governor of Kentucky and the other Kentucky employee's defendants, to protect the Governor in his reelection bid, for Mr. Bonnie.

Petitioner Flint will now argue the facts Judge Heyburn used in his Memorandum opinion and order that dismissed the case dated April 26, 2011.

Judge Heyburn never held a hearing on this case and in this section he draws conclusion based on facts submitted by the Defendant in their Brief, on motion to dismiss. Judge Heyburn took the word of all defendants, and did his own interpretation of their facts and said Flint's facts was wrong and MetLife and the defendants were right. Judge Heyburn was not a neutral judge. Flint asked for a jury trial and not a trial by a judge. The facts Judge Heyburn used are wrong and self-serving. Example, Flint alleged MetLife has never applied correctly for the rate increases that MetLife is charging. No properly hearing was held before Kentucky approved the rates. Most of the facts stated by Judge Heyburn are wrong.

The actuary that gave the figures to Kentucky Department of Insurance was hired on a $340,000 (667,000) no-bid contact and never broke down the different long term care types of policies. He lumped all types of policies together and gave Kentucky the same rate for all policies. There are many different types of long term care policies. Some policies have a set amount of money only to use, and other have different variations, some have a number of days, some have weeks or some have both.

The facts in this case show that the amount of dollars in insurance could use would remain the same for Flint if he used the policy. In 1996 when Plaintiff signed up for his policy he purchased $273,750.00 coverage, not so many days or so many weeks, but a set dollar amount His coverage has remained the same $273,000.00 and will never change, but his premiums have now been increased 37%. MetLife contends Flint policy could be increased every year, even though the pay out money to Flint will never change. In Flint's Response to MetLife's motion to dismiss Flint told the judge the following about his policy and what it said about his policy and the trial judge completely ignored the facts. Flint statement to the trial judge was as follows as cut from the original statement.

GUARANTEED RENEWABLE FOR LIFE

"As long as the premium is paid when due, we cannot change any provision of this policy or cancel it during your, life time. **PREMIUMS MAY BE CHANGED ON A CLASS BASIS ONLY"**

MetLife is saying that when they receive a premium increase of any kind on long term care from the State of Kentucky that it is a blanket increase and they can use the increase to raise the premium on all policies regardless of the type of policies or the structure of the policies.

Flint states that the record shows that his type of policy has never been evaluated by Kentucky as a separate type of policy. Flint is stating that insurance companies write all type of policies in long term care and some policies are based on paying so much per week for a person care, and not a set dollar amount. Flint's policy had a specific dollar amount, not so many days or weeks and when that dollar amount runs out MetLife has no more responsibilities. Flint's type of policy has no more cost to MetLife now than it did in 1996; $273,750.00 is still the total payout. Flint still has $273,750.00 worth of insurance. The cost of other types of policy can cost the insurance company more each year because of inflation or cost of the medical field. Flint's policy will only buy him about forty percent (40%) of health care now of what it would have in 1996 when he took out the policy, but he is paying 37% more and MetLife is reaping the profits. MetLife has a scheme to keep raising premiums each year and when the cost becomes so high that a person can't afford to carry the policy, then the policy holder drops the policy, MetLife then keeps the entire premium paid in for years and have no expense, which makes a big profit for MetLife. Travelers never once attempted to raise the premium, but when MetLife took them over they are raising premiums every year. The records will show that the Kentucky Insurance Department never evaluated the premiums cost on long term care policies; they let outside companies with close ties to one of the Defendants, Milliman Inc do the analyzing of the policies and they did it as an entire group and didn't break down the different types of policies. The Kentucky Department of Insurance never questioned them, but accepted their figures as being the truth. Someone or a number of employees are getting cuts from this actions and Judge Heyburn didn't want Flint to pursue the matter to find out whom.

Courts Order II

Heyburn stated **"Flint claims against MetLife fail for the following reason. First the filed rate doctrine operates as a complete bar to Flints claims for damages. Pursuant to this doctrine and as recognized by the Kentucky Court of Appeals and numerous federal and state courts around the country, insurance rates filed with state regulators are per, se, reasonable and are not subject to collateral attack."** Judge Heyburn submitted no authority to back up his claim and Flint claims Judge Heyburn's words are nothing but double talk that he made up, trying to throw an old man who's Pro,Se, off and wanted Flint believe him. Can this court image what would happen if all states said to all insurance company "just send your rates in and we will accept them as reasonable and won't let anyone attack your rates?" Judge Heyburn had no reason to dismiss this case and he made up stuff like this and he wants this panel to protect him. All states have statutes and regulations and a duty to protect their citizens and make sure the rate increase are justified. For Judge Heyburn to claim that rate increase submitted by insurance company is not subject to collateral attack is laughable. Judge Heyburn in his statement showed he has no feelings for Kentucky citizens, and he only cares about helping his friends who hire him and he wants this panel of judges to back him up by jeopardizing their judgeship and integrity.

Heyburn stated MetLife properly filed the premium increase at issue with the Kentucky DOI pursuant to Kentucky's comprehensive insurance statutory and regulatory scheme and these rates were duly approved prior to their implementation and this is not true, to this day Kentucky Insurance Department has never issue a document that approved the increase that MetLife is charging.

Judge Heyburn did not know what he was talking about, he used his friendly Defendant's pleadings and Judge Heyburn never gave Flint a forum to present different facts. Flint has alleged that the rates were not properly approved. The Kentucky Insurance Department employees that Flint sued never approved the rates in official records and they never held hearings on the rate increase according to requirements of Kentucky statutes and regulations. Flint has claimed in his complaint that MetLife breached his contract. Again Judge Heyburn judged what he wanted to and failed to give Flint a fair and honest trial by jury.

COURT ORDER III

3. Heyburn stated Flint has sued state officials apparently for actions taken in their official capacities, the Eleventh Amendment of the United States Constitution bars suits brought in federal courts against the state or its agencies or its employees acting in their official capacities unless the state has waived its sovereign immunity or otherwise consented to be sued in federal court. Flint states that he sued the Kentucky employees as individuals who violated their Fiduciary Duty to the citizens of Kentucky. They violated laws and regulations in their efforts they did not live up to their duty. The constitution only protects those who does not violate their duty and who does not violate Kentucky rules, regulations or laws. Many Kentucky employees have been sued for violation of laws, regulations and duty, and as individuals for years.

4. Baker v. Fletcher, 204 S.W. 589 (Ky. 2006) pertains to the Governor of Kentucky, who is charged under section 81 of the Kentucky Constitution, with the responsibility to "take care, that the laws be faithfully executed." And then they would be granted absolute immunity for official acts why in office. The key is the "Laws Be Faithfully Executed." and if the laws of Kentucky were not faithfully executed, then the Governor is not granted immunity.

Kentucky employees are sued regularly in courts for violating Kentucky rules regulations or laws. Every employee hired by the state of Kentucky, owes and has a fiduciary duty to ever citizen of Kentucky.

Again Judge Heyburn has judged the case before facts are presented; he used in his opinion only the facts from Defendants pleadings and not Flint's. He turned a blind eye to Flint's pleadings. Judge Heyburn didn't understand the facts of the case and this is why a jury trial is required. Flint's complaint is very clear on what he has alleged against the employees of Kentucky as individuals.

COURT ORDER IV

Judge Heyburn says it is difficult to know the precise nature of Flint claim against Milliman. If he didn't know then he should not put it in the memorandum. Flint states his complaint is very clear and I quote directly from the complaint as follows.

Plaintiff believes that Defendant Milliman Inc. who is an agent for MetLife has on behalf of MetLife has given the state of Kentucky wrong information and has

**mislead the state of Kentucky and has not obeyed all Kentucky's rules and stat-
utes and their action has harmed Plaintiff and the citizens of Kentucky. Plaintiff
also alleges that there may be personal reasons in their actions**

Flint gave to the Court of Appeals in his pleadings document exhibits for the record regarding some of the allegations in the complaint.

1- EXHIBIT-4- a letter dated July 19 from Flint to Bradley Nelson at the Kentucky Department Insurance showing correspondence regarding the issue of increasing Flint premiums and the meaning of Flint's policy.

2- EXHIBIT-5- a letter date February 19, 2010 from Milliman to Sharon Clark Commissioner of Insurance Kentucky Department of Insurance regarding Premium rates regarding long term care. This letter contains what MetLife is seeking in premiums increases. This letter shows that no Kentucky employee name is on the approval. The only approval given was by Mr. Burkhart the actuary hired gun.

3- EXHIBIT-6- an email from Ed Flint to Sharron Burton the General Counsel for the Kentucky Insurance Department, showing that she didn't want to cooperate on giving Flint the records on the non-bid contract and was trying to stop Flint. Kentucky Department of Insurance would not give Flint the records he asked for under the open records law and would go to any means to stop Flint.

4- EXHIBIT-7- a document dated 4/6/2010 regarding Solicitation # 1000000378. This document shows that only one company was asked to bid for the $668,000 contract.

5- EXHIBIT-8- a 4 page document dated August 03, 2010. These documents were given to Flint by Sharron Burton the General Counsel for Kentucky Insurance Department as the documents Flint asked for in his request. The first page is a letter informing Wakely Consulting Group being awarded a Personal Service Contract, by the Kentucky Insurance Company. The other 3 pages are first pages from the contract. Flint in his complaint stated that Kentucky had given a non-bid contract for $340,000; however after coping these 3 exhibits pages for this brief and studying them further, the 3 pages show the contract is for a total of $668,000, as the contract is for 2 years, the years 2011 and 2012.

There are a number of other alleged issues that Judge Heyburn did not confront in his memorandum opinion and order and all allegations must be put before a jury to determine guilt. Some allegations Judge Heyburn didn't confront are as follows

1- MetLife has been selling insurance in Kentucky without being registered and license with the Secretary of the State.

2- Kentucky employees did not proper authorize the increase in premiums to MetLife in the best interest of Kentucky citizens and cannot present any official Kentucky Insurance document showing approval, because it doesn't exist.

3- Kentucky statutes and regulations and their duty was not followed by all employees listed as defendants and there may be more defendants from the John Doe list, still to be added as defendants

4- MetLife forged and intentionally misrepresented to Flint what his policy was.

5- The interpretation of the words "PREMIUMS MAY BE CHANGED ON A CLASS BASIS ONLY" in Flints policy must be determine by a jury as the two parties disagree to the meaning.

6- Flint alleges that Fraud was committed by defendants in the actions taken regarding the premiums increase and other actions taken.

7- Flint alleges that MetLife hired Milliman to represent them in Kentucky and Milliman did not properly fulfill their duty and their actions harmed Flint and others.

8- Flint alleges that employees of the State of Kentucky violated their Fiduciary Duty to the citizens of Kentucky.

9- This court like the trial court owes Flint and the citizens of Kentucky the right to prove the allegations made in this complaint.

10- Flint has alleged the actions by MetLife are a rip off scheme.

11- Flint alleged that approving a $340, 000 (668,000) no bid contract by Kentucky employees was a violation of Kentucky statues and regulations.

12- Flint alleges that the 36.2 % increase in premiums was not properly issued and MetLife has charged customers a higher premium than they should have.

This case should not be about politics, or friendship, It should be judged about the type of government Kentucky's should have, about people buying insurance for retirement and knowing that when you get old and after you have paid thousands of dollars for the policy, someone in not going to get you to give it up because you can no long afford the higher premiums or else you will have to pay higher premiums with money from your retirement funds that you work for all your life. This type of scheme by insurance companies could spread to every state. This type of treatment to old people is like conning or robbing them, because they are easy prey. What would each member of this court do if a person was in front of them, had robbed an old person? Would you try the crook or would you dismiss charges against the crook?

Flint and the citizens of Kentucky needs and deserves to know the truth about their government, their employees, and their suppliers of products and the circumstances of no-bid contracts and premium increases to MetLife. The guilty must be investigated and held accountable.

There was no legal reason for this case to be dismissed and there is no legal reason why it cannot precede to trial, unless this panel believes that insurance companies should be given the right to rape old people and government turns its head.

REASONS FOR GRANTING THE WRIT

1- Congress knew what they were doing when they passed U.S. Code 28 #455 and the Supreme Court in 1988 knew how important it was to have a fair unbiased judge handling every case. This court should uphold the law.

2- Judge Heyburn under 28 U.S.C. #455 should have recused himself from this case when he was asked by Flint in a motion 6 days after the case was assigned to him.

3- Judge Heyburn should have never ruled in this case after being asked to recuse himself.

4- There are a number of allegations in the complaint that no attempt was made to answer by the trial judge.

5- MetLife was not registered with the Kentucky Secretary of State as they were required to do, in order to do business in Kentucky and everything they did should be voided

6- The district court cited the file-rate doctrine as a reason to dismiss this case. There is no such doctrine for the insurance industry. The trial court stated in his order the following, "First the filed rate doctrine operates as a complete bar to Flint's claims for damages. Pursuant to this doctrine, and as recognized by the Kentucky Court of Appeals and numerous federal and state courts around the country, Insurance rates filed with regulators are per se reasonable, and are not properly subject to collateral attack." Judge Heyburn made up a law that he wanted it to be, but couldn't find any law that proves it is correct. He lied, he could not cite the Kentucky Court of Appeals case that recognized the file-rate doctrine and the numerous federal and state courts around the country, as he stated. Therefore they filed-rate doctrine is an imagination in the judge's head only

7- The Court of Appeals on the same filed-rate doctrine, quoted this, "Although the fixed-rate doctrine originated in the context of challenges to rates filed with federal agencies, "most states have adopted the file rate doctrine, and many apply it to insurance regulation," The Court of Appeals lied also. Why didn't the appeals court tell us who the states are that has adopted it and the many states who have applied it? There is no such thing and the Court of Appeals is only protecting the trial court and in doing so is making a mockery out of the justice system. The filed-rate doctrine does not exist for insurance, it only exists for the trucking industry and even that is not constitutional.

8- This court can turn its head and ignore this case and not grant certiorari, but this court knows that what Judge Heyburn did was wrong and not the way our forefather wanted justice to be, for the people. MetLife will be raising everyone's premium across America if this court lets them get by with it. This court should not protect companies that buy judges, so they can rape to people.

9- This case should not have been dismissed in the first place. Judge Heyburn took advantage of an old man who was Pro, Se, to get even.

10- The lack of actions by this court in this case will tell America that this court doesn't really care about justice; that all this court really cares about is protecting judges.

11- Justice can only be assured, by judges obeying the laws and principle of our forefathers.

CONCLUSION

12- This court knows that Judge Heyburn was wrong and this is not what, the United States Constitution says.

13- Because Judge Heyburn is the attorney for and good friend of Minority Leader Mitch McConnell is no reason he should be allowed to do as he pleases with the law. Because Chief Judge Roberts has put Judge Heyburn on a national committee is no reason to let Judge Heyburn violate 28 U.S.C. #455 and not recuse himself

14- This Court knows what 28 U.S.C. #455 means and what its purpose was, honest judges.

15- This court knows that if companies can swindle people and get by with it, the public won't stand for it.

16- This Court knows Petitioner has a good complaint and should not been dismissed.

17- This court should know that the movements in this country like Occupy Wall Street are only the beginning. Those people know there something wrong in this country they just don't know what the problems are, that they are protesting about, but they don't want to continue living it, like it is now, but any smart judge should know that they want only what our forefathers came for, a fair and honest justice system, freedom of speech and freedom of religion. Only by everyone having these will this country survive.

18- This court knows what is being done by judges in district courts and appeals courts. Judges don't care about justice; they only care about getting their way. They know they are protected for life; however this court's ruling in years gone by has made it to where judges don't even think about justice. Is this the type of justice you want to leave for your family's future?

19- Petitioner knows that some members on this court have a high opinion of themselves as Scholars and hopefully these scholars will recognize that judges must obey 28 U.S.C. #455 Petitioner hopes and prays that five (5) of this court judges do care about justice and will vote to grant certiorari.

20- This Courts duty is to protect the all citizens of this country and not just judges.

21- The Judges in the Western District of Kentucky has become dictator not judges. Framers of the constitution did everything in their power to   keep this type of justice from happening in

America. The Mayflower people came to get away from Kings and Dictators and this court must use every muscle in it brain to keep this from happening in America.

22- The filed-rate doctrine does not apply to insurance companies increasing rates and is unconstitutional.

23- Flint complaint was a factual complaint and should have never been dismissed.

24- Kentucky has never issued an official document, approving MetLife's request for a rate increase.

25- A jury should have determine, what is the meaning of this paragraph, in Flint policy?

"GUARANTEED RENEWABLE FOR LIFE

As long as the premium is paid when due, we cannot change any provision of this policy or cancel it during your, life time. **PREMIUMS MAY BE CHANGED ON A CLASS BASIS ONLY"**

Petitioner knows that some members of this court have large egos and take great pride, when it comes to other judges, but fair and honest justice for all, is why this great county was founded. Justice means for everyone, not just a few, who corrupt themselves.

Petitioner prays that at least five (5) members of this court cares about true and fair justice and will grant certiorari and review this case.

Respectfully submitted,
s/ Edward H. Flint, Pro, Se.

The Supreme Court refused to look at the case

The Judge in this case was Judge Heyburn, Senator McConnell friend.

The judges at the Court of Appeals and the Supreme Court covered up fraud by MetLife, Milliman, the Governor of Kentucky, and official of the state of Kentucky.

CHAPTER 12

LAWSUIT FLINT V. GOVERNOR OF KENTUCKY ET AL

**** The complaint was assigned to Judge Simpson

UNITED STATES DISTRICT COURT
WESTERN DISTRICT OF KENTUCKY
LOUISVILLE DIVISON

CASE NO 3:11-CV-276-S

EDWARD H. FLINT   PLAINTIFF

VS

COMPLAINT

DEFENDANTS

STEVE BESHEAR- INDIVIDUAL- GOVERNOR OF KENTUCKY

BRADLEY P. RHOADS- INDIVIDUAL- APPOINTED TO JUDGE CERTAIN CASES ON THE KENTUCKY SUPREME COURT

JOHN S. REED- INDIVIDUAL- APPOINTED TO JUDGE CERTAIN CASES ON THE KENTUCKY SUPREME COURT

MARY C. NOBLE-INDIVDUAL- A MEMBER OF THE KENTUCKY SUPREME COURT

LISABETH HUGHES ABRAMSON-INDIVDUAL-A MEMBER OF THE KENTUCKY SUPREME COURT

Jane Does and John Does

COMPLAINT

The Case was Assigned to Judge Simpson and Judge Simpson's order stated, "For the reasons set forth in the Memorandum Opinion entered this date, and being otherwise sufficiently advised, **IT IS ORDERED** that this action is dismissed for lack of subject –matter jurisdiction pursuant to this court's authority under Fed. R. Civ. P. 12(h) (3) and Apple v. Glenn, 183 F.3d 477(6th Cir. 1999)

Date; May 12, 2011   Charles R. Simpson III Judge

I appealed the District Court order- to The Sixth Circuit Court of Appeals and they upheld Judge Simpson's order and the Court affirmed Judge Simpson's order.

Accordingly, we affirm the district court's order. Rule 34U)(2)(C), Rules of the Sixth Court

ENTERED BY ORDER OF THE COURT   LEONARD GREEN--CLERK

I appealed and My Petition to the Supreme Court starts here*

N0._____

In The
Supreme Court of the United States

Edward H. Flint   Petitioner,

Versus

STEVE BESHEAR et al.   Respondents

PETITION FOR WRIT OF CERTIORARI

QUESTIONS PRESENTED

1- If a judge disqualifies his self under title 28 U.S.C. #455, in a case, isn't he disqualified after that on all cases assigned to his court by the same Plaintiff?

2- Must all judges comply and honor, a congress law, that this court has stated, **"that the purpose of section 455(a) is to promote public confidence in the integrity of the judicial process," the Court also observed that "such confidence "does not depend upon whether or not the judge actually knew of facts creating an appearance of impropriety, so long as the public might reasonably believe that he or she knew."**?

3- Does the United States Constitution give this Supreme Court the right to protect judges against liabilities by giving them absolute judicial immunity that denies United States citizens the right to due process and the right to protect their property?

4- Is Apple v. Glenn, 183, F.d 477 (6th cir. 1999) constitutional, as used in this case by both district and appeals courts in dismissing cases by granting judges immunity and denying plaintiffs a due process trial?

5- Does the Rooker-Feldman doctrine apply when a state's governor appointed two (2) judges to hear cases on a party in the states Supreme Court when the Governor had been sued by the Plaintiff party, thereby creating a conflict of interest?

6- Was a Governor entitle to immunity after appointing judges in a case where the suing party has sued him before he appointed the two judges?

7- Do judges appointed to hear cases due to a vacancy in a state's Supreme Court, have to be trained and educated in judging before setting?

STATEMENT OF THE CASE

PROCEDURAL HISTORY

Flint would like to start by saying that he is an 81 year old Pro, Se and he deserves a review on his Petition the same as any attorney. This Court has refused to hear a number of cases by Petitioner even though he has showed this court how judges are violating laws and rules in Jefferson County, KY and this court has turned a deaf ear to his pleadings. Petitioner is concern about our country. This court is destroying America because they won't or can't control judges across America from violating rules and laws.

This case involves Steve Beshear Governor of Kentucky, two persons who were appointed to serve as judges in Petitioners cases before the Kentucky Supreme Court, and two members of the Kentucky Supreme Court.

The District court hung its dismissal on Rooker-Feldman doctrine and Apple v. Glenn 183 F.3d at 477(6th Cir. 1999) and Fed. R. Civ. P. 12(h)(3).

Petitioner filed a motion two day (2) before Judge Simpson issued his order asking Judge Simpson to recuse himself from the case for being bias against Flint and he refused to answer the motion. Flint had sued him in Federal Court and asked him to recuse himself because of biases in other cases. He recused himself from a Churchill Downs case No. 3:10-CV-00202-S. The case was assigned to Judge Charles R. Simpson. Two days later on April 1, 2010 Judge Simpson without a reason except he stated 28 U.C.

Code #455 to recuse himself, Kentucky Western District Court has a local rule that states a judge cannot recuse himself from a case without a reason and it's in the best interest of justice. Judge Simpson gave no other reason in his order why he was recusing himself

Judge Simpson violated the local rule, in his order except as he stated; he cited 28 U.S. Code #455, which is a reason if a judge is bias.

Judge Simpson by citing 28 U.S.C. #455 in the Churchill Downs case to recuse himself should have disqualified his self from every case that Flint filed after that, which was assigned to him, because he was bias in every case.

Judge Simpson hung his rulings on the Rooker-Feldman doctrine and the Court of Appeals said the doctrine didn't fit this case and they dismissed that part of the trial court's rulings. See the Appeal courts two orders in this case Appendix 1 and 2. The Appeals court should have sent it back to the trial court, but the court made up and used other cases. The trial court Memorandum and opinion bears this out, see Appendix 3 and 4 and compare it to Appendix 1 and 2.

The trial court and the appeals court stated that governor of Kentucky had protection under the eleventh amendment of the constitution and could not be sued because of sovereign immunity. Petitioner claims that he had sued the Governor in another case and the Governor used his power to appoint two people to judge Flint's cases at the Kentucky Supreme Court. Two people who had no experience or training, to make sure Flint would loss his cases in the Supreme Court. With the governor going in with two of the five votes needed, was a good way to be vindictive and get even.

Flint claims that Governor Beshear was vindictive because Flint sued him in another case. Flint in the other case alleged that Governor Beshear let a no bid contract that cost the people of Kentucky, $670,000. He appointed two attorneys that had never been a judge and had not been trained in judging other. The records shows that the two was announced one day and the next day or two they judged the cases that involved Flint. Is this justice? The two appointed judges were large donors to the Governor's election campaign. The Governor should have tried to be fair and appoint two former judges, but he chose to appoint only those he could rely on to make sure Flint didn't win his cases. Governor Beshear should have recused himself and let the Chief Judge of the Kentucky Supreme Court chose the two needed. The Kentucky legislators in all other statutes give the Chief Judge the right to choose and replace judges that are needed. Petitioner sued the Governor as an individual and not as Governor. The Governor actions denied Flint a Due Process fair and honest trial and his actions violated Flint's civil rights. **Baker v. Fletcher, 204 S.W. 589 (Ky. 2006) pertains to the Governor of Kentucky, who is charged under section 81 of the Kentucky Constitution, with the** responsibility to "take care, that the laws be faithfully executed." And then they would be granted absolute immunity for official acts why in office. The key is the "Laws Be Faithfully Executed." and if the laws of Kentucky were not faithfully executed, then the Governor is not granted immunity. The Governor could have recused himself from his duties and to do the right thing and not harm Flint; all the governor had to do was let the Chief Judge replace the judges needed. The Chief Judge was in position to know and appoint educated and trained judges, to hear cases in the highest court Kentucky and an honest Governor would think about all of the people and not about being malicious and mean against Flint.

Flint filed a complaint against all parties and the complaint was as follows.

COMPLAINT

Comes now the Plaintiff, Edward H. Flint, Pro, Se, acting as his own counsel against Defendants.

This case is about actions by the all defendants to harm Plaintiff Flint, which was to see that Flint didn't win any of his three cases that was before the Kentucky Supreme Court and all defendants was going to be against Flint regardless of the facts in the cases. Flint alleges that The Kentucky Supreme Court members along other things did not want to rule against Circuit Court judges who Plaintiff alleged violated court rules and Kentucky laws. Flint alleges that all of the Defendants conspired against him, although not necessary for the same reasons, but all reasons was based on the same three Flint cases in front of the Supreme Court. Plaintiff alleges Defendant Beshear appointed two persons to set on the Supreme Court as judges, fifteen (15) days after Plaintiff served a lawsuit against him that had been filed in Federal Court. Plaintiff alleges that besides conspiring against him by all defendants, Flint has also been denied Due Process to a fair and honest trial by all of the Defendants, along with being denied his civil rights and other allegation which harmed Plaintiff both physically and mentally. Plaintiff will outline other allegations below.

The Plaintiff and Defendants are as follows:

1- Plaintiff lives at

2- Defendant Steve Beshear an individual who was elected to be Governor of the State of Kentucky.

3- Defendant Bradley P. Rhoads an individual from Owensboro Kentucky who was appointed by Defendant Beshear to judge certain Flint's cases on the Kentucky Supreme Court

4- Defendant John S. Reed an individual from Louisville, Kentucky who was appointed by Defendant Beshear to judge certain Flint's cases on the Kentucky Supreme Court

5- Defendant Mary C. Noble an individual who was elected to the Kentucky Supreme Court

6- Defendant Lisabeth Abramson an individual who was elected to the Kentucky Supreme Court

7- Defendants Jane and John Does are persons unknown at this time, but if one or more appears doing discovery, they will be added to the complaint by their real name.

Plaintiff's Other Allegations is as follows.

1- Plaintiff alleges that Defendant Beshear harmed Plaintiff Flint, to get back at Flint, because Flint had sued him personally.

2- Plaintiff alleges that Defendant Beshear failed to perform his constitutional duty, when he appointed two judges to hear Flint's cases.

3- Plaintiff alleges that Defendant Beshear abused his elected office when he appointed the two Defendants Rhoads and Reed to serve on the Kentucky Supreme Court, to judge Flint's Cases.

4- Plaintiff alleges that Defendant Beshear should have asked the courts who to transfer the authority to, to appoint judges to the Supreme Court since he had a conflict of interest in the matter.

5- Plaintiff alleges that Defendant Beshear conspired against Plaintiff Flint; because he wanted to get even with Flint and or to get Flint to back down from the lawsuit had filed against him

6- Plaintiff alleges that Defendant Beshear had a conflict of interest when he appointed Defendants Rhoads and Reed to the Supreme Court as judges and should not have appointed them to a position as judge on the Supreme Court to judge Flint's Cases.

7- Plaintiff alleges that Defendant Beshear failed to live up to his fiduciary responsibly and duty to his elected office.

8- Plaintiff alleges that Defendant Beshear actions were done deliberately to harm Flint.

9- Plaintiff alleges that Defendant Beshear appointed the two Defendants Rhoads and Reed to sit as judges and the two defendants were not qualified to be Supreme Court judges.

10- Plaintiff alleges that Defendant Beshear appointed Rhoads and Reed because he knew they would vote against Plaintiff Flint and when Beshear appointed them he had a conflict of interest and he violated ethics laws which he knew better than to do.

11- Plaintiff alleges that Defendants Rhoads accepted the appointment to Kentucky Supreme Court to please the Governor of Kentucky and to help him out, so he could be given State of Kentucky contracts.

12- Plaintiff alleges that Defendants Rhoads was not qualified to be a judge on the Kentucky Supreme Court.

13- Plaintiff alleges that Defendants Rhoads actions that he took why sitting on the court were done deliberately to harm Flint.

14- Plaintiff alleges that Defendant Rhoads did not judge Flint's cases by the Supreme Court rules SCR 4.300

15- Plaintiff alleges that Defendant Rhoads conspired against Flint

16- Plaintiff alleges that Defendants Reed's actions that he took why sitting on the court were done deliberately to harm Flint.

17- Plaintiff alleges that Defendant Reed conspired against Flint

18- Plaintiff alleges that Defendants Reed accepted the appointment to Kentucky Supreme Court to please the Governor of Kentucky and to help him out, so they would be given State of Kentucky contracts.

19- Plaintiff alleges that Defendant Reed did not judge Flint's cases by the Supreme Court rules SCR 4.300

20- Plaintiff alleges that Defendant Abramson became involved in harming Flint by influencing other Defendants to vote against Flint and for her friend Mr. Dennis Stilger.

21- Plaintiff alleges that Defendant Abramson violated her duty as a member of the Supreme Court.

22- Plaintiff alleges that Defendant Abramson had a conflict of interest in this matter and by becoming involved she violate Kentucky Court's rules and ethics.

23- Plaintiff alleges that the actions of all Defendants harmed Flint, by denying him Due Process of a fair and honest trial as called for in the constitution.

24- the 14th amendment to the United States constitution,

25- Plaintiff alleges that the actions of all Defendants violated his civil rights.

26- Plaintiff alleges that all defendants harm him both physical and mentally by their actions.

27- Plaintiff alleges that all defendants' judges in Flint's cases did not live up to their duty and did not adhere to the Kentucky Supreme Court's Rule SCR 4.300. And they knew their actions were wrong and they knew that their actions would harm Flint.

28- Plaintiff alleges that all defendants sitting as judges in all cases in which Flint was involved, conspired to harm Flint and to make sure Flint did not win any cases that were before them. And defendants knew their actions was wrong and they knew that their actions would harm Flint

29- Plaintiff alleges that all Defendants that were setting as judges on the Kentucky Supreme Court violated court rules and ethics when they voted against Flint, because Flint had accused three Circuit Court judges in one of the cases of violating Kentucky Supreme Court rules and the members of the Kentucky Supreme Court did not want to rule against the three judges that was on the record. The Court chose to harm Flint instead.

30- Plaintiff alleges that all Defendants that were setting as judges on the Kentucky Supreme Court violated court rules and ethics, when they voted against Flint because Flint had accused a Circuit Court judge in a case of violating Kentucky Supreme Court rules by refusing to recuse himself after Plaintiff sued him in Federal Court and the members of the Kentucky Supreme Court did not want to rule against the judges on the record. The Court chose to harm Flint instead.

31- Plaintiff alleges that all defendants setting in judgments against Flint conspired against Flint and did so in order to help another defendant Judge Abramson, who had recused herself from the cases. Judge Abramson wanted help for her and her husband's friend, who was also her husband's associate in teaching students in law, Mr. Dennis Stilger. Judge Abramson's friend Mr. Stilger was the Defendant in a slander lawsuit in one of Flint's cases before the court at that time. Mr. Stilger was Counsel for the Defendants in another of Flint's case that was before the court and ruled on at the time. Judge Abramson only recused herself from Flint's cases only did so after Flint in letters, complained about Judge Abramson helping the attorney Mr. Stilger and after Judge Abramson recused herself, she didn't drop the effort; Judge Abramson enlisted her court cohorts, the defendants to help her rule for her friend Mr. Stilger and against Flint.

32- Plaintiff alleges that defendant Abramson actions was deliberately to harm Flint

33- Plaintiff alleges that the Defendants members of the Kentucky Supreme Court were prejudice for Mr. Stilger and were bias against Flint.

34- Plaintiff alleges that the Defendants members of the Supreme Court violated the court's rules and court's ethics by letting Mr. Stilger file a pleading after time had expired, but before they granted him discretionary review.

35- Plaintiff alleges that the defendant members of the court let Mr. Stilger file a pleading after the deadline so they would have a reason to change the Court of Appeals ruling against Mr. Stilger.

36- Plaintiff alleges that all defendants who were sitting as judges on the Supreme Court knew that the person Judge Abramson wanted to help, Mr. Stilger, had been found guilty of slander against Plaintiff Flint by the Kentucky Court of Appeals and the Defendants judges chose to help violate the court rules and ethics, rather than uphold the law.

37- Plaintiff alleges that Defendant Mary Noble, who was acting as Chief Judge in the three Flint cases, issued three orders on April 13, 2011 that intentionally left information off, that should have been on the order and Judge Noble did this to hide the information from Plaintiff.

38- Plaintiff alleges that Defendant Mary Noble when acting as Chief Judge in the cases against

Flint did not fully inform the full court of the vote against Flint's cases and misled some of the members.

39- Plaintiff alleges that all Defendants, although maybe for different reasons, found working together against Flint was to their benefit in their cause in seeing Flint did not win any of his cases.

40- Plaintiff alleges that some judges setting on Flint's cases voted against Flint for no factual reason or didn't hear the full discussion of the cases and they voted as they were told to vote, against Flint.

41- Plaintiff alleges that all sitting judges on the Supreme Court on Flint cases were prejudice against Flint.

42- Plaintiff alleges that some judges failed to know all of the facts in the cases when they voted against Flint's cases and should not have judged the cases.

43- All sitting defendant judges on the Supreme Court on Flint cases knew they had a conflict of interest when they voted against Flint in his cases and should not have judged the cases. Defendants knew that what they were doing is against all ethics.

44- Plaintiff alleges that the actions of all Defendants in this case were committing fraud against the Plaintiff.

45- Plaintiff alleges that Flint cases may not have been judged as required by the courts and the judgment orders against him may not have been by a majority of the sitting court judges.

46- Plaintiff alleges that the Defendants who are judges had a dislike for Flint because Flint sued judges who violated Court rules and violated laws and stood up for justice for the people.

47- Plaintiff alleges that all Defendant judges was out to get Flint because the judges didn't want to rule by rules and laws but by their own believes and wants and Flint was standing in their way, by fighting corrupt judges and attorneys.

48- Plaintiff alleges that all of the judges did not even have known how each judge voted.

DEMANDS

Plaintiff makes the following demands

1- A trial by jury.

2- On any allegations in this complaint which a jury finds any Party guilty, Plaintiff is awarded both compensatory and punitive damages from each party found guilty in the amount determined by a jury.

3- Any defendant found guilty of any allegation in this complaint by a jury is removed from the office they were elected to by the citizens of Kentucky or appointed as judges by the Governor of Kentucky.

4- That all of Flint's lawsuits that was dismissed by the actions of those defendants sitting as judges are found guilty on any allegation in this complaint be reinstated to the Supreme Court and heard by an elected Kentucky Supreme Court that does not contain any of those found guilty and Flint be allowed to attend all hearing held on any case that is returned to the court.

5- All cost of this complaint by Plaintiff

6- For any other relief to which said Plaintiff may appear entitled.

REASONS FOR GRANTING THE WRIT

1- Congress knew what they were doing when they passed U.S. Code 28 #455 and the Supreme Court in 1988 knew how important it was to have a fair unbiased judge handling every case. This court must uphold that law.

2- Judge Simpson under 28 U.S.C. #455 recused himself from the Churchill Downs case for being bias and then refused to recuse himself from this case He knew instantly in the Churchill case he was bias, and he recused himself two (2) day after being assigned the case, but refuse to recuse himself on this case. He was going to get Flint at all cost regardless of justice.

3- Judge Simpson hung his memorandum opinion and order on the Rooker-Feldman doctrine and he knew this doctrine was not constitutional and could not be used. The Court of Appeals dropped Rooker-Feldman as a reason for dismissing the case. The Court of Appeals should have sent the case back to the trial court for trial, but instead they searched for other law what was not part of the case for which Flint knew nothing about and had never argued. The trial court decision shows Judge Simpson wanted to hurt Flint and would do anything to harm him. The court of Appeals wanted to uphold the district court and tried to find another way to uphold the dismissal order.

4- Based on 3 above this case stinks as far as justice being served by a federal justice system, but they both did anything to deny Flint his due process and civil rights.

5- Governor Beshear by his actions took away Flint's rights to a fair and honest Due Process trial.

6- The two judges appointed to hear Flint's case was not trained to serve as Supreme Court judges.

CONCLUSION

1- This Court knows what 28 U.S.C. #455 means and what its purpose was, honest judges. Judge Simpson should have recused himself without hesitating and never should have heard the case.

2- Immunity granted under Apple v. Glenn is false because the complaint Flint filed was a good complaint with factual issues and therefore immunity should have not been granted.

3- The district court dismissed this case on based on the Rooker-Feldman doctrine and the Court of Appeals threw that reason out and then had to try and find one to keep the case alive. This Court knows Petitioner has a good complaint that should not been dismissed.

4- This court knows that the movements in this country like Occupy Wall Street are only the beginning. Those people know there is something wrong in this country, they just don't know what the problems are, and they are protesting unfairness.

5- This court knows what is being done by judges in district courts and appeals courts. Judges don't care about justice; they only care about getting their way. They know they are protected for life.

6- Some members on this court have a high opinion of themselves as scholars and hopefully these scholars will recognize that judges must obey 28 U.S.C. #455 and the dismissing the case was wrong. Petitioner hopes and prays that five (5) of this court judges do care about justice and will vote to grant certiorari.

7- Flint was judged by two people who had never been trained as a judge and never set as a judge.

8- The Mayflower people came to get away from Kings and Dictators and this court must use every muscle in it brain and moral fiber to keep dictators and bully judges from being in America.

9- If Judge Simpson was bias in the Churchill Downs case he was bias in this case and all other cases after the Churchill Downs case.

Fair and honest justice for all, is why this great county was founded. Justice means for all, not just a few, especially those who corrupts themselves.

Petitioner prays that at least five (5) members of this court cares about true and fair justice and will grant certiorari and review this case and do justice in this case .

Respectfully submitted, s/ Edward H. Flint, Pro, Se.

The Supreme Court refused to look at the case

CHAPTER 13

LAWSUIT FLINT V. JUDGE DAVE WHALIN

The case was assigned to Judge John Heyburn

The Complaint starts here

UNITED STATES DISTRICT COURT
WESTERN DISTRICT OF KENTUCKY
LOUISVILLE DIVISON

CASE NO 3:11CV-316-H

EDWARD H. FLINT   PLAINTIFF

VS

COMPLAINT

DAVE WHALIN, Magistrate Judge -
AN INDIVIVDUAL   DEFENDANT

Comes the Plaintiff Edward H. Flint acting as his own counsel against Defendant who is a magistrate judge in Federal Court in Louisville, KY.

1- **Plaintiff, Edward H. Flint lives at**

2- **Defendant Dave Whalin is an individual who is a magistrate judge in Western District of Kentucky Federal Court.**

3- **Plaintiff filed a complaint in Federal Western District Court on September 20, 2011 against Hewlett Packard Company with a number of allegations in the complaint.**

4- **The complaint was assigned a case No. 3:10-CV-597-S.**

5- The case was assigned to Judge Charles Simpson.

6- The court for some reason assigned the case to Judge Dave Whalin, the Defendant which is against the Federal court rules.

7- Plaintiff alleges that Defendant Whalin is bias against him in the case.

8- Plaintiff alleges that Defendant Whalin has taken actions in the case that has harmed Plaintiff, physically.

9- Plaintiff alleges that Defendant Whalin has taken actions in the case that has harmed Plaintiff mentally

10- Plaintiff alleges that Defendant Whalin actions is denying Plaintiff receiving Due Process fair and honest trial under the 14th amendment to the constitution.

11- Plaintiff alleges that Defendant Whalin has refused to recuse himself from this case after being asked by Plaintiff a number of times and Judge Whalin's actions shows that he is prejudice for Hewlett Packard and bias against Plaintiff.

12- Plaintiff alleges that Judge Whalin has a personal connection to counsel for Hewlett Packard and has used his bias for them against Plaintiff.

13- Plaintiff alleges that Defendant Whalin has and is violating courts rules.

14- Plaintiff alleges that Defendant Whalin is using the court system to determine the outcome of a case rather than doing his duty of trying to find the truth.

15- Plaintiff alleges that Defendant Whalin' actions shows he wants to judge the complaint rather that a jury and he is interpreting the complaint rather than let a jury.

16- Plaintiff alleges that Defendant Whalin is using power that he doesn't have by Federal rules or Federal laws.

17- Plaintiff alleges that Defendant Whalin is attempting to be a judge of the law and he doesn't have that power.

18- Plaintiff alleges that Defendant Whalin has conspired with Hewlett Packard to take advantage of Plaintiff.

19- Plaintiff alleges that Defendant Whalin is taking advantage of an old person.

20- Plaintiff alleges that Defendant Whalin is taking advantage of a Pro, Se, non-educated in legal law person to get his way and easy control the case.

21- Plaintiff alleges that Defendant Whalin should have bent over to help a Pro, Se person and by not doing so gave the advantage to Plaintiff's opponent Hewlett Packard.

22- Plaintiff alleges that Defendant Whalin's duty was to find the truth between the parties and let a jury determine who was right and who was wrong and he has not done that.

23- Plaintiff alleges that Defendant Whalin's actions has denied Plaintiff his civil rights in the case

24- Plaintiff alleges that Defendant Whalin is prejudice against Plaintiff in his rulings and actions.

25- Plaintiff alleges that Defendant Whalin did not conduct himself the way a judge should.

26- Plaintiff alleges that Defendant Whalin has violated the court of conduct rules that all judges must adhere to.

27- Plaintiff alleges that Defendant Whalin has violated the courts rules and laws of ethics in his handling of the case against Plaintiff.

28- Plaintiff alleges Defendant Whalin made up rulings that fit his own wants, thereby pulling the justice system down from being fair and honest.

29- Plaintiff alleges that Defendant Whalin by his actions is trying to take advantage of Plaintiff's inexperience and is not judging by Cannons conduct ethics.

30- Plaintiff alleges that Defendant Whalin violated court rules to make sure he was in control of the case and therefore he would control the court's actions against Plaintiff.

31- Plaintiff alleges that Defendant Whalin wants Hewlett Packard to win the case and has taken actions to assure that it happened.

32- Plaintiff alleges that for some reason yet to be determined Judge Whalin is siding with Hewlett Packard on every issue of value.

33- Plaintiff alleges that Defendant Whalin violated courts rules and laws to keep Plaintiff from receiving discoveries due him by the courts rules.

34- Plaintiff alleges that Judge Whalin was on Hewlett Packard's side from the beginning of the case and his actions against Plaintiff were done with intent to make sure Hewlett Packard wins the case, which thereby harmed Plaintiff.

35- Plaintiff alleges that Defendant Whalin is on Hewlett Packard's side in this case.

36- Plaintiff alleges that Defendant Whalin is feeding his ego, rather than search for the truth which was his duty to his office.

37- Plaintiff alleges that Defendant Whalin from the beginning knew the outcome that he wanted and he bent and violated rules and laws to do it, regardless of the truth.

38- Plaintiff alleges that Defendant Whalin knew how he was going to rule in the case before the case was started in discovery and he knew his actions would harm Plaintiff.

39- Plaintiff alleges that Defendant Whalin by his actions has stopped Plaintiff from receiving evidence that Plaintiff is entitled to by court Rules.

40- Plaintiff alleges that Defendant Whalin refused to conduct himself to the oath he took to this country.

41- Plaintiff alleges that Defendant Russell knew he violated court rules by his actions and did nothing to correct his mistakes.

42- Plaintiff alleges that Defendant Whalin is not concerned about Plaintiff's rights.

43- Plaintiff alleges that Defendant Whalin was assigned this case by Chief Judge Russell to get Plaintiff because Plaintiff wrote a book titled "Corrupt Judges" about a case Judge Russell mishandled and Defendant Whalin did what Judge Russell wanted even though it was against courts rules, ethics and integrity.

44- Plaintiff will ask this court to amend the complaint if other allegations appear or other defendants appear.

DEMANDS

Plaintiff makes the following demands

1- A trial by a jury

2- **If the Defendant is found guilty by a jury of any allegations in this complaint, Plaintiff is awarded both compensatory and punitive damages from the Defendant in an amount determine by a jury.**

3- **If the Defendant is found guilty on any allegation in this complaint, he must at once be removed as a Federal Magistrate Judge and never seek another position with any court system again.**

4- **All cost of this complaint by Plaintiff**

5- **For all other relief to which said Plaintiff may appear entitled.**

Respectfully submitted
Edward H. Flint Pro, Se
*** The Complaint stops here****

The District Courts order stated that Judge Whalin had absolute immunity and Judge Heyburn in his order warned me that he would fine me if I filed any more lawsuits. Judge Heyburn took away my rights to sue anyone. The Constitution says I can sue, but Judge Heyburn took away my constitutional rights.

The order in part said,

Generally, a district court may not sua sponte dismiss a complaint where the filings fee has been paid unless the court gives the plaintiff the opportunity to amend the complaint. See Apple v. Glenn, 183 F.3d at 479. However where a complaint is "totally implausible, attenuated, unsubstantial, frivolous, devoid of merit, or no longer open to discussion," the district court need not afford the plaintiff an opportunity to amend the complaint. Id. (citing Hagans v. Lavine, 415 U.S. 528, 536 (1974).

Judges are entitled to absolute immunity for actions arising out of all acts performed in exercise of their judicial functions. Mitchell v. Forsyth, 472 U.S. 511, 526 (1985). "Accordingly, judicial immunity is not overcome by allegations of bad faith or malice, the existence of which ordinarily cannot be resolved without engaging in discovery or eventual trial." Mireles v. waco, 502 U.S. 9, 11 (1991). "Immunity applies even when the judge is accused of acting maliciously and corruptly." Harlow v. Fitzgerald 457 U.S. 800, 825-19 (1982). The United States Supreme Court has made clear that immunity is overcome in only two sets of circumstances: [f}irst, a judge is not immune from liability for non-judicial actions.... [s]econd a judge is not immune for actions, though judicial in nature, taken in complete absence of all jurisdictions." Mireless, 502 U.S. at 12.

Up on review, the court concludes that sua sponte dismissal under Apple v. Glenn is appropriate because it is "no longer open to discussion" that Plaintiff's claims of all legal merit. See Metzenbaum v. Nugent, 55 F App'x 729 (6th cir. 2003) (upholding district court's sua sponte. Dismissal of a complaint under Apple v. Glenn because the named defendant, a judge, was entitled to absolute immunity); Forbush v. Zaleski, 20 F. App'x 481 (6ᵗʰ cir. 2001) (same).

Accordingly, the court will enter a separate Order of Dismissal.

Flint is <u>WARNED</u> that he will be sanctioned in the amount of $700.00 per suit should he file any additional lawsuits in this Court against federal or state judges on the grounds that he believes they were biased against him, made incorrect rulings or otherwise improperly oversaw any of his cases. Additionally, filing any additional such lawsuit could result in the imposition of additional sanctions, including the imposition of filing restrictions.

Date June 21, 2011   John G. Heyburn II Judge

United States District Court

This judge is Senator Mitch McConnell's friend, again. Judge Whalin, who I sued, violated courts rules. I asked him by motion 13 times to recuse himself from the case. He refused. I sent copies of a number of the motion asking him to recuse himself to Chief Judge John Roberts and Judge Roberts refuse to do anything to help me. Judge Roberts is close to Senator McConnell. Judge Roberts and Judge Whalin both violated a law of Congress.

I appealed to the Court Of Appeals and their order starts here

UNITED STATES COURT OF APPEALS
FOR THE SIXTH CIRCUIT

NO. 11-5809

EDWARD H. FLINT,   Plaintiff-Appellant

v.

DAVE WHALIN, Judge   Defendant-Appellee

On Appeal from the United States District
Court for the Western District of Kentucky

FILED October 18, 2011

Before: KEITH, GUY, and Gibbons, Circuit Judges.

Edward H. Flint, a Kentucky resident proceeding pro se, appeals from a district court order dismissing his civil complaint. This case has been referred to a panel of the court pursuant to Rule 34(j) (1), rules of the Sixth Circuit. Upon examination, this panel unanimously agrees that oral argument is not needed. Fed. R. App. P. 34(a)

Seeking monetary and equitable relief, Flint sued United States District Court Magistrate Judge Dave Whalin, claiming the magistrate judge: a) violated his Fourteenth Amendment due process rights by ruling in favor of Hewlett-Packard in a prior lawsuit: b) attempted to act as a judge without authority under law: and c) refused to recuse himself from Flint's case even though he had a "personal connection" with Hewlett-Packard's counsel and was bias against Flint. The district court sua sponte dismissed Flint's complaint, pursuant to Apple v. Glenn, 183 F3d 477 (6th Cir. 1999) concluding that the record established that Flint's complaint is devoid of legal merit because Magistrate Judge Whalin was entitled to absolute judicial immunity.

On appeal, Flint argues that Magistrate Judge Whalin is not entitled to judicial immunity because he engaged in numerous improper actions to ensure that Hewlett-Packard would prevail in Flint's underlying lawsuit, including conducting a meeting with Flint outside the presence of defense counsel about settling the case, sealing the transcript of the meeting with Flint, failing to permit Flint to amend his complaint or to seek discovery, attempting to improperly dismiss the lawsuit based on lack of diversity jurisdiction, and making misleading statements and untruths about the facts of the case. Flint argues that the magistrate judge's conduct did not constitute normal judicial functions. Flint argues that his complaint was not subject to dismissal under Apple because his claims are not frivolous or devoid of merit. Flint maintains that Magistrate Judge Whalin should have recused himself from the case to avoid the appearance of impropriety. He also maintains that, as a pro se litigant, he should not be held to the same pleading standards as an attorney.

Flint spends a significant portion of his appellate brief arguing that Judge Heyburn, who dismissed his complaint against Magistrate Judge Whalin, is biased against him. He maintains that Judge Heyburn should have recused himself from ruling on Flint's lawsuit against Magistrate Judge Whalin because he had previously sued the judge and that Judge Heyburn made several incorrect factual findings in dismissing the instant complaint.

We reviewed de novo a district court's sua sponte dismissal of a complaint. See Apple, 183 F.3d at 480(dismissal pursuant to federal Rule of Civil Procedure 12(b)(1). A district court may dismiss a complaint for lack of subject jurisdiction if the purported federal claims are "so attenuated and unsubstantial as to be absolute devoid of merit."

Hagans v. Lavine, 415 U.S. 528, 536 (1974). A fee-paid complaint may be dismissed by the district court sua sponte for lack of subject matter jurisdiction where it is completely implausible or frivolous. Apple, 183 F.3d at 479. where a complaint is "totally implausible, attenuated, unsubstantial, frivolous, devoid of merit or no longer open to discussion" the district court need not afford the plaintiff an opportunity to amend the complaint, especially where the district court has determined that it lacks subject matter jurisdiction over the action. Id. (citing Hagans, 415 U.S. at 536-37).

The district court property concluded that Flint's complaint was devoid of legal merit because Magistrate Judge Whalin is entitled to absolute judicial immunity. Absolute judicial immunity attaches only to actions undertaken in a judicial capacity." Barnes v. Winchell, 105 F3d 1111, 1116 96th Cir. 1997). "Whether an act is judicial depends on the nature and function of the act, not the act itself." Id.(internal quotation marks omitted). "in examining the functions normally performed by a judge, courts have found that paradigmatic judicial acts are those that involve resolving disputes between parties who have invoked the jurisdiction of a court." Id. Internal quotation marks omitted). Moreover, a "judge will not be deprived of immunity because the action he took was in error, was done maliciously, or was in excess of his authority." Stump v. Sparkman, 435, U.S. 349, 36 (1978). Absolute judicial immunity is overcome only when a judges engages in non-judicial absence of all jurisdiction." Mire v. Waco, 502 U, S. 9, 12 (1991).

Neither of these circumstances exists here. Flint sued Magistrate Judge Whalin based on his allegedly improper action in accepting the assignment of Flint's case against Hewlett-Packard and ruling in favor of Hewlett-Packard bases on his bias against Flint. Magistrate Judge Whalin's rulings clearly involve judicial decisions and were made within the authority granted a magistrate judge. Contrary to Flint's arguments, Magistrate Judge Whalin had jurisdiction to issue orders on nondispositive pretrial matters and to submit proposed findings of facts and recommendations on dispositive motions without the consent of the parties. See 28 U. S. C. #636 (b)(1)(A)-(B).

Flint argues that Magistrate Judge Whalin's during the lawsuit against Hewlett-Packard were improper and taken in bad faith. However, even if the alleged actions were improper, a judge will not be deprived of immunity because the action he took was in error. See Stump U. S. at 356-57. Hence, the district court properly concluded that Magistrate Judge Whalin was entitled to absolute immunity.

Finally, contrary to Flint's arguments, the record does not support his claim that Magistrate Judge Whalin should have recused himself from Flint's lawsuit. To justify recusal, the judge's prejudice or bias must be personal or extrajudicial. United States v. Jamieson, 427 F3d 394,405 (6th Cir. 2005) (citing United States v. Hartsel, 199 F3d 812, 820 (6th Cir. 1999). Although Flint argues that the magistrate judge had a personal connection with Hewlett-Packard's counsel and made up his mind to take action to ensure that Hewlett-Packard prevailed in the case, Flint's allegations are insufficient to establish that Magistrate Judge Whalin's rulings were based on personal bias. Flint provided no persuasive arguments or evidence to support his self-serving allegations that the magistrate judge sought to improperly dismiss his lawsuit in order to protect Hewlett-Packard.

Likewise, Flint has not established that Judge Heyburn should have recused himself from ruling on the lawsuit against Magistrate Judge Whalin. See Jamieson, 427 F3d at 405. The fact that Flint had previously sued Judge Heyburn did not require his recusal. See Azubuko v. Royal, 443 F3d 302, 304 (3d Cir. 2006). Furthermore, although Judge Heyburn inadvertently stated that Flint that Flint alleged that Magistrate Judge Whalin was biased because Flint had written a book about him, this misstatement did not affect the analysis of the case or its outcome. Flint's remaining complaints against Judge Heyburn are more properly raised in the appeal from the dismissal of his lawsuit against Judge Heyburn.

Accordingly, we affirm the district court's order. Rule 34(j)(2)(c), Rules of the Sixth Circuit.

ENTERED BY ORDER OF THE COURT

Leonard Green--Clerk

I appealed and file a Petition to the Supreme Court which starts here

No._____

In The
Supreme Court of the United States

Edward H. Flint   Petitioner,

Versus

DAVE WHALIN, JUDGE   Respondent

PETITION FOR WRIT OF CERTIORARI

Edward H. Flint Pro, Se

QUESTIONS PRESENTED

1- Does a Citizen loose his right to Due Process because he wouldn't give in to a Federal judge's demands that the citizen settle the case?

2- Does a Federal Judges have to abide by and honor 28 U.S. Code #455 which pertains to when a judge must disqualify themselves?

3- Did the 1988 United States Supreme Court get it right in their ruling in Liljeberg v. Health Servs. Acquisition Corp., 486 U.S. 847, 860 n.8 (1988).

4- Should a judge have disqualified himself from a case under 28 U.S.C #455 when requested by petitioner, when the recoded records shows that at a settlement hearing set by the judge, the judge dismissed the counsel for the other party from the hearing and when alone, brow beat the Petitioner, attempting to make him settle the case? Is this American justice by the constitution?

5- Should a Federal judge have disqualified himself after Petitioner had requested him to recuse himself in 3 other cases before this case?

6- Did a judge show bias when he told and threaten the Petitioner not to file any more lawsuit in Federal Court and threaten him with sanctions if he did?

7- Does the United States Constitution grant judges immunity when they have violated court rules and laws of the United States, including laws of Congress pertaining to when a judge must recuse them self from a case, in their handing of a case.

STATEMENT OF THE CASE

PROCEDURAL HISTORY

Flint would like to start by saying that he is an 81 year old Pro, Se and he deserves a review on his Petition the same as any attorney. This Court has refused to hear cases by Petitioner even though he has showed this court how judges are violating laws and rules in Jefferson County, KY and this court has turned a dumb ear to his pleadings. Petitioner is concern about our country. This court is destroying America because they don't or can't control judges across America from violating rules and laws. They should know that if one judge can be corrupt and get by with it, others judge will think its ok to be corrupt also. Petitioner has filed a number of petitions for certiorari regarding immunity granted by this court in Stump v. Sparkman and numerous other cases feeding off of Stump v, Sparkman. Petitioner believes that the judges on this court either does not know how to correct this problem or don't have the will to do the right thing, to fix the America justice system to make it as fair for everyone as the constitution calls for.

This case involves two judges that refused to recuse them self when they both was clearly bias. Flint filed a lawsuit against Hewlett Packard on September 20, 2010. The case was assigned to Judge Charles Simpson, case No. 3:10-CV-597-S. Judge Simpson issued an order for a settlement hearing and turned the case over to Magistrate Judge Dave Whalin to handle.

Judge Simpson in his order, instructed both parties to present a brief out lining the case.

Petitioner Flint attended the settlement hearing as ordered by Judge Simpson for January 20, 2011. Flint ordered a copy of the transcript. Flint received the copy ordered, but a note was put in the transcript that the transcript was ordered sealed by Judge Whalin. Flint on February 8, 2011 filed a motion that told of what happen at the meeting and after the hearing. Flint has copied the motion he filed with the court and it follows.

Comes the Plaintiff Edward H. Flint Pro, Se demanding that Judge Dave Whalin be removed from this case and the part of the transcript of the January 20, 2011 scheduling conference hearing that has been sealed, be open to the public. On January 20, 2011 there was a hearing held by Judge Whalin regarding a scheduling conference, regarding this case. Judge Whalin during the hearing asked Mr. Hardesty, Counsel for Hewlett Packard to leave the room and for no reason. After Mr. Hardesty left the room, Judge Whalin continued to discuss with Plaintiff the case. Judge Whalin only purpose in asking Mr. Hardesty to leave, was so he could intimidate Plaintiff. There was no reason for Judge Whalin's actions and he knows that he should not discuss a case with one party without the other being present, without a reason, which he didn't have. Plaintiff states that Judge Whalin is bias against him and is bias for defendant Hewlett Packard. His motive for conducting the hearing without Mr. Hardesty out of the room was to try and take advantage of Plaintiff's lack of experience and try to steer the case to where he wanted it to go. Judge Whalin was upset he couldn't control the actions of Plaintiff. Judge Whalin has no has no regards for courts ethics. There was absolute no reason for him to attempt to get Plaintiff to settle this case, after Plaintiff told him that he was not interested in settling the case

After Plaintiff told him he was not interested in settling the case is when Judge Whalin asked Mr. Hardesty to leave the room. Judge Whalin motive was to intimidate Plaintiff in settling the case. He doesn't care about equal justice; he just believes in justice his way. Judge Whalin wanted the case settled because he wanted to protect Hewlett Packard. Judge Whalin's action was out of bounds based on a judge's duty. Judge Whalin, even when the meeting resumed with Mr. Hardesty, was still upset in his mind and Judge Whalin threaten Plaintiff about discoveries.

In addition the ruling that Judge Whalin made at the hearing, was not the same as the order that he signed contained. The signed order was different and was in the favor of Hewlett Packard the Defendant. Judge Whalin actions show he is bias against Plaintiff.

Plaintiff has filed a motion to vacate that order and issue a correct order to what he ruled on from the bench.

Judge Simpson should take this case over himself and make sure Plaintiff receives a fair and honest trial. Judges are not Gods; they are only performing a job, a job that has rules and ethics that they must abide by. Plaintiff is entitled to a Due Process fair and honest trial.

Plaintiff asked for a transcript of the January 20, 2011 hearing. After receiving the transcript Plaintiff was shocked to find there were two transcripts. One of the transcripts was marked sealed. The sealed transcript was the part of the hearing held between Judge Whalin and Plaintiff. Plaintiff never asked for the transcript to be sealed and is upset that a court would seal a transcript for no reason, accept trying to keep it out of the public hands. But a bigger question arises and that is why it was it sealed.

Therefore Plaintiff demands that Judge Whalin be removed from this case and that the transcript be unsealed. Plaintiff asks Judge Simpson to handle the case himself. In addition Plaintiff would like to know why the judge ordered the transcript sealed and what reason was given for sealing the transcript. Plaintiff never received a copy of the order from the judge that sealed the transcript. Petitioner Flint has asked Judge Whalin Fourteen times to recuse himself and he has refused each time. Judge Whalin fused to grant Flint leave to amend the complaint and add Office Depot to the complaint. Office Depot sold Flint the Hewlett Packard printer.

Judge Heyburn the trial Judge should have recused himself the moment he was assigned the case. Flint had sued him and Flint had asked him to recuse himself in other cases before he was assigned this case. But Judge Heyburn in his memorandum opinion to dismiss shows his bias a number of times, but the last sentence of his opinion showed not only bias but his hatred for Petitioner Flint. The last sentence reads as follows.

Accordingly, Flint is WARNED that he will be sanctioned in the amount of $700.00 per suit should he file any additional lawsuits in this Court against federal or state judges on the grounds that he believes they were biased against him, made incorrect rulings or otherwise improperly oversaw any of his cases. Additionally, filing any additional such lawsuit could result in the imposition of additional sanctions, including the imposition of filing restrictions.

Judge Heyburn action and remarks not only shows his hatred for Flint, but takes away Flint constitutional right to defend himself.

By 28 U.S.C. #455 both Judge Heyburn and Judge Whalin should have disqualify themself. In Liljeberg v. Health Services Acquisition Corp., 486 U.S. 847, 860 n.8 (1988) **The Supreme Court noted that the purpose of section 455(a) is to promote**

public confidence in the integrity of the judicial process, the Court observed that such confidence "does not depend upon whether or not the judge actually knew of facts creating an appearance of impropriety, so long as the public might reasonably believe that he or she knew."'

The Supreme Court has never asked Congress to delete the law and there can be no question that in *Liljeberg* v. *Health Services Acquisition Corp.* that Supreme Court studied the law thoroughly and concluded that the integrity of the court system was the most important thing of all, if this country was going to have a truly fair and honest justice system. The founders of our country came and established this court for three reasons, a fair and honest justice, Freedom of speech and freedom to worship. This court should do everything possible to their last breath to see that these three principals live forever.   This case shows how terrible the Stump v. Sparkman decision was and what a bad experiment it was.

Both Judge Whalin and Judge Heyburn, by not recusing himself, knew what they were doing, but it was on purpose, to control on how they wanted the outcome of the case to be.

Judge Heyburn controlled every case that came before him regarding Flint and his actions harmed Flint badly. Judge Whalin also violated Cannons laws and the record shows he was bias against Flint every step of the way.

REASONS FOR GRANTING THE WRIT

1- Congress knew what they were doing   when the passed U.S. Code 28 #455 and the Supreme Court in 1988 knew how important it was to have a fair unbiased judge handling every case. This court should uphold the law.

2- This country has major problems and they will continue to grow unless this court fixes the justice system. The Supreme Court in Stump v. Sparkman stated "we could try this." They were saying that something needed to be done to speed up a growing system, something that our forefathers didn't confront in the constitution. The experiment since 1978 has grown into a monster. Someone has to lead this country out of its problems and as long as this court fights to keep it the way it is, the public will do just what the court does, they will fight for their beliefs instead of doing what is right for America. Each side in America is fighting for their belief because the Supreme Court does it. This is destroying America

3- No honest open minded judge can say that Judge Heyburn and Judge Whalin have not violated U. S. Code 28 #455.

4- This court can turn its head and ignore this case and not grant certiorari, but this court knows that what Judge Heyburn and what Judge Whalin did was wrong and not the way our forefather wanted justice to be for the people and this court knows that it is happening in every court in America, and this court knows that the same thing is happening in every Court of Appeals Circuit Court. Does getting your way and showing the other side you have power and can stop almost anything before it, lead America?

5- The lack of actions by this court in this case will tell America that this court doesn't really care about justice that this court only cares about their selfish selves and protecting judges.

6- Justice can only be assured by obeying the laws and principle of our forefathers.

<u>CONCLUSION</u>

1- This court knows that Judge Heyburn and Judge Whalin were wrong and was not what, the United States Constitution states.

2- This Court knows what 28 U.S.C. #455 means and what it was intended to do.

3- This court knows that Stump v. Sparkman is a failed experiment and must be changed.

4- This court knows that if companies continue making and selling defective produces and getting by with it, the public won't stand for it.

5- This Court knows Petitioner has a good complaint and the trial court should never have dismissed the case against Judge Whalin.

6- This Court knows that the words in Judge Heyburn's actions prove he was bias.

7- This court should know that uprising movements in this country like Occupy Wall Street are only the beginning. Those people know something in this country is wrong and they don't want to continue living it like it is, they just don't what the problems are they are protesting about, but any judge should know that only what our forefathers came for, a fair and honest justice system, freedom of speech and freedom of religion, will this country survive.

8- This court knows what is taking place by judges in district courts and appeals courts. Judges don't care about justice they only care about doing it their way. Judges know they are protected for life; however this court's ruling in years gone by has made it to where judges don't even think about justice. Is this the type of justice you want to leave for your family's future?

9- This court can see that the reason given for dismissal is wrong, that Petitioner complaint did fall into the Apple v. Glenn case, given by the trial court for a reason to dismiss.

10- Petitioner knows that some members on this court have a high opinion of themselves as Scholars and hopefully these scholars will recognize that judges were never given immunity in the constitution. Petitioner hopes and prays that five (5) of judges do care about justice and will vote to grant certiorari.

11- This court has an opportunity to correct the American Justice system from the harm done by Stump v. Sparkman in 1978, by holding judges responsible for violating laws and rules of the court. If this court takes away the immunity clause for violations of court rules and laws, ninety (90) percentages of the problems of the court system would go away. The fathers of our country did not put judges on a higher plateau than the people, but the Supreme Court did, by making dictators out of the judges and America is being destroyed.

12- This Courts duty is to protect the citizens of this country and not just judges, by interpreting the Constitution and this court cannot find anywhere in the constitution where judges are to have immunity. This court's ruling in Stump v. Sparkman is a direct assault on the citizen of this country and this court should find a way to protect and assure that each and every citizen receives a fair and honest trial regardless of how small the complaint or how large a company is. This court should not make laws, but interpret how justice is to protect the citizens of this county and how justice is to be run as defined by the constitution. The court system has had more to do with the unrest that is taking place in America than all of other elements combined.

13- How can this court do nothing when a Federal judge threatens to put sanctions on a person for filing a lawsuit and also threatens to not let him file a lawsuit? The Judges in the Western District of Kentucky has become dictator not judges. Framers of the constitution did everything in their power to keep this type of justice from happening in America. The Mayflower people came to get away from Kings and Dictators and this court must use every muscle in it brain to keep this from happening in America, Stump v. Sparkman is a failed experiment and must be changed.

This court should throw out the Stump v. Sparkman ruling and take away immunity for all judges that do not adhere to Cannons Law, Court Rules and statue laws. The Constitution does not grant immunity to judges.

Petitioner prays that at least five (5) judges on this court cares about America having true and fair justice for its people and will grant certiorari and review this case.

Petitioner also asks this court to interpret the Constitution regarding immunity for judges and put America back the way it was once. This court's members should leave an honest and fair court system for their families and for America.

Respectfully submitted,
s/ Edward H. Flint, Pro, Se.

THE SUPREME COURT REFUSED TO REVIEW THE CASE

The Court of Appeals refused to anything. The Supreme Court refused to do anything. Judge Whalin violated court rules. I asked him 13 times to rescue himself, under a law that Congress passed and the Supreme Court sweeps in under the rug.

Judge Heyburn took away my rights to file lawsuits and the Supreme Court did nothing.

CHAPTER 14

LAWSUIT FLINT V. JUDGE THOMAS B. RUSSELL

This case was assigned to Judge Simpson

UNITED STATES DISTRICT COURT
WESTERN DISTRICT OF KENTUCKY
LOUISVILLE DIVISON

CASE NO 3:11-CV-291-S

*** The complaint starts here***

EDWARD H. FLINT   PLAINTIFF

VS

COMPLAINT

THOMAS B. RUSSELL, Judge- AN INDIVIVDUAL DEFENDANT

Comes the Plaintiff Edward H. Flint acting as his own counsel against Defendant who is a judge in Federal Court Western District in Louisville, KY.

1- Plaintiff, Edward H. Flint lives at

2- Defendant Thomas B. Russell is an individual who is a judge in Western District of Kentucky Federal Court.

3- Plaintiff filed a complaint in Jefferson Country KY Circuit Court against Target Corporation in October 2007.

4- Target asked that the case be moved to Federal Western District of Kentucky Court.

5- Judge Russell Defendant signed an order on December 11, 2007 moving the case to the Federal Court and the case was assigned to Judge Russell. The case was NO. 3:07-CV-600-R

6- Plaintiff alleges that Defendant Russell was bias against him in the case.

7- Plaintiff alleges that Defendant Russell actions harmed Plaintiff, physically.

8- Plaintiff alleges that Defendant Russell actions harmed Plaintiff mentally

9- Plaintiff alleges that Defendant Russell actions denied Plaintiff from receiving Due Process fair and honest trial under the 14th amendment to the constitution.

10- Plaintiff alleges that Defendant Russell took advantage of an old person.

11- Plaintiff alleges that Defendant Russell took advantage of a Pro, Se, non-educated in legal law person to get his way and easy control the case.

12- Plaintiff alleges that Defendant Russell should have bent over to help a Pro, Se person and by not doing so gave the advantage to Plaintiff's opponent Target.

13- Plaintiff alleges that Defendant Russell duty was to find the truth between the parties and let a jury determine who was right and who was wrong.

14- Plaintiff alleges that Defendant Russell liked Plaintiff being pro, se and inexperience, which made Judge Russell, fell great in side and feel like a big man.

15- Plaintiff alleges that Defendant Russell denied Plaintiff his civil rights in the case

16- Plaintiff alleges that Defendant Russell was prejudice against Plaintiff in his rulings.

17- Plaintiff alleges that Defendant Russell did not conduct himself the way a judge should.

18- Plaintiff alleges that Defendant Russell has violated the court of conduct rules that all judges must adhere to.

19- Plaintiff alleges that Defendant Russell violated the courts rules and laws of ethics in his handling of the case against Plaintiff.

20- Plaintiff alleges Defendant Russell made up rulings that fit his own wants, thereby pulling the justice system down from being fair and honest.

21- Plaintiff alleges that Defendant Russell in his actions took advantage of Plaintiff's inexperience and did not judge by Cannons conduct ethics.

22- Plaintiff alleges that Defendant Russell violated court rules to make sure he was in control of the case and therefore he would control the court's actions against Plaintiff.

23- Plaintiff alleges that Defendant Russell wanted Target to win the case and took actions to assure that it happened.

24- Plaintiff alleges that Defendant Russell violated courts rules and laws to keep Plaintiff from receiving discoveries due him by the courts rules.

25- Plaintiff alleges that Judge Russell was on Target side from the beginning of the case and his actions against Plaintiff were done with intent to make sure Target won the case, which thereby harmed Plaintiff.

26- Plaintiff alleges that Defendant Russell help Target sell illegal drugs.

27- Plaintiff alleges that Defendant Russell was told and knew that illegal drugs was being produced and sold in America and took no actions to stop it or to notify the authorities.

28- Plaintiff alleges that Defendant Russell mislead the Federal Court of Appeals with his rulings and writings.

29- Plaintiff alleges that Defendant Russell was on the take from Target.

30- Plaintiff alleges that Defendant Russell feed his ego rather than search for the truth which was his duty to his office.

31- Plaintiff alleges that Defendant Russell from the beginning knew the outcome that he wanted and he bent and violated rules and laws to do it, regardless of the truth.

32- Plaintiff alleges that Defendant Russell knew how he was going to rule in the case before the case was started in discovery and he knew his actions would harm Plaintiff.

33- Plaintiff alleges that Defendant Russell by his actions stopped Plaintiff from receiving evidence that Plaintiff was entitled to by court Rules.

34- Plaintiff alleges that Defendant Russell refused to conduct himself to the oath he took to this country.

35- Plaintiff alleges that Defendant Russell influenced others to harm Plaintiff.

36- Plaintiff alleges that Defendant Russell ordered others to do his deeds even though he knew the deeds where wrong and violated court rules and laws.

37- Plaintiff alleges that Defendant Russell solicited others to help him pull off his scheme to harm Plaintiff or to protect Target.

38- Plaintiff alleges that Defendant Russell at no time had intentions of giving Plaintiff a fair trial.

39- Plaintiff alleges that Defendant Russell did not care about illegal drugs being given to customers and did nothing to check to see if they were sold by Target and two other companies and took no actions to stop the illegal actions, even though he knew the drugs was illegal.

40- Plaintiff alleges that Defendant Russell had no feeling for anyone but Target and himself in this case.

41- Plaintiff alleges that Defendant Russell knew he violated court rules by his actions and did nothing to correct his mistakes.

42- Plaintiff alleges that Defendant Russell was being paid off by Target in order to protect Targets reputation with the public and to keep the public consumers from knowing that Target was selling illegal drugs to customers.

43- Plaintiff alleges that Defendant Russell was not concerned about Plaintiff's rights and ignored facts that he should have investigated, by Federal agencies.

44- Plaintiff alleges that Defendant Russell actions in this case made a mockery out of the Unite States of America's court system.

45- Plaintiff will ask this court to amend the complaint if other allegations appear or other defendants appear.

The money Plaintiff asks for in this complaint exceeds
money the requirements of this court

Respectfully submitted
Edward H. Flint Pro, Se

*** The Complaint ends here***

***** The District Court order starts here***

ORDER

For the reasons set forth in the memorandum Opinion & Order entered this date and being otherwise sufficiently advised, **IT IS ORDERED** that Plaintiff's claims are dismissed pursuant to this court's authority under Apple v. Glenn, 183 F3d 477 (6th Cir. 1999), because it is "no longer open to discussion" that plaintiff's claims are devoid of legal merit under the doctrine of absolute judicial immunity.

There being no just reason for delay in its entry, this is a **final Order.**

Date: May 13, 2011   Charles R. Simpson, Judge

United States District Court

Judge Simpson stated the case is no longer open for discussion
and Judge Russell has absolute immunity.

*** I appealed to the Court of Appeals and my Brief starts here***

CASE NO. 11-5726

UNITED STATES COURT OF APPEALS
FOR THE SIXTH CIRCUIT

EDWARD H. FLINT,   Plaintiff – Appellant

v.

THOMAS B. RUSSELL   Defendant-Appellee

On Appeal from the United States District Court
For the Western District of Kentucky
Louisville Division

Honorable Charles R. Simpson III

Civil Case No. 3:11-CV-00291-S

BRIEF FOR APPELLANT/ PLAINTIFF

STATEMENT OF FACTS AND BACK GROUND INFORMATION REGARDING THIS CASE

Appellant Flint is 81 years old and is Pro, Se, states he has lived his live believing that Judges was the most respected people, along with Doctors in America. However

Flint has discovered that some judges like to use their power to show those before them, that they don't care how people perceive them and they believe that their power of a judge makes them chosen ones and will get them in Heaven, just like the religious leaders did with Jesus, but how wrong they were. Flint believes in truth and it doing the right thing if life. He has seen and lived World War II, Hitler and everything that has come after that. Flint believes in Jesus and in God. Jesus said that Satan was the father of lies and Flint can't believe that some Judges doesn't care about justice that they only care about using their devil power and they believe other judges from will protect them when they commit acts of corruption. Judges like everyone, will someday become equal to all others, when they get old and on judgment day. **Jesus said on judgment day, we will all be judge by the thoughts we had in our mind and by the deeds we did, not by the words we said**.

Flint also states that; there is a constitutional question in this case that this court must address. Flint is entitled to a Due Process fair and honest trial as called for in the Constitution.

Flint wants to also remind this court that the court's duty by the constitution is to find the truth, over and above anything else. No person who is Pro,Se can possible write a pleading, know the Federal rules of civil procedures and cite laws and for any court to expect a Pro, SE to follow all of the rules and cite laws is in violation of granting a person a Due Process trial. The Court's rules of civil procedures only exist to keep order among trained lawyers and are not the only way to determine the truth.

When a Pro, Se is involved, a court has to overlook some of the presentation by a Pro, Se and arrive at the truth by other means, regardless of what it takes. No fair minded judge or the framers of the constitution would expect a non-educated person to compete with a person who has been educated and trained for a number of years. There is nothing in the United States Constitution that says that the Court's Rule of Civil procedures must be adhered to by Pro, Se's. Nothing can supersede the 14th amendment to the constitution, which gives everyone Due Process, to a fair and honest trial.

Therefore any misstatement made or lack of presenting the proper federal law or rule in pleadings to a court, cannot be held against a Pro, Se. If any court holds in their rulings that a Pro, Se didn't adhere to the rules of civil procedures or cite the right authority, then the court is giving the educated lawyer an unfair advantage over the pro, se, and denying the Pro, Se a Due Process fair trial. The court its self would be discriminating against a Pro, Se.

Court's Rules of Civil Procedure are court drafted rules and are not constitution mandated for a due process fair trial. Example, when a Plaintiff says he has been harmed by a defendant action and doesn't spell out which Federal law or civil rule should be used, does mean that Plaintiff's case should be thrown out,. The truth which a court must find is was Plaintiff harmed by any method, whether it is physical or civil rights or property. The 14ᵗʰ Amendment gives every person the right to protect their property and that is what Flint was doing in this complaint he filed with the trial court. Pro, se's under all circumstances must be protected by this court, from the harassing done by any Defendant, in not conforming to the courts rules on discovery, if any exits. A Pro, Se person have a right to explain their case the best they can and a court must take the time to get to the truth, even if everything is not done by the Courts rules.

A courts duty is to get the truth in the case, regardless of anything else and regardless of what time and effort it takes the court to find the truth.

Chief Judge of the United States Supreme Court John Roberts stated at his confirmation hearing with the United States Senate replied when asked what a judge's duty was, and I quote,

"Judges are like umpires. Umpires don't make the rules. They apply them. The role of an umpire and a judge is critical. The make sure everybody plays by the rules. But it is a limited role. Nobody ever went to a ball game to see the umpires." His jurisprudence would be characterized by "modesty and humility"

No one can disagree with John Roberts's statements. The constitution gives every person Due Process of a fair and honest trial, regardless of what it takes and this court must see that Flint receives a Due Process fair and honest trial, especially if hot shots attorneys try to take advantage of a Pro, Se's lack of experience. When a judge makes up their own rules or ignores and expands the court's rules and or legal laws, or judges by their feelings, the Justice System breaks down and fails. When the Justice system fails, social order fails.

The trial judge gave Judge Russell absolute immunity, which can only be overcome by two ways. In **Stump v Sparkman 435 U.S. 349, 357 (1978)** The majority opinion of the Supreme court went on to decide that the factors determining whether an act by a judge is a judicial act "relate to the nature of the act itself":

1. whether it is a function normally performed by a judge; and

2. whether the parties dealt with the judge in his judicial capacity.

This leaves Appellant to have to prove that Judge Russell violated one of the two or both. Flint contents that violating the 14ᵗʰ amendment to the constitution by denying Flint Due Process would not be a function normally performed by a judge. Every person should automatically receive Due Process and by Judge Russell violating it means, he was violating his normal function duty. A judge to deny a person Due Process has to go out of his way and internationally performs a non-normal function action. Violating court's rules and laws are no a function normally performed by a judge and violating rules and laws are not in a judges jurisdiction, it is the opposite of his duty. A judge's duty is to punish violators of rules and laws, not to be one.

Judge Russell has violated his sworn duty to be a fair and honest judge in all cases that became before him and has not lived up to his duty regarding Appellant.

The District Judge in her order in this case used as authority Apple v. Glenn 183 F. 3d 477 (6th Cir 1999). The trial judge dismissed this case to protect a fellow judge. Under Apple v. Glenn the judge stated, "The plaintiff's case is devoid of merit and also state as a judge he has absolute immunity from suit." These statements are not correct and Flint complaint shows different. The trial judge, judged the case without looking at the facts in the complaint and what evidence would have been presented if the Appellee had filed for a dismissal of the case. The trial judge wanted the results to be what he ordered, before looking at any evidence. The trial judge was bias and he wanted to take advantage of a Pro, Se, to hell with justice and law. (Attached is **EXHIBIT 1**-Flint's complaint filed on May13, 2011 against Appellee Russell.)

Flint filed this complaint on May 13, 2011 and the trial court issued an order dismissing the case on the same day May 13, 2011. The trial court did not allow Appellant time to submit any pleadings or to amend his complaint. The trial judge has violated Cannons, Court Rules and Due Process by not allowing Flint to present his evidence. The judge's order stated and I quote, "no longer open to discussion" that the plaintiff claims is devoid of merit under the doctrine of absolute immunity. How can a fair and honest judge make such remarks when the Appellant has not had a chance to submit evidence or to chance to change his complaint and the complaint clearly showed plenty of facts, especially violating local court's rules The judge didn't allow Flint to do anything, he had her mind made up before he started. The court dismissed the case pursuant to its authority under Apple v. Glenn 183, F.3d at 479. (6th Cir. 1999)

The trial court stated the following, "Generally, a district may not *sua sponte* dismiss a complaint where the filing fee has been paid, unless the court gives the plaintiff the opportunity to amend the complaint. See Apple v. Glenn 183, F.3d at 479. However where a complaint is "totally implausible, attenuated, unsubstantial, frivolous, devoid of merit, or no longer open to discussion" the district court need not afford the plaintiff an opportunity to amend the complaint" The Appellant states the complaint **EXHIBIT 1** had plenty of facts and merit. The trial judge was going to dismiss this case regardless of the content in the complaint. The trial judge flat out goofed and wants this panel to protect him. The trial court judge had no integrity and wants you to give up yours to agree with him. The trial court should have let Flint respond to a motion to dismiss before issuing an order dismissing the case.

The next issue is absolute immunity. The trial court stated and I quote, "The United States Supreme Court has made clear the immunity is overcome in only two set of circumstances: "[f]irst a judge is not immune from liability for nor-judicial actions…;[s] second a judge is not immune for actions, though judicial in nature, taken in complete absence of all jurisdiction." This puts the burden on Flint 1) to show where Judge Russell is liable to Flint because Judge Russell did not perform functions that a judge would normally perform and 2) to show where Judge Russell is liable to Flint also for actions taken by Judge Russell against Flint on issues that was in complete absence of all jurisdictions.

ARGUMENT

We as a society live by laws and rules. Our lives are controlled by laws and rules. What would sports be without referees or umpires? If a referee or umpire let their friends do as the want and not the others players in a game, what type of game would it be? If a policeman let his friends drive 80 miles put hour in a 30 mile an hour zone, what would happen? There has never been a law or rule written that everybody agreed with; however we all have to live by the rules we have, not what we want them to be. A judge is the referee or umpire or policeman who makes everyone obey the laws and rules. When a judge says in a court I don't like the way a rule is written, so I will just let it set on it and not making a ruling to keep the case moving my way. What will become of our society?

Every judge knew the laws and rules when they were appointed to their position, so why should they be allowed to violate rules and harm someone? Is this type of action fair to judges who are honest? Is every judge bound to judge by cannons and Supreme Courts rules? Was Chief Judge John Roberts wrong when he told the United States Senate, **"Judges are like umpires. Umpires don't make the rules. They apply them. The role of an umpire and a judge is critical. The make sure everybody plays by the rules. But it is a limited role. Nobody ever went to a ball game to see the umpires." His jurisprudence would be characterized by "modesty and humility"**

If a judge violates a law or rule, are they any different than a robber or a con artist who cons money from old people or a company who sells bad products and won't take them back or a drug dealer who sells dope to people or store that sells alcohol to 10 year olds?

A judge has a duty to make a call on motions or other pleadings that require a judge's action. A judge cannot skip over motions and other pleadings and then issue a summary judgment, which is what Judge Russell did in this case. Judge Russell by not making rulings on all issue that came before him did not perform functions that a judge would normally perform and was a non-juridical act and not performing his duty on issues that was before the court was in complete absence of all jurisdictions. A court cannot function if a judge fails to perform his daily duty. There is no jurisdiction that says a judge can just set and do nothing and then issue a summary judgment when plaintiff's evidence was not taken in consideration. If all cases were handled like this, there would be no system. Flint had forty-seven (47) motions that were never ruled on my Judge Russell, including not enforcing court issued subpoenas and motions for leave for Flint to amend the complaint and add two (2) other defendants. If Flint was allowed to amend the complaint then Judge Russell would not have at reason to grant summary judgment to Target. Judge Russell had a personal reason not to see Target loose his case and he let Target get by with not producing discovery to Flint, which is not part of a judge's normal function.

A judge's duty is to find the truth, not stop the truth. Judge Russell stopped the truth in this case. Judge Russell had his mind made up before the case started who was going to win. He didn't figure an old man who had never filed a lawsuit before would be able to compete with an experience group of lawyers. Judge Russell didn't know that God through the Holy Spirit told Flint to file the lawsuit. The Holy Spirit told Flint he would give him the actions and words to use in the lawsuit. Judge Russell didn't care that Flint was injured by illegal non FDA approved drug from Target, that didn't matter; it was Target's reputation that mattered. Target wanted to maintain their reputation so bad they would do and pay anything to keep the truth about selling non-approved drugs to a person that harmed him. The only way Target could win this case was by and trough Judge Russell's action. Target gave a drug to Flint that was 230% heavier in weight and what Flint was supposed to receive. The drug had 10 different in-active chemicals in it, which it should not have. Judge Russell granted summary judge based on a Kentucky law that said Flint had to hold the manufacturer or distributor responsible. Flint tried to add the manufacturer and distributor as Defendants, but Judge Russell refused to rule on Flint's motion for leave to amend the complaint to add the two additional defendants, because Target would still be in the lawsuit for a number of violations they did in the case.

Judge Russell could have granted summary judgment on the one issue and Flint sill had a case against Target on a number of other issues, such as actions they took on the way they handled the prescription fill and on the documents they gave to Flint, regarding selling non FDA approved drug, but Judge Russell chose to protect Target by doing nothing on Flint's motions and pleadings. Judge Russell figured out that Flint knew what he was doing. There can be no question that Judge Russell was going to protect Target no matter what Flint did or proved. The actions of doing nothing are not an everyday function of a judge and therefore according to the United States Supreme Court he cannot receive immunity. The Supreme Court in Stump v. Sparkman ruled that a wrong decision by a judge can be appealed, so wrong decisions can be reversed, however no decisions cannot be reversed so there is nothing to reverse.

Therefore based on the court's reasoning, no decisions made is not a judicial act and therefore is part of a judge's normal function and therefore cannot be part of a judge's jurisdiction, so therefore not a reason to grant judge immunity.

If this panel wants to defend a Judge who did the things Judge Russell did, then Flint knows he can't win, but this panel must figure out in their minds if this is direction they want the justice system in America to go in the future. This court must realize and know that justice rulings is like rows of dominos, once they start falling they keep on falling, like by bad laws written by corrupt judges, keeps being used by other judges as authority.

Appellant Flint filed this lawsuit in October 2007 in Jefferson Circuit Court and Target through counsel had Judge Russell move the case to Federal Court with Judge Russell as the judge.

Flint can only give this court Exhibits of documents with explanation of what Judge Russell did with each document and let the panel decide if Judge Russell preformed his duty on each one and if such action of not ruling on motions by Judge Russell was in his jurisdiction to act this way, then Judge Roberts answer to the Senate was wrong. These are part of the 47 motions or pleadings that was never ruled on by the court in the Target case. Flint will now list a few of the motions or pleading not ruled on by Judge Russell which meet the Supreme Court's criteria for not being granted immunity to a judge.

EXHIBIT 2- Is a copy of the original complaint Flint filed against Target filed in October 2007.

EXHIBIT 3- Is Flint's motion asking for leave with an attached amended copy to amend the original complaint, which the court never ruled on.

EXHIBIT 4- Is a copy Flint's response to defendant's motion to quash to take the deposition of a Mr. Gregg Steinhaffel, President of Target Corporation. The court granted the Defendants motion to quash the deposition with a statement that Flint would never be allowed to take this person's deposition.

EXHIBIT 5- Flint's motion for a reconsideration of the court's order quashing the deposition of Mr. Steinhaffel. The court never responded to this motion

EXHIBIT 6- Flint's Motion requesting Target to produce a person to testify about FDA approval of drugs. The court never responded to the motion.

EXHIBIT 7- Plaintiff's motion objecting to defendant's motion to remand its motion for summary judgment. The court never responded to Flint motion, granted defendants motion to remand and granted defendants summary judgment.

EXHIBIT 8- Plaintiff's Motion for leave to join two (2) other parties into the complaint as defendants. The court never responded to this motion

EXHIBIT 9- Flint's motion for an extension of time for discovery. The court never responded to this motion. Target refused to give discovery to Flint by the Federal Rules of Civil Procedures and Flint wanted more time, but Judge Russell did nothing about ruling.

EXHIBIT 10- Flint's Motion for leave to file the attached amend complaint which also joins two (2) other defendants to the complaint and if this motion is granted-Plaintiff is asking to remand the motion he filed on June 13, 2008 to amend the original complaint. The court never responded to this motion. Judge Russell was not going to give Flint a differed complaint with two (2) new defendants. The two new defendants was the manufacturer and distributor and this actions ruined Judge Russell plan.

EXHIBIT 11- Flint's response and objection to defendant's response to Plaintiff's motion to hold defendant in contempt of court and to have defendant compel on a total of fifteen (15) discoveries that was not answered or the answers were changed when submitted to interrogatories that were not ordered to be answered by this court. The court never responded to this matter

EXHIBIT 12- Plaintiff's motion to hold Breckenridge Pharmaceutical in contempt of court and compel them to give a deposition after refusing to honor a **subpoena**. The court never responded to this matter.

EXHIBIT 13- Plaintiff's response and object to defendant's response to Plaintiff's motion for defendants to explain and reproduce documents and documents produced are not to be used and if defendants cannot show legitimate reasons why these documents was a mistake, then this court hold them in contempt. The court never responded to this matter

EXHIBIT 14- Plaintiff's motion to hold Ms. Ann Curatola of Breckenridge Pharmaceutical Inc. in contempt of court and compel her to give a deposition and hold Breckenridge Pharmaceutical Inc. in contempt for refusing to produce document and to order Breckenridge to compel the document that was listed in the **subpoena**. The court never responded to this motion

EXHIBIT 15- Plaintiff's motion to compel Mr. Aron Podell to give a deposition and to hold Mr. Podell in contempt of court for refusing to appear for his **subpoenaed** deposition and for failing to produce the documents that was listed in the subpoena and in the notice of deposition and to hold Contract Pharmacal corporation in contempt of court. The court never responded to this motion.

The Trial court should have granted Flint leave to file his last amended complaint to add two other defendants to the lawsuit under **Federal Rules of Civil Procedures-Rule 15 Amended and Supplemental Pleadings amendments before trial (2) other Amendments the rule states "the court should freely give leave when justice so requires"** Judge Russell violated the Supreme Court's criteria for immunity by doing nothing. This type of action is what the Supreme Court had in mind when it wrote the criteria for liability by judges in Stump v. Sparkman. Judge Russell knew from the first day when Target asked for the case to be moved to Federal Court who was going to win the case and his way to accomplish that was to do nothing to help Flint, which in effect stopped Flint.

CONCLUSION

Flint argues that Judge Russell has violated Flint's right to a Due Process trial. The fourteenth amendment gives a party the right to due process, a fair and honest trial. Such violation is not a normal function performed by a judge and certainly is an issue that is not in a judge's jurisdiction.

Judge Russell's actions have denied Flint his Civil Rights. This is not a normal function performed by a judge and certainly is not an issue that is with-in a judge jurisdiction.

Ignoring and not abiding by court's and Cannons laws is not a function normally performed by a judge and is not within their jurisdiction.

Flint alleges that Judge Russell has by his actions of no action in this case, has violated Cannons and Supreme Court Rules.

Judge Russell's actions of no action were an intentional act against Flint because he was bias and because Judges Russell was going to protect Target regardless of what he had to do. The question is why did Judge Russell do nothing, but protect Target's reputation.

There can be no question that Judge Russell violated the court's rule, and other laws. He thought that he could depend on his fellow judges in the 6[Th] circuit to protect him. He doesn't care if he jeopardized the other judge's positions or integrity as long as he got his way, as long as Flint had no hard evidence. Judge Russell could not grant Flint's motion to add two other defendants in the case, and the only way he could make sure was to do nothing regarding Flint's motions. Judge Russell is a user of other people to get his way and never gives it a thought about what harm he may be causing other judges. A person's integrity is the only thing we each have that cannot be taken from them, we can give it up, but not one can take it. Judge Russell wants this panel of judges to give up their integrity for him. He believes that all judges think and act like he does, by not judging by the rules, by not judging what's right and wrong, but ruling by greed, he believes that if he is corrupt then all other judges are corrupt. Flint is positive that Judge Russell will call the members of the panel hearing this case or another judge in the 6th circuit and call Flint every name in the book and say he doesn't know what he is doing, he is a trouble maker. He doesn't like Flint because Flint believes in Jesus Christ and truth, and truth is against his way of judging and he is against being Pro, Se. Judge Russell to do what he did either cared about favors from others or about showing a Pro,Se that he doesn't like Pro, Se's. In his heart he looks down on anyone who didn't go to school like he did and he believes they shouldn't ever win in a court. He doesn't believe we are all equal and shouldn't be treated as equals. He couldn't give Flint a reason that the Court of Appeals would have to overturn his ruling in favor of Target.

There is no reason why an honest judge should take advantage of a Pro, Se. and no honest judge would. No honest judge would do to any party what Judge Russell did unless they was bias against the Plaintiff, or unless they had a financial or personal interest in the case with the other party or had once a financial or personal interest with another party in the case.

Violating a court's rule is not a normal function by a judge and it is certainly not in his jurisdiction. In fact it is the opposite of a normal function by a judge and it is certainly not in his jurisdiction.

We all have to be accountable for our deeds in life and this panel will someday have to account for the actions they take in this case, to the only judge that counts, and that is Jesus Christ. Jesus says that he won't judge you based on what you say on earth, but he will judge you on the thoughts you had and the deeds you did on earth, that is how he will judge each of us.

Flint cannot put it in the best legal language, but this panel must rule that Judge Russell can be held liable under the Supreme Court rulings "a function not normally preformed" and his actions was not in the jurisdictions of his court. What other explanation can there be for the Supreme Court language? No actions taken cannot is not a juridical act. Judge Russell took no actions and thereby denied Flint a Due Process trial. If this panel did nothing on this brief, would the lack of action be a judicial act that they normally do and would it be in the panel's jurisdiction if it took no actions?

Flint therefore asks this panel to overturn the trial court on granting Judge Russell immunity. Flint also asks this court to define if Pro, Se's are bound by the court's rules the same as an educated attorney and are judges supposed to hold a pro, se to the same standards as educated attorneys and how are judges supposed to treat pro, se's.

Appellant therefore has met the United States Supreme Court's criteria for Judge Russell to receiving immunity and asks this court to reverse the trial court and sent the case back and let discovery begins and a trial take place.

Respectfully submitted
Edward H. Flint Pro, Se

**** The Court of Appeals order starts here***

UNITED STATES COURT OF APPEALS
FOR THE SIXTH CIRCUIT

NO. 11-5726

EDWARD H. FLINT,   Plaintiff-Appellant

v.

Thomas B. Russell   Defendant-Appellee

On Appeal from the United States District
Court for the Western District of Kentucky

FILED October 18, 2011

ORDER

Before: KEITH, GUY, and Gibbons, Circuit Judges.

Edward H. Flint, a Kentucky resident proceeding pro se, appeals from a district court order dismissing his civil complaint. This case has been referred to a panel of the court pursuant to Rule 34(j) (1), rules of the Sixth Circuit. Upon examination, this panel unanimously agrees that oral argument is not needed. Fed. R. App. P. 34(a)

Seeking monetary and equitable relief, Flint sued United States District Court Judge Thomas B. Russell, claiming that Judge Russell: a) violated his Fourteenth Amendment due process rights by denying him a fair trial in a 2007 lawsuit against Target Corporation (Target); b) violated court rules to ensure that the lawsuit against Target was assigned to him; c) exhibited bias against Flint, as a pro se litigant and made rulings to ensure that Target would prevail in the lawsuit; d) prevented Flint from obtaining discovery. The district court sua spone dismissed the complaint pursuant to Apple v. Glenn 183 F 3D 477 (6ᵗʰ Cir, 1999), concluding that Flint's claim was devoid of merit because Judge Russell was entitled to absolute immunity from suit.

On appeal, Flint argues that Judge Russell is not entitled to judicial immunity because his actions during the lawsuit against Target did not constitute normal judicial functions. He maintains that Judge Russell violated his right to due process and exhibited bias against Flint bases on his age and status as a pro se litigant. He also argues that Judge Russell is not entitled to immunity because he failed to rule on approximately forty-seven of Flint's motions, including a motion to amend his complaint to add additional defendants. Flint maintains that Judge Russell failure to rule on these motions cannot be equated with a "judicial act" because the judge took no action at all. He also maintains that, as a pro se litigant, he should not be held to the same pleading standard as an attorney.

We review de novo a district court's sua spone dismissal of a complaint. See Apple, 183 F 3d at 480 (dismissal pursuant to Federal Rule of Civil Procedure 12 (b) (1). A district court may dismiss a complaint for lack of subject matter jurisdiction if the purported claims are "so attenuated and unsubstantial as to be absolutely devoid of merit." Hagans v. Lavine, U.S.. 528, 526 (1074). A fee-paid complaint may be dismissed by the district court sua sponte for lack of subject matter jurisdiction where it is completely implausible or frivolous. Apple, 183 F. 3d at 479. such a dismissal is appropriate in only the rarest of circumstances where…the complaint is deemed totally implausible." *Id* at 480. The pleadings of a pro se litigants are liberally construed and held to a less stringent standard that those drafted by attorneys. Martin v. Overton, 391 F.3d 710, 712 (6ᵗʰ Cir. 2004) (citing Haines v. Kerner, 404 U.S. 519, 520-21 (1972). Nonetheless, where a complaint is "totally implausible, attenuated, unsubstantial, frivolous, devoid of merit, or no longer open to discussion." The district court need not afford the plaintiff an opportunity to amend the complaint, especially where the district court has determined that it lacks a subject matter jurisdiction over the action. Apple, 183 F. 3d at 479 (citing Hagans, 415 U.S. at 536-37.

The district court properly concluded that Judge Russell is entitled to absolute judicial immunity. "Absolute judicial attaches only to actions undertaken in a judicial capacity." Barnes v. Winchell, 105 F. 3d 1111, 1116 (6ᵗʰ Cir 1997). Whether an act is judicial depends on the nature and functions of the act, not the act itself." *Id.* (internal quotation marks omitted). "in examining the functions normally performed by a judge, courts have found that paradigmatic judicial acts are those involve resolving disputes between parties who have invoked the jurisdiction of a court." Id. (internal quotation marks omitted).

Contrary to Flint's arguments, neither of these circumstances exists here. Although Flint argues that Judge Russell did not act in a "normal" judicial capacity when he allegedly violated Flint's right to due process and exhibited bias against him, Flint's allegations clearly show that he sued Judge Russell based on the judge's alleged illegal actions in obtaining control over his lawsuit against Target and ruling in favor of Target. These actions clearly involved judicial decisions and were clearly made within the judge's jurisdiction.

Further, Flint argues that Judge Russell acted in bad faith and intentionally failed to rule on several of Flint's motions in order to prevent the truth about Target's illegal actions from coming to light. Even if Judge Russell erred by failing to rule on some of Flint's motions, a judge will not be deprived of immunity because the action he took was in error. See Stump. 435, U.S. at 356-57.

Finally, Flint argues that the district court improperly dismissed his complaint without affording him an opportunity to pursue discovery. However, he points to no potential discovery information that would have changed the outcome of this case in light of Judge Russell's entitlement of absolute judicial immunity.

Accordingly, we affirm the district court's order. Rule 34 (j) (2)(c), Rules of the Sixth Circuit.

ENTERED BY ORDER OF THE COURT

Leonard Green-Clerk

*** THE COURT OF APPEALS ORDER STOPPED HERE***

*** My Petition for Certiorari to the Supreme Court starts here ***

In The
Supreme Court of the United States

Edward H. Flint   Petitioner,

Versus

THOMAS B. RUSSELL   Respondent

PETITION FOR WRIT OF CERTIORARI

QUESTIONS PRESENTED

1- Does the United States Constitution grant judges immunity after the judges have violated court rules, cannons and laws of the United States, including a law that Congress made, regarding when a judge must recuse them self from a case.

2- Does a judge have the right to absolute immunity after he granted summary judgment to a company after Petitioner showed and proved that the company was selling illegal drugs to consumers?

3- Does a judge that refuses to rule on forty-seven (47) of a Petitioner's motions in a case, which violates Cannons, have the right to absolute immunity?

4- Does a judge that refuses to grant a Petitioner leave to amend their complaint, which would add two new defendants to the complaint; have the right to absolute immunity?

5- Does a Federal Judges have to abide by and honor 28 U.S. Code #455 which pertains to when a judge must disqualify themselves?

6- Does the constitution protect citizens from harmful illegal drugs regardless of who sells them?

7- Is Kentucky statute KRS 411.340 constitutional?

STATEMENT OF THE CASE

PROCEDURAL HISTORY

Flint would like to start by saying that he is an 81 year old Pro, Se and he deserves a review on his Petition the same as any attorney. This Court has refused to hear a number of cases by Petitioner even though he has showed this court how judges are violating laws and rules in Jefferson County, KY and this court has turned a dumb ear to his pleadings. Petitioner is concern about our country. This court is destroying America because they don't or can't control judges across America from violating rules and laws. They should know that if one judge can be corrupt and get by with it, others judge will know its ok to be corrupt also. Petitioner has filed a number of petitions for certiorari regarding immunity granted by this court in Stump v. Sparkman and numerous other cases feeding off of Stump v, Sparkman. Petitioner believes that the judges on this court either does not know how to correct this problem or don't have the will to do the right thing, to fix the America justice system to make it as fair for everyone as the constitution calls for.

This case involves a judge who had determined the outcome of a case before it had started. The case was assigned to Judge Russell who in returned assigned the case to a Magistrate judge. After the Magistrate judge issued an order, part of the order is as follows. "Target's representations to the court and to Mr. Flint cause the court concern. The statements imply, if not arguably state, that Target sent a

representative sample of the pills in its possession and used to fill Mr. Flint's prescription to Breckinridge for testing, that those pills were in fact tested, and that Mr. Flint was sent a copy of the test results pertaining to the specific pills that had been sent to Breckinridge by Target. The problem with these statements is that they seem to be misleading and appear to the court to be untrue. The only test results referenced by Target, either in its pleadings, or in open court, have been those contained in the CPC QC Report. That report, however, could not have been an analysis of the specific pills sent to Breckinridge by Target, as Target claims. Mr. Flint's prescription was not filled until December 2006, and he did not raise the issue of his alleged allergic reaction with Target, until after he had taken several of the pills. The CPC QC Report, however, pertains to an analysis of pills from a particular lot, which may indeed be the same lot of medication that was ultimately dispensed to Mr. Flint, but the analysis was performed in <u>September 2006</u>. Accordingly, the test results provided to Mr. Flint are not an analysis of the specific pills returned to Breckinridge by Target, and could not reasonably have been offered as such, but appear to be merely the results of a random lot sample performed pre-distribution by the manufacturer as part of its required FDA compliance efforts.

The court has accepted the representation of Target's counsel, as an officer of the court, that the CPC QC Report is the only laboratory analysis in Target's possession, custody, or control, and the court has no reason to doubt the veracity of this statement. That does not, however, address what seem to be Target's misleading statements regarding what the CPC QC Report actually represents. Although given ample opportunity by the court during its recent hearing, at which this issue and Mr. Flint's concerns about it were discussed at some length, Target's representative did nothing to clarify the matter. Target must do so now, within <u>ten </u>days of the date of entry of this order. Either Target sent specific pills to the manufacturer or distributor for testing and has the results of the qualitative analysis pertaining to those actual pills, or it does not."

After the order was issued, the Defendant Target asked for a hearing, which the Magistrate judge held. After the hearing with nothing new being added or said, the Magistrate judge vacated the order. It became clear at that time and on everything else involving the case thereafter, that Judge Russell had seized control of the case from behind the scene, for the entire case.

Petitioners will now copy the Complaint he filed.

Comes the Plaintiff Edward H. Flint acting as his own counsel against Defendant who is a judge in Federal Court Western District in Louisville, KY.

1. **Plaintiff, Edward H. Flint lives at**

2. **Defendant Thomas B. Russell is an individual who is a judge in Western District of Kentucky Federal Court.**

3. **Plaintiff filed a complaint in Jefferson Country KY Circuit Court against Target Corporation in October 2007.**

4. **Target asked that the case be moved to Federal Western District of Kentucky Court.**

5. **Judge Russell Defendant signed an order on December 11, 2007 moving the case to the Federal Court and the case was assigned to Judge Russell. The case was NO. 3:07-CV-600-R**

6. **Plaintiff alleges that Defendant Russell was bias against him in the case.**

7. **Plaintiff alleges that Defendant Russell actions harmed Plaintiff, physically.**

1. **Plaintiff alleges that Defendant Russell actions harmed Plaintiff mentally**

2. **Plaintiff alleges that Defendant Russell actions denied Plaintiff from receiving Due Process fair and honest trial under the 14th amendment to the constitution.**

3. **Plaintiff alleges that Defendant Russell took advantage of an old person.**

4. **Plaintiff alleges that Defendant Russell took advantage of a Pro, Se, non-educated in legal law person to get his way and easy control the case.**

5. **Plaintiff alleges that Defendant Russell should have bent over to help a Pro, Se person and by not doing so gave the advantage to Plaintiff's opponent Target.**

6. **Plaintiff alleges that Defendant Russell duty was to find the truth between the parties and let a jury determine who was right and who was wrong.**

7. **Plaintiff alleges that Defendant Russell liked Plaintiff being pro, se and in-experience, which made Judge Russell, fell great in side and feel like a big man.**

8. **Plaintiff alleges that Defendant Russell denied Plaintiff his civil rights in the case**

9. Plaintiff alleges that Defendant Russell was prejudice against Plaintiff in his rulings.

10. Plaintiff alleges that Defendant Russell did not conduct himself the way a judge should.

11. Plaintiff alleges that Defendant Russell has violated the court of conduct rules that all judges must adhere to.

12. Plaintiff alleges that Defendant Russell violated the courts rules and laws of ethics in his handling of the case against Plaintiff.

13. Plaintiff alleges Defendant Russell made up rulings that fit his own wants, thereby pulling the justice system down from being fair and honest.

14. Plaintiff alleges that Defendant Russell in his actions took advantage of Plaintiff's inexperience and did not judge by Cannons conduct ethics.

15. Plaintiff alleges that Defendant Russell violated court rules to make sure he was in control of the case and therefore he would control the court's actions against Plaintiff.

16. Plaintiff alleges that Defendant Russell wanted Target to win the case and took actions to assure that it happened.

17. Plaintiff alleges that Defendant Russell violated courts rules and laws to keep Plaintiff from receiving discoveries due him by the courts rules.

18. Plaintiff alleges that Judge Russell was on Target side from the beginning of the case and his actions against Plaintiff were done with intent to make sure Target won the case, which thereby harmed Plaintiff.

19. Plaintiff alleges that Defendant Russell help Target sell illegal drugs.

20. Plaintiff alleges that Defendant Russell was told and knew that illegal drugs was being produced and sold in America and took no actions to stop it or to notify the authorities.

21. Plaintiff alleges that Defendant Russell mislead the Federal Court of Appeals with his rulings and writings.

22. Plaintiff alleges that Defendant Russell was on the take from Target.

23. Plaintiff alleges that Defendant Russell feed his ego rather than search for the truth which was his duty to his office.

24. **Plaintiff alleges that Defendant Russell from the beginning knew the outcome that he wanted and he bent and violated rules and laws to do it, regardless of the truth.**

25. **Plaintiff alleges that Defendant Russell knew how he was going to rule in the case before the case was started in discovery and he knew his actions would harm Plaintiff.**

26. **Plaintiff alleges that Defendant Russell by his actions stopped Plaintiff from receiving evidence that Plaintiff was entitled to by court Rules.**

27. **Plaintiff alleges that Defendant Russell refused to conduct himself to the oath he took to this country.**

28. **Plaintiff alleges that Defendant Russell influenced others to harm Plaintiff.**

29. **Plaintiff alleges that Defendant Russell ordered others to do his deeds even though he knew the deeds where wrong and violated court rules and laws.**

30. **Plaintiff alleges that Defendant Russell solicited others to help him pull off his scheme to harm Plaintiff or to protect Target.**

31. **Plaintiff alleges that Defendant Russell at no time had intentions of giving Plaintiff a fair trial.**

32. **Plaintiff alleges that Defendant Russell did not care about illegal drugs being given to customers and did nothing to check to see if they were sold by Target and two other companies and took no actions to stop the illegal actions, even though he knew the drugs was illegal.**

33. **Plaintiff alleges that Defendant Russell had no feeling for anyone, but Target and himself in this case.**

34. **Plaintiff alleges that Defendant Russell knew he violated court rules by his actions and did nothing to correct his mistakes.**

35. **Plaintiff alleges that Defendant Russell was being paid off by Target in order to protect Targets reputation with the public and to keep the public consumers from knowing that Target was selling illegal drugs to customers.**

36. **Plaintiff alleges that Defendant Russell was not concerned about Plaintiff's rights and ignored facts that he should have investigated, by Federal agencies.**

37. **Plaintiff alleges that Defendant Russell actions in this case made a mockery out of the United States of America's court system.**

45- sPlaintiff will ask this court to amend the complaint if other allegations appear or other defendants appear.

The trial court and the Court of Appeals dismissed the case under Apple v. Glenn, 183 F. 3d at 479 stating a fee-paid complaint may be dismissed by the district court sua sponte for lack of subject matter jurisdiction where it is completely implausible or frivolous. The courts stated such a dismissal is appropriate in only the rarest of circumstances where…the complaint is deemed totally implausible. No judge can look at Petitioner's complaint and say that it is implausible or frivolous or devoid of merit.

By 28 U.S.C. #455 Judge Russell should have disqualify himself. In *Liljeberg* v. *Health Services Acquisition Corp., 486 U.S. 847, 860 n.8 (1988)* **The Supreme Court noted that the purpose of section 455(a) is to promote public confidence in the integrity of the judicial process, the Court observed that such confidence "does not depend upon whether or not the judge actually knew of facts creating an appearance of impropriety, so long as the public might reasonably believe that he or she knew."**

The Supreme Court has never asked Congress to delete the law and there can be no question that in *Liljeberg* v. *Health Services Acquisition Corp.* the Supreme Court studied the law thoroughly and concluded that the integrity of the court system was the most important thing of all, if this country was going to have a truly fair and honest justice system. The founders of our country came and established this court for three reasons, a fair and honest justice system, Freedom of speech and freedom to worship. This court should do everything possible to their last breath to see that these three principals live forever.

This case shows how terrible the Stump v. Sparkman decision was and what a horrifying experiment it turned out to be.

Judge Russell should have recused himself because his actions showed he was bias against Flint and bias for Target.

Judge Russell refused to grant leave to Flint to amend his complaint. Flint wanted to add two companies who were the Manufacturer and the Distributor.

Petitioner amended complaint that Judge Russell refused to accept is as follows.

This is the amended complaint that was attached to the leave motion above.

UNITED STATES DISTRICT COURT
WESTERN DISTRICT OF KENTUCKY
LOUISVILLE DIVISON

CASE NO 3:07CV600-R

EDWARD H. FLINT   PLAINTIFF

VS

TARGET CORPORATION   DEFENDANTS

BRECKENRIDGE PHARMACEUTICAL
1141 S. Rogers Circle, Suite 3
Boca Raton, FL 33487

CONTRACT PHARMACAL
135 Adams Avenue
Hauppauge NY 11788

AMENDED COMPLAINT JOINING TWO OTHER DEFENDANTS AND AMENDING THE ORIGINAL COMPLAINT

Comes the Plaintiff, Edward H. Flint Pro, Se amending his original complaint and joining two (2) other Defendants to the complaint:

1- Plaintiff is a resident of Louisville, Jefferson County, Kentucky, and resides therein at

2- On or about November 15, 2006 Plaintiff was operated on for prostate cancer, On November 16, 2006 plaintiff was given a prescription by his doctor, with 2 additional refills for a drug named Pyridium (Phenazopyridine). Plaintiff had the prescription filled later the same day at a Target Store located at 4174 Westport Road in Louisville, Kentucky and was directed to take three (3) pills per day. Plaintiff took the prescription as directed and with no problem.

3- On November 26, 2006 Plaintiff had the prescription refilled at the same store, again with no problems.

4- On December 6, 2006 plaintiff had the same prescription refilled again. The pills given him December 6, 2006 were a different shape and size. The pills purchased on December caused the Plaintiff to break out with red spots (hives) that itched and caused his mouth to draw up inside with small bumps or ridges, causing his tongue to go numb and Plaintiff stopped tasting food, and developed other problems.

5- After taking 8 of the pills purchased on December 6, 2007 Plaintiff quit taking the pills, and called his doctor, who confirmed not taking them.

6- On December 11, 2006 the plaintiff went to the Target store where the pills was purchased and spoke with the pharmacist Mr. Rob Warford, who was the pharmacy manager, about his problems from the pills. Plaintiff was told by Mr. Warford that he was not given the wrong medicine, but the pills were from a different company. Mr. Warford said all he could do for the Plaintiff was refund his cost of the pills. After Plaintiff complained further, Mr. Warford stated that the problem should go away in several days after Plaintiff stopped taking the pills. Rob the manager stated, Plaintiff should call Defendant's customer services if the problem didn't start to clear up in a couple of days. Plaintiff asked for the phone number and Mr. Warford gave him a card with a customer service number.

7- Before calling Target's customer service, Plaintiff waited a few days, as Mr. Warford suggested, and after getting no relief, Plaintiff called the Target customer service phone number on December 20, 2006 and told the person answering the phone, what happen with the drug. The person took the complaint, asking questions about what transpired, and said they would put the complaint into the computer and send it to the right department, and someone from that department would call Plaintiff in four (4) days.

8- The Plaintiff waited and after not hearing from anyone at Target, called the customer service phone number again on January 10, 2007. The person answering Plaintiff's call this time told the Plaintiff that his complaint from December 20, 2006 was in the computer, but she would put it in again. Plaintiff asked if there was someone else he could talk with about his problem. The person then gave Plaintiff a phone number saying it was the department who was responsible for this type of complaint.

9- Plaintiff called the number of the responsible department and a person by the name of Jenny answered the phone, Jenny was pleasant and very concerned. Jenny stated she would make sure the complaint was put in the computer again and said the person who would handle this complaint in the future was a person named Cindy. Jenny went to fine find Cindy at that time. Jenny could not find Cindy. Jenny stated she would have Cindy call the Plaintiff the next morning. The next morning when Cindy did not call Plaintiff, the Plaintiff called Cindy's number, her voice mail answered the phone, and Plaintiff left word for her to call, stating it was urgent. At 3:00P.M. Cindy called the Plaintiff and was very rude. Plaintiff then asked to speak with Cindy's boss. She said he was in a meeting and she would give him a message and Plaintiff's phone number.

10- A Mr. Wright returned the call about two (2) hours later, stating he was Cindy's boss. The Plaintiff told Mr. Wright the problem he was having. Mr. Wright said he would have another person call. The next day a Mr. Paul Wirkkala called Plaintiff and stated he was now handling the case. Mr. Wirkkala told Plaintiff that Target could not do anything about this problem, Target was not responsible for the pills content, and that they only sold the pills that Plaintiff should contact the manufacture of the pills for relief. Plaintiff communicated with Mr. Wirkkala about this matter, a number of times after that conversation, by both phone and letters, attempting to find the answer to who the manufacture was and what was in the pills that made him lose his taste and caused his injury.

11- Target refused to help Plaintiff find the solution to his injury and put the burden on the Plaintiff to find the solution. Plaintiff was told by Target that the manufacture was responsible, not Target.

12- Plaintiff alleges that he had expected to receive the same medication on December 6, 2006 as he received on November 16, 2006 and November 26, 2006 and Target failed to deliver the same medication.

13- Plaintiff alleges that Target failed to live by its own policy by not notifying Plaintiff that it changed suppliers, regarding the pills Plaintiff received pills on December 6, 2006. The pills and type of drug dispended to Plaintiff on December 6, 2006 were from a different manufacture, than the first two fills of pills he received on November 16, 2006 and November 26, 2006. Target has a written policy that states, when it dispenses subsequent refills of prescriptions to quest that are manufactured by a different company than prior fills, Target notifies quests of the change by placing a green sticker on the bottle that states "This is the same medication you have been getting. Color, size or shape may appear different". Target did not place a green sticker on the bottle that contained the pills Plaintiff was given on December 6, 2006. The medication was not the same as in the first two fills.

14- Plaintiff alleges that with the pills Target dispensed to Plaintiff on December 6, 2007, Target also gave Plaintiff a "Patient Card," which stated the pills side effects could be Headaches and Belly Pain. The Patient Card never notified Plaintiff that the pills would cause hives. The dispended pills Plaintiff received on December 6, 2006 caused him to break out with hives over his body including his lips, tongue and mouth. The hives caused Plaintiff to lose his taste and other injuries to his body.

15- Plaintiff alleges that the thirty (30) pills he received on December 6, 2006 which contained one (1) active ingredient and fifteen (15) in-active ingredients, were defective. The pills compositions were different in types of materials, in weight of pill and in size of pill than the pills were from the two fills Plaintiff had received in November, 2006.

16- Plaintiff contents that Defendants cannot shrug off the blame for defective drugs and put the blame on Plaintiff. It is clear that the system Target has set up on obtaining drugs has faults. Plaintiff did not and could not control the quality of drugs Target receives.

17- Plaintiff has learned that the pills that injured him was manufactured by Contract Pharmacal, who the sold the pills to Breckenridge Pharmaceutical, who in turn sold them to McKesson Corporation, who then sold them to Target.

18- Plaintiff alleges that over twenty-five percent of the pills sold to him on December 6, 2006 were out of the Manufacture's Specification tolerance limit in weight; and these pills should have been rejected and never sold to any customers.

19- Plaintiff alleges that Target sent two pills from the batch that Plaintiff's pills came from, to Breckenridge to be tested and Defendants refuses to give Plaintiff the test results.

20- Plaintiff alleges that one or more Defendants were neglectful in their responsibility to Plaintiff.

21- Plaintiff alleges that one or more of the Defendants had no consideration for the health of customers.

22- Plaintiff alleges one or more Defendants did not test the complete finished pills after the pills were manufactured, thereby ignoring safety for consumers, before selling to Plaintiff.

23- Plaintiff alleges that one or more Defendants were more concern about their own profits than about customer's health.

24- Plaintiff alleges that one or more of the Defendants had no control over the drugs before they were sold to Plaintiff.

25- Plaintiff alleges that one or more of the Defendants sold drugs to Plaintiff that they didn't know was safe and thereby injuring Plaintiff.

26- Plaintiff alleges that one or more of the Defendants at no time had control and never attempted to have control over the quality of the pills that was sold to Plaintiff. One or more of the Defendants never had an agreement with any supplier that the pills shipped would be certified safe for human consumers. One or more Defendants had failed to establish a safety program regarding drugs consumed by humans purchased from them.

27- Plaintiff alleges that one or more of the Defendants has set up a supply system, starting at purchasing; all the way through to delivery to consumers, without any consideration for consumer's safety or any system that guarantees consumer's drug safety.

28- Plaintiff alleges that one or more of the Defendants refused to hold their supplier responsible to identify the ingredient in the pill which caused plaintiff's problems.

29- Plaintiff alleges that one or more of the Defendants has refused to attempt to find a solution to clear up the Plaintiff's health problems, except to give Plaintiff at his request, some information about who manufactured the pills in question, and the active and in-active materials contained in the pills.

30- Plaintiff alleges that one or more Defendants had a Fiduciary Duty and Responsibility to consumers and failed to perform that Duty and Responsibility before selling the flawed pills that injured Plaintiff.

31- Plaintiff alleges one or more of the Defendants sold or dispensed drugs to Plaintiff over which they had no control over at any time and their lack of control injured Plaintiff.

32- Plaintiff alleges that one or more Defendants pushed Plaintiff's health to the side and refused to find the source of what caused Plaintiff's injury.

33- Plaintiff alleges that one or more Defendants had never attempted to have their suppliers certify the in-active materials in their prescriptions drugs as being safe for customers.

34- Plaintiff alleges that one or more Defendants failed to take Plaintiff injury and complaint serious.

35- Target failed to write up Plaintiff's injury and complaint as an incidence report, required by their own policies.

36- Plaintiff alleges that after he warned one or more of the Defendants they refused to take serious that other customers could be affected, by the pills, which harmed the Plaintiff.

37- Plaintiff alleges that one or more of the Defendants knew that when applying for the right to do business in Kentucky, they took on the responsibility to supply safe drugs to customers, they also knew they would have to take all steps to correct any harm done to their customers caused by their produces and failed to live to this responsibility.

38- Plaintiff alleges that one or more of the Defendants broke the trust that the State of Kentucky granted them by granting them the right to do business in Kentucky. Target when applying for the right to do business in Kentucky, knew that with the right, there was a trust to sell safe products to consumers.

39- Plaintiff alleges that when one or more Defendants applied for and received the right to do business in the State of Kentucky; they took on the responsibility and duty to deliver safe drugs to all Kentucky citizens. If the burden of such Responsibility and Duty was too heavy for Defendants to carry, Defendants should not have applied for or accepted the right to sell drugs in Kentucky.

40- Plaintiff alleges that one or more Defendants had a duty to customers to completely investigate serious health complaints.

41- Plaintiff alleges that Defendants sold Plaintiff pills that were not FDA approved and that FDA unapproved pills injured him.

42- Plaintiff alleges that the Defendants failed to apply to the FDA for approval to produce and sell the drugs that injured Plaintiff.

43- Plaintiff alleges that a trust exists between Doctor, Patient, Pharmacies, and that trust was breached when Plaintiff was sold flawed pills. One or more Defendants had the responsibility to assure the pills were safe.

44- Plaintiff alleges one or more of the Defendants failed to run test on all ingredients that were contained in the pills in question, attempting to find out if foreign materials or material overage of each ingredient was in the pills.

45- Plaintiff alleges that one or more of the Defendants attempted to diagnose Plaintiff's injury without seeing him and thereby was practicing medicine and ignoring Plaintiff's injury.

46- Plaintiff alleges that one or more of the Defendants discussed and put in writing to others, information about Plaintiff's health prior to his injury from the pills.

47- Plaintiff alleges that one or more of the Defendants has tampered with documents in this case to hide true discoveries, from Plaintiff.

48- Plaintiff alleges one or more of the Defendants has refused to demand that Breckenridge produce the test results, which Breckenridge stated they ran on the two pills, which had been sent to them by the Target store in Louisville. The two pills sent were from the same container as the pills that injured Plaintiff came from.

49- Plaintiff contends that Defendants may have broken other laws or regulations that have not come forward as of this time, that may before or during trial.

WHEREFORE, the Plaintiff demands the following relief

1- A trial by jury

2- If one or more of the Defendant is found guilty of any allegation in this complaint, or found guilty of neglect on any other issue that was due to Plaintiff, or broke any law or regulation that may come forward during trial, then Plaintiff demands Defendant be held accountable by the demands in the following paragraphs.

3- Defendants is ordered to use all efforts possible and to pay all cost necessary, to find the cause and cure for Plaintiff's health problems cause by the pills sold to Plaintiff on December 6, 2006

4- Plaintiff is award financial damages as determined by a jury, both compensatory and punitive damages.

5- Plaintiff also demands that this court orders the Defendants to develop a policy that states, "all in-active materials in prescription drugs that they sell, are certified to contain no harmful materials" and those Defendants with retail outlets, hang a sign it their stores stating the policy.

6- For all cost of this suit.

7- For any other relief to which said plaintiff may appear entitled.

Respectfully submitted
Edward H. Flint Pro, Se

REASONS FOR GRANTING THE WRIT

1- Congress knew what they were doing when they passed U.S. Code 28 #455 and the Supreme Court in 1988 knew how important it was to have a fair unbiased judge handling every case. This court should uphold the law.

2- This country has major problems and they will continue to grow unless this court takes the time to fixes the justice system. The Supreme Court in Stump v. Sparkman stated "we could try this." They were saying that something needed to be done to speed up a growing system, something that our forefathers didn't confront in the constitution. The experiment since 1978 has grown into a monster. The innocence gets hurt. Someone has to lead this country out of its problems and as long as this court fights to keep it the way it is, the public will do just what the court does, they will fight for their beliefs instead of doing what is right for America. Each side in America is fighting for their belief because the Supreme Court does it and get by with it. This is destroying America

3- No honest open minded judge can say that Judge Russell has not violated U. S. Code 28 #455.

4- This court can turn its head and ignore this case and not grant certiorari, but this court knows that what Judge Russell did was wrong and not the way our forefather wanted justice to be, for the people and this court knows that it is happening in every court in America, every day. This court keeps turning its head hoping it will go away, but it won't it will get worse. Does getting your way and showing the other side you have power, and can stop almost anything before it, lead America? Will it leave you a good legacy? The way that judges are now treating parties that is before it, is no different than raping a person. Judges have become rapist.

5- The lack of actions by this court in this case will tell America that this court doesn't really care about justice; all this court really cares about is their selfish selves and protecting judges.

6- Justice, can only be assured, by judges obeying the laws and principle of our forefathers.

7- Kentucky law KRS 411.340 is unconstitional.

CONCLUSION

1- This court knows that Judge Russell was wrong and this is not what, the United States Constitution says.

2- This Court knows what 28 U.S.C. #455 means and what it was intended to do.

3- This court knows that Stump v. Sparkman is a failed experiment and must be changed.

4- This court knows that if companies continue making and selling bad produces and getting by with it, the public won't stand for it.

5- This Court knows Petitioner has a good complaint and the trial court should never have dismissed his case against Judge Russell.

6- This court should know that the movements in this country like Occupy Wall Street are only the beginning. Those people know there something wrong in this country they just don't know what the problems are, that they are protesting about, but they don't want to continue living it, like it is now, but any smart judge should know that they want only what our forefathers came for, a fair and honest justice system, freedom of speech and freedom of religion. Only by everyone having these will this country survive.

7- This court knows what is being done by judges in district courts and appeals courts. Judges don't care about justice they only care about getting their way. They know they are protected for life; however this court's ruling in years gone by has made it to where judges don't even think about justice. Is this the type of justice you want to leave for your family's future?

8- This court can see that the reason given for dismissal in this case is wrong, that Petitioner complaint did fall into the Apple v. Glenn case, given by the trial court as for a reason to dismiss.

9- Petitioner knows that some members on this court have a high opinion of themselves as Scholars and hopefully these scholars will recognize that judges were never given immunity by the constitution. Petitioner hopes and prays that five (5) of judges do care about justice and will vote to grant certiorari.

10- This court has an opportunity to correct the American Justice system from the harm done by Stump v. Sparkman in 1978, by holding judges responsible for violating laws and rules of the court. If this court takes away the immunity clause for violations of court rules and laws, ninety (90%) percentages of the problems of the court system would go away. The fathers of our country did not put judges on a higher plateau than the people, but the Supreme Court did, by making dictators out of the judges and America is being destroyed.

11- This Courts duty is to protect the all citizens of this country and not just judges, by interpreting the Constitution correctly and this court cannot find anywhere in the constitution where judges are to have immunity. This court's ruling in Stump v. Sparkman is a direct assault on the citizen of this country and this court should find a way to protect and assure that each and every citizen receives a fair and honest trial, regardless of how small the complaint or how large a company is. This court should not make laws, but interpret how justice is to protect the citizens of this county and how justice is to be run as defined by the constitution. The court system has had more to do with the unrest that is taking place in America than all of other elements combined.

12- The Judges in the Western District of Kentucky has become dictator not judges. Framers of the constitution did everything in their power to keep this type of justice from happening in America. The Mayflower people came to get away from Kings and Dictators and this court must use every muscle in it brain to keep this from happening in America, Stump v. Sparkman is a failed experiment that must be changed. This court should throw out the Stump v. Sparkman ruling and take away immunity for all judges that do not adhere to Cannons Law, Court Rules and statue laws. The Constitution does not grant immunity to judges.

13- Stump v. Sparkman was a self-serving law created by a court that was too concerned about their own ego and friends, to make true judgment verdicts. A judge on every decision they make, must choose between ego and truth. A judge must choose ego or justice in every case before it. Jesus chose justice and didn't have an ego. In fact Jesus didn't hate but a few things, however he didn't like people who put themselves above right and wrong. Where does each of you fit in this subject?

14- Kentucky, KRS 411.340 is unconstitional.

Although Petitioner knows that some members of this court would destroy America rather that give in to their ego and pride, Petitioner prays that at least five (5) member of this court cares about true and fair justice and will grant certiorari and review this case. Petitioner also asks this court to interpret the constitution regarding immunity for judges and put America back the way it was once.

This court's members should crave for and leave an honest and fair court system for their families and for America.

Respectfully submitted,
S/ Edward H. Flint, Pro, Se.

The Supreme Court refused to review the case

Judge Russell could not afford to let me add the two companies, because if I had been allowed to file the Amend complaint, then Judge Russell could not have let Target go free, without a trial. Judge Russell granted summary judgment based on a Kentucky law that says a party must sue the manufacturer or distributor and not the place where you buy it.

Judge Russell hung his so called decision on Kentucky law KRS 411.340 When wholesaler, distributor or retailer to be held liable. The Kentucky law below states

"In any product liability action, if the manufacturer is identified and subject to the jurisdiction of the court, a wholesaler, distributor, or retailer who distributes or sells a product, upon his showing by a preponderance of the evidence that said product was sold by him in its original manufactured condition or package, or in the same condition such product was in when received by said wholesaler, distributor or retailer, shall not be liable to the plaintiff for damages arising solely from the distribution or sale of such product, unless such wholesaler, distributor or retailer, breached an express warranty or knew or should have known at the

time of distribution or sale of such product that the product was in a defective condition, unreasonably dangerous to the user or consumer. "

Judge Russell not only refused to let Flint amend his complaint adding the manufacturer and distributor, but he squash the subpoena for a deposition served on the President of Target Corporation. Judge Russell refused to compel on three court served subpoenas for depositions. The three was employees of the Manufacturer and distributor, after they failed to appear. Flint filed a motion to compel and Judge Russell refuse to sign an order to compel on them.

Petitioner Flint had other allegations that Target was responsible for regardless of the so called Kentucky law the judge used. Target, at least, should have been tried by a jury on Para's 11-12-13-14-15-18-41 of Petitioner's complaint.

Judge Russell had his mind made up from the beginning about who was going to win the case. Judge Russell was bias for Target. Judge Russell and the Court of Appeals and the Supreme Court approved of Target selling illegal drugs.

CHAPTER 15

LAWSUIT FLINT V. HEWLETT PACKARD COMPANY

UNITED STATES DISTRICT COURT
WESTERN DISTRICT OF KENTUCKY
LOUISVILLE DIVISON

CASE NO 3:10-CV-597-S

**** Next is the amended Complaint that I tried to file, Every person by court rules is allowed to amend their original complaint one time, with no questions, but this court refused to allow me to file this amended complaint****

EDWARD H. FLINT   PLAINTIFF

VS

AMENDED COMPLAINT AND JOINING
OFFICE DEPOT TO LAWSUIT

HEWLETT-PACKARD COMPANY   DEFENDANTS

OFFICE DEPOT
6600 North Military Trail
Boca Raton FL 33496

AMENDED COMPLAINT

Comes now the Plaintiff, Edward H. Flint Pro, Se acting as his own counsel, moving the court for leave to amend his original complaint, which joins Office Depot as a Defendant along with Hewlett-Packard Company in a complaint against them, for selling Plaintiff a defective 4 in 1 printer product with a so called warranty and not fixing the printer and for creating a monopoly, regarding ink cartridges without informing potential customers such as Plaintiff of such monopoly and for this cause of action and other causes, Plaintiff states as follows:

1- Plaintiff Edward H. Flint lives at 5800 Coach Gate Wynde #293, Louisville, KY 40207 and is eighty (80) years old and has a hearing problem.

2- Hewlett-Packard (HP) is a company in Palo Alto California that produces and sells printing equipment for use with computes or standing by them self, for coping documents, coping pictures, sending faxes and scanning documents into a computer. Hewlett-Packard is one of the world's largest producers of computers and printers. Hewlett Packard also sells printers to various companies like Office Depot for resell to consumers

3- Office Depot is a company in Boca Raton Florida that buys printers from Hewlett Packard and other manufacturers and resells them to consumers.

4- Plaintiff purchased` a HP Office Jet model J4580 four in one printer from Office Depot in good faith, based on advertised facts that the printer had been reengineered from past models and tested and promoted as a great printer and Plaintiff wouldn't have any problems with the equipment when used for its 4 in 1 objective. The printer came with a warranty that Defendants implied that if the printer didn't work, Defendants as promised would correct any faults, so it would perform as promised. Therefore Plaintiff alleges that Defendants put on the market a product that was not properly designed and had not been proven to operate the way consumers was led to believe it would. Office Depot advertised in its stores and by word of mouth from employees at their store that the model printer was an upgrade from the previous HP 4 in 1 printer. Hewlett Packard also advertised on their web site that the printer would perform better and faster that their prior model.

5- Plaintiff alleges that Defendants rushed the printer into production to be sold, before it was proven to work correctly and efficiency, as advertise, because they wanted the sales from the ink cartridges that the printer used. Defendant makes more money on the ink cartridges that on the printers themselves and the sale of ink was their aim and they didn't care how much trouble they put consumers through. They knew the printer was not ready to be sold and they knew the printer had a lot of flaws in it, when they released the printer for sale.

6- Plaintiff alleges that Defendants wasn't concern about the hardship caused to consumers, only about profits from the ink. They intentionally made the printer so it would not use ink from another manufacture or a refill of their own cartridges or use their ink cartridges after a certain time frame, which forced a consumer to buy their ink cartridges and thereby created a monopoly on the ink cartridges for Defendants printers. They created this monopoly, but defendants didn't tell or warn the customers the facts before or doing the sales, that the printer would only use HP ink cartridges and had variation from their past 4 in 1 printers.

7- Plaintiff alleges that Defendants had so many problems with the printer they finally had to discontinue producing it. Defendants created a monopoly by designing their printers, so it will only use Defendants ink cartridges, and they do not warn or tell potential consumers of this fact before or when the consumer buys the printer.

8- Plaintiff alleges that Defendant's actions and printer caused Plaintiff harm and distress.

9- Plaintiff alleges that Defendant's actions injured Plaintiff both mentally and physically.

10- Plaintiff alleges that Defendant's equipment failed to perform as promised and as warranted and Defendants couldn't or wouldn't fix it.

11- Plaintiff alleges that Defendants uses customers instead of their own salaried personal to fix and correct problems with their equipment, which is not what defendant says in their warranties.

12- Plaintiff alleges that Defendants uses old people, or tech ignorant people and or young people, who are not capable of fixing HP printers, but who have no choice but to try and fix their printer in order to have a printer and consumers aren't told of these fact before or when purchasing printers and this deed is time consuming and nerve wrecking to consumers This is like buying a new car and when something doesn't work the car dealer reads instructions over the phone to the car's owner and the owner does the work.

13- Plaintiff alleges that Defendants doesn't take in to account the fact that some consumers have handicaps and Defendants require these people to fix the problems on bad products that's under warranty, that Hewlett-Packard manufactures and sells.

14- Plaintiff alleges that Hewlett-Packard post on their web site, corporate objectives and shared values to help sell the image of Hewlett-Packard and to help sell their products. Hewlett-Packard ignores these objectives and values when it comes to costing the company money and they fail to live by the objectives and shared values when it comes to customers.

15- Plaintiff alleges that Hewlett-Packard uses misleading wording in their sales tactics regarding warranties.

16- Plaintiff alleges that Defendants failed to perform their ethical responsibility to the Plaintiff and to the general public who buys their equipment.

17- Plaintiff alleges that Defendants only cares about making a profit and has no feelings for its customers, once it gets the customer's money.

18- Plaintiff alleges that after customers purchase equipment from them, Defendants intentionally has a phone system that only confuses customers who needs repairs to their equipment; however the Defendants know how to make it easy and simple to buy printers from them, but not to repair them.

19- Plaintiff alleges that Defendants conspires within their company against consumers who has purchased equipment from them, by not living up to their promises and then passing the problem from person to person.

20- Plaintiff alleges that Defendants routes technical problems to technicians in the country of India or some other foreign country and uses technicians that speaks broken English, some speak very bad broken English, which makes it difficult for English speaking customers to understand. The technician and consumers spend hours just trying to commutate with each other, when attempting to get the customer's equipment fixed, without success at times. This action is harmful to consumers.

21- Plaintiff alleges that Defendants should have put their customer first, even before other profits, after they have received the consumer's money. Defendants owe their customers technicians who speak clear English. Even if Hewlett-Packard goes to another country to save money on hiring technician, they still had a duty to their customers to hire clear English speaking technicians.

22- Plaintiff alleges that Defendants actions cause's consumers to loose valuable time and such actions are frustrating, costly and harmful to customer's nerves.

23- Plaintiff alleges that on September 9, 2010 after the words "tri-color ink cartridge is incomparable" kept scrolling on his printer. A technician, who is employed by Defendants, stated that he could not make the equipment work and the technician turned Plaintiff over to his supervisor. The supervisor told Plaintiff that another person who is employed by Defendants would call Plaintiff and that person would ship a new printer to Plaintiff. Plaintiff could choose a new printer from any printer Defendants, sells. The supervisor employee stated the person would call Plaintiff on Friday September 10, 2010.

24- Plaintiff alleges that no one called Plaintiff on that Friday and Plaintiff after not receiving a phone call from anyone, started Saturday calling technicians in India to find out why the person hadn't called about shipping a new printer, with no luck.

25- Plaintiff alleges that after making a number of phone calls to various other employees of Defendants, on Monday September 13, 2010, Plaintiff was finally put on the line with a person named Diana who claimed to be a case manager. After going through the story with Diana, she stated that the model printer Plaintiff has, has been discontinued, but she would sell Plaintiff a newer model printer for $119.00. Plaintiff told case manager Diana 4 or 5 times what he had been promised by the Supervisor and Diana said the supervisor didn't have the authority to say those things to Plaintiff and Plaintiff needed to buy a printer..

26- Plaintiff alleges that Defendants sold a printer that was so poorly made, that its own ink cartridges wouldn't work in their own printer, and all at the expense of the consumers. Defendants hid this fact from the consumers, rather than recall all of the printers.

27- Plaintiff alleges that Defendants has a program within their company that rewards employees by either paying bonuses or the employees are told what they have to do to keep their job or to obtain promotions to better jobs, all which are based on profits their unit earns. The employees are to convict the customers to do things that will enhance Defendants profit line and the customers has to bear the blunt of the actions taken by the employees.

28- Plaintiff alleges that Defendants actions created mental and physical harm to Plaintiff, over the greed of profit for Defendants.

29- Plaintiff alleges the ink cartridge problem happens on a regular bases in Defendants printers and Defendants failed to notify customers of the problems the printers are having and Defendants hid the truth from buyers, both old and new buyers, even when their technicians knew what the problems was.

30- Plaintiff alleges that he had a right to know before purchasing the printer that only Defendants ink cartridges would work in the printer. Defendants hid the fact from him. Even when the technicians knew Plaintiff's problem; he would not tell Plaintiff the truth. The technician gave Plaintiff's problem to his supervisor and the supervisor after knowing Plaintiff printer couldn't be fixed, promised to get a new printer for Plaintiff and promised Plaintiff he could choose a printer from all printers that Defendants makes. Plaintiff now believes the supervisor was saying pick a different one than what you have now, because this model won't work. Someone at Defendants must of have told the Supervisor, no to giving a new printer to Plaintiff and Defendants has refused to honor an employee word.

31- Plaintiff alleges that Defendant's employees play a delay game, hoping the customer will give up and do what Defendants wants. Plaintiff is his adventure with his problem was given the name and phone number of Reece at the Defendant headquarters and after telling Reece the problem, Reece asked where the printer was purchased. Plaintiff said he didn't have the records in front of him and then asked what different does than matter. Plaintiff stated he purchased if from one or the other Defendants. Plaintiff asked, can't you look it up. Reece then said Plaintiff didn't buy it direct from Hewlett –Packard, so there was nothing he could do about the problem. Plaintiff asked him why and he said the record shows it was not purchased from Hewlett Packard, so he gave Plaintiff a phone number to another unit. So the pass it on to somebody else game continued on and on. However later Plaintiff checked his records and he bought the printer from one of the Defendants, Office Depot.

32- Plaintiff alleges that by Defendants not telling consumers about ink cartridges from other manufactures, not working in Defendant's printers or needing both cartridges with ink in the printer or it won't work or a time limit on the manufactured date, on defendant's ink, have committed fraud on public consumers. Not telling the public consumers is fraud on Defendant's part.

33- Plaintiff believes that other actions or promises have been broken and when these facts come forward, Plaintiff will ask this court for leave to amend this complaint.

Therefore Plaintiff demands that Defendants be held liable for their actions in the above allegations, and Plaintiff makes the following demands.

1- A trial by jury.

2- On any or all allegations in this complaint which a jury finds either Defendant guilty, Plaintiff is awarded both compensatory and punitive damages from each defendant found guilty, in the amount determined by a jury.

3- If either one of the Defendants is found guilty on any alleged issue in this complaint, 1) that each defendant found guilty be ordered to place a full page ad in the top 100 newspaper across America, apologizing, for the way Defendants has treated customers and 2) further each Defendant found guilty guarantees to correct and simplify their procedures for repairing consumers equipment problems in the further, including using technicians who speaks clear English, and 3) if either is found guilty of creating or trying to create a monopoly whereby only their ink cartridges can be used or establish a time frame when cartridges must be used by in their printers or both ink cartridges must be in the printer at the same time for the printer to work and or both cartridges must have ink in them for the printer to work correctly, Defendant is to redesign all printers both past and future, to where the printer can use ink manufactured by other companies and has no time requirement when cartridges must be used and no requirements that the printer must have both cartridges in the machine at the same time and both cartridges must have ink in them and 4) agree not to create a monopoly on any printer using ink cartridges in the future without advertising said fact and telling each potential customer said fact and 5) to recall all printer previously sold to anyone and to fix them where consumers can use ink cartridges produced by other companies.

4- If either one of the Defendants are found guilty by a jury of committing fraud on public consumers, then the guilty Defendant be fined fifty million (50,000,000) dollars, which Plaintiff must give to charities that are approved by this court, and if both are found guilty, then both be fined fifty million (50,000,000) dollars each, which Plaintiff must give to charities that are approved by this court..

5- All cost of this complaint by Plaintiff

6- For any other relief to which said Plaintiff may appear entitled.

Respectfully submitted
Edward H. Flint Pro, Se

*** The complaint ends here***

The judge ordered each party to submit a brief, outlining what the case was about and what each party's position was and the judge scheduled a hearing to discuss the case.

*** **My Brief the judge requested starts here*** **

UNITED STATES DISTRICT COURT
WESTERN DISTRICT OF KENTUCKY
LOUISVILLE DIVISON

CASE NO 3:10-CV-597-S

EDWARD H. FLINT   PLAINTIFF

VS

PLAINTIFF BRIEF AND POSITION PER COURT ORDER FOR THE SCHEDULING CONFERENCE TO BE HELD ON JANUARY 20, 2011

HEWLETT-PACKARD COMPANY   DEFENDANT

Comes the Plaintiff, Edward H. Flint Pro, Se, presenting his brief and position regarding this case as ordered by the court for the Scheduling Conference to be held on January 20, 2011.

Plaintiff purchased a Hewlett Packard printer from Office Depot. Plaintiff was told that the printer had a warranty and there shouldn't be any problems, that they work great, but if a problem came about, that Plaintiff could call the H-P tech center and they would fix the printer.

H-P will attempting to change the meaning of the warranty and Plaintiff declares this is an issue for a jury to decide, the meaning of the warranty versus what happens after the machine has problems, including the design and the con game that went with the printer Plaintiff purchased. H-P is trying to get out of welshing on an employee's word.

The printer had all kinds of problems that required calling a technician to fix each problem, if the problem could be solved. After many calls, the technician stated they couldn't fix the printer and they would have to send Plaintiff another printer.

H-P records these calls and should have the recordings to be heard by a jury.

After the second printer arrived Plaintiff had to repackage the old printer, take it to a UPS store and ship it. Plaintiff was told to put everything that came with the first printer into the same packaging as the shipped container and return it with the shipping label and return it per the shipping instruction.

After receiving the new printer Plaintiff had to install the printer. The package did not contain a warranty. Plaintiff had a 4200 model and assumed that the warranty was the same. After installing, the new printer, the printer had mores of the same problems as the first one. Plaintiff had to call the technicians' numberless times. Plaintiff on September 3, 2010 was told by the technician that the warranty was about to expire on his printer. Plaintiff renewed the warranty on September 3, 2010 by credit card. On September 9, 2010 Plaintiff's printer quite working again and a warning message came on a screen that said "tri-color ink cartridge is incomparable". Plaintiff called the technician and after hours of trying, the technician said that he couldn't fix the printer and for Plaintiff to hold on and talk with his supervision.

The supervision came on the line and Plaintiff's printer would have to be replaced and said that Hewlett Packard would have to send another printer and Plaintiff could pick out any printer he wanted from H-P line of printers. He said H-P would call the next morning from a different department of Hewlett Packard.

Plaintiff after not hearing from anyone about replacing the printer on September 13, 2010 started calling H-P. After calling a number of numbers and getting kicked around from department to department, Plaintiff was finally given the person who said she was the case manager, her name was Diana. After Plaintiff told Diana the story, she said the supervision didn't have the authority to tell Plaintiff what he did. Diana said the model number printer Plaintiff had had been discontinued. However she said she had another model that she would sell Plaintiff for $119.00.

PLAINTIFF'S POSITION

Plaintiff now tells this court that Hewlett Packard makes a profit of over 10 billion dollars a year. Hewlett Packard makes 10 Billion dollars a year in profit; by selling horrible designed printers, printers that are designed to suck money out of consumer's pockets as Plaintiff will show below.

Hewlett Packard deliberately designed a different series of 4 in 1 printers that was out of the norm for printers used to hook up to computers. The design was produced so consumers have to buy more ink than was the normal for 4 in 1 printers were, including their printers.

They sold printers;

1- That required both the color and black cartridges had to be in the printer, in unison.

2- That required that both cartridges had to have ink in them at all time. However even when the color ink cartridge contained ink, the printer would stop functioning. Thereby they created a monopoly.

3- That wouldn't function with an ink cartridge that was produced by another company, thereby creating a monopoly

4- That would not function with a cartridge, including those sold by Hewlett Packard that was refilled with ink by other companies. This designed produced a monopoly for Hewlett Packard and keeps consumers from being able to save money and forced them to buy original H-P ink cartridges.

5- That has a built in program that won't function if a certain date is stamped on the cartridge even if the cartridges are made and sold by Hewlett Packard. This endeavor forces consumers to use a cartridge by a certain date or by a new one. This is a monopoly created to make consumers buy more Hewlett Packard ink cartridges. A consumer buy a printer and buy ink cartridges from H-P and H-P says that if you don't use the ink by a certain date, you must throw it away and buy a new cartridges of ink.

6- That the printer's scanner was faulty doesn't function correctly and screws up other programs in the computer.

7- That the printer would not print envelopes correctly, like normal printers

Hewlett Packard once had a series of 4 in 1 printers that didn't have the requirements stated above and Hewlett Packard redesigned those printers to create a monopoly to sell more ink by requiring the above.

H-P created a monopoly to sell more ink and hid the facts from the consumer; H-P created a monster and as one person said "a piece of junk."

Hewlett Packard never informed consumers of these facts before selling them the printer and Plaintiff states that H-P action are at the expense of consumers.

Plaintiff argues that H-P owes it to consumers to advise them of the facts before the sale of the printer. H-P has set up a rip-off on their customers and doesn't tell their customers because they know that no one would buy such a printer, if the told the truth.

The resigned printers H-P put on the market had horrible flaws in the design and the printers don't operate correctly and the consumers are paying for the defects. Plaintiff will prove that Hewlett Packard deliberately designed the printer to more sell ink cartridges, which is where all of the profits are in the Printer business. Consumers have a right to be told the truth before they buy a produce.

H-P will attempt to hide behind a catch all warranty, in this case. The warranty and action of H-P is a swindle on the consuming public, and Plaintiff will prove such to a jury.

When a consumer buys an H-P printer, the consumers are told there is a warranty on the printer and H-P will make good on any problems. After Plaintiff brought the printer he had to call Hewlett Packard's technicians frequent times to try and get it fixed and the technicians are in India.

When you call Hewlett Packard and they asked which department you want and when you say tech support, Hewlett Packard says have your information regarding the printer ready for the technician and if the product is out of warranty you will be charged a fee. The technicians that a consumer gets are nothing but readers of manuals, which tells the consumers what to do to fix the printer. H-P is not repairing the printers; the buyers of the printers are, if they can be fixed. The consumers must do everything to make the printer function, that includes taking apart some of the printer, etc. Hewlett Packard does not tell, but should tell consumers what to expect, before selling printers to consumers. If Plaintiff had been told what he would have to go through, Plaintiff would have never brought the printer and doesn't believe any other person would either. Hewlett Packard designed a printer around more ink profits, which created a monopoly for H-P.

Plaintiff states that H-P warranty does not tell or notify a consumer what to expect if he needs help, except to call their nearest service center. H-P uses a catch all warranty to swindle their consumers. Hewlett Packard sells a cheap printer to attract consumers, but hides the information about the ink cartridges.

In addition, when you call a Hewlett Packard technician, you expect to be able to communicate with a technician you can understand. All technicians that answered the phone when Plaintiff called them were in India and all spoke very bad broken English. The Plaintiff could not hear or understand them. A call to Hewlett Packard for technical help takes hours and hours, rather than minutes because of the poor communication. Plaintiff states that at the very least Hewlett Packard owes the consumer a technician they can understand. If Hewlett Packard had told Plaintiff to expect such problems, Plaintiff would have never purchased the printer. Hewlett Packard owes the public a simple easy way of fixing printers or they should be told truth and H-P shouldn't be selling printers that don't meet those expectations. Hewlett Packard put the consumers at risk and took advantage of customers by shipping the jobs of technicians to India for cheap labor. H-P saves money, but consumers pay dearly for the hassle and ineffective service. If the America public knew what H-P does they would quit buying HP produces

Plaintiff now believes that what the supervisor was telling him, was he needed another printer and Plaintiff could take his pick from any H-P printers, but don't pick this one, he was telling Plaintiff that the product he had was so bad they couldn't fix it and you need a different model.

Hewlett Packard welched on their employee's word, and instead of replacing Plaintiff's printer, they offered to sell Plaintiff a printer.

Hewlett Packard has an incentive program that pays employees bonuses based on the profits they earn. That program is the reason for the faulty printer, the people in either the engineering department or the sales department seen dollars signs instead of consumers when putting this printer on the market. Sell ink, the hell with problems. Plaintiff claims that once H-P sells you a despicable designed printer, they have you in a position, that they keep squeezing you to buy more ink, before you completely understand the problems. Plaintiff wonders how many people H-P has done this to. The so called case worked tried to squeeze Plaintiff out of money. This may be another reason they make over 10 billion dollars a year profit.

Hewlett Packard went back on their word that Plaintiff would receive a printer of his choice. Plaintiff claims that the person who denied Plaintiff the promise that the supervisor made and who said she was the case manager, receives a bonus based on profits made. She attempted to create more profits for H-P rather than make good on the supervisor word. When she made the statement, she was really saying, H-P doesn't care if you have problems, we need to make more profits and you need to buy a new printer and forget about all of the labor, heartache, pain, etc. that H-P has cause you, I can only receive a bonus if you buy something, I won't receive a bonus if we give away printers.

H-P's printer that Plaintiff purchased also does work properly on printing envelopes and on scanning documents.

Plaintiff is writing a book titled "Corrupt Judges". The book is a true story about an actual lawsuit case and the content of his book is 80% legal court documents regarding the case. Plaintiff scanned these documents and the scanning from the printer screwed up Plaintiff computer so bad, that he spent three weeks straighten out his computer. Plaintiff is going to write another book title "Corrupt Judges Kill Justice," and he is trying to figure out how to scan legal court documents.

Before Plaintiff can print an address on an envelope properly he has to unfold the envelope before he puts it into the printer. The H-P technicians were never able to fix the problem. H-P put the printer on the market before it working properly, because they were in a hurry to make profits.

Hewlett Packard owes consumers the truth about their product before they sell a product. H-P puts fancy printing on their documents; about what the printer is supposed to do. But H-P prints nothing about what is required to make it function properly, nothing about the ink. H-P owes the public a printer that is properly designed before putting it on the market and they put a printer on the market that was never designed properly. Discovery will show that H-P knew they had problems with printer and sold it to customers anyhow, so they could sell more ink. What does their warranty mean? What are consumers entitled to for their money? What do consumers need to know about the meaning of a warranty before they buy it, not after? What does the consumer need to know about how the printer functions? What Hewlett Packard has done and is doing, is tricky deception on consumers. Hewlett Packard designed and sold a printer that was flawed from the start and they never fixed it to run properly. H-P should not be allowed by this court to treat consumers this way.

H-P should have recalled all of the flawed printers after finding out they didn't function properly, just like automobile manufactures have to, by federal government demands. This court should rule that they must recall the printers. Plaintiff states that H-P had an obligation to recall these printers and they chose to keep on making money at the consumer's expense, they never recalled the horrible printers. H-P didn't want to tell the consumers the truth, which they were obligated to do. Hewlett Packard has at this time three (3) class actions suits against them over the ink cartridges in these machines, that they have agreed to settle.

A jury should decide the allegations Plaintiff has made against Hewlett Packard. Plaintiff is sure that somewhere down the line of this case, H-P will ask the judge for summary judgment in this case; they don't want a jury to decide guilt or innocence based on the evidence. Plaintiff hopes this case never become a subject for one of his books.

Plaintiff was called by Hewlett Packard right after he filed his complaint and H-P asked him to make an offer to settle. All though Plaintiff wasn't interested in settling the case, he did make an offer and Hewlett Packard refused to accept the offer. An offer at this time from Plaintiff would be greater that the first offer.

Plaintiff states and alleges that Hewlett Packard's handling and design of the printer was nothing but a con game for making profits. In addition they committed fraud on Plaintiff and lied to Plaintiff, and they created a monopoly on Plaintiff and other consumers by deception. No person or company should be allowed to profit on a monopoly that is based on fraud.

A jury trial is necessary to determine the truth and to determine if Hewlett Packard is guilty as Plaintiff alleges. Plaintiff has attached his proposed case schedule and there is no reason why Plaintiff's schedule should not be granted. Plaintiff needs at least the time he has asked for and if H-P drags their feet on discovery, Plaintiff will have to request additional time from this court. In the name of justice, Plaintiff will ask this court for leave to amend his complaint after discovery, after the wrongs done by Defendant, become clearer. This case is important for consumers of printers throughout the world and this court should grant Plaintiff all of the time he needs to obtain his discovery.

Respectfully submitted
Edward H. Flint Pro, Se

*** My Brief on my position and about the case, ends here***

*** The Court issued the following two orders which starts here***

UNITED STATES DISTRICT COURT
WESTERN DISTRICT OF KENTUCKY
AT LOUISVILLE

EDWARD H. FLINT   PLAINTIFF

v.

CIVIL ACTION NO. 3:10CV-597-S

HEWLETT-PACKARD CONPANY   DEFENDANT

ORDER- 2

On August 26, 2011, this court entered a memorandum opinion and an accompanying order dismissing this matter without prejudice for lack of subject matter jurisdiction. Those items were docketed on August 30, 2011. On December 5, 2011, the plaintiff, Edward H. Flint, filed a motion requesting, *inter alia,* that this court vacate the memorandum opinion and accompanying order because he did not receive copies and therefore did not have an opportunity to appeal within the time period allowed.

A review of the docket sheet indicates that the Clerk of Court provided a copy of the memorandum opinion and accompanying order to counsel. There is no indication that copies were provided to the plaintiff, who is acting *pro se.*

Thus, the plaintiff's contention that he did not receive copies is apparently well taken.

The omission by the Clerk of Court to serve copies upon the plaintiff requires rectification. Accordingly, the memorandum opinion and the accompanying order entered by the court on August 26, 2011 and docketed on August 30, 2011 (DN 68 and 69) are hereby **WITHDRAWN.**

For the reasons stated therein, said memorandum opinion (now DN 78) and the accompanying order (now DN 79) will be **RE-ENTERED** this date. **The Clerk of Court is directed to provide copies to counsel of record and to the plaintiff acting** *pro se.*

There being no just reason for delay in entry, the order (now DN 79) is a final order.

IT IS SO ORDERED this December 8, 2011

Charles R. Simpson III, Judge

ORDER- 1

This matter having come before the court for consideration whether the amount in controversy exceeds the sum of $75,000, exclusive of interest and costs, in satisfaction of the jurisdictional prerequisite of 28 U.S.C. § 1332(a)(1) and the court having determined to a legal certainty that the jurisdictional minimum has not been met, and the court being otherwise sufficiently advised, **IT IS HEREBY ORDERED AND ADJUDGED** that this action is **DISMISSED WITHOUT PREJUDICE** for lack of subject matter jurisdiction. There being no reason for delay in its entry, this is a final order.

IT IS SO ORDERED.

August 26, 2011

Charles R. Simpson III, Judge
United States District Court

*** The District Court submitted two orders and the judge explained the order dated August 26, 2011 number 1 is the correct order.

I appealed the case to the Court of Appeals with this Brief, which starts here

CASE NO. 11-6523/12-5100

UNITED STATES COURT OF APPEALS
FOR THE SIXTH CIRCUIT

EDWARD H. FLINT,   Plaintiff – Appellant

v.

HEWLETT PACKARD COMPANY   Defendant-Appellee

On Appeal from the United States District Court
For the Western District of Kentucky
Louisville Division

Civil Case No. 3:11-CV-597-CRS-DW

BRIEF FOR APPELLANT/ PLAINTIFF

Respectfully submitted
Edward H. Flint Pro, Se

STATEMENT OF FACTS AND BACK GROUND INFORMATION REGARDING THIS CASE

Appellant Flint is 81 years old and is Pro, Se, states he has lived his live believing that Judges was the most respected people along with Doctors in America. However Flint has discovered that some judges like to use their power to show parties before them, that they don't care how people perceive them and they think that this will get them in Heaven, just like the religious leaders did with Jesus, but how wrong they were. Flint believes in truth and it doing the right thing if life. He has seen and lived World War II, Hitler and everything that has come after that. Flint believes in Jesus and in God. Jesus said that Satan was the father of lies and Flint can't believe that some Judges doesn't care about justice, they only care about using their power and they believe in protecting other judges from everything a judge does corrupt. Judges like everyone will someday become equal to all others on judgment day. **Jesus said on judgment day, we will all be judged, by the thoughts we had in our mind and by the deeds we did, not by the words we said**.

History of the case, as seen from the court's docket file and Appellant Argument.

1) Appellant purchased a printer from Appellee and it was a piece of junk. See complaint Docket (#**1**).The complaint spell out the outline of over 25 allegations.

2) The case was assigned to Judge Charles Simpson, who referred it to Magistrate Judge Dave Whalin. See Docket (#**7**)

3_ Judge Simpson entered an order on 11/15/2010 setting forth a Scheduling Conference on 1/20/2011 See Docket (#**7**)

4) Appellant submitted a brief and position statement as requested by the court on 1/11/2011 regarding appellant's allegation of what the case is about. See Docket (#**12**)

5) The scheduling conference was held and Judge Whalin violated the courts rule when he told the Appellee attorney to leave the hearing, leaving Flint alone with Judge Whalin and Judge Whalin brow beat appellant, trying to get him to settle the case.

6) Appellant on 2/03/2011 filed a motion to compel See Docket (#**19**). The court refused to answer the motion.

7) Appellant on 2/8/11 file a motion requesting Judge Whalin be moved and to un-seal the part of the transcript that was sealed by the court. See Docket (#**24**). The court refused to move Judge Whalin. Judge Whalin signed an order refusing to recuse himself. See Docket (#29). Appellant filed a motion asking for reconsideration on 2/18/2011. See docket (# **24**) and order (# **33.**)

8) Appellant on 2/08/2011 filed a motion to compel Appellee to answer interrogatories and produce documents. See Docket (#**25**.) The court answered this motion as moot and Appellant responded to the court order with Docket (# **31**)

9) Appellant filed a Motion for leave to file an amended complaint number 2 on 2/14/2011. See Docket (#**27**). The court refused to answer this motion. Flint was adding Office Deport to the complaint

10) Appellant filed on 2/17/2011 a motion to compel and hold in contempt Hewlett Packet for refusing to answer interrogatives and for failure to produce document. See Docket (# **33**) the court refused to answer the motion.

11) Appellant filed on 4/21/20 a motion reminding Judge Whalin that he had stated he would rule quickly on all motion and about a Constitution question. See Docket (# **43**). The court never ruled on all motions and about the constitution question.

12   Judge Whalin issued an order dated 4/20/2011 stating there would be a status conference on the pending non-dispositive motion filed by the Plaintiff for 5/4/2011 See Docket (# **48)**. Judge Whalin in his Docket (#**48)** order calling for a status conference hearing for May 4, 2011 regarding motions that had been filed, but the real purpose for the hearing was to find a way to dismiss the case. Judge Whalin's order stated **"that the court notifies the parties of its concern about the diversity of jurisdiction of the court to hear the present case under 28 U.S.C. 28 #1332. In particular, the court requires impute from the parties on the question of whether the lawsuit as pled satisfies the jurisdictional amount requirement statute. To address this potential problem the court will elaborate on its concern at the status hearing and will enter a briefing schedule at that time, if necessary."**

God through the Holy Spirit has told Appellant to file this appeal.

Appellant knows that this court can and will do as it please. Judges believes that they are special and they are, on this earth. However there will be another life and in that eternal life God is special and Jesus will judge all who wants to spent eternal life with God. Of course if judges want to be with the Devil then Appellant is wasting his time. So if this court rules against Appellant, Jesus will know that these three judges were warned.

Appellant bought a printer and it was junk. Hewlett Packard replaced it once. The second printer was worse that the first. Flint tried every way to make it work. The people oversea in Indian that Hewlett Packard uses as technicians told Flint to get another kind; this one is bad and can't be made to work. Flint was told by the technicians that Hewlett Packard would give him a different type, but the person at Hewlett Packard refuse to care what Flint was told, they wanted to sell Flint another printer. Flint checked the Hewlett Packard website and found out that 9 out of ten people who bought this model would say it was junk. Hewlett Packard was selling junk at other people expense, so Flint decided to make the public aware of what was going on with Hewlett Packard.

Flint asked for a lot of money in his demands, but not for himself, but for charity. Hewlett Packard would have settled this case easy, but Flint refused to. When Flint refused to settle with Hewlett Packard, they bought two judges. If this panel wants to protect corrupt judges, Flint knows you will regardless of what he says. Flint understand the law as good as this panel. Flint knows that this panel can twist and turn the case anyway they like. But Jesus will know and your Holy Spirit (everyone has one) will inform Jesus. Hewlett Packard wanted this panel to dismiss the case on the first appeal when they asked for the case to be dismissed.

This panel will act on how they see two issues, One being, is Flint asking for too much and some judges believe high awards is causing America's problems. Flint says it is the opposite. The big companies like Hewlett Packard don't make the best product they can; they send bad products out the door at the expense of poor people, because H-P know the courts will protect them and it saves them money. It cheaper for them to fight lawsuits, rather than produce good products.

The other reason is the trial court judges who are on the take will ask their fellow judges to protect them. Appeal judges protect those who corrupt, but the appeal courts judges don't get part of it. Judges are protecting all of the bad and corrupt people because they don't want to see high awards. Flint could have settled this case at the beginning, but he refuse to accept life the way it is in America now. America wasn't like this 30 years ago, because back then judges let lawsuits be tried.

Judge Whalin and Judge Simpson did everything to Flint they could. Flint asked them to recuse themselves, under Cannons, under the Court's rules, but most of all under Title 28, #455 which is about honest justice and in the name of justice. Flint asked, as the record shows a number of times. Judge Simpson and Judge Whalin think they got by with it, but Jesus is waiting to tell them to go see the Devil and tell him what a good job they did for him.

Judge Whalin and Judge Simpson could not get Flint to agree to settle the case and their client did not want this case to go to trial, because they knew Flint had the evidence to convince them as charged, by a jury and they struggled every way they could to find a way to defeat Flint. After the hearing on May, 4, 2011 Flint sent to the court a Memorandum dated May 9, 2011. The memorandum's heading was "**MEMORANDUM TO ANSWER JUDGES WHALIN'S ORDER CONCERNING THE HEARING HELD BETWEEN THE PARTIES AND JUDGE WHALIN ON MAY 4, 2011.**"

Flint on May 18, 2012 asked the court's clerk to send him a copy of the docket. When Flint received the docket, he found that the Memorandum filed May 9, 2011 did not appear on the docket. The Clerk of the Court told Flint to send a copy of the May 9, 2011 Memorandum to the court and they would add it to the docket. Flint has attached a copy of the document and a copy of the pleading sent to the court on May 22, 2012. (See **EXHIBIT 1** copy of letter to the court and memorandum dated May 9, 2012) The court's clerk said she had no idea why it didn't get put on the docket, and Flint believes it was deliberately left off. But the point being the judge didn't have it when he made his ruling.

The Memorandum shows that Hewlett Packard the Appellee didn't raise the question of diversity jurisdiction, $75,000 dollars but the court raised it. The court should have raised the question at the beginning of the case, if there was a question. There is no question, Judge Whalin couldn't get Flint to settle the case and Judge Whalin thought that Flint being Pro, Se didn't understand the law or the rules and how courts operate. Judge Simpson issued his order dismissing the case without seeing **Exhibit 1**. However any honest judge can look at the complaint, including Flint's demands and look at the brief Flint submitted to the court in docket #12, regarding how he seen the case and not know that the case was worth more than $75,000, which Judge Simpson said it was not worth and the reason for dismissing the case. Even without **Exhibit 1**, a judge knows the case if judged by a jury was worth millions of dollars. Hewlett Packard knew it was worth more or they would not have bought the judges.

Judge Simpson issued a Memorandum and opinion DATED August 26, 2011 dismissing the complaint for want of a subject matter jurisdiction See Docket (**# 68**). However Flint never received a copy until November 29, 2011. Judge Simpson at the same time issued an order to go along with the Memorandum See Docket (**# 69**.) Appellant Flint never received a copy this August 26, 2011 order.

Appellant on December 2, 2011 sent a motion to Judge Simpson to remand and vacate the August 26, 2011 order and reissue under Fed. Rule 60. See Docket (**# 75**).

Docket (**# 77**) shows that Judge Simpson issued an order on December 8, 2012 that states Docket (**# 68**) and (**# 69**) are withdrawn; Memorandum Opinion and order will be re-entered this date. Flint received a copy of the Memorandum and order; however it still had the August 26, 2012 date. Flint appealed the December 8, 2011 order and Memorandum to the Court of Appeals, (**# 80**) however he does not have, nor does the trial court have a copy of the Memorandum and Opinion dated December 8, 2012. Appellant has discussed this with the Courts clerk and she said that the clerk did what Judge stated to do. She said the judge didn't say to re-date the document just re-enter it in to the record and send a copy to counsel. Appellant is basing his appeal on the December 8, 2011 docket (**#77**) and using the one with an August 26, 2001 date.

Flint has tried to get this matter straighten out by motions asking for the Memorandum be send to him with a current date, the date it was issued. Flint filed motion in dockets #81 and #86, which the judge denied.. The court has a major problem in understanding, between the judge and clerk of the court. Flint has done all he could to get the Memorandum sent to him with the correct date. Flint filed for appeal based on this statement and the Court of Appeals must get it straighten out, however there is no reason that this panel cannot proceed.

Judge Simpson ruling to dismiss is based the suit wasn't worth $75,000. Flint's demand was more than $75,000 and no judge can say that when Flint asked for millions, he didn't ask for enough to meet the required under 28 U.S.C. #1332. Juries determine how much a Plaintiff receives not the judges in a jury trial. Judge Simpson doesn't care about law or justice; he only cares about winning for his clients.

Appellant based on the action of the two judges Judge Simpson and Judge Whalin had that asked that both recuse them self from the case a number of time. Not only has Judge Whalin violated the rules of the court and Cannons, but he also refuses to honor 28 U.S.C. #455.

Because of other lawsuits and because Flint has sued him, Judge Simpson should have recused himself. By 28 U.S.C. #455 Judge Simpson should have disqualify himself from this case. **In** *Liljeberg* v. *Health Services Acquisition Corp., 486 U.S. 847, 860 n.8 (1988)* **the Supreme Court noted that the purpose of section 455(a) is to promote public confidence in the integrity of the judicial process, the Court observed that such confidence "does not depend upon whether or not the judge actually knew of facts creating an appearance of impropriety, so long as the public might reasonably believe that he or she knew."'**

No Court in America, including this court, can replace 28 U.S. Code #455. This code is a law passed by Congress and it is clear. The trial judges failed to do anything, but give their personal opinion on why they would not recuse themselves. Congress created and passed this law and the Supreme Court in 1988 has stated, it good for justice, so a judge doesn't have a say in to recusing themselves.

Flint will quote from the Federal Judicial Center an Analysis of case law 28 U.S.C. #455.

The document states,

The new section 455(a) replaced the subjective standard of the 1948 state with an objective standard. It is no longer that a judge should recuse where "in his opinion" sitting would be improper, but rather where his or her impartiality "might reasonably be questioned." Also, section 455(b) spells out certain situations in which partiality is presumed and recusal is required.

Judges should keep in mind that sections 455(a) and (b) provide separate (though substantially overlapping) bases for recusal. The formal deals exclusively with the appearance of partiality in any circumstance, whereas the latter pertains to conflicts of interest in specific instances. Thus, the existence of the facts listed in section 455(b) requires recusal, even if the judge believes impartiality might reasonably be questioned, whether or not touched on in section 455(b), requires recusal under section 455(a)

In addition, where section 455(b) sets forth a particular situation requiring recusal, it will tend to control any section 4559A) analysis with respect to that specific circumstance. For example, section 455 (b)(5) requires recusal where one of the parties is a third degree of relationship to the judge

The analysis also stated the following:

There is a second respect, apart from application of the reasonable person standard, in which the determination under section 455(a) is objective. The Supreme Court has held that a violation of section 455(a) takes place even if the judge is unaware of the circumstance that created the appearance of impropriety. In *Liljeberg* v. *Health Services Acquisition Corp.,486 U.S. 847, 860 n.8 (1988)* the trial judge was a member of the board of trustees of a university that had a financial interest in the litigation, but he was unaware of the financial interest when he conducted a bench trial and ruled in the case. The court of appeals nevertheless vacated the judgment under Fed. R. Civ. P 60(b) because the judge failed to recuse himself pursuant to section 455(a) and the Supreme Court agreed. Noting that the purpose of section 455(a) is to promote public confidence in the integrity of the judicial process, the Court observed that such confidence "does not depend upon whether or not the judge actually knew of facts creating an appearance of impropriety, so long as the public might reasonably believe that he or she knew."

Flint and any fair minded person would agree that the impartiality of both judges' actions was questioned and both Judge Simpson and Judge Whalin should have disqualified themselves, without question; they cannot use his own feelings or beliefs to make a ruling on this issue, but must use the law, which is 28 U.S.C. #455.

The court's records in this case shows that Flint has asked Judge Simpson to recuse himself a number of times, at least nine (9) in this case, as well as in other cases. Judge Simpson has no respect for law, he only does what he wants to, because he believes that the Court of Appeals judges will have no integrity and will not do anything to him, but uphold his decision not to recuse himself.

For this court to uphold Judge Simpson and Judge Whalin orders you will have to state that 28 U. S. Code #455 has no bearing on judges; judges can do as we please. Even Cannons laws which every judge must adhere to, states that Judge Simpson and Judge Whalin must recuse themselves, based on their actions in this case.

Appellant asked Judge Whalin thirteen (13) times to recuse himself and he refused

CONCLUSION

1- Any questions about Flint filing the appeals on time and properly is a problem that the trial judge or the court clerk created and not Appellant. Flint did everything a person can do to keep the record right and the court acted like the Keystone Cops in the way the issue was handled

2- Judge Whalin and Judge Simpson both should have recused themselves when first was asked to recuse themselves. Both judges wanted their way and thought they could run over a Pro, Se. They felt like big men running over a non-law educated person. They are small men pretending to be honest judges, when they are not. Hewlett Packard bought them before the case started and for a company that makes 10 billion dollars a year profit off of hard working people, this is a disgrace on the human race.

3- For this panel to rule that Judge Simpson and Judge Whalin did not to recuse themselves by 28 U.S. C. #455, would be saying that the court system doesn't care what laws Congress passes, we are going by our rules and not by Congress's rules.

4- Appellant has attached a filing as EXHIBIT 1 to this brief and the pleading was never put on the trial court's docket. It was intentionally left off of the docket in order Judge Simpson could make the ruling he did of dismissing the case. Even Judge Simpson couldn't dismiss this case with EXHIBIT 1 in front of him. Exhibit 1 proves without a doubt that the case was filed in the right court. Someone in the courts clerk's office left Exhibit 1 off intentionally, either the judge or the Clerk of the Court's staff.

5- Judge Whalin raised the issue of diversity jurisdiction thinking Flint being Pro, se, couldn't properly answer the question of diversity jurisdiction.

6- Judge Whalin and Judge Simpson did everything they could to take advantage of Flint and when everything else failed, they came up with the diversity jurisdiction issue. Every honest judge in America knows that Flint complaint was a good complaint and every honest judge knows that Flint complaint was in the proper jurisdiction. But Hewlett Packard became nervous and didn't want the case tried, they knew they sold a bad product and were doing everything to contain the fire storm they built and started with their junk equipment. Judge Whalin orders regarding diversity jurisdiction read like orders written by a 6th grade school kid.

7- The issue of did Flint file the case in the right court should no longer be a question. The demands in Flint's complaint clearly showed that there were a number of allegations that each in their own right was over a million dollars each. The damage to Flint alone he believes is over $75,000, not counting all of the other demands he made, one for charity.

8- Flint in exhibit 1 shows what he believes the judgment should be. It's up to a jury to determine the amount. It's not up to judge to look at such a major case like this and rule that its worth less than $75,000. Such action only shows how bias Judge

Simpson is against Flint and how prejudice he is for Hewlett Packard. It's hard to image a judge being so open about his prejudice.

9- Hewlett Packard the Appelles never questioned the diversity jurisdiction issue; Judge Whalin did only after months had gone by, after the complaint was filed. Judge Whalin knew it was a good filing, but he was desperate for a way to stop Flint. He knew Flint had the evidence to win a jury trial, but he wanted Hewlett Packard to win, because for some reason they owned him in this case.

10- Judge Whalin should have questioned the $75,000 issue at the start of the case, if there was an issue to be questioned, but he didn't. He raised the issue because he was so desperate wanting the case dismissed. He violated the courts rule trying to get Flint to settle the case at the January 20, 2011 hearing. This is corruption not justice.

11- Appellant Flint was not allowed to amend the complaint by the court, which would have added Office Depot as a Defendant. Adding Office Depot as a defendant would have increased the amount Flint could have received and added to the demand. Why wasn't Flint allowed to amend his complaint, which he was entitled to by Federal Rules?

12- Judge Simpson and Judge Whalin by not allowing Flint to amend the complaint proves that they were working for Hewlett Packard, who wanted Flint stopped at all cost and the judges did what Hewlett Packard wanted.

13- Between all of the other things that was done to Flint and then the trial court didn't add Exhibit 1 to the docket and the court wouldn't straighten out the mess of giving Flint the right Memorandum and order, but instead gave him one Dated August 26, 2011 to throw him off, so he couldn't appeal the case and he couldn't pursue the case. And wouldn't let him added Office Depot to the complaint. This is corruption at it worse and makes the justice system look like there is no justice system in America.

14- This case should be referred to Congress to consider impeaching Judge Simpson and Judge Whalin.

15- Hewlett Packard should be investigated by Congress and the FBI for tampering with the court system and for denying Flint his right to Due Process and his civil rights.

16- This panel should send this case to the FBI and have it investigated, unless this panel believes in the kind of justice that reaps with corruption, as in this case. Either the judge ordered, or the clerk's office staff withheld from posting court pleadings and not handing the judges memorandum and order properly.

17- Flint has done nothing wrong in this case and does not deserve to be treated like he is an idiot, but he was.

18- To prove how someone from the court has done everything to beat Flint all one has to do is look at the first page of the docket. At the top where the summary of the case is stated under Demand is $50,000,000. Someone knew what the demand was but Judge Simpson dismissed the case because he stated it the case didn't have the $75,000 threshold needed to meet the jurisdiction of 28 U.S.C. #1332. This shows that Judge Simpson did what he was hired to do. Also at the top it shows the case was terminated on 8/30.2011, which was the day that Judge Simpson signed the order dismissing the case. Someone was trying to make the Pro, Se thinks the case was over and there was nothing else he could do. The Western District Court of Kentucky has a real problem, either Judge Simpson or Judge Whalin or both was doing everything they could to stop Flint or the Clerk of the court has a problem with what their staff was doing or both. Appellant believes that the two judges had the court staff helping them keep Flint from winning this case. Flint said in pleadings to the court in this case that he belief that one the Counsel for Hewlett Packard was kin to someone in the court system in Louisville. Only an investigation by the FBI will the truth come out. There is one thing clear in the Louisville Court system and that is Flint was treated worse than a criminal.

The Plaintiff states he deserves to be granted as a Pro, Se, some leniency in the way he types and presents his briefs, however the truth must be found by this court, regardless of what it takes.

The trial court in its dismissing the case not only didn't search for the truth, but ignored it completely. The trial court based its dismissal order only on the fact that it didn't want Flint to have justice under any circumstances; the judge wanted his friends or clients to win this case. Flint prays that the panel reviewing this case believes in true and honest justice and will judge accordingly. Flint hopes the panel will read the entire records. Flint has been beat to a pulp by judges in the last 3 years, by judges who like to beat up on Pro, Se's and by judges who ignore the law, which means they put themselves above the law. If this panel chooses to defend Judge Simpson and Whalin, Flint will lose this case. Judges should remember that when they take sides, another side gets harmed. The only winners in the justice system are the judges who judge by the law. Judge Simpson harmed thousands of citizens by dismissing this case. The public which in this case is mostly young kids and old people who can't afford to buy top of the line printers and who believes it when a big company like Hewlett Packard advertises a product as being good and it turns out to be junk.

Flint also states that; there is a constitutional question in this case that this court must address. Flint is entitled to a Due Process fair and honest trial as called for in the Constitution. Flint wants to also remind this court that the court duty by the constitution is to find the truth, over and above anything else. No person who is Pro,Se can possible know the Federal rules of civil procedures and cite laws like educated attorneys and for any court to expect a Pro, SE to follow all of the rules and cite laws is in violation of granting a person a Due Process trial. The Court's rules of civil procedures only exist to keep order among trained lawyers and are not the only way to determine the truth.

When a Pro, Se is involved, a court has to overlook some of the way it is presented by a Pro, Se and arrive at the truth by other means, regardless of what it takes. The framers of our constitution or a fair minded judge would not expect a non-educated person in law to compete with a person who has been educated and trained for a number of years. There is nothing in the United States Constitution that says that the Court's Rule of Civil procedures must be adhered to by Pro, Se's. Nothing can supersede the 14th amendment to the constitution giving everyone Due Process, to a fair and honest trial.

Therefore any misstatement made or lack of presenting the proper federal law or rule in pleadings to a court, should not be held against a Pro, Se. If any court holds in their mind or in rulings that a Pro, Se didn't adhere to the rules of civil procedures or cite the right authority, then the court is giving the educated lawyer an unfair advantage over the pro, se, and denying the Pro, Se a Due Process fair trial. The court its self would be discriminating against a Pro, Se.

Court's Rules of Civil Procedure are court drafted rules and are not constitution mandated for a due process fair trial. Example, when a Plaintiff says he has been harmed by a defendant action and doesn't spell out which Federal law or civil rule should be used, doesn't mean that Plaintiff's case should be thrown out, like Judge Simpson did to Flint. The truth which a court must find is, was the Plaintiff harmed by any method, whether it is physical or civil rights or property. The 14th Amendment gives every person the right to protect their property and that is what Flint was doing in his complaint. Pro, se's under all circumstances must be protected by this court, from the harassing done by any Defendant, in not conforming to the courts rules on discovery, if any exits. A Pro, Se person has a right to explain their case the best they can and a court must take the time to get to the truth, even if everything is not done by the Courts rules.

A courts duty is to get the truth in the case, regardless of anything else and regardless of what time and effort it takes the court to find the truth.

Chief Judge of the United States Supreme Court John Roberts stated at his confirmation hearing with the United States Senate replied, when asked what a judge's duty was, and I quote,

"Judges are like umpires. Umpires don't make the rules. They apply them. The role of an umpire and a judge is critical. The make sure everybody plays by the rules. But it is a limited role. Nobody ever went to a ball game to see the umpires." His jurisprudence would be characterized by "modesty and humility"

No one can disagree with John Roberts's statements. The constitution gives every person Due Process of a fair and honest trial, regardless of what it takes and this court must see that Flint receives a Due Process fair and honest trial, especially if hot shots attorneys or judges try to take advantage of a Pro, Se's lack of experience. When a judge(s) makes up their own rules or ignores and expands the court's rules and or legal laws, or judges by their personal feelings, the Justice System breaks down and fails. When the Justice system fails, social order fails.

As I told you at the beginning, Jesus is watching this case, because he has a personal interest in the case. Therefore Appellant Flint asks this court to overrule and dismiss the trial court's order that dismissed this case and to send the case back to the trial court for discovery and trial, and see that an honest non-bias judge oversees the trial of this case.

Respectfully submitted
Edward H. Flint Pro, Se

*** My Brief Ends here***

The court of Appeals order Starts Here

Nos. *11-6523/ 12-5100*

UNITED STATES COURT OF APPEALS
FOR THE SIXTH CIRCUIT

EDWARD H. FLINT,   Plaintiff-Appellant,

v.

HEWLETT-PACKARD,   Defendant-Appellee

ORDER FROM THE UNITED STATES DISTRICT COURT
FOR THE WESTERN District OF KENTUCKY

Before: SILER, MOORE, and McKEAGUE, Circuit Judges.

Edward H. Flint, a Kentucky resident processing pro se, appeals district court orders denying his motion for recusal and denying his motion requesting the district court to re-issue its order dismissing his complaint. These consolidated cases have been referred to a panel of the court pursuant to Federal Rule of Appellate Procedure 34(a) (2)(C). Upon examination, we unanimously agree that oral argument is not needed. Fed. R. App. P. 34(a).

Seeking monetary and equitable relief, Flint sued Hewlett-Packard Company (HP), alleging that he purchased a defective printer from HP and that HP failed to honor its warranty for the printer. Following an initial scheduling conference, Flint filed a motion to amend his complaint. He also filed a motion requesting that Magistrate Judge Dave Whalin be removed from the case. The magistrate judge denied the motion for recusal. Following a status conference hearing, the magistrate judge asked the parties to submit briefs addressing whether Flint's claim for relief satisfied the $75,000 amount-in-controversy requirement for diversity jurisdiction, and stayed any ruling on Flint's pending motions.

Flint filed additional motions asking Judge Charles Simpson and Magistrate Judge Whalin to recuse themselves from the case. Following briefing on jurisdiction, the district court issued an order, dated August 26, 2011, in which it concluded that the amount in controversy did not exceed $75,000, and dismissed the complaint without prejudice for lack of subject matter jurisdiction.

However, Flint continued filing motions seeking the recusal of the magistrate judge and Judge Simpson. The district court denied Flint's request for recusal. Furthermore, in an effort to ensure that Flint was made aware that his complaint had been dismissed, the district court forwarded a copy of the dismissal order to Flint. Flint filed a motion requesting that the district court "remand and vacate" the August 26, 2011, order because he never received a copy of the order. On December 12, 2011, the district court again denied Flint's request for Judge Simpson to recuse himself from the case. The district court also directed the clerk's office to withdraw the August 26, 2011, memorandum and order and re-enter them on the docket as of that date. The signature page of the order still reflected the August 26, 2011, date. Flint filed a notice of appeal, specifying that he was appealing the order denying his motions for recusal. (Case No. 11-6523).

On December 19, 2011, Flint filed a motion for the court to again re- issue the memorandum and order dismissing his complaint, but with a currently dated signature page. On January 10, 2012, Flint filed a second motion requesting that the district court reissue the order of dismissal with a current date. On January 23, 2012, the district court denied Flint's motions, explaining that the new entry date began the appeal period. Flint appealed. (Case No. 12-5100).

On appeal, Flint reasserts his arguments that Judge Simpson and Magistrate Judge Whalin exhibited bias against him and that they should have recused themselves from his case. Flint also argues that the district court erred when it concluded that he did not satisfy the amount-in- controversy element in order to establish diversity jurisdiction because he sought damages in the "millions" of dollars. We denied the government's motion to dismiss the appeals, but instructed the parties that they could further brief the issue of appellate jurisdiction for Case No. 12-5100 if they deemed it appropriate. The government reasserts its motion to dismiss Flint's attempt to appeal the dismissal of his complaint for lack of subject matter jurisdiction.

Flint has not established that either Judge Simpson or Magistrate Judge Whalin should have recused himself from presiding over his lawsuit. We review the denial of a motion to recuse for an abuse of discretion. *Johnson v. Mitchell,* 585 F.3d 923, 945 (6th Cir. 2009). To justify recusal, the judge's prejudice or bias must be personal or extra-judicial. *United States* v. *Jamieson,* 427 F. 3 d 394, 405 (6th Cir. 2005) (citing *United States* v. *Hartsel,* 199 F.3d 812,820 (6th Cir. 1999»). Flint's Allegations of bias do not warrant the recusal of either Judge Simpson or Magistrate Judge Whalin.

Flint sought Magistrate Judge Whalin's recusal because he alleged that, during a conference hearing, the magistrate judge asked HP's counsel to leave the room and attempted to "brow-beat" Flint into settling the case. Flint maintains that the magistrate judge acted improperly by discussing the case without both parties being present and by trying to intimidate Flint. However, Flint has not established that the magistrate judge's alleged bias was personal or extrajudicial. Even if the magistrate judge attempted to convince Flint to settle the case, Flint has presented no allegations sufficient to show any impropriety in the magistrate judge's recommendation that Flint's complaint did not meet the requirements for diversity jurisdiction. In addition, Judge Simpson was not required to recuse himself from the case merely because Flint had previously named Judge Simpson in a prior lawsuit. *See Azubuko* v. *Royal,* 443 F.3d 302,304 (3d Cir. 2006). Flint's assertions that the judge's failure to include all of his documents on the docket sheet and the judge's refusal to address Flint's pro se motions do not establish any extrajudicial bias. Indeed, the district court specifically advised Flint that his motions were being stayed pending the resolution of the question of whether the court had subject matter jurisdiction in this case. In light of the finding that the court did *not* have jurisdiction, the failure to rule on Flint's pending motions does not establish that either Magistrate Judge Whalin or Judge Simpson was biased against Flint.

The district court properly dismissed Flint's case for lack of subject matter jurisdiction. Initially, we conclude that we have jurisdiction to review the district court's order dismissing Flint's complaint for lack of subject matter jurisdiction. As we stated previously in the order denying the government's motion to dismiss Flint's appeals, Flint's motion for the court to again re-issue its order dismissing his complaint may be construed as a Rule 59(e) motion because it was filed within he fourteen-day appeal period. *See Inge* v. *Rock Fin. Corp.,* 281 F .3d 613, 617 (6th Cir. 2002); *seealso Smith* v.

Dretke, 119 F. App 'x 691, 692 (5th Cir. 2005) ("[D]espite the label affixed by this pro se litigant, the post judgment filing must be regarded as a Rule 59(e) motion because it was filed within 10 days of the entry of judgment."). Moreover, because Flint filed a timely notice of appeal from the order denying his Rule 59(e) motion, we have jurisdiction to consider the underlying judgment. "A Rule 59(e) motion relates to the underlying final judgment ... and, as a general matter, the appeal from the denial of a Rule 59(e) motion is treated as an appeal from the underlying judgment itself." *GenCorp, Inc.* v. *Am. Int'l Underwriters,* 178 F.3d 804, 832-33 (6th Cir. 1999).

We review de novo a district court's dismissal of an action for lack of subject matter jurisdiction. *Wagenknecht* v. *United States,* 533 F .3d 412,415 (6th Cir. 2008). Diversity jurisdiction requires that the amount in controversy exceed $75,000 and that no plaintiff is a citizen of the same state as any defendant. *See Lincoln Prop. Co.* v. *Roche,* 546 u.s. 81, 89 (2005). Here, the parties are citizens of different states - Flint resides in Kentucky and HP is located in California. However, the district court properly concluded that Flint did not satisfy the amount-in- controversy element needed to establish jurisdiction. Flint purchased an allegedly defective HP printer from Home Depot for $84.79. Although the printer was eventually replaced, Flint alleged that the replacement was also defective, and that the printers were designed to work with only HP ink cartridges. Although Flint stated that the printers were under warranty, the record reflects that the warranty limited Flint's remedy to having the printer repaired or replaced - a limitation that is permitted under Kentucky law. *See* KRS 355.2-719(1)(a). Therefore, even though Flint's claim for relief included a "50 million" dollar fine for HP's alleged fraud on the public and for his pain and suffering, HP's limited warranty limits its liability to the cost of repairing or replacing the allegedly defective printer. Likewise, Flint's conclusory allegation that HP created a "monopoly" for its ink cartridges, by producing printers that work with only HP ink cartridges, is insufficient to state an anti-trust claim, and also fails to satisfy the amount-in-controversy element for diversity jurisdiction. Flint does not allege that he purchased any HP ink cartridges.

Finally, the district court did not err when it denied Flint's motion to again reissue its order dismissing his complaint for lack of subject matter jurisdiction. Although the order was re-issued with the original August, 26, **2011,** entry date, the appearance of the original entry date did not prevent Flint from pursuing a timely appeal because the order dismissing the complaint was clearly withdrawn and re-entered on December 12, 2011.

Accordingly, we deny the motion to dismiss and affirm the district court's orders. Fed. R. App. P. 34(a)(2)(C).

ENTERED BY ORDER OF THE COURT

Deborah S. Hunt, Clerk

*** The District Court's order ends her***

*** I appealed to the Supreme Court. I file a Petition
for Certiorari that begins here ***

NO._____

In The
Supreme Court of the United States

Edward H. Flint   Petitioner,

Versus

HEWLETT PACKARD CCOMPANY   Respondents

PETITION FOR WRIT OF CERTIORARI

QUESTIONS PRESENTED

1- **Has a person been denied Due Process under the 14th amendment to the constitution when the second Court of Appeals panel denies Petitioner's appeal after the first Court of Appeals panel ruled that the petitioner was in the proper jurisdiction. The Trial Court had dismissed the case on one issue only and that being and I quote from the trial court's order dated December 8, 2011, "IT IS HEREBY ORDERED AND ADJUDGED that this action is DISMISSED WITHOUT PREJUDICE for lack of subject matter jurisdiction." The First Court of Appeals panel ruled for Petitioner and then after a changed of panels for no reason, the second ruled against Petitioner.**

2- **Does an Appeal panel have the right to change another Appeal panel's ruling based on no new evidence and after the first panel published their ruling.**

3- **Does the Constitution give the Court of Appeals the rights to deny a person Due Process because the issue in the complaint goes against the court's personal beliefs, which happened in this case?**

4- **Is there at least five (5) members on this Supreme Court who believe that our forefathers meant for all Complaints that were requested to be tried by a jury are tried by jury, and not judges, judging the case.**

5- **Is there at least five (5) members on this court who believes that companies who cheat and swindle people by selling junk products and refuses to fix and or replace the products, should have to answer to a jury to determine guilty? Who believes that the middle class people should have their day in court and who believe that judges should stick to the issue appealed and not change issues to protect a company?**

STATEMENT OF THE CASE AND ARGUEMENT

PROCEDURAL HISTORY

Flint would like to start by saying that he is an 81 year old Pro, Se and he deserves a review on his Petition the same as any attorney. It seems some judges on this court don't believe that a person should be a pro, se. This Court has refused to hear a number of cases by Petitioner even though he has showed this court how judges are violating laws and rules in Jefferson County, KY and this court has turned a deaf ear to his pleadings. Petitioner is concern about our country.

Surely this court has five (5) members who care about true justice. Five members who believes that large companies that makes billions of dollars each year shouldn't be protected by this court when they have committed horrible acts that has harmed America and its citizens.

Petitioner has been lied to, deceived and mistreated by two District Court judges and by a second panel of judge on the Sixth Circuit Court of Appeals. The First panel issued an order on May 15, 2012 denying Hewlett Packard's motion to dismiss the case. That panel issued an order and published the order.

When a Pro, Se is involved, a court has to overlook some of the actions by a Pro, Se and arrive at the truth by other means, regardless of what it takes. No fair minded judge or the framers of the constitution would expect a non-educated person to complete with a person who has been educated and trained for a number of years or judges that has all of the power. There is nothing in the United States Constitution that says that the Court's Rule of Civil procedures must be adhered to by Pro, Se's. A pro, se actions must me judge by the pro, se's action and their intent. Nothing can supersede the 14th amendment to the constitution giving everyone Due Process, to a fair and honest trial.

Therefore any mis-action made or lack of presenting the proper federal law or rule in pleadings to a court, cannot be held against a Pro, Se. If any court holds in their rulings that a Pro, Se didn't adhere to the rules of civil procedures or cite the right authority, then the court is giving the educated lawyer an unfair advantage over the pro, se, and denying the Pro, Se a Due Process fair trial. The court its self would be discriminating against a Pro, Se.

Court's Rules of Civil Procedure are court drafted rules and are not constitution mandated for a due process fair trial. The truth which a court must find is was Plaintiff harmed by any method, whether it is physical or civil rights or property. The 14th Amendment gives every person the right to protect their property and that is what Flint was doing in this complaint he filed with the trial court. Pro, se's under all circumstances must be protected by this court, from the harassing done by any party including judges in not conforming to the courts rules on discovery, if any exits. A Pro, Se person have a right to explain their case the best they can and a court must take the time to get to the truth, even if everything is not done by the Courts rules.

A courts duty is to get the truth in the case, regardless of anything else and regardless of what time and effort it takes the court to find the truth.

What the trial court and the second panel of the Appeals court did to Flint are dictator and they have no desire for true justice.

This case involves Hewlett Packard (here after HP) a large company that makes computers and printers.

Petitioner Flint purchased a printer from the respondent HP and they printer would not function properly. Flint worked with HP's technicians for months trying to make the printer work, Finally HP technicians said they couldn't make it work properly and would have another printer sent to Flint to replace the printer. After Flint received the replacement printer he and HP technicians couldn't make it function properly. HP technicians finally gave up and said they would have another printer sent to replace the printer. The technicians stated that Flint should choose another model of his chose from HP's line of printers that the model Flint had purchased could not be made to function properly. The technicians said they would have someone from HP call and discuss the transaction with Flint.

Finally after Flint could not get the issue settled he filed a complaint in Federal Court.

Flint will now copy a portion of the complaint he filed in this case in September of 2010.

A PORTION OF FLINT'S COMPLAINT

Comes now the Plaintiff, Edward H. Flint Pro, Se acting as his own counsel against Defendant Hewlett-Packard Company in a complaint against them for selling Plaintiff a defective product with a so called warranty and not fixing the printer and for creating a monopoly regarding ink cartridges without informing potential customers such as Plaintiff of such monopoly and for this cause of action and other causes, Plaintiff states as follows:

1- Plaintiff Edward H. Flint lives at

2- Hewlett-Packard (HP) is a company in Palo Alto California that produces and sells printing equipment for use with computes or standing by them self, for coping documents, coping pictures, sending faxes and scanning documents into a computer. Hewlett-Packard is one of the world's largest producers of computers and printers

3- Plaintiff purchased` a Office Jet model J4580 all in one printer from HP on good faith, based on facts that the printer had been engineered and tested and promoted as a great machine and Plaintiff wouldn't have any problems with the equipment when used for its intended purposes. The printer came with a warranty that Hewlett-Packard implied that if the printer didn't work, Hewlett-Packard as promised would correct any faults, so it would perform as promised. Therefore Plaintiff alleges that HP put on the market a product that was not properly designed and had not been proven to operate the way consumers was led to believe it would.

4- Plaintiff alleges that HP rushed the printer into production to be sold, before it was proven to work correctly and efficiency, because they wanted the sales from the ink cartridges that the printer used. Defendant made more money on the ink cartridges that on the machine and the sale of ink was their aim and they didn't care how much trouble they put consumers through. They knew the printer was not ready to be sold and they knew the printer had a lot of flaws in it, when they released the printer for sale.

5- Plaintiff alleges that HP wasn't concern about the hardship on consumers, only about profits from the ink. They intentionally made the printer so it could not use ink from another manufacture or a refill of their own cartridges, which forced a consumer to buy their ink cartridges and thereby created a monopoly on the ink cartridges for Hewlett-Packard printers. They created this monopoly didn't tell or warn the customers before or doing the sales that the printer would only use HP ink cartridges.

6- Plaintiff alleges that HP had so many problems with the printer they finally had to discontinue producing it. Hewlett-Packard created a monopoly by designing their printers so it will only use HP ink cartridges, and they do not warn or tell potential consumers of this fact before or when the consumer buys the printer.

7- Plaintiff alleges that Hewlett-Packard's actions and printer caused Plaintiff harm and distress.

8- Plaintiff alleges that Hewlett-Packard's actions injured Plaintiff both mentally and physically.

9- Plaintiff alleges that Hewlett- Packard's equipment failed to perform as promised and as warranted and HP couldn't fix it.

10- Plaintiff alleges that HP uses customers instead of their own salaried personal to fix and correct problems with their equipment, which is against what defendant says in their warranties.

11- Plaintiff alleges that Hewlett-Packard uses old people, tech ignorant people and young people, who are not capable of fixing HP printers, but have no choice but to try and fix their printer and consumers aren't told of this fact before or when purchasing printers and is time consuming and nerve wrecking to consumers This is like buying a new car and when something doesn't work the car dealer reads instructions over the phone to the car's owner and the owner does the work.

12- Plaintiff alleges that Hewlett-Packard doesn't take in to account the fact that some consumers have handicaps and HP require these people to fix the problems on bad products that's under warranty that Hewlett-Packard manufactures and sells.

13- Plaintiff alleges that Hewlett-Packard post on their web site, corporate objectives and shared values to help sell the image of Hewlett-Packard and to help sell their products. Hewlett-Packard ignores these objectives and values when it comes to costing the company money and they fail to live by the objectives and shared values when it comes to customers.

14- Plaintiff alleges that Hewlett-Packard uses misleading wording in their sales tactics regarding warranties.

15- Plaintiff alleges that Hewlett-Packard failed to perform their ethical responsibility to the Plaintiff and to the general public who buys their equipment.

16- Plaintiff alleges that Hewlett-Packard only cares about making a profit and has no feelings for its customers, once it gets the customer's money.

17- Plaintiff alleges that after customers purchase equipment from them, Hewlett-Packard intentionally has a phone system that only confuses customers who needs repairs to their equipment; however the Defendants know how to make it easy and simple to buy printers from them, but not to repair them.

18- Plaintiff alleges that Hewlett-Packard conspires within their company against consumers who has purchased equipment from them, by not living up to their promises and then passing the problem from person to person.

19- Plaintiff alleges that Hewlett-Packard routes technical problems to technicians in the country of India or some other foreign country and uses technicians that speaks broken English, some speak very bad broken English, which makes it difficult for English speaking customers to understand. The technician and consumers spend hours just trying to commutate with each other, when attempting to get the customer's equipment fixed, without success at times. This action is harmful to consumers.

20- Plaintiff alleges that Hewlett-Packard should have put their customer first, even before other profits, after they have received the consumer's money. Hewlett-Packard owes their customers, technicians who speak clear English. Even if Hewlett-Packard goes to another country to save money on hiring technician, they still had a duty to their customers to hire clear English speaking technicians.

21- Plaintiff alleges that Hewlett-Packard actions cause's consumers to loose valuable time and such actions are frustrating, costly and harmful to customer's nerves.

22- Plaintiff alleges that on September 9, 2010 after the words "tri-color ink cartridge is incomparable" kept scrolling on his printer. The technician, who is employed by Hewlett-Packard, stated that he could not make the equipment work and the technician turned Plaintiff over to his supervisor. The supervisor told Plaintiff that another person who is employed by Hewlett-Packard would call Plaintiff and that person would ship a new printer to Plaintiff. Plaintiff could choose a new printer from any printer Hewlett-Packard, sells. The supervisor employee stated the person would call Plaintiff on Friday September 10, 2010.

22- Plaintiff alleges that no one called Plaintiff on that Friday and Plaintiff after not receiving a phone call from anyone, started Saturday calling technicians in India to find out why the person hadn't called about shipping a new printer, with no luck.

23- Plaintiff alleges that after making a number of phone calls to various other employees of Hewlett-Packard, on Monday September 13, 2010, Plaintiff was finally put on the line with a person named Diana who claimed to be a case manager. After going through the story with Diana, she stated that the model printer

Plaintiff has, has been discontinued, but she would sell Plaintiff a newer model printer for $119.00. Plaintiff told case manager Diana 4 or 5 times what he had been promised by the Supervisor and Diana said the supervisor didn't have the authority to say those things to Plaintiff and Plaintiff needed to buy a printer.

24- Plaintiff alleges that Hewlett-Packard sold a printer that was so poorly made, that its own ink cartridges wouldn't work in their own printer, and all at the expense of the consumers. HP hid this fact from the consumers, rather than recall all of the printers.

25- Plaintiff alleges that Hewlett-Packard has a program within their company that rewards employees by either paying bonuses or the employees are told what they have to do to keep their job or to obtain promotions to better jobs, all which are based on profits their unit earns. The employees are to convict the customers to do things that will enhance Hewlett-Packard profit line and the customers has to bear the blunt of the actions taken by the employees.

26- Plaintiff alleges that Hewlett-Packard actions created mental and physical harm to Plaintiff, over the greed of profit for HP.

27- Plaintiff alleges the ink cartridge problem happens on a regular bases in HP printers and Hewlett-Packard failed to notify customers of the problems the printers are having and HP hid the truth from buyers, both old and new buyers, even when their technicians knew what the problems was.

28- Plaintiff alleges that by Hewlett-Packard not telling consumers about ink cartridges from other manufactures not working in HP printers have committed fraud on public consumers. Not telling the public consumers is fraud on HP's part.

Therefore Plaintiff demands that Hewlett Packard be held liable for their actions in the above allegations, and Plaintiff makes the following demands.

1- A trial by jury.

2- On any or all allegations in this complaint which a jury finds the Defendant guilty, Plaintiff is awarded both compensatory and punitive damages from defendant in the amount determined by a jury.

3- If Hewlett-Packard is found guilty on any alleged issue in this complaint, 1)defendant is ordered to place full page ad in the top 100 newspaper across America, apologizing, for the way Hewlett-Packard has treated customers and 2) further Hewlett-Packard guarantees to correct and simplify their procedures for repairing consumers equipment problems in the further, including using technicians who speaks clear English, and 3) if found guilty of creating or trying to create a monopoly whereby only their ink cartridges can be used in their printers, Hewlett-Packard is to redesign all printers both past and future, to where the printer can use ink manufactured by other companies and 4) agree not to create a monopoly on any printer using ink cartridges in the future without advertising said fact and telling each potential customer said fact and 5) to recall all printer previously sold to anyone and to fix them where consumers can use ink cartridges produced by other companies.

4- If Hewlett-Packard is found guilty by a jury of committing fraud on public consumers, they be fined fifty million (50,000,000) dollars, which Plaintiff must give to charities that are approved by this court.

5- All cost of this complaint by Plaintiff

6- For any other relief to which said Plaintiff may appear entitled.

Respectfully submitted
Edward H. Flint Pro, Se

The Trial judge ordered each party to file a brief stating what the case was about and scheduled a conference hearing for January 20, 2011.

Flint filed his brief in December 2010 and he now copies a portion of his brief which follows.

Comes the Plaintiff, Edward H. Flint Pro, Se, presenting his brief and position regarding this case as ordered by the court for the Scheduling Conference to be held on January 20, 2011.

Plaintiff purchased a Hewlett Packard printer from Office Depot. Plaintiff was told that the printer had a warranty and there shouldn't be any problems, that they work great, but if a problem came about, that Plaintiff could call the H-P tech center and they would fix the printer.

H-P will attempt to change the meaning of the warranty and Plaintiff declares this is an issue for a jury to decide, the meaning of the warranty versus what happens after the machine has problems, including the design and the con game that went with the printer Plaintiff purchased. H-P is trying to get out of welshing on an employee's word.

The printer had all kinds of problems that required calling a technician to fix each problem, if the problem could be solved. After many calls, the technician stated they couldn't fix the printer and they would have to send Plaintiff another printer.

H-P records these calls and should have the recordings to be heard by a jury.

After the second printer arrived Plaintiff had to repackage the old printer, take it to a UPS store and ship it. Plaintiff was told to put everything that came with the first printer into the same packaging as the shipped container and return it with the shipping label and return it per the shipping instruction.

After receiving the new printer Plaintiff had to install the printer. The package did not contain a warranty. Plaintiff had a 4200 model and assumed that the warranty was the same. After installing, the new printer, the printer had mores of the same problems as the first one. Plaintiff had to call the technicians' numberless times. Plaintiff on September 3, 2010 was told by the technician that the warranty was about to expire on his printer. Plaintiff renewed the warranty on September 3, 2010 by credit card. On September 9, 2010 Plaintiff's printer quite working again and a warning message came on a screen that said "tri-color ink cartridge is incomparable". Plaintiff called the technician and after hours of trying, the technician said that he couldn't fix the printer and for Plaintiff to hold on and talk with his supervision.

The supervision came on the line and Plaintiff's printer would have to be replaced and said that Hewlett Packard would have to send another printer and Plaintiff could pick out any printer he wanted from H-P line of printers. He said H-P would call the next morning from a different department of Hewlett Packard.

Plaintiff after not hearing from anyone about replacing the printer on September 13, 2010 started calling H-P. After calling a number of numbers and getting kicked around from department to department, Plaintiff was finally given the person who said she was the case manager, her name was Diana. After Plaintiff told Diana the story, she said the supervision didn't have the authority to tell Plaintiff what he did. Diana said the model number printer Plaintiff had, had been discontinued. However she said she had another model that she would sell Plaintiff for $119.00.

PLAINTIFF'S POSITION

Plaintiff now tells this court that Hewlett Packard makes a profit of over 10 billion dollars a year. Hewlett Packard makes 10 Billion dollars a year in profit; by selling horrible designed printers, printers that are designed to suck money out of consumer's pockets as Plaintiff will show below.

Hewlett Packard deliberately designed a different series of 4 in 1 printers that was out of the norm for printers used to hook up to computers. The design was produced so consumers have to buy more ink than was the normal for 4 in 1 printers were, including their printers.

They sold printers;

12- That required both the color and black cartridges had to be in the printer, in unison.

13- That required that both cartridges had to have ink in them at all time. However even when the color ink cartridge contained ink, the printer would stop functioning. Thereby they created a monopoly.

14- That wouldn't function with an ink cartridge that was produced by another company, thereby creating a monopoly

15- That would not function with a cartridge, including those sold by Hewlett Packard that was refilled with ink by other companies. This designed produced a monopoly for Hewlett Packard and keeps consumers from being able to save money and forced them to buy original H-P ink cartridges.

16- That has a built in program that won't function if a certain date is stamped on the cartridge even if the cartridges are made and sold by Hewlett Packard. This endeavor forces consumers to use a cartridge by a certain date or by a new one. This is a monopoly created to make consumers buy more Hewlett Packard ink cartridges. A consumer buy a printer and buy ink cartridges from H-P and H-P says that if you don't use the ink by a certain date, you must throw it away and buy a new cartridges of ink.

6- That the printer's scanner was faulty doesn't function correctly and screws up other programs in the computer.

7- That the printer would not print envelopes correctly, like normal printers

8- Hewlett Packard once had a series of 4 in 1 printers that didn't have the requirements stated above and Hewlett Packard redesigned those printers to create a monopoly to sell more ink by requiring the above.

9- H-P created a monopoly to sell more ink and hid the facts from the consumer; H-P created a monster and as one person said "a piece of junk."

10- Hewlett Packard never informed consumers of these facts before selling them the printer and Plaintiff states that H-P action are at the expense of consumers.

11- Plaintiff argues that H-P owes it to consumers to advise them of the facts before the sale of the printer. H-P has set up a rip-off on their customers and doesn't tell their customers because they know that no one would buy such a printer, if the told the truth..

12- The resigned printers H-P put on the market had horrible flaws in the design and the printers don't operate correctly and the consumers are paying for the defects.

Plaintiff will prove that Hewlett Packard deliberately designed the printer to more sell ink cartridges, which is where all of the profits are in the Printer business. Consumers have a right to be told the truth before they buy a produce.

13- H-P will attempt to hide behind a catch all warranty, in this case. The warranty and action of H-P is a swindle on the consuming public, and Plaintiff will prove such to a jury.

14- When a consumer buys an H-P printer, the consumers are told there is a warranty on the printer and H-P will make good on any problems. After Plaintiff brought the printer he had to call Hewlett Packard's technicians frequent times to try and get it fixed and the technicians are in India.

15- When you call Hewlett Packard and they asked which department you want and when you say tech support, Hewlett Packard says have your information regarding the printer ready for the technician and if the product is out of warranty you will be charged a fee. The technicians that a consumer gets are nothing but readers of manuals, which tells the consumers what to do to fix the printer. H-P is not repairing the printers; the buyers of the printers are, if they can be fixed. The consumers must do everything to make the printer function, that includes taking apart some of the printer, etc. Hewlett Packard does not tell, but should tell consumers what to expect, before selling printers to consumers. If Plaintiff had been told what he would have to go through, Plaintiff would have never brought the printer and doesn't believe any other person would either. Hewlett Packard designed a printer around more ink profits, which created a monopoly for H-P.

16- Plaintiff states that H-P warranty does not tell or notify a consumer what to expect if he needs help, except to call their nearest service center. H-P uses a catch all warranty to swindle their consumers. Hewlett Packard sells a cheap printer to attract consumers, but hides the information about the ink cartridges.

In addition, when you call a Hewlett Packard technician, you expect to be able to communicate with a technician you can understand. All technicians that answered the phone when Plaintiff called them were in India and all spoke very bad broken English. The Plaintiff could not hear or understand them. A call to Hewlett Packard for technical help takes hours and hours, rather than minutes because of the poor communication. Plaintiff states that at the very least Hewlett Packard owes the consumer a technician they can understand. If Hewlett Packard had told Plaintiff to expect such problems, Plaintiff would have never purchased the printer. Hewlett Packard owes the public a simple easy way of fixing printers or they should be told truth and H-P shouldn't be selling printers that don't meet those expectations. Hewlett Packard put the consumers at risk and took advantage of customers by shipping the jobs of technicians to India for cheap labor. H-P saves money, but consumers pay dearly for the hassle and ineffective service. If the America public knew what H-P does they would quit buying HP produces.

Plaintiff now believes that what the supervisor was telling him, was he needed another printer and Plaintiff could take his pick from any H-P printers, but don't pick this one, he was telling Plaintiff that the product he had was so bad they couldn't fix it and you need a different model.

Hewlett Packard welched on their employee's word, and instead of replacing Plaintiff's printer, they offered to sell Plaintiff a printer.

Hewlett Packard has an incentive program that pays employees bonuses based on the profits they earn. That program is the reason for the faulty printer, the people in either the engineering department or the sales department seen dollars signs instead of consumers when putting this printer on the market. Sell ink, the hell with problems. Plaintiff claims that once H-P sells you a despicable designed printer, they have you in a position, that they keep squeezing you to buy more ink, before you completely understand the problems. Plaintiff wonders how many people H-P has done this to. The so called case worked tried to squeeze Plaintiff out of money. This may be another reason they make over 10 billion dollars a year profit.

Hewlett Packard went back on their word that Plaintiff would receive a printer of his choice. Plaintiff claims that the person who denied Plaintiff the promise that the supervisor made and who said she was the case manager, receives a bonus based on profits made. She attempted to create more profits for H-P rather than make good on the supervisor word. When she made the statement, she was really saying, H-P doesn't care if you have problems, we need to make more profits and you need to buy a new printer and forget about all of the labor, heartache, pain, etc. that H-P has cause you, I can only receive a bonus if you buy something, I won't receive a bonus if we give away printers.

H-P's printer that Plaintiff purchased also does work properly on printing envelopes and on scanning documents.

Plaintiff is writing a book titled "Corrupt Judges". The book is a true story about an actual lawsuit case and the content of his book is 80% legal court documents regarding the case. Plaintiff scanned these documents and the scanning from the printer screwed up Plaintiff computer so bad, that he spent three weeks straighten out his computer. Plaintiff is going to write another book title "Corrupt Judges Kill Justice," and he is trying to figure out how to scan legal court documents.

Before Plaintiff can print an address on an envelope properly he has to unfold the envelope before he puts it into the printer. The H-P technicians were never able to fix the problem. H-

P put the printer on the market before it working properly, because they were in a hurry to make profits.

Hewlett Packard owes consumers the truth about their product before they sell a product. H-P puts fancy printing on their documents; about what the printer is supposed to do. But H-P prints nothing about what is required to make it function properly, nothing about the ink. H-P owes the public a printer that is properly designed before putting it on the market and they put a printer on the market that was never designed properly. Discovery will show that H-P knew they had problems with printer and sold it to customers anyhow, so they could sell more ink. What does their warranty mean? What are consumers entitled to for their money? What do consumers need to know about the meaning of a warranty before they buy it, not after? What does the consumer need to know about how the printer functions? What Hewlett Packard has done and is doing, is tricky deception on consumers. Hewlett Packard designed and sold a printer that was flawed from the start and they never fixed it to run properly. H-P should not be allowed by this court to treat consumers this way.

H-P should have recalled all of the flawed printers after finding out they didn't function properly, just like automobile manufactures have to, by federal government demands. This court should rule that they must recall the printers. Plaintiff states that H-P had an obligation to recall these printers and they chose to keep on making money at the consumer's expense, they never recalled the horrible printers. H-P didn't want to tell the consumers the truth, which they were obligated to do. Hewlett Packard has at this time three (3) class actions suits against them over the ink cartridges in these machines, that they have agreed to settle.

A jury should decide the allegations Plaintiff has made against Hewlett Packard. Plaintiff is sure that somewhere down the line of this case, H-P will ask the judge for summary judgment in this case; they don't want a jury to decide guilt or innocence based on the evidence. Plaintiff hopes this case never become a subject for one of his books.

Plaintiff was called by Hewlett Packard right after he filed his complaint and H-P asked him to make an offer to settle. All though Plaintiff wasn't interested in settling the case, he did make an offer and Hewlett Packard refused to accept the offer. An offer at this time from Plaintiff would be greater that the first offer.

Plaintiff states and alleges that Hewlett Packard's handling and design of the printer was nothing but a con game for making profits. In addition they committed fraud on Plaintiff and lied to Plaintiff, and they created a monopoly on Plaintiff and other consumers by deception. No person or company should be allowed to profit on a monopoly that is based on fraud.

A jury trial is necessary to determine the truth and to determine if Hewlett Packard is guilty as Plaintiff alleges. Plaintiff has attached his proposed case schedule and there is no reason why Plaintiff's schedule should not be granted.

After months of HP refusing to turn over discovery and the trial court refusing to grant Flint leave to amend the complaint and add Office Depot to the complaint as a Defendant, the trial court issued an order regarding jurisdiction. The trial court Seven (7) months after the complaint was filed and with no one questioning the issue of jurisdiction, set a hearing and ordered a brief on jurisdiction by both parties. The following is Flint Memorandum as ordered by the trial court

MEMORANDUM TO ANSWER JUDGE WHALIN'S ORDER CONCERNING THE HEARING HELD BETWEEN THE PARTIES AND JUDGE WHALIN ON MAY 4, 2011

MEMORANDUM

Comes the Plaintiff Edward H. Flint Pro, Se filing this memorandum to answer Judge Whalin's order given on a number of issues at a hearing held on May 4, 2011.

Plaintiff first states he is confused by why the hearing was held by Judge Whalin, but will comment on each issue that Judge Whalin stated at the hearing.

1- Judge Whalin stated he is denying Plaintiff's motion for Judge Whaling to recuse himself from this case. Plaintiff contends that Judge Whalin by holding the May 4, 2011 hearing again proved that Judge Whalin is bias against Plaintiff in this case. Plaintiff is being denied a Due Process fair trial by Judge Whalin's actions and in addition Plaintiff is not being judge by the Rules of how a judge should react according to the court's rules and by the ethics outlined in the court's rules and by Cannons laws. Judge Whalin is determine that the outcome out this case will be the way he wants and not by truths and facts

2- Judge Whalin stated that he was staying all discoveries and all scheduled dates in this case. This is telling Plaintiff that the outcome will be against you, so there is no reason for Plaintiff to ask for or to expect any discoveries because you are not going to get any discoveries and you are not going to get any trial, because I Judge Whalin has determined the outcome, so why waste time.

3- Judge Whalin stated and issued an order that he wanted Plaintiff to justify why this case is in this court based on the court concern about the diversity jurisdiction of the court to hear the present case under 28 U.S.C. # 1332. Plaintiff asks Judge Whalin why this court has raised this issue. Plaintiff filed his complaint on September 20, 2010. Now Seven Months (7) later this court orders a hearing and Judge Whalin orders Plaintiff to justify why the case should be heard by this court. The Defendant Hewlett Packard did not question the issue of diversity jurisdiction when the complaint was filed and as of this time Hewlett Packard has not raised the question about jurisdiction. Judge Whalin on his owned raised the question and Plaintiff is loss for a reason, except Judge Whalin wants Hewlett Packard to win this case and is bias for Hewlett Packard. The court is to be neutral in cases before it, but Judge Whalin wants to do it his way and not by the Courts rules and ethics.

Judge Whalin didn't question if Hewlett Packard was qualified to be sued in this court.

Plaintiff states that Hewlett Packard is a resident of Kentucky. Hewlett Packard has been registered with the Secretary of the State of Kentucky as a resident of Kentucky since at least 2001 and has a registered agent to do business for them in Kentucky. Plaintiff contents that under U.S.C. 28 #1391 the complaint against Hewlett Packard prevails and therefore there is no diversity of citizenship as Judge Whalin is attempting to raise. Hewlett Packard is subject to be sued in Kentucky for any amount.

Plaintiff believes that Hewlett Packard is bribing Judge Whalin who has done everything possible to keep the case from proceeding from the very start. Plaintiff states that by Hewlett Packard actions of bribing Judge Whalin would be consistent with the allegations Plaintiff has made against Hewlett Packard and the way Hewlett Packard has handled this case, against the court's rules with no integrity. It is unbelievable that a judge of a Federal Court in America would do everything against the courts rules and ethics do what Judge Whalin has done to Plaintiff in this case.

4. Now to answer Judge Whalin about whether this complaint satisfies the jurisdictional amount required by 28 U.S.C. #1332. This section that Judge Whalin is attempting to using, states among other things that there must be a controversy that exceeds a value of $75,000.00. Plaintiff in his demands believes that the allegations he made is in Plaintiff mind and eyes has a value of over $60,000,000.00. The amount in controversy far exceeds the statute amount. If Defendant Hewlett Packard had a question on the amount of Plaintiff's demands, they should have put in as a controversy when the complaint was filed. Hewlett Packard did not raise the controversy at the time the complaint was filed and Hewlett Packard still has not raised the controversy about the amount in question. Only Judge Whalin has raised the subject and this is not the court's duty. As Plaintiff as told this court in a number of pleading Chief Judge of the United States Supreme Court state to the United

States Senate at his confirmation hearing when asked what a judges duty was, he stated and I quote, **"Judges are like umpires. Umpires don't make the rules. They apply them. The role of an umpire and a judge is critical. The make sure everybody plays by the rules. But it is a limited role. Nobody ever went to a ball game to see the umpires." His jurisprudence would be characterized by "modesty and humility."** Judge Whalin has stepped out of bounds in his actions of raising the diversity of citizenship issue. A Judge is not to look for what's in a complaint, that is the other parties responsible and Hewlett Packard did not raise the issue.

a) Plaintiff in his complaint in his demands asked for in No. 2- Plaintiff is awarded both compensatory and punitive damages. Plaintiff would at the time asked the jury for two hundred thousand (200,000) dollars in compensatory damages plus punitive damages and since the case has started, based on the way Hewlett Packard has acted and not obeyed the court rules which hurt Plaintiff, Plaintiff would now ask the jury for one million (1,000,000) in compensatory damages, plus punitive damages.

b) Plaintiff in his complaint in his demands asked for in his No. 3- a full page ad in the top one hundred (100) newspapers across America, with Hewlett Packard apologizing for the way Hewlett Packard has treated customers which Plaintiff believes will cost $5000.00 per page for a total cost of five hundred thousand ($500,000.00) and

c) in No. 2 of 3- Plaintiff asked that Hewlett Packard correct and simplify their procedures for repairing consumers equipment problems, which Plaintiff believes will cost Hewlett Packard over two million (2, 000,000) and d) in No. 3 of 3- Hewlett Packard is to resign printers, which Plaintiff believes will cost Hewlett Packard over two million (2,000,000) dollars and e) in No. 5 of 3- Hewlett Packard to recall all printers sold and repair them, which Plaintiff believes will cost a minimum of two million (2,000,000) dollars

f) in 4- of Plaintiff complaint Plaintiff asked that if Hewlett Packard be fined fifty million (50, 000,000) dollars.

Plaintiff states that for a company that makes 10 billion (10,000,000,000) dollars per year profit, this would be a small amount compared to what they make per year.

The requirement of the court for jurisdiction is $75,000. Even questioning the jurisdiction is an insult to the justice system and makes a mockery out of the courts. Plaintiff again states that Judge Whalin wants Hewlett Packard to win this case and it seems he will do anything to see that they do. No honest and fair court can look at Plaintiff complaint and question if the case meets the courts requirement as far as the amount of money.

Hewlett Packard has shown in the way they designed the printer and treated customers, they have no regards for customers; the way they acted in this case they have no regards for the courts or laws or rules and or ethics and now getting a judge to question if an amount of $75,000 is involved, have no integrity whatsoever. Hewlett Packard proves that for money some companies will do anything.

This court must send a message to companies that consumers of products must come first.

Therefore this court must accept that the complaint is in the right jurisdiction, reset the dates for trial, compel Hewlett Packard on discovery, must rule on every motion and other documents before this court and Judge Whalin must recuse himself from this case in the name of justice.

On August 26, 2011 the trial court issued an order and reentered the same order on December 8, 2011 that stated "IT IS HEREBY ORDERED AND ADJUDGED that this action is DISMISSED WITHOUT PREJUDICE for lack of subject matter jurisdiction."

Petition Flint appealed two separate orders of the trial court the to the Sixth Circuit Court of Appeals and the Court of Appeals put the all issues in to one case (11-6523-12-5100). The first panel agreed that the complaint was in the proper venue. The second Court of Appeals panel twisted and turned the facts of the case because they assumed that Flint was too dumb to know the different

Respondent Hewlett Packard filed a motion to dismiss based on jurisdiction. The first Court of Appeals panel denied the motion to dismiss Hewlett Packard's motion by order on May 15, 2012 and consolidated the appealed ordered and ordered a briefing scheduled on the other appealed issue. The case wound up being consolidated the cases into 11-6523-12-5100.

Because the majority of judges in the appeals court are conservatives' judges they are in control of that court. The judge of the district court in Louisville regarding this case was a law partner of Senator Mitch McConnell. He never sees a neural case. If any case is against a company he is against that party and he has the majority of the Court of Appeals with him. Hewlett Packard filed a motion with the Court of Appeals to dismiss this case for lack of jurisdiction. The Court of Appeals panel hearing that motion ruled on May 15, 2012 that Flint was in the right jurisdiction and then set a scheduling date for briefs on the other issue. Someone at the Court of Appeals took the case away from the panel that ruled in favor of Flint and gave it to a panel who favors the two judges. How can this court let these things happen? Being conservatives should make you sell your soul and this court should let not a pro, se be taken advantage of. If a sham ever existed in a law case this tops the list.

The new panel on the Court of Appeals issued an order dated September 27, 2012 against Flint. The order was full of non-truthful facts and twist words and they changed the facts to fit their wants.

Petitioner Flint filed with the Court of Appeals a motion for rehearing, parts of which follows. Flint will point out below some of the content of his Motion for a rehearing, because too print the entire motion would make the Petition go over the word limit of this court.

PORTION OF MOTION FOR REHEARING

Comes the Appellant requesting a rehearing on Case 11-6523/12-5100

Appellant disagrees with the interpretation, used by the court in regards to the issues of this case. The court in its order of May 15, 2012 found that the appellant jurisdiction is proper and denied the motions to dismiss. The judges that ordered the May 15, 2012 order were Kennedy, Siler and Sutton. The Judges that ruled on the September 27, 2012 order was different judges, these, they were Siler, Moore and McKeague. Appellant questions why a different set of judges was used on the last hearing on September 27, 2012 rather than the first. It looks like someone didn't like the ruling on the May 15, 2012 and switched judges to get the results it's wanted

The court in its September 27, 2012 ruling stated that Judges Whalin and cited Johnson v, Mitchell (6th Cir. 2009) as its authority. IT stated that, "to justify recusal the judge's prejudice or bias must be personal and extrajudicial." Judge Whalin violated court rules and the records shows he was bias. Appellant in his brief to this court stated, "Appellant based on the action of the two judges Judge Simpson and Judge Whalin had that asked that both recuse them self from the case a number of time. Not only has Judge Whalin violated the rules of the court and Cannons, but he also refuses to honor 28 U.S.C. #455.

Because of other lawsuits and because Flint has sued him, Judge Simpson should have recused himself. By 28 U.S.C. #455 Judge Simpson should have disqualify himself from this case at once.

Judge Simpson and Judge Whalin by not recusing themselves under 28 U.S. Code #455 are saying they don't have to obey Congresses law. They can do as they please.

This court stated the record reflects that the warranty limited Flint's remedy to have the printer repaired or replaced a limitation that is permitted under Kentucky law. See KRS 355.2-719 (1((a). This court cited one small part of a very large Kentucky statute. The Statute has other parts that the court failed to cite. Citing same KRS 355.2-719 (2) it states "Where circumstances cause an exclusive or limited remedy to fail its essential purpose remedy may be had as provided in this chapter." Kentucky's KRS 355.2-721 states "Remedies for material misrepresentation or fraud include all remedies available under the article for nonfraudulent breach. Neither rescission or a claim for a rescission of the contract for sale nor rejection or return of the goods shall bar or be deemed inconsistent with a claim for damages or other remedy." Appellant has accused Hewlett

Packard of Fraud in a number of issues in the case records, regarding the printer and their actions.

This court has failed to read the complaint, and Appellants pleadings filed in the records of this case.

The Trial Court dismissed the case on one issue only and that being and I quote from the trial court's August 26, 2011 order and reentered order dated December 8, 2011, IT IS HEREBY ORDERED AND ADJUDGED that this action is DISMISSED WITHOUT PREJUDICE for lack of subject matter jurisdiction."

There can be no question that the Appellant demands meet the criteria of 28 U.S.C #1332 (a)(1), however the trial court stated it did not and the reason for dismissal.

All other issues involved are for a jury to decide and not this court.

This court is searching for issues to rule against Flint, to protect their fellow judges.

Flint's complaint was filed correctly. The judges in this case both Judge Simpson and Judge Whalin should have reused them self from the case when asked the first time, but they refused after Flint asked Judge Simpson to recuse himself at least nine (9) times and Judge Whalin 13 times.

(1) Why did the court change judges from the panel who heard the first issue and then used a different panel before to new judges in the last hearing of the case?

(2) Why didn't the court confront the only issue before it and that issue is, Judge Simpson's August 26, 2011 order, that states "IT IS HEREBY ORDERED AND ADJUDGED that this action is DISMISSED WITHOUT PREJUDICE for lack of subject matter jurisdiction," and took up issues that are not in the trial court order that dismissed the case

Appellant Flint is asking this court to directly answer these two questions.

The Court of Appeals on December 3, 2012 denied Flint's Petition for a rehearing. The Sixth Circuit Court of Appeals for no reason switched judges from the panel who heard the first hearing to a second panel and, again for no reason except to protect the two trial judges and Hewlett Packard, a extreme large company who produced and sold junk products to poor people.

REASONS FOR GRANTING THE WRIT

1- The Sixth Circuit Court of Appeals was bias against Petitioner Flint and switch panels to make sure that Flint's case was dismissed

2- Flint was denied Due Process because the second panel of Court of Appeals only had one issue before them, but ruled on issues that were neither appealed nor briefed nor true. The second panel of Court of Appeals was either bias or didn't understand the case. The second panel of Court of Appeals made up issues that were not in the appeal, in order to reach the conclusion they wanted, to protect the trial judges.

3- Flint asked for a trial by a jury and the trial court refused to give him a jury trial but dismiss on lack of jurisdiction

4- Out forefathers foremost wanted all people to have trials by juries if they desired, instead of judges. In this case the Appeal Court judged issues that a jury should judge.

5- Courts are to see that every party gets justice and the trial court and the second Court of Appeals panel by their actions, protected the rich large company.

6- If a business ran its office and handled paper work the way the District Court of Kentucky did, the company wouldn't stay in business for a month. Flint believed that the trial judge had the paper work mishandled on purpose to throw him off and not know which way to turn and would give up pursuing his case.

CONCLUSION

1- Flint filed a proper complaint and in the proper jurisdiction and asked for a trial by jury.

2- The second Court of Appeals panel judged the wrong issue and failed to judge the issue that Flint appealed which was the judges recusing themselves

3- Both trial judges in the name of justice should have disqualified them self from the case.

4- The second Court of Appeals panel should have ruled on the issue of judges recusing them self only. Flint was denied Due Process because of the second panel of Court of Appeals was bias.

5- This court should grant certiorari and let this case be tried in District court by a jury.

6- The Court of Appeals judges even used wrong dates and facts in their order

7- This court should be concerned about the issues of fair and honest justice and about trials by a jury, as our forefathers wanted and so stated in the constitution.

8- This court should look at the constitution for how all parties should be treated and just how the rich and large companies are to be protected.

9- There were only two orders from the District Court judges that directly affected the outcome of this case and one was dismissing the case for lack of jurisdiction and the second was the two judges refusing to recuse themselves. The First issue regarding the dismissing the case for lack of jurisdiction was settled when the first panel of judges found that that the case should not have been dismissed because the case was filed in the right jurisdiction. The second panel action was protecting the District judges and a very large company, a company that makes over 10 billion dollars a year profit. Regarding the issue of the judges recusing themselves, the judges and the second Appeals Court judges are sayings that a judge can do anything and not have to recuse himself. The law that Congress passed meant nothing to the courts and Flint doesn't deserve justice, only the ones the judges wants to win, wins.

10- If the Supreme Court handled paper work including orders the way that the District Court did in this case, the Court couldn't function and America could not exist.

11- This court should do the right things and judge on what our forefathers wanted and grant certiorari.

12- The Mayflower people came to get away from Kings and Dictators. George Washington refused to be a king or dictator so he would stay a common man and this court must use every muscle in it brain and moral fiber to keep dictators and corrupt judges from existing in America.

13- The District Court judges and the second panel of the Court of Appeals judges twisted Flint like a straw in a tornado.

14- It is Flint's desire that this court will use its wisdom and God given talent to change every federal court in America to where every common middle class person receives justice and the large companies have to answer to a jury for their actions.

15- The act of changing Court of Appeals judge panels was an intentional act to harm Flint. If the judge(s) at the Court of Appeals who gave the approval to switch judges was in violation of their duty, they should be reported to Congress for impeachment.

16- This court owes it to America to make sure that there is no corruption in any court in America; this court owes it to America to make sure that no company is allowed to escape from being tried by a jury, when producing and selling defective products to consumers, this court owes it to America to make sure that the rich is not treated better that the poor, this court owes it to America to make sure that no person who harms another person or another person's property, escapes from being tried by a jury.

Fair and honest justice for all, was the reason this great county was founded. Justice for all, not for just a few is a right in America. Justice is not a game it's the most precious thing free people can receive, after life.

Petitioner Flints begs this court not to sleep with the Devil.

Petitioner prays that at least five (5) or more members of this court care about fair and honest justice.

Flint reminds the member of this court that Jesus Chris said that on judgment day he would judge us by the thoughts we had in our minds and the deeds we did on earth and not by the words we said.

Respectfully submitted,

s/ Edward H. Flint, Pro, Se.

*** The Supreme Court refused to review the case***

This case is the most troubling case of all. Hewlett Packard was selling a terrible designed and poorly manufactured printer. Hewlett Packard wanted to sell ink and they produced a printer to make the product use more ink than was needed. They were robbing their customers.

Hewlett Packard makes 10 billion dollars per year profit and treats customers as an enemy. The courts protected H-P. The courts actions harmed the consumers; they must have wanted H-P to make more than 10 billion dollars per year.

After I filed my lawsuit suit, a judge ordered a hearing. At the hearing the judge had the other attorney in the lawsuit, leave the court room and it was just him and me. This action was against the court's rules

At the hearing the judge brow beat me, trying to get me to settle the case for a new printer. I have a transcript of the hearing to prove what the judge did and said.

I asked this judge 13 times to recuse himself from the case and each time he refused.

There were two judges assigned to the case and I asked the other Judge 9 times to recuse himself and he refused. Both judges were bias and showed it.

The judge could only find one reason to dismiss the case. He ruled that I filed the case in the wrong jurisdiction. The Appeals Court at first said I was in the right jurisdiction. And then the court of appeals gave the case to another panel. The new panel said I was in the wrong jurisdiction.

The Supreme Court refused to review the case.

CHAPTER 16

LETTERS TO JUDGE ROBERTS AND SENATOR LEAHY AND OTHER JUSTICES OF THE SUPREME COURT

I hope that you have read the pages regarding the lawsuits, I will now start listing the letters that I wrote and as I go through them, I will explain them, although they speak for themselves.

I never filed a lawsuit that I couldn't win in a fair court. What the Federal Courts did to me is hard to believe. The entire Federal Court system was involved in making sure I never won a case.

It's hard to believe that there is not one judge that was fair and honest, although there were a couple of times that I believe the judge wanted to be fair and honest, but someone had pressure on them, not to let me win at all cost.

The Holy Spirit told me to write to the Chief Judge of the Supreme Court, John Roberts.

I became convinced that Senator Mitch McConnell, who I knew well and I knew how he operated, was involved. Two of the judges in the Louisville, Kentucky Federal District Court were friends and former counsels for Senator McConnell.

I had no choice but file the lawsuits in the Louisville court, by the rules of the court.

After I filed the Churchill Downs lawsuit and based on the treatment I received from the judge, it hit me that I was treading on unfriendly water. Churchill Downs was friendly to Senator McConnell. Churchill Downs and I had fought for years.

I was President in Kentucky and also nationally of an origination that represented owners and trainers of thoroughbred horses, that race at racetracks, through-out America.

Churchill Downs and I didn't see many things alike. We fought every session in the General Assembly of Kentucky, over money for owner's purses and any other issues that affected horse racing.

Senator McConnell was for seven years, Judge Executive of Jefferson County, Kentucky. He and I didn't see eye to eye. I was active in politics, behind the scene. We came from different sides on most issues.

I tell the story in Chapter 9 of about a friend of Senator McConnell that I terminated as counsel for the horsemen origination that I was president of, that represented the horse owners and trainers.

I became mad as hell; I knew our country was going to hell regarding the court system. The courts are rigged. The Holy Spirit told me to write Chief Judge John Roberts of the Supreme Court. I wrote a series of letters to Judge Roberts. Five letters to Judge Roberts follows.

On March 6, 2011 I wrote the following letter to Judge Roberts.

March 6, 2011

ATTN. Chief Judge John Roberts
Supreme Court of the United States
Attention Office of the Clerk
1 First Street, N. E.
Washington, DC 20543

Chief Judge Roberts:

I have enclosed a book that I wrote. In the book I quoted you a number of times and therefore I wanted you to see the book.

The title of the book is "Corrupt Judges"

The book is based on an actual case in Federal Court in Louisville Kentucky.

The justice system is destroying its self by corrupt judges.

I have sued seven judges and the courts keep protecting them. The corruption keeps spreading, when one judge sees another judge gets by with it.

There is a simple way to stop this madness.

I pray that you read the book and can do something to correct the justice system and the corrupt judges that exist, which there are many.

You are the only person who can correct the system. May God be with you on correcting the system.

Thanks for your time and I hope the book gives you some insight in how the judges are operating.

Ed Flint

I never received a reply from Judge Roberts

I wrote a letter to Judge Roberts dated June 27, 2011 regarding Judge Heyburn. It is inserted now.

June 27, 2011

Supreme Court of the United States
Attention Chief Judge John Roberts
1 First Street, N. E.
Washington, DC 20543

Chief Judge Roberts:

My name is Ed Flint. I am 81 years old and I am Pro, Se in a number of lawsuits. I understand how the law works.

I have enclosed a copy of an order from Judge Heyburn of Western District Court of Kentucky at Louisville. Judge Heyburn has threatened me. I have filed a number of lawsuits, some of them against judges. The attached copy of the order says I cannot sue any judge in state court or federal court.

The judges in Kentucky are corrupt and do as they please. I know they are after me because I am pro, se, and interfere with them being paid off by attorneys and companies, however I am entitled to Due Process fair and honest trial on each case and the judges won't give it to me.

I have asked the sued judges to disqualify themselves and the refuse to do so. I have sued Judge Heyburn, who you have put on a national committee and he refuses to disqualify himself.

I believe in truth and honesty at all times. I have never filed a frivolous law suit. When I sued a company it was because they harmed me some way. If I sued a judge it was because they violated Court's rules and laws. The 6th Circuit Court of Appeals is no help, because they protect the judges.

My question to you is how I get relief from the attached order, who can I appeal it to besides the Court of Appeals. The 6th Circuit rubber stamp everything the Western district sends them.

The judges in Louisville won't let me file a pleading and submit the facts to them; they use this as an excuse to dismiss the case. If I sued a judge; they dismiss it without finding out the facts by not giving me a chance, they say because it is clear that Plaintiff's complaint is devoid of all legal merit. I have attached a copy of the complaint Flint v. Hewlett, Case NO. 3:11CV-316-H. My complaint deserve to be heard or at lease let me submit a pleading to explain my allegations

Judge Heyburn's case was dismissed without a hearing or a pleading being filed explaining why the judge should recuse himself. Where is honest justice in this action?

Judge Whalin's case was dismissed without a pleading being filed explaining why the case should not be dismissed.

I also have enclosed a copy of my Brief to the Court of Appeals regarding my lawsuit against Judge Heyburn. In my brief I have outlined my case against Judge Heyburn and why he should disqualify himself.

I filed the Brief to the 6th Circuit on June 14, 2011 and sent Judge Heyburn a copy the same day. After receiving my motion to recuse him and the brief I filed with the Court of Appeals he keeps on judging my cases. All Judges in Louisville does the same thing, the refuse to recuse them self. They are being bought by attorneys and companies and don't want to be honest judges.

The justice system in America is leading America to destroy itself. Judges only let their friends win. Laws and rules mean nothing to judges any more. They know the system lets them do as they please.

If you read Judge Heyburn's Memorandum and Order and think this is how a person should be treated, then the justice system is finished in America.

I deserve a fair and honest trial and have not received one yet in Louisville. I have also enclosed copies of the Motions for Judge Heyburn and Judge Whalin to recuse them self. Under 28 U.S.C. #455 these judges should disqualify themselves. I am entitled to be trial by a judge that I haven't sued. Any judge a party sued will be prejudiced against me. Judge Heyburn says I am judge shopping, but that is no true, I am looking for and honest judge. Judge Heyburn's action is another attempt to write another law for corrupt judges to cite as authority. Judge Heyburn doesn't want to abide by the law but wants to write his own law to what he thinks it should be not want Congress passed. Until 28 U.S.C. #455 is changed by congress the law is clear, that a judge must disqualify themselves.

I ask you to read these documents and if you believe Judge Heyburn is right, and then let me know.

I asked you to please stop the madness going on in the courts across America.

You are the only person who can save America's justice system, but it takes guts and wisdom.

God through the Holy Spirit told me to write this letter to you.

I would be pleased to come to Washington to present my case to the Court, along my thoughts

I would like some kind of reply after you have read this letter and the enclosed documents.

Thanks and may God be with you on the endeavor of repairing the Justice System.

Edward Flint

I never received a reply from Judge Roberts about the letter and nothing was done about Judge Heyburn threatening me.

On August 21, 2011, I wrote the following letter to judge Roberts.

August 21, 2011

Attention: Chief Judge John Roberts
Supreme Court of the United States
1 First Street, N. E.
Washington, DC 20543

Chief Judge Roberts:

My name is Ed Flint. I am 81 years old and I am Pro, Se in a number of lawsuits. I understand how the law works.

I have enclosed a copy of two motions I filed in Louisville Kentucky, attempting to have two judges disqualified and replaced with another judge. The dates filed are August 1, 2011 and August 13, 2011. The August 13, 2011 has a letter to the district court chief judge attached. The judges refuse to recuse themselves. My case is not moving.

By Cannons Rules a judge should do something. Can you have the case moved along or can you tell me how I can get the case moving along for trial. Do I have a way to appeal to someone? I am entitled to a trial of some kind. These judges are violating the 14th amendment to the constitution, regarding Due Process for me.

I am entitled to America justice by a trial with an unbiased judge

I have written to you before and have not heard from you, it was about Judge Heyburn threatening me.

I have appealed a number of cases to your court, petitioning for certiorari against corrupt judges and your court refuses to grant certiorari. Your court is protecting judges who violate court rules and federal and state laws and I don't understand that. These corrupt judges are destroying America.

Regarding the issue that I am writing about I don't understand what the judges are going to do with this case, hold it forever, hoping I die? The case is against Hewlett Packard and Hewlett Packard selling junk printers, swindling money from people. I have asked for leave to amend my complaint an add Office Depot and the court refuses to rule on my motion. I have come to believe that one of the judges is akin to one of the attorneys for Hewlett Packard and the judge doesn't want them to lose. I would have to hire an investigator to find out for sure about kinship. Can the Court hold my case forever and do nothing? If they do nothing, this would be a dictatorship, not justice. There are other judges in the district that is capable of judging this case.

What is the America justice system coming to when two judges can hold a case forever? There has to be a reason and it has to be a personal reason for one of them or both a normal judge who is not bias would rule. If it is personal then that is even more reason they must disqualify themselves. I beg you to either get the case moving or tell me what I have to do to get it moving. The justice system is deteriorating rapid in America.

The justice system in America is responsible for America being destroying like it is doing. Judges only let their friends win or by their philosophy, but not truth and facts. Laws and Rules mean nothing to judges anymore. They know that appeal judges let give them a pass and that includes the Supreme Court and bless whatever they do

I asked you to please, stop the madness going on in the courts across America. You are the only person who can save America's justice system, but it takes guts and wisdom. Surely you have the votes on the court to do that.

I ask that you review this case; you will see that the judges in Kentucky have done everything bad to me possible. I have filed only good complaints, but because I am Pro, Se the judges think I don't understand what they are doing. The judges don't like it because a Pro, Se can be smart. Truth and facts doesn't come into the judge's mind. Please check out any case I have had before your court, just to satisfy your mind that I have filed only good cases.

God through the Holy Spirit told me to write this letter to you.

I would appreciate some kind of reply after you have read this letter and the enclosed documents.

Thanks for reading my letter and May God be with you on the endeavor of fixing the Justice System.

Edward H. Flint

I never received a reply from Judge Roberts regarding this letter.

I wrote Judge Roberts the following letter on September 15, 2011.

September 15, 2011

Attention: Chief Judge John Roberts
Supreme Court of the United States
1 First Street, N. E.
Washington, DC 20543

Chief Judge Roberts:

My name is Ed Flint. I am 81 years old and I am Pro, Se in a number of lawsuits. I understand how the law works. I have forward to you a couple of letters to you about my case. The case in the Western District of Kentucky at Louisville is CASE NO. 3:10-CV-597-S

I have enclosed a copy another motion I filed in Louisville Kentucky, attempting to have two judges disqualified and replaced with another judge. The judges refuse to recuse themselves. My case is not moving. How can we say that America has a fair and honest court system when judges do this to anyone?

By Cannons Rules a judge should do something. Can you have the case moved along or can you tell me how I can get the case moving along for trial. Do I have a way to appeal to someone? I am entitled to a trial of some kind. These judges are violating the 14th amendment to the constitution, regarding Due Process for me.

I am entitled to America justice by a trial with an unbiased judge

I have written to you before and have not heard from you, it was about Judge Heyburn threatening me.

I have appealed a number of cases to your court, petitioning for certiorari against corrupt judges and your court refuses to grant certiorari. Your court is protecting judges who violate court rules and federal and state laws and I don't understand that. These corrupt judges are destroying America.

Regarding the issue that I am writing about I don't understand what the judges are going to do with this case, hold it forever, hoping I die? The case is against Hewlett Packard and Hewlett Packard selling junk printers, swindling money from people. I have asked for leave to amend my complaint an add Office Depot and the court refuses to rule on my motion. I have come to believe that one of the judges is akin to one of the attorneys for Hewlett Packard and the judge doesn't want them to lose. I would have to hire an investigator to find out for sure about kinship. Can the Court hold my case forever and do nothing? If they do nothing, this would be a dictatorship, not justice. There are other judges in the district that is capable of judging this case.

What is the America justice system coming to when two judges can hold a case forever? There has to be a reason and it has to be a personal reason for one of them or both a normal judge who is not bias would rule. If it is personal then that is even more reason they must disqualify themselves. I beg you to either get the case moving or tell me what I have to do to get it moving. The justice system is deteriorating rapid in America.

The justice system in America is responsible for America being destroying like it is doing. Judges only let their friends win or by their philosophy, but not truth and facts. Laws and Rules mean nothing to judges anymore. They know that appeal judges let give them a pass and that includes the Supreme Court and bless whatever they do

I asked you to please, stop the madness going on in the courts across America. You are the only person who can save America's justice system, but it takes guts and wisdom. Surely you have the votes on the court to do that.

I ask that you review this case; you will see that the judges in Kentucky have done everything bad to me possible. I have filed only good complaints, but because I am Pro, Se the judges think I don't understand what they are doing. The judges don't like it because a Pro, Se can be smart. Truth and facts doesn't come into the judge's mind. Please check out any case I have had before your court, just to satisfy your mind that I have filed only good cases.

God through the Holy Spirit told me to write this letter to you.

I would appreciate some kind of reply after you have read this letter and the enclosed documents.

Thanks for reading my letter and May God be with you on the endeavor of fixing the Justice System.

Edward H. Flint

I never received a reply from Judge Roberts on this letter

I wrote the following letter to Judge Roberts on October 29, 2011

October 29, 2011

Attention: Chief Judge John Roberts
Supreme Court of the United States
1 First Street, N. E.
Washington, DC 20543

Chief Judge Roberts:

My name is Ed Flint. I am 81 years old and I am Pro, Se in a number of lawsuits. I understand how the law works.

I have enclosed another copy of the motion dated October 29, 2011 that I filed in Western District Court of Kentucky, Louisville, Division attempting to have two judges disqualified and replaced with another judge. The judges refuse to recuse themselves. My case is not moving.

By Cannons Rules a judge should do something. Can you have the case moved along or can you tell me how I can get the case moving along for trial. Do I have a way to appeal to someone? I am entitled to a trial of some kind. These judges are violating the 14th amendment to the constitution, regarding Due Process for me.

I am entitled to America justice by a trial with an unbiased judge.

I have been treated like I was a theorist from another country in this case and a number of other cases. The Supreme Court refuses to look at them.

Why does this court not live up to it duty to check cases that judges mis-handle. It seems that being an America hurts in our court system.

The justice system in America is responsible for America being destroying like it is doing. Judges only let their friends win or by their philosophy, but not truth and facts. Laws and Rules mean nothing to judges anymore. They know that appeal judges let give them a pass and that includes the Supreme Court and bless whatever they do. No free country can exist without and honest court system.

I asked you to please, stop the madness going on in the courts across America. You are the only person who can save America's justice system, but it takes guts and wisdom. Surely you have the votes on the court to do that.

God through the Holy Spirit told me to write this letter to you.

I would appreciate some kind of reply after you have read this letter and the enclosed documents.

Thanks for reading my letter and May God be with you on the endeavor of fixing the Justice System.

Edward H. Flint
5800 Coach Gate Wynde #293
Louisville, KY 40207
502-896-1219

I never received an answer from Judge Roberts on this letter.

I wrote the following letter to Judge Roberts on December 2, 2011

December 2, 2011

Attention: Chief Judge John Roberts
Supreme Court of the United States
1 First Street, N. E.
Washington, DC 20543

Chief Judge Roberts:

My name is Ed Flint. I am 81 years old and I am Pro, Se in a number of lawsuits. I understand how the law works.

I have enclosed another copy of the motion dated December 2, 2011 that I filed in Western District Court of Kentucky, Louisville Division.

Judge Simpson has sent me an answer in my case. He has back dated an order. I never received at order he said was sent.

My motion explains what is happening.

I have a question for you. Are there any honest judges anymore? I have lost every case and I assure you that if you take the time to read my cases you will see I did not file a bad lawsuit.

I want to give you an example. In my complaint against Hewlett Packard I asked that if they are found guilty of treating customers the way I claim and that is by selling junk for printers that the court make them pay 50 million dollars to charities and the charities be approved by the court. The judges in Louisville make it look like I want the money. Money is not what I was after. Hewlett Packard makes 10 billion dollars a year and most of it is off of people who buy their junk. As big as Hewlett Packard is, they have fired two Presidents of the company in 18 months. The last one was fired about 3 months ago and they gave him I think 30 million dollars pay when they fired him. His pay came from hard working people who just want a good printer for their computer.

The justice system in America is responsible for America being destroying like it is doing. Judges only let their friends win or by their philosophy, but not truth and facts. Laws and Rules mean nothing to judges anymore. They know that appeal judges let give them a pass and that includes the Supreme Court and bless whatever they do. No free country can exist without and honest court system.

I asked you to please, stop the madness going on in the courts across America. You are the only person who can save America's justice system, but it takes guts and wisdom. Surely you have the votes on the court to do that.

God through the Holy Spirit told me to write this letter to you.

Thanks for reading my letter and May God be with you on the endeavor of fixing the Justice System.

Edward H. Flint

I never heard from Judge Roberts on this letter.

Judge Roberts never answered any of my letters.

He kept letting the District judges and the Court of Appeals, beat me up; he kept letting his judges, be corrupt. There was no way he was going to let a hearing, about the court system, take place.

CHAPTER 17

The Holy Spirit told me to research everything I could and to keep writing letters about immunity for judges.

I found in my research, a blog from, "Justice Integrity Project," I didn't and still don't know who they are.

The article said that Senator Leahy Chairman of the Senate Judiciary Committee and other Democrat Senators had written a letter to Judge Roberts saying they were concern about oversight of federal judges.

The article said and I quote, "The federal courts function honestly," according to the annual report that Supreme Court Justice John Roberts issued on December 31. 2011.

Judge Roberts's report stated and I quote, "I have complete confidence in the capability of my colleagues to determine when recusal is warranted. They are jurists of exceptional integrity and experience. I know that they each give careful consideration to any recusal questions that arise in the course of their judicial duties."

The article stated that the Roberts's report was released at 6: 00 pm. Saturday, which was New Year week-end, thus guaranteeing minimal attention from the public.

The blog stated the report was "whitewash."

The article stated and I quote, "Every American, every day is affected by issues before the Supreme Court". The article also said that Roberts stated, "The federal judiciary needs no reforms because its members seek to address their duties in an ethical manner."

Judge Roberts lives in a different world that the rest of America does, believe me what he said was "whitewash."

Judge Roberts lied based in the report he issued on December 31, 2011. The five letters that I wrote to Judge Roberts in Chapter 16, that you just finished reading, showed him what the corrupt judges was doing in Louisville. Those judges was Senator McConnell friends and Judge Roberts was not about to do the right thing and go against Senator McConnell. I became ill after reading what Judge Roberts said in his December 31, 2011 report.

After I read this article I figured that Senator Leahy had complaints from someone or some group (s) about federal judges.

So on February 2, 2012 I wrote Senator Leahy the following letter.

February 2, 2012

Senator Patrick Leahy
437 Russell Senate Bldg
United States Senate
Washington, DC 20510

Dear Senator Leahy:

My name is Ed Flint. I live in Louisville, Ky. and I am 81 years old. I am pro se in a number of cases.

I am writing you this letter to tell you that America is in serious trouble and the main cause of this, is the justice system we have in America. The problems start with the United States Supreme Court. The justice system cannot keep up with the growth we have in law cases, so the Supreme Court gives judges across America immunity. The Supreme Court action has made more corrupt that the criminals that they lock up. I am talking about judges at all levels, local, state and Federal.

The Supreme Court started this problem back in the 1970's and the problems grow with each day. The Supreme Court in 1978 gave absolute immunity from liability to all judges and it has grown to where we don't have honest judges anymore. In Stump v. Sparkman 435 U.S. 349 the court stated that a judge had immunity regardless of his actions The Supreme Court stated

"A judge will not be deprived of immunity because the action he took was in error, was done maliciously, or was in excess of his authority; rather, he will be subject to liability only when he has acted in the 'clear absence of all jurisdictions.'

A judge can error, can do it maliciously and can do it in excess of his authority, but is given absolute immunity.

What other business or government or services or any group that is connected with human, is grant absolute immunity in a country that is supposed to be free, and have justice, do you know of? The courts should not be allowed to make their own rules and laws and give immunity. The court's decision put the judges a head of free people, over every other citizen of our country. This is not what the constitution says or was meant to say.

I have not found one case where it was in clear absence of all jurisdictions. For it to be in clear absence of all jurisdiction it would have to be where a judge signed another judge's order, without the assigned judge knowing about it. So any ruling judges' makes on any case that is assigned to them, they have absolute immunity to do anything they wish or make any ruling they would like to make. This is not justice, but dictatorship.

Bases on this ruling, today there is no justice, because a judge, the Court of Appeals and the Supreme Court won't even hear a case where the judge has violated Federal laws, or courts rules and Cannons. A judge in America is more powerful that any king who ever lived or the worse dictators that ever lived and even more powerful that Hitler. Hitler would have had to answer to a world court, but America's judges don't have to answer to anyone.

The United States Supreme Court could change their ruling, but refuse to.

I have enclosed two copies of filing for Petition for writ of certiorari to the Supreme Court that I filed. One of the judges involved is Minority leader Senator Mitch McConnell's lawyer and good friend. The Supreme Court will not hear any of these cases. I have filed about ten of these in the last 4 years and the Supreme Court upholds all of them. I believe if a judge shot someone in a case, the court would give that judge immunity.

I write to beg you to take some action to save this country and do something about this problem. Can you imagine what this county would be like if the people who was responsible for all decisions made, was given immunity, example, all industries, all government bodies, all sporting events, all doctors, all lawyers, all groups that touch people's lives was given immunity. Any time a human is given absolute immunity you can bet they will use it for their own benefit and not for the benefit of the public. Can you imagine that if designers of cars were given immunity what would happen? Can you imagine that if banks were given immunity what would happen? Can you imagine that if Doctors was given immunity, what would happen? Can you imagine that if pharmaceuticals manufacturers were given immunity what would happen? A dishonest judge can have as much or more effect on a human as those I just listed.

I was sold by a large chain pharmacy, Target Corporation, a drug that was not FDA approved and was never tested by anyone including the manufacturer. The drug injured me and I will have the injury till I die. The Federal Court granted summary judgment to Target. The judge refused to let me amend the complaint, refused to let me take depositions from employees of the manufacturer of the drug after I served them with subpoenas and add two other companies, the judge refuse to rule on 47 of my motions.

The Supreme Court decision has created dishonest judge who are on the take. Large companies are buying judges to keep from being found guilty by a jury of producing bad produces. The Supreme Court have found a way to keep the poor man from suing Doctors or other large companies, by judges protecting large corporations by granting judges immunity and knowing they have immunity.

I wrote a book titled "Corrupt Judges" that was mostly court documents. The Court of Appeals and the Supreme Court refused to do anything. Their actions allowed illegal drugs to be sold by pharmacies. I will send you a copy of the book and I hope you or one of your staff will read it.

Judges violating laws and court rules are as common, as you starting your car.

Congress passed a law; title 28 U.S.C. #445 that pertains to judges recusing themselves from cases. This law means nothing to judges, they refuse to recuse them self and the Supreme Court turns their heads and do nothing. I grew up believing that judges were honest. Now I don't believe any are honest. Today judges believe they can do as they please and this is why.

The best thing you could do is hold hearings and make the public aware of how bad the Supreme Court has become and how the court is not what our forefathers wanted in the constitution.

Maybe with pressure from the public the Supreme Court would write a sensible law that gave judges immunity from ruling unless the judges violated laws, rules of the courts and Cannons, like our forefathers meant for it to be. Judges need to be held liability like any other person for violating laws, Court rules and Cannons.

Or maybe there are laws that Congress could pass to stop the crumbing of our country from a doctoral Supreme Court that has gone amuck.

Think about this, judges are appointed for life and are given absolute immunity from liability. Does any person with a half brain think that judges are going to be honest after they receive appointments for life and immunity.

The public needs to know the truth about how terrible our justice system is,

If I can answer any questions, have your staff contact me, I have a lot of examples of what is taking place in the court system.

Thanks for your time.

Edward H. Flint

I never heard from Senator Leahy

The next day February 3, 2012 I wrote Senator DeMint who is a Republican the same letter as I wrote to Senator Leahy. I was optimistic this issue might be a non-partisan issue.

The following is the letter to Senator DeMint

February 3, 2012

Senator Jim DeMint
167 Russell Senate Bldg
United States Senate
Washington, DC 20510

Dear Senator DeMint

My name is Ed Flint. I live in Louisville, Ky. and I am 81 years old. I am pro se in a number of cases.

I am writing you this letter to tell you that America is in serious trouble and the main cause of this, is the justice system we have in America. The problems start with the United States Supreme Court. The justice system cannot keep up with the growth we have in law cases, so the Supreme Court by giving immunity to judges across America have made the judges become more corrupt than the criminals that they lock up. I am talking about judges at all levels, local, state and Federal.

The Supreme Court started this problem back in the 1970's and the problems grow with each day. The Supreme Court in 1978 gave absolute immunity from liability to all judges and it has grown to where we don't have honest judges anymore. In Stump v. Sparkman 435 U.S. 349 the court stated that a judge had immunity regardless of his actions The Supreme Court stated

"A judge will not be deprived of immunity because the action he took was in error, was done maliciously, or was in excess of his authority; rather, he will be subject to liability only when he has acted in the 'clear absence of all jurisdictions.'

A judge can error, can do it maliciously and can do it in excess of his authority, but is given absolute immunity.

What other business or government or services or any group that is connected with human, is grant absolute immunity in a country that is supposed to be free, and have justice, do you know of? The courts should not be allowed to make their own rules and laws and give immunity. The court's decision put the judges a head of free people, over every other citizen of our country. This is not what the constitution says or was meant to say.

I have not found one case where it was in clear absence of all jurisdictions. For it to be in clear absence of all jurisdiction it would have to be where a judge signed another judge's order, without the assigned judge knowing about it. So any ruling judges' makes on any case that is assigned to them, they have absolute immunity to do anything they wish or make any ruling they would like to make. This is not justice, but dictatorship.

Bases on this ruling, today there is no justice, because a judge, the Court of Appeals and the Supreme Court won't even hear a case where the judge has violated Federal laws, or courts rules and Cannons. A judge in America is more powerful that any king who ever lived or the worse dictators that ever lived and even more powerful that Hitler. Hitler would have had to answer to a world court, but America's judges don't have to answer to anyone.

The United States Supreme Court could change their ruling, but refuse to.

I have enclosed two copies of filing for Petition for writ of certiorari to the Supreme Court that I filed. One of the judges involved is Minority leader Senator Mitch McConnell's lawyer and good friend. The Supreme Court will not hear any of these cases. I have filed about ten of these in the last 4 years and the Supreme Court upholds all of them. I believe if a judge shot someone in a case, the court would give that judge immunity.

I write to beg you to take some action to save this country and do something about this problem. Can you imagine what this county would be like if the people who was responsible for all decisions made, was given immunity, example, all industries, all government bodies, all sporting events, all doctors, all lawyers, all groups that touch people's lives was given immunity. Any time a human is given absolute immunity you can bet they will use it for their own benefit and not for the benefit of the public. Can you imagine that if designers of cars were given immunity what would happen? Can you imagine that if banks were given immunity what would happen? Can you imagine that if Doctors was given immunity, what would happen? Can you imagine that if pharmaceuticals manufacturers were given immunity what would happen? A dishonest judge can have as much or more effect on a human as those I just listed.

I was sold by a large chain pharmacy, Target Corporation, a drug that was not FDA approved and was never tested by anyone including the manufacturer. The drug injured me and I will have the injury till I die. The Federal Court granted summary judgment to Target. The judge refused to let me amend the complaint, refused to let me take depositions from employees of the manufacturer of the drug after I served them with subpoenas and add two other companies, the judge refuse to rule on 47 of my motions.

The Supreme Court decision has created dishonest judge who are on the take. Large companies are buying judges to keep from being found guilty by a jury of producing bad produces. The Supreme Court have found a way to keep the poor man from suing Doctors or other large companies, by judges protecting large corporations by granting judges immunity and knowing they have immunity.

I wrote a book titled "Corrupt Judges" that was mostly court documents. The Court of Appeals and the Supreme Court refused to do anything. Their actions allowed illegal drugs to be sold by pharmacies. I will send you a copy of the book and I hope you or one of your staff will read it.

Judges violating court rules are as common as you starting your car.

Congress passed a law; title 28 U.S.C. #445 that pertains to judges recusing themselves from cases. This law means nothing to judges, they refuse to recuse them self and the Supreme Court turns their heads and do nothing. I grew up believing that judges were honest. Now I don't believe any are honest.

The best Congress could do is hold hearings and make the public aware of how bad the Supreme Court has become and how the court is not what our forefathers wanted in the constitution.

Maybe with pressure from the public the Supreme Court would write a sensible law that gave judges immunity from ruling unless the judges violated laws, rules of the courts and Cannons, like our forefathers meant for it to be. Judges need to be held liability like any other person for violating laws, Court rules and Cannons.

Or maybe there are laws that Congress could pass to stop the crumbing of our country from a doctoral Supreme Court that has gone amuck.

The public needs to know the truth about how terrible our justice system is,

If I can answer any questions, have your staff contact me, I have a lot of examples of what is taking place in the court system.

Thanks for your time.

Edward H. Flint

I never heard from either senator. However the Holy Spirit told me to just write to Senator Leahy in the future, that Senator DeMint would not become involved. I didn't know why, but I found out later that he resigned from the senate.

My February 2, 2011 letter explained what the judges in District and Appeals courts and Supreme Court was doing and I asked him to hold a hearing in the senate. I told him I would testify about my cases.

It seems that after Senator Leahy received my letter of February 2, 2012. Senator Leahy and four (4) other Senators wrote to Judge Roberts, again, asking for a code of conduct for federal judges.

So it looks like Senator Leahy wrote another letter to Judge Roberts after he received my letter February 2 letter and before February 20, 2011, when Judge Roberts rejected adopting a Code of Conduct.

My letter gave Senator Leahy facts and history about judges. I don't believe Senator Leahy had these types of facts and history of lawsuits when he wrote to Judge Roberts back in December, 2011. After receiving my letter he wrote to Judge Roberts again.

In my research for other information, I found that on February 21, 2012 the Washington Post and other news print Medias, had articles where Judge Roberts had sent Senate Leahy a one page letter.

The articles stated Senator Leahy and four other Democratic Senators on the Judiciary Committee had signed a letter to Judge Roberts saying and I quote, "We hope to increase public trust and confidence in all of our institutions, including the Supreme Court."

The four Senators were Durbin, Whitehouse, Blumenthal and Franken. The five said, they "did not intent to question or impugn the ethic of any individual Justice,"

The Washington Post article stated that members of Congress, a group of law professors and other side groups had called upon the court to adopt the Code of Conduct. So this means a lot of others groups wanted a Code of Conduct regarding judges.

Judge Roberts told the five Senators for the second time, that the Supreme Court was not going to formally adopt a judicial code of conduct that governs the actions of other federal judges.

When I saw that, I was mad as hell. What a selfish attitude, I was determined more than ever, that something had to be done to stop this madness.

I sent additional letters to Senator Leahy.

I wrote to Senator Leahy, three other letters that gave him more facts and more history, regarding judge's actions. The letters were written on February 22, 2012 and February 23, 2012 and February 29, 2012.

The three letters are inserted next.

February 22, 2012

Senator Patrick Leahy
437 Russell Senate Bldg
United States Senate
Washington, DC 20510

Dear Senator Leahy:

My name is Ed Flint. I live in Louisville, Ky. and I am 81 years old. I am pro se in a number of cases. I wrote to you on February 2, 2012 and included two cases I filed with the United States Supreme Court. I also sent you a book.

I have now filed another case with the Supreme Court and have enclosed a copy of it with this letter and I hope you will read it.

Something has to be done to stop the madness that is going on in the Federal Courts by the judges.

I read in today's newspaper that Chief Judge Roberts turned you down on your request for changes in the court.

If you held a hearing I would come and testify about what has happen in my cases. There is a lot more that what I have sent you.

Thanks for your time.

Edward H. Flint

I never heard from Senator Leahy.

On February 23, 2012, I wrote Senator Leahy the following letter
February 23, 2012

Senator Patrick Leahy
437 Russell Senate Bldg.
United States Senate
Washington, DC 20510

Dear Senator Leahy:

My name is Ed Flint. I live in Louisville, Ky. and I am 81 years old. I am pro se in a number of cases. I wrote to you on February 2, 2012 and February 22, 2012 and included cases that I filed with the United States Supreme Court. I also sent you a book.

Our country is in serious trouble and it is my belief that the Justice System is leading to the decay of America. The Supreme Court is not only protecting judges, but the courts across America are protecting big business. I have filed suits against MetLife insurance and Hewlett Packard and the court system dismissed my cases. I could try and explain both of them to you but the best way to explain to start is enclose copies of the two cases briefs to the Court of Appeals, they have not reached the Supreme Court yet, but the briefs will explain. I am sure that your staff can copy the case history on the Hewlett Packard case in the court system.

I have enclosed another case to the Supreme Court, this one is Flint v. New York Stock Exchange et al. I asked for Petition for writ of certiorari and the Supreme Court turned me down. The court is protecting Wall Street. The Petition shows that Congress gave immunity to the SEC back a long time ago. But the court rules it is for everyone connected in any way to the SEC. The insiders have learned how to beat the system and the court system gives immunity to everyone involved. The stock market is a con game. By reading my Petition it will all become clear.

The morals of our country is decaying badly and giving judges immunity has and is leading the charge. The only thing that our strict morals' have held up in, in this country is the armed services. Can you imagine what would happen if soldiers was given immunity using the same words that the Supreme Court used in Stump v. Sparkman or any type of immunity for that matter. We would have no armed services. Can you think of one entity that would remain honest, if they were granted immunity?

If you held a hearing I would come and testify about what has happen in my cases. I would make a great witness.

Thanks for your time.

Edward H. Flint

I never heard from Senator Leahy, but the Holy Spirit told me to keep writing him. And I did.

On February 29, 2012 I wrote Senator Leahy the following letter.

February 29, 2012

Senator Patrick Leahy
437 Russell Senate Bldg.
United States Senate
Washington, DC 20510

Dear Senator Leahy:

My name is Ed Flint. I live in Louisville, Ky. and I am 81 years old. I am pro se in a number of cases. I wrote to you on February 2, 2012 and February 22, 2012 and February 23, 2012 a letter which included cases that I filed with the United States Supreme Court. I also sent you a book.

As I stated in my letters, our country is in serious trouble and it is my belief that the Justice System is leading to the decay of America. The Supreme Court is not only protecting judges, but the courts across America are protecting big businesses.

I have enclosed new pages 21 thru 29 of one of the cases I sent you. The case was Flint v. Whalin. The Supreme Court's clerk made me do the case over and resubmit it. I had copied some of the pages in my Petition from filings I filed to the trial court and it was in "Times Romans" type and the Supreme Court's rules says all of the pleading had to me in "Gothic" type. So when I made the changes and I resubmitted the Petition and I made some additional changes and added to "REASON FOR GRANTING THE WRIT" I added No. 7 on page 22 and in Conclusion I added No. 14 on page 24 and No. 15 and No. 16 on page 25. I through you might want to see the new parts I added. It concerns immunity for members of our military.

As I expressed previously in my letters the justice system of America is going to hell and thereby it is taking our country with it.

There is no way immunity can be given to a group of any type that the group doesn't become corrupt with most of those in the group. As I stated in my Petition for Certiorari that if there was any group of people deserving of immunity in America the soldiers in our military does. If soldiers were given immunity (the exact wording that Stump v. Sparkman gave judges) there would be deaths to no end and we would have no control over our military. This is exactly what is happening to the justice system and the Supreme Court refuses to clean this issue up and the longer they refuse, the more judges will become will become corrupt. Right now there are a lot more corrupt judges in America than there are honest judges.

The other problem that creates corrupt judges is life time appointments. Our constitution needs to be change to where all federal judges must either be reappointed or elected every some many years or they have limited terms.

Granting immunity to judges and giving them life time appointments has open up the opportunity for judges to be brought by the highest bidder. Judges can be brought just like in any industry or organization with the less chance of getting caught.

If you held a hearing and wanted me to testify about these matters, I would come and testify about what has happen in my cases and how rules and laws are being violated. I would make a great witness. I have filed in Federal Courts since 2007 about 12 lawsuits and the story that I can tell would make your head spin. I can do things that licensed attorneys, that make a living in practicing law, cannot do. A judge cannot intimidate me and or hurt me in my lively hood, because I don't need them. If you are interested in get the truth out to the public and in passing laws to correct the inequities that are going on in every court in America. I can and will tell you, the other Senators, and the world the truth about how corrupt the judges are, from the District Courts to the Supreme Courts. I can hold my own against anyone in testifying about this subject.

Thanks for your time.

Edward H. Flint

I never heard from him regarding this letter.

By this time the judges in the Louisville Federal Court was treating me like I was dirt, being hard on me. If I told them in a pleading that the paper was white, they would send back an order saying I was wrong, it was red.

I sent another letter to Senator Leahy dated March 17, 2012. This letter pointed out that Senator Mitch McConnell the Minority Leader in the Senate, and the judge, Judge Heyburn had worked together in Louisville. Judge Heyburn was General Counsel for Senator McConnell.

Judge Heyburn was the judge in my case against MetLife Insurance and the Governor of Kentucky. Judge Heyburn's ruling was a joke. That letter is now inserted.

March 17, 2012

Senator Patrick Leahy
437 Russell Senate Bldg.
United States Senate
Washington, DC 20510

Dear Senator Leahy:

My name is Ed Flint and I have recently sent you letters and copies of Petitions for Writ of Certiorari. I have enclosed another Petition for Certiorari to the Supreme Court. The new one is Flint v. MetLife insurance company. I mailed this on March 17, 2012

The judge in this case was again Minority Leader Mitch McConnell's attorney in Kentucky. I am sure that if a Republican is elected President, this judge will be pushed by Mitch for the Supreme Court. A second year law student could have done a better job of judging the Flint v. MetLife case. I hope you will read it and judge for yourself.

I beg you to do something to put justice back into our country, because America doesn't have an honest and fair justice system now and it gets worse with each passing day. All of the judges both Democrats and Republicans have become nothing but bullies or dictators. The Courts of Appeals are useless and should not be in existence, they cause more harm that they do good. Circuit judges are being brought by companies or by friendly attorneys. Circuit judges don't care about fair and honest justice. The Courts of Appeals do nothing, except rubber stamp what the Circuit Judges rules on and protect any corrupt judges. The United States Supreme Court only wants to hear cases that are either high publicly or case that they personally care about. They do not want to do anything but protect judges, regardless of how bad or wrong the judge acted or rule. Our country does not have the justice system that our forefathers thought they laid out. The system has out grown what I forefathers had in mind. The only way to preserve the current system is to make it tougher on a judge when he deviates from the way the system was intended to be and to make it more likely a judge could lose their job. Our forefather at the time only had honest judges in mind when they wrote the constitution; they could not vision what dishonesty would come. Only Congress can save America.

I will list some examples of what is occurring by judges, each and every day across America by Federal judges.

1)- Congress passed a law which was title 28 U.S. CODE #455, which pertains to judges recusing them self from cases. The Supreme Court ruled in *Liljeberg* v. *Health Services Acquisition Corp., 486 U.S. 847, 860 n.8 (1988)* regarding this law along with their opinion on what the law means. The Federal Judicial Center Analysis of case law on this title follows.

I will quote some from, Federal Judicial Center an Analysis of case law 28 U.S.C. #455.

The new section 455(a) replaced the subjective standard of the 1948 state with an objective standard. It is no longer that a judge should recuse where "in his opinion" sitting would be improper, but rather where his or her impartiality "might reasonably be questioned." Also, section 455(b) spells out certain situations in which partiality is presumed and recusal is required.

Judges should keep in mind that sections 455(a) and (b) provide separate (though substantially overlapping) bases for recusal. The formal deals exclusively with the appearance of partiality in any circumstance, whereas the latter pertains to conflicts of interest in specific instances. Thus, the existence of the facts listed in section 455(b) requires recusal, even if the judge believes impartiality might reasonably be questioned, whether or not touched on in section 455(b), requires recusal under section 455(a)

In addition, where section 455(b) sets forth a particular situation requiring recusal, it will tend to control any section 455(a) analysis with respect to that specific circumstance. For example, section 455 (b) (5) requires recusal where one of the parties is a third degree of relationship to the judge.

The analysis also stated the following:

There is a second respect, apart from application of the reasonable person standard, in which the determination under section 455(a) is objective. The Supreme Court has held that a violation of section 455(a) takes place even if the judge is unaware of the circumstance that created the appearance of impropriety. In *Liljeberg* v. *Health Services Acquisition Corp., 486 U.S. 847, 860 n.8 (1988)* the trial judge was a member of the board of trustees of a university that had a financial interest in the litigation, but he was unaware of the financial interest when he conducted a bench trial and ruled in the case. The court of appeals nevertheless vacated the judgment under Fed. R. Civ. P 60(b) because the judge failed to recuse himself pursuant to section 455(a) and the Supreme Court agreed. Noting that the purpose of section 455(a) is to promote public confidence in the integrity of the judicial process, the Court observed that such confidence "does not depend upon whether or not the judge actually knew of facts creating an appearance of impropriety, so long as the public might reasonably believe that he or she knew.'"

the Supreme Court agreed that the purpose of section 455(a) is, to promote public confidence in the integrity of the judicial process, the Court observed that such confidence "does not depend upon whether or not the judge actually knew of facts creating an appearance of impropriety, so long as the public might reasonably believe that he or she knew." The Supreme Court also held that a violation of section #455 (a) takes place even if the judge is unaware of the circumstance that created the appearance of impropriety.

The document states,

The new section 455(a) replaced the subjective standard of the 1948 state with an objective standard. It is no longer that a judge should recuse where "in his opinion" sitting would be improper, but rather where his or her impartiality **"might reasonably be questioned."** Also, section 455(b) spells out certain situations in which partiality is presumed and recusal is required.

The courts, Circuit, Appeals and Supreme Court ignore this statute every day and refuse to honor the law. There is no reason why a judge would want to retain a case unless they were involved personally. The statute needs to be changed so a judge has no choice, but to recuse them, when a party point out there was bias. This is a tough law to word, however it should lean on the side of the parties and not the judge.

2)- As I stated before, but will state once again. Does anyone believe that if a person or a group of people are given a life time position and immunity, they won't start to do as they please and become corrupt? Most like to feel the power, knowing full well that no one can harm them or stop them.

Judges are given immunity for not doing their job. If any group of people deserved immunity it would be members of our armed services. If we gave immunity to members of the armed services we wouldn't have an armed services, because they would start shooting and killing everyone. Based on history any group of people who is given immunity has to become corrupt.

Just think that if a soldier was given the same immunity reasons a judge is given what would happen. A judge is now given absolute immunity if and I quote, **"A judge will not be deprived of immunity because the action he took was in error, was done maliciously, or was in excess of his authority; rather, he will be subject to liability only when he has acted in the 'clear absence of all jurisdiction.'** Can you imagine what would happen if members of the armed services was given the same wording, **"A member of our armed services will not be deprived of immunity because the action he took was in error, was done maliciously, or was in excess of his authority; rather, he will be subject to liability only when he has acted in the 'clear absence of being a member of the United States armed services.'**

How about all policemen receiving immunity, the same thing would happen as to a soldier.

A statute should be passed that states, "any federal employees including judges can be held liable and judged by a jury in a court of law for violating any Federal or state law, any rule of a court issued by the Supreme Court of the United States or any state Supreme Court and Cannons." This would not take care of all of the problems, but it would be a large start and after a few judges got sued, the others would start too straight up. In the same statute it could state that "any federal employee found guilty by a jury in a court of law of any charge, could be dismissed from employment and judges appointed by under the constitution, can be bought up for impeachment, by congress."

3)- The constitution give every party the right to a trial by jury, however these days the judges use summary judgment and other ways to keep from given a person a jury trial. The judges have become lazy, they want to control the outcome of each case, either because their friends are on one side or they have been brought by someone. A trial by a jury is rare these days. I would have won all 14 of my cases if I had a jury trial.

The question I have laid before you is, the citizens of this country no longer have a justice system the way our forefathers meant for America to be. If some way is not found to correct this, our country will not stand much longer. As you and everyone else know, we as a country are in serious trouble and I personally believe that most of the problem is cause by unfair justice. Companies rip people off every day, they produce bad products and get by with it, and judges protect them, because they can buy the judges.

Why is a judge treated special, compared to ordinary people, which can be sued? I cannot get an answer to this question. Would you ask Chief Judge Roberts for an answer?

Also Chief Judge Roberts at his Senate confirmation hearings when asked, what is a judge's job and duty, he stated "Judges are like umpires. Umpires don't make the rules. They apply them. The role of an umpire and a judge is critical. The make sure everybody plays by the rules. But it is a limited role. Nobody ever went to a ball game to see the umpires." His jurisprudence would be characterized by "modesty and humility"

If every judge did what Chief Judge Roberts stated, judges would not need immunity, so why doesn't Chief Judge Roberts ask the other judges on his court to join him and change Stump v. Sparkman, to his statement?

No one can disagree with John Roberts's statements. However when judges makes up their own rules or ignores and expands the court's rules and or ignore or change legal laws, the Justice System breaks down and fails. When the Justice system fails, social order fails.

I am concerned, but not for myself, but for the future of our country. I am 81 years old and won't be around much longer.

I sent you a Petition for Writ, regarding Flint v. New Your Stock Exchange et al. Congress originally gave the Security Exchange Commission immunity. The Supreme Court has ruled that the immunity applies to everyone that comes in contact with the SEC. I know I can prove that the stock market is manipulated. I asked the Supreme Court to rule how far down the line does immunity go and they refused to grant certiorari.

Billions of dollars is lost each year by hard working people and the courts don't want to stop this from happening. Please read my Petition that I sent.

Until 2007 I had never filed a law suit. I have no training in law. I only have a 9th grade education. I filed my first lawsuit because the Holy Spirit told me God wanted these problems out in the public, so humans would change the laws and give everyone equal treatment in court system.

I lobbied in the Kentucky General assembly for 20 plus years, representing the race horse industry. I understand the legislative system.

I have not put the problems concerning the judges and courts in the best of language, but you and your staff will be able to know what the problems are from my writings.

At one time this country had lots of con artists. Today the con artists have become judges in courts of law, they rape the public of fair and honest justice, and get their power because they have immunity from being corrupt, and Congress blesses their work.

I believe there should be a separation of the three branches of government; however that doesn't mean that each branch can control their branch the way they want. Our forefathers mean for the three branches to watch over each other, however congress has to be the watch dog of the judicial branches. The justice system should not be allowed to make their own rules, on how to punish their employees, including judges, and the America public expects congress to set the rules and to set the punishment for violators. The judicial system took congress's duty away from congress in 1970's. Congress has given up their responsibility and must take their duty back.

If you are interested in fixing some of the legal problems about judges, I will, as I told you before, testify about what has happened in all of the 14 cases that I have filed with the Supreme Court. I will tell you how judges have become the greatest rip off artists of all times. How judges receive help from other employees of the court system to do their coning. My testimony will freak out the American public, because they won't believe how bad our system has deteriorated. It's more than just immunity, it how they manipulate the system to get their way and use their employees to help them rape the public. I believe that once the public knows the truth they will demand an investigation of the system and I believe there are thousands of attorneys who will come forth and tell the same stories I will tell.

The public will be bewildered when they hear the truth about what the courts are doing. Most attorneys feel as I do, that the system needs to be made fair and equal for everyone. Most attorneys can't and won't testify the way I can. Honest attorneys are receiving the same treatment as I have. This should not be a partisan issue.

Since I am Pro, Se I cannot be hurt by judges. I do my own work, I do my own typing and I don't know how to type. I know most there is to know, about what is wrong and can explain it to your committee, if requested. I will testify so all Americans know how corrupt and dishonest our system is. No judge can hurt me, so I can speak the truth about the system. I would love the opportunity to be questioned by your committee. Get the information out to the public and let the truth be heard.

If you have any doubts about me, have one of your staff call me and question me or have them come to Louisville and spend a day or week questioning me.

Thanks

Ed Flint-

I never heard from him about this letter.

On March 19, 2012 I sent Senator Leahy another letter. This letter was about something new, that happen.

I received a document from the Solicitor General of the United States regarding a case that I had filed in the Supreme Court.

The case was a lawsuit where I had sued Judge John Heyburn. Judge Heyburn worked with and for Senator Mitch McConnell the Minority Leader.

This case was referred to the Solicitor General of The United States to handle, by either Judge Heyburn or Senator McConnell and this told me, that they didn't want to take a chance, that the Supreme Court would review the case or they was now starting to worry about how much I was pushing these cases. The letter to Senator Leahy is now inserted.

March 19, 2012

Senator Patrick Leahy
437 Russell Senate Bldg.
United States Senate
Washington, DC 20510

Dear Senator Leahy:

My name is Ed Flint and I have recently sent you letters and copies of Petitions for Writ of Certiorari. I have attached with this letter, a document that I received from the Solicitor General of the United States.

The document is a waiver regarding Flint v. Heyburn. I recently filed a Petition for Writ of Certiorari with the Supreme Court regarding this case and I sent you a copy of it.

I do not know what this document means. I have filed about 10 to 12 Petitions for Certiorari with the Supreme Court and this is the first time I have received anything from the Solicitor General about any of my cases. I send this to you for your valuation; I thought it might be of interest to you. I have no idea who notified the Solicitor General, about the case.

Thanks

Ed Flint-

I never heard from him about this letter.

I kept sending Senator Leahy letters. I sent him a letter on April 18, 2012, another on May 17, 2012 and another on June 2, 2012. These three are inserted now

April 18, 2012

Senator Patrick Leahy
437 Russell Senate Bldg.
United States Senate
Washington, DC 20510

Dear Senator Leahy:

I have enclosed a copy of a document where the Supreme Court denied me certiorari in my case against Judge John G. Heyburn II, who was Minority Leader Mitch McConnell's attorney.

The Supreme Court has become a bunch of bullies and dictators. You must find a way to fix the Supreme Court and make it the people's court again.

Absolute immunity for judges I hope can be overcome by legislation I hope, also being able to sue those who are manipulating the stock market.

I don't expect to be granted certiorari in none of my cases. I will send them to you as I get them for your review..

Thanks, for taking the time to read my letters, I wish you the best of luck.

Ed Flint-
I never heard from him about this letter.

On May 17, 2012 I wrote the following letter to Senator Leahy.

May 17, 2012

Senator Patrick Leahy
437 Russell Senate Bldg.
United States Senate
Washington, DC 20510

Dear Senator Leahy:

My name is Ed Flint and I have recently sent you a number of letters and copies of Petitions for Writ of Certiorari and the Supreme Court.

I have enclosed with this letter, two new orders from the United Supreme Court denying more of my petitions for certiorari. I wanted you to see these since I sent you copies of my petitions

I read where you put the Supreme Court on notice about the health care bill.

There is no way they will approve of the health care bill.

I have asked you to hold a hearing about how the courts protect judges. If you want the Independent votes then hold hearings on the Supreme Court and how judges are given immunity. If you hold a hearing about immunity for judges 90% of the Independents will vote for Obama.

You and your committee are the only hope that America has to have a good justice system.

Thanks

Ed Flint-

I never heard from him about this letter.

On June 2, 2012 I wrote Senator Leahy the following letter.

June 2, 2012

Senator Patrick Leahy
437 Russell Senate Bldg.
United States Senate
Washington, DC 20510

Dear Senator Leahy:

My name is Ed Flint and I have recently sent you a number of letters and copies of Petitions for Writ of Certiorari and the Supreme Court.

You may be getting tired of my letters but I want you to know how bad and corrupt the Federal Court system is and how bad and corrupt Federal judges are.

I have enclosed a copy of a brief that I will be sending this week to the Sixth Circuit Court of Appeals. It's a disgrace that we have these types of judges in our courts. And then to really hurt the citizens, the Supreme Court gives these judges absolute immunity.

The brief that I have enclosed is Flint v. Hewlett Packard.

Thanks

Ed Flint-

I never heard from him about this letter.

At this point, I want to point out how close some of the players are tied together.

Of the 14 cases that I have inserted into the book, six (6) of them was assigned to Judge Heyburn and five (5) was assigned to Judge Simpson. This didn't happen by chance, there were other judges in the Kentucky District that the cases could have been assigned to. Someone in the Louisville court had their finger on everything I did and they had it from the start.

Senator Mitch McConnell was Judge-Executive of Jefferson County Kentucky for 7 years, from 1978 to 1985.

Both of these judges, Heyburn and Simpson were nominated to be Federal judges by Senator McConnell.

Judge Heyburn was Special Counsel to Mitch McConnell when Senator McConnell was the Judge-Executive of Jefferson County for the 7 years.

Judge Simpson was also counsel to Mitch McConnell as Judge –Executive for the 7 years.

Judge Simpson had practiced law with Senator McConnell.

Also in 2007, Chief Judge Roberts appointed Judge Heyburn to a Supreme Court committee. He was the Chair of the Judicial Panel on Mulit. District

Litigation. I am sure that Judge Roberts appointed him, only after being ask to do so by Senator McConnell

The Supreme Court Chief Judges appoints judges to panels to build their resume, getting them ready for the Supreme Court.

Senator McConnell was grooming Judge Heyburn to be appointed to the Supreme Court. If Governor Romney had been elected as President, I am sure that Judge Heyburn would have been nominated to the Supreme Court. This is how important the election was.

Judge Heyburn was certainly no stranger to Chief Judge Roberts.

I have known Senator McConnell for a long time and I know that he thinks ahead, in everything he does.

Judges Roberts twice had refused to put a Code of Conduct for judges, into a rule (law) of the Supreme Court.

The Holy Spirit told me that Senator Leahy started putting in motion a hearing on Code of Conduct for judges. After he received my letters of February 22, 23, and 29, 2012 and the March, and April letters.

I believe Senator Leahy and or another senator went to Senator McConnell and told him there would be hearings scheduled, regarding the Code of Conduct for judges. I believed that they told Senator McConnell that his friend Judge Heyburn would be invited to testify at the hearing and maybe he was told I would come and testify.

After Senator Leahy received the March 17 and 19 letters he shared them with Senator McConnell.

Senator McConnell would not want me to testify, He knew about my cases and he knew that I was capable of testifying and he knew what I would testify about. He knew that I did my homework and would know thoroughly the subject matter. He also knew that I would not be timid in front of the Judiciary committee.

Senator McConnell has a history of taking care of himself, first. He also takes care of the things that mean something to him personally. His personal goals come before anything else or anybody else.

Judge Roberts did not want hearings regarding the subject that Senator Leahy would hold the hearing on. Judge Roberts was trying to find a way to have the hearing not take place.

The entire Supreme Court also knew about me, and about the subjects that I would testify about. I had told them.

I wrote Judge Roberts the following letter on January 10, 2012 and sent copies to all Justices on the Supreme Court.

January 10, 2012

Attention: Chief Judge John Roberts
Supreme Court of the United States
1 First Street, N. E.
Washington, DC 20543

Chief Judge Roberts:

My name is Ed Flint. I am 81 years old and I am Pro, Se in a number of lawsuits. I understand how the law works. I have written to you a number of times about the treatment I am receiving from judges in the Western District of Kentucky, in Louisville Kentucky. The judges in this court have done everything in their power to deny me a fair and honest trial. Justice does not exist in the Federal Court in Kentucky. Your court has denied me certiorari a number of times. Most of my charges are being denied due process and corrupt judges violating rules and laws. Don't enough members of the Supreme Court have the guts to change the past court decisions about protecting judge throughout America?

Member of this court can say the man is crazy or he doesn't understand the justice system, but they are wrong. I know this court is busy, but this court has a moral obligation to see the courts through-out America are fair and honest to all people. This court must put a stop to courts running mad, harming the people by corrupt judges. All it takes is for this court to have the guts to render the proper ruling to overturn the terrible ruling made in Stump v. Sparkman and take away immunity from judges who violate court rules and statues.

If this was happening to each of you, then you would do something about it. Some judges on the court have the bighead and think its ok to eliminate fair and honest trials for the people, because it doesn't fit what they believe. Jesus won't buy that story on judgment day.

I have a case in Louisville where the courts are doing everything to stop me from a trial against a big company, because the company hired attorneys who are close to the judge.

I have enclosed just three motions from the case to show you how bad it has become.

The members of this court swore to uphold the rules and laws and to give justice to the people. I know the court is busy, but it must do its duty regardless.

I have told this court before, but I will tell you again, this country is in serious trouble and it starts with corrupt justice .This court can and must lead this country out of its problems by assuring an absolute fair and honest justice system.

I ask that you read the enclosed pleadings and see if this is how you want the justice system to be run in America. It takes so little to make a horrible ruling, right, if you really care about justice for all, like our forefather did. I ask that you be humans and not just powerful people with any heart for the common person.

I thank you for taking the time to read this letter.

Edward H. Flint

Cc to

Judge Samuel Alito
Judge Anthony Kennedy
Judge Ruth Bader Ginsburg
Judge Antonin Scalia
Judge Clarence Thomas
Judge Sonia Sotomayor
Judge Stephen Beyer
Judge Elena Kagan

One would have thought that at least one judge would have replied. I never received a reply from any member of the Supreme Court

---

I had sent Justice Kennedy a letter on October 9, 2011 and he knew what was going on. I will now insert the letter to Justice Kennedy.

October 9, 2011

ATTN. Judge Anthony M. Kennedy
Supreme Court of the United States
Attention Office of the Clerk
1 First Street, N. E.
Washington, DC 20543

Dear Judge Kennedy:

My name is Edward Flint, I am 81 years old, and I live in Louisville Ky. Like me, your time on this earth is limited. I am writing to you to ask that you clean up the justice system in America, to make it fair and honest. America has no justice system because most all judges across America are corrupt. Those who may not be corrupt have big egos and want cases decided to match their feelings and not law. The worse thing that is happening in America is judges protecting each other at all cost, no matter how wrong the judge was in his actions or decisions. America cannot last without a fair and honest justice system. Without a fair and honest justice system we will someday become a dictatorship.

I am not a lawyer, I have never studied law, and in fact I only went to the 9th grade in school. I have been blessed by the good Lord and because he gave me a good mind, I was able to have three successful careers. I found out that law is nothing but common sense. I filed my first lawsuit at the age of 77. I had no idea what I was doing and there is still a lot I don't know and will never know.

But in my first lawsuit three judges violated the rules of the courts because they wanted me to lose my case. I sued the three judges and lost that case. I appeal it to your court and as normal your court denied me Certiorari. I sued other judges because I discovered that most all judges are corrupt. I wrote a book about one of my cases and sent you a copy of it. The title is "Corrupt Judges." I have filed other lawsuits and that is when I discovered that all most all judges are corrupt. I appealed every case to your court and lost every one of them. But I decided that one case Stump v. Sparkman 1978 has caused the justice system to fail. If a judge can't be sued then they have no reason to do anything except what they want to do. Writing a rule that will make the judges' honest will take 10 minutes.

Only by the Supreme Court putting a harness with a burden on the judges will the system ever change except for the worse.

I have enclosed a case that I have now in Federal Court in Kentucky and the two judges involved refuse to move the case or refuse to recuse themselves. If you take the time to read the enclosed pleading and you will see what I am trying to tell you. The court system where it be, state or federal, doesn't matter, they are all the same.

I could tell you many stories about how the judges corruptly operate, and get by with it, they are all the same and it wouldn't do any good unless you and your court decide to help clean the system up. I say again that the only way that a judge will do the right thing is he knows if he can be tried in a court and that it will cost him, both money and his position as a judge. You can write a rule and sell it to the court for a legacy

As I said, the time I have left on this earth is limited and then the court system can't hurt me anymore, but I hate to think what the court system will be like in another 5 to ten years. The framers of our country would take it all back if they could have seen the future. But you and I have the ability to see how bad it is going to get. Without an honest justice system our great country will not survive.

Think back to how different the court system is now compared to 1978 when your court wrote a much divided opinion in Stump v. Sparkman. I know the court at that time thought they was helping the system, but they in realty made honest caring judges into corrupt judges. With every passing year the judges are becoming more corrupt across America.

You are fair minded and have an open mind. These are rare traits these days in judges.

You have an opportunity to create something great for the future of America.

Every human should have to obey the laws and every judge should have to obey the laws and the rules of the courts.

I beg you to take action to change the system and make an honest and fair system again for those who will follow you and me.

I thank you for your time and I pray God is watching over you and he is waiting for you.

Ed Flint
I never heard from Judge Kennedy

I had been sending Judge Roberts's letters for a long time and he knew what was taking place in the Federal Courts in Kentucky, between the judges and me. He knew that I was out to find justice. Judge Roberts was weak and did nothing.

Also Judge Roberts along with the other justices on the Supreme Court had read all of the Petitions for Certiorari that I filed with the court, so they knew.

I knew Judge Roberts would not want a hearing about the Code of Conduct subject or any subject that would give me a chance to tell the world about the corrupt federal justice system.

The Holy Spirit told me what happened, regarding other facts, thereafter. Senator McConnell told Judge Roberts that Senator Leahy was serious about holding hearings about the Code of Conduct for judges

I believe that Judge Roberts didn't know what to do about the hearing. He was hoping that I or the subject would go away. Judge Roberts asked Senator McConnell if he could stop the hearing by Senator Leahy.

Senator McConnell told Judge Roberts that he couldn't stop the Senate hearings.

Senator McConnell told Judge Roberts that he might be able to stop Senator Leahy from holding the hearing on the subject of Code of Conduct for judges. But it might take a deal on the Obamacare mandate.

Senator Leahy, the four Democrat Senators and President Obama wanted the Obamacare law, more than anything else, more that the hearing on Code of Conduct for judges.

Some of the conservative judges on the Supreme Court were told what was going on by Judge Roberts. Those judges also didn't want the hearings to take place; they didn't want to have to answer to the America public, about the issues, I would testify about.

Judge Roberts didn't know what to do about Senator Leahy's hearings, after he talked with Senator McConnell and a few members of his court.

Senator Leahy, the other four Senators and President Obama would rather have the Obamacare law become the law of the land, more that they wanted the hearing on judges. So they started putting pressure on Judge Roberts.

Senator McConnell didn't want his judge friends being raked over the coals. He also knew that if a hearing was held and I testified, then everything would be brought out for the America public to hear. He knew that the Supreme Court would be harmed by my testimony and he told Judge Roberts so.

Senator McConnell and Judge Roberts were chatting about this subject, fairly often.

President Obama in April started putting pressure on Judge Roberts. In April during a Rose Garden ceremony the President spoke out, saying "Ultimately, I'm confident that the Supreme Court will not take what would be an unprecedented extraordinary step to overturning a law that was passed by a strong majority of a democratically elected Congress."

Senator Leahy on May 14th made a long speech from the floor of the Senate.

Regarding the subject of Senator Leahy's speech and Judge Roberts, I found an article written by a Mr. Stewart Baker, I don't know Mr. Baker. He stated in his article that there were countless news articles in May warning of the damage to the court and to Roberts's reputation, if the court struck down the mandate. He stated, he had no such sources, but the internal clues in the opinions certainly seem consistent with such a switched by judge Roberts.

This article contained a large report regarding Senator Leahy's speech and I will quote from it. The article stated that Senator Leahy's speech was addressed to Judge Roberts in a sharply partisan tone to keep the law, passed in 2010, in place.

The article stated it was unusual for a member of Congress to tell the high court, how it should vote. Mr. Baker also stated that he wondered at the time, would the chairman of the Judiciary Committee risk the appearance of trying to strong-arm the Court when his remarks wouldn't make a difference.

The article went on and on, about Senator Leahy's speech and it stated that CBS reported, "Judge Roberts was the defenders only hope and that it started to look "gettable" around the time of Senator Leahy's remarks. Suddenly, the Senator's remarks looked a lot less foolhardy. In fact they look like a miraculously prescient and well-timed gamble.

I found another article stated that Jan Crawford a reporter for CBS reported, that Judge Roberts initially aligned with the four conservatives against the mandate, but at some point switched his vote. She also reported, "Relying on two anonymous sources to provide details that would seem to be known only to the justices and their law clerks."

After Senator Leahy speech, Senator McConnell again told Judge Roberts that he couldn't stop the hearing from taking place and Judge Roberts needed to decide what to do.

Judge Roberts knew he had to choose between what he and other conservatives believed or he had to give Senator Leahy and the President what they wanted.

A deal was finally cut between Judge Roberts and Senator Leahy. The deal was brokered by Senator McConnell. The deal was that Judge Roberts would vote in favor of the Obamacare law and Senator Leahy wouldn't hold hearings on Code of Conduct for judges.

For Judge Roberts, voting for the Obamacare law was a lot better than having the senate holds hearing and letting me testify.

The deal was made after Senator Leahy went to the floor of the Senate on May 14, 2012 and gave the long speech to Chief Judge Roberts, about Obamacare.

That speech showed Judge Roberts that Senator Leahy wasn't fooling, he was serious. His speech really said, Judge Roberts, which do you want the hearing or give us your vote on Obamacare.

Judge Roberts after making the deal had his staff draft the opinion that he voted for, which was made public.

Senator McConnell had saved his friends from being confirmed as corrupt judges. Senator McConnell's friends meant more to him than the Obamacare law. The Republicans needed an issue that would stir up their base against President Obama and to raise money on and to also use as an issue to run against, in the 2014 elections.

I got shoved under the bus; my lawsuits are still the same, nothing has changed, in fact worse.

On June 28, 2012, 2012, I wrote Senator Leahy the following letter. I knew when I heard the news about how the Supreme Court voted on Obamacare, that the letters that God had me write, had hit pay dirt.

God had delivered the President and the Senate Democrats a gift from Heaven.

I insert the letter of June 28, 2012 now.

June 28, 2012

Senator Patrick Leahy
437 Russell Senate Bldg.
United States Senate
Washington, DC 20510

Dear Senator Leahy:

This is Ed Flint, again, and I had to write one more time. Today the Supreme Court gave the President a victory regarding health care.

I believe that Chief Judge John Roberts voted with the President in order to keep you from bringing up the immunity to judges issues. He knows the court is wrong for granting judges immunity, to do as they please, but he doesn't know how to face the issue. Judge Scalia is fighting the issue of taking immunity away from the judges and Judge Roberts is not able to control him.

I hope that you hold a hearing on the issue of immunity and other things corrupt things the judges have been doing. I hope Judge Robert's vote doesn't stop you.

America must get the issue of corrupt judges straighten out. Please don't stop. Please get the issue out for all America to see and know.

Thanks, for taking the time to read my letters, I wish you the best of luck.

Ed Flint-   I never heard from him about this letter.

CHAPTER 18

After the Supreme Court approved Obamacare, I had a good talk with myself.

I was happy that God and Jesus got one of the two things that they wanted and that being health insurance for the poor. Jesus performed a lot of miracles while he was on this earth. He healed the poorly, he raised the dead and he feed thousands with very little. Making people well and comfortable was Jesus' goal. Jesus in the Gospel of **Matthew chapter 19** said. **"If you want to be perfect, go and sell all you have and give the money to the poor and you will have treasure in heaven. Then come follow me."** Jesus though-out the New Testament talked about taking care of the poor.

The second thing God and Jesus wanted was equal justice. In **Matthews 5- Jesus in his sermon on the mount**, said **"God blesses those who are hungry and thirsty for justice."** The only way humans on earth can get justice is the way our forefathers wanted justice. That being equal justice for all, by fair and honest judges at all times. The Holy Spirit said God's will was not over; we still had a way to go.

I asked myself, what will happen now, about the Senate holding a hearing about immunity for judges and the other changes that is badly needed in the America Justice System?

As the Holy Spirit told me to do, I kept searching the internet for articles about the entire subject. I wrote letters to Judge Roberts and Senator Leahy inquiring about copies of letters between them. I soon discovered that nobody would cooperate.

Also I knew that if I told anyone about what I had done and what I knew, a lot of people would deny that these letters had anything to do with Judge Roberts switching his vote. I had to try and find out what else happen between the Senator and Judge Roberts, to persuade him to change his mind.

On July 21, 2012, I wrote two letters to Judge Roberts. In one I asked him for letters between himself and Senator Leahy. In the second letter, I asked for the history on how the judges voted in my cases. The first letter to Judge Roberts follows.

July 21, 2012

Attention: Chief Judge John Roberts
Supreme Court of the United States
1 First Street, N. E.
Washington, DC 20543

Chief Judge Roberts:

My name is Ed Flint. I am 82 years old and I am Pro, Se in a number of lawsuits. I understand how the law system works.

I am requesting a copy of all corresponds between Senator Leahy and yourself, regarding the subject of "Judicial Code of Conduct that governs actions by Federal judges."

I discovered in my research of some law cases, that there was a series of letters written, between Senator Patrick Leahy and yourself, regarding the subject of "Judicial Code of Conduct that governs actions by Federal judges."

My research shows that beginning in late 2011 and until the present is when the communications took place. I understand the first letter to you from Senator Leahy, also contained the signature of four (4) other senators.

I look forward to receiving the requested documents from you and hopefully at once.

If more information is needed from me, please advise.

I thank you for your time and effort.

Edward H. Flint

I never heard from Judge Roberts about the letters.

The second letter to Judge Roberts was about the history of my cases the letter was dated July 21, 2012 and a copy follows. I wanted to know if all of the judges voted against me or if only the conservatives' judges did.

July 21, 2012

Attention: Chief Judge John Roberts
Supreme Court of the United States

1 First Street, N. E.
Washington, DC 20543

Chief Judge Roberts:

My name is Ed Flint. I am 82 years old and I am Pro, Se in a number of lawsuits. I understand how the law works.

In the years of 2010, 2011 and 2012 I filed with the Supreme Court fifteen (15) Petitions for Certiorari. I was denied certiorari in every case.

I am now requesting from the Supreme Court, the history on each case. I would like to know what Supreme Court judge made the motion to deny each Petition for Certiorari and how each judge voted on each case. Who voted to deny the petition and who voted to grant the petition in each petition?

The cases are all styled Edward H. Flint v. xxxxxxxxxxx. I will now list the Respondent in each case for you.

1- Target Corporation
2- Churchill Downs Inc.
3- New York Stock Exchange et al
4- Judge A.C. McKay Chauvin
5- Judge John Heyburn
6- Judge Dave Whalin
7- Coach House Inc. et al (No.1)
8- Judge Donald Armstrong
9- Judge Thomas Russell
10- Coach House Inc. et al (No.2)
11- Judge Charles Simpson
12- Judge Katie King
13- Judge James Shake et al
14- MetLife et al
15- Steve Beshear et al

I never heard from Judge Roberts about this letter.

When I didn't receive a reply from Judge Roberts, I wrote a letter Dated August 10, 2012 to the Clerk of the Supreme Court, Mr. Suter. I was asking for information about the letters between Judge Roberts and Senator Leahy and about how the judges voted in my cases. A copy follows.

August 10, 2012

Attn: William K. Suter Clerk of the Court
Supreme Court of the United States
Attention Office of the Clerk
1 First Street, N. E.
Washington, DC 20543

Dear Mr. Suter:

I have enclosed two letters, both dated July 21, 2012, that I sent to Chief Judge John Roberts of the United States Supreme Court.

As you can see, the letters are about, 1) "Judicial Code of Conduct that governs actions by Federal Judges" and the second is about the history of each case that I filed with the court asking for certiorari and I was denied each time.

I ask that you send me all of the documents that I referred to in the enclosed letters to Chief Judge John Roberts.

If you are not in a position to supply m with the requested documents, then I ask you to forward me the name and address of the person who can.

I have called a number of departments at the Supreme Court and I keep getting the run around.

I believe that the information requested is open public records, and I am entitled to review and obtain a copy of them. If the information is confidential, please advise me of that fact. If there are any cost please inform me and I will sent the amount that you tell me I owe,

If you need more information, please contact me.
Thanks
Edward H Flint
I never heard from Mr. Suter regarding this letter.

I wrote the following letter to Senator Leahy on July 23, 2012, regarding the series of letters, between him and Judge Roberts. I sent the letter by fax. I insert it now.

July 23, 2012   FAX PHONE NUMBER 1-202-224-9516

Senator Patrick Leahy
437 Russell Senate Bldg.
United States Senate
Washington, DC 20510

Dear Senator Leahy:

My name is Ed Flint and I have recently sent you a number of letters and copies of Petitions for Writ of Certiorari and the Supreme Court.

I called your office last Friday July 20, 2012 and spoke with a person who said his name was Charlie. I ask him to send me copies of letters between Chief Judge John Roberts of the Supreme Court and yourself. He acknowledged knowing about some of the letters and mentioned a letter in February 2012. He asked for my email address and said he would check it out and send me an email that day with the information. I did not hear from him.

Today Monday July 23, 212 I called and asked for Charlie and I was told that he was not in. I ask to put a message on his voice mail and I was told it was full. So therefore I am writing this letter to you and sending in by fax.

The letters are a series of letters that started in late 2011 and continued until recently. The subject of the letters was "Judicial Code of Conduct that governs the actions of judges. I read where Judge Roberts sent one of the letters to you late on December 31, 2011.

Could you please ask your staff to send me copies of all of the letters?
Thanks

Ed Flint-
I never heard from him about this letter.

On August 5, 2012 I wrote a letter to Senator Leahy that was sent via fax. The letter was concerning the letters between the Judge Roberts and Senator. The letter is as follows.

August 5, 2012   FAX PHONE NUMBER 1-202-224-9516

Senator Patrick Leahy
437 Russell Senate Bldg.
United States Senate
Washington, DC 20510

Attn: Charles, who is Senator Leahy's Assistant

Dear Charles:

This is Ed Flint. I received your phone message that you left on my home phone, on Friday August 3, 2012. Finally after about 7 different phone calls and a letter between us regarding letters about "Judicial Code of Conduct that governs the actions of judges", between Senator Leahy and Chief Judge Roberts, we might be making some head way by the message you left me. Your message stated there was 2 letters, but was between Senator Durbin and Chief Judge Roberts of the Supreme Court, not Senator Leahy. Your message stated one letter was from Senator Durbin and five other Senators and not Senator Leahy and the second letter was from Chief Judge Roberts to Senator Durbin.

You further stated that you would put me in touch with Senator Durbin's staff and they would send me copies of the two letters. I appreciate your help. Will you please explain to Senator Durbin's staff what I am looking for and please give Senator Durbin's staff my phone number and ask them to call me about sending me the letters, or give me their name and phone number, and I will call them.

I am disappointed that you have only accounted for two letters between the Senate and Chief Judge Roberts regarding the subject "Judicial Code of Conduct that governs the actions of judges." When we spoke the first time you stated you knew something about a letter sent in February 2012 and the letter from Judge Roberts was dated December 31, 2011. Also when we spoke on Friday August 3, 2012, before you called me back and left the message pertaining to the 2 letters, you offered to read me a letter and I told you, that I was looking for the whole series of letter, that I believe to be 6 or 7 total.

You have told me a number of times that you and your staff were looking for the 6 or 7 letters that I inquired about on July 12, 2012 and couldn't find them. I asked you in our phone call Friday that if the President of the United States called and wanted a copy of them, would Senate Leahy's staff tell him that they could not find them. I thought that my letter to Senator Leahy, which I faxed on July 23, 2012, was clear and in our conversations you did not have any questions about what I was looking for.

We talked about the letters being confidential and you agreed they weren't confidential. So, please have Senator Durbin's staff send me the 2 that you said the Senator wrote and received and I look forward to receiving the balance from you.

Thanks
Ed Flint

I never received any answers from anyone regarding the subject of letters between Senator Leahy and Judge Roberts.

Neither Judge Roberts, nor Senator Leahy nor the Clerk of the Supreme Court would send me the information I requested, regarding the series of letters between Judge Roberts and Senator Leahy, about "Judicial Code of Conduct that governs actions by Federal judges."

I have continued sending letters to Senator Leahy; still trying to have a hearing. Senator Leahy has never said he wouldn't hold the hearings. I also started sending copies of the letters to Senator Dick Durbin and President Obama. Senator Durbin is in leadership and also on the judiciary committee. The Holy Spirit has not told me the Senate wouldn't hold the hearings. The Holy Spirit keeps telling me to keep sending Senator Leahy letters. I still have hopes that Congress will do the right thing and make the badly needed changes regarding justice in America.

I will now insert letters that I sent to Senator Leahy and Senator Durbin and President Obama after the vote by Judge Roberts on Obamacare.

January 18, 2013

Senator Richard Durbin
711 Hart Senate Office Building
United States Senate
Washington, DC. 20510

Senator Patrick Leahy
437 Russell Senate Bldg.
United States Senate
Washington, DC 20510

Dear Senator Leahy: and Durbin

I have written to both of you about the court system in America and how the Supreme Court is protecting terrible corrupt judges. I have begged you to hold hearing of the Senate Judiciary Committee about corrupt practices and exposed the corruption of the Republican controlled Supreme Court.

Until you do something to stop what is happening, you are letting the Republicans in America grow in strength. The average citizen of this county is being crucified by the court system. Senator Mitch McConnell has to go and only you can make it happen.

I have attached an article from the Courier-Journal newspaper in Louisville, KY. Mitch has the President tied up and he intends to control the appointment to the court. He will only let judges be confirmed that will dance to his tune. The President and all citizens of America are being sent to the slaughter house by Mitch McConnell. The man is sick in the head over power and wants his way or he will destroy America. In the article it refers to two judges, Judge Simpson and Judge Heyburn. Judge Simpson was Mitch's Law Partner and Judge Heyburn was counsel for Mitch when he was Jefferson County KY Executive Judge.

I have sued both of these judges for violating laws and court rules, but the Supreme Court of the United States protects them. Only you can put a stop to this. I told you once that I would testify to your committee what has happen to me. Mitch McConnell has absolute control over the President's appointments. I will testify to all issues and hold nothing back. I am not scared to speech to the public.

I beg you to hold hearings.

Thanks
Ed Flint

Cc to President Obama

I never heard back from any of the three

January 24, 2013

Senator Richard Durbin
711 Hart Senate Office Building
United States Senate
Washington, DC. 20510

Senator Patrick Leahy
437 Russell Senate Bldg.
United States Senate
Washington, DC 20510

Dear Senator Leahy: and Durbin

I have written to both of you about the court system in America and how the Supreme Court is protecting terrible corrupt judges. I have begged you to hold hearing of the Senate Judiciary Committee about corrupt practices and exposed the corruption of the Republican controlled Supreme Court. With this letter, I again beg you to hold hearings.

I have enclosed pleadings in a court case that I am involved in Kentucky. The judge in this case is Judge Simpson who was Senator McConnell law partner here in Louisville. Please ask one of your staff to review these documents. The courts are beating me to death.

I have enclosed a CD video to review. The Jefferson County judges in Circuit Court refused to let me defendant myself. The judge issued an order that I could not file any more lawsuits in Kentucky. I filed a complaint in federal court and the judge's attorney filed a motion to dismiss for failure to state a claim. I am sending the documents that have been filed since the complaint was filed. The judge dismissed my case and the judge has stopped me from filing lawsuits. My rights to file lawsuit has been taken away from me. If it happens to me it will spread to all people who don't think like the conservatives do.

If you look at the CD Video and the judge's order, you will see that the Louisville judge, Judge Simpson granted immunity to the judge who committed this horrible act. As you watch the video you will find that it is hard to believe that this happened in America. 250 years since the United States Constitution was written, this is going on in our courts.

This has been going on for 4 years with me in a number of cases and the United States Supreme Court will not review my cases. They give judges absolute immunity and say a judge can do everything they want and it's OK. I have told you about my cases before. I and every party that the judges don't like don't have a shot in court.

What the judges in Kentucky are doing is the same thing that Senator McConnell does and that is be in absolute control and walk over everyone who gets in their way. The judges know that Senator McConnell will protect them with the Supreme Court.

I know that you know Senator McConnell wants to control everything and will say and do everything to beat another person down. What Senator McConnell did to President Obama is what he does to everyone who will stand up to him. I personal believe that Senator McConnell has a mental problem, over power.

The only way to get my problems straighten out is by the Senate exposing the Supreme Court and their protection of judges. America needs and deserves to know how the court system lets judges do anything and then they receive immunity for their acts.

Until you do something to stop what is happening, you are letting the Republicans in America grow in strength. The average citizen of this county is being crucified by the court system. Senator Mitch McConnell has to go and only you can make it happen. I beg you to hold hearings and expose the system.

I need help with the United States Supreme Court, but don't know how to get it. It seems to me that the 4 Democrats on the court should be against the absolute immunity issue and I keep hoping that one of the other 5 will switch their vote and take a look at the Stump v. Sparkman issue and the court will reverse their position on immunity for judges.

I know that you are fighting the Republicans over their move to take over America and I tell you that until and unless the immunity issue for judges is, changed they will succeed. For America middle class you must succeed or this county is going to explode and a great civil war will take place. The justice system must be changed to where every person is treated equal.

Our county has a system of corrupt judges who can do anything they like and get by with it. It started in 1978 with the Supreme Court's ruling in Stump v. Sparkman and other cases. The system becomes more corrupt with each passing day. I am convinced that only the Senate holding hearing and letting the public know about our system will it change. Only when the public demands change will it become about. No other part of our society has absolute immunity for doing corruption; even congress does not enjoy the immunity that the court system has given themselves.

Our country cannot and will not survive on corruption in the justice system.

Thanks
Ed Flint

Cc to President Obama

I never heard from any of the three

March 12, 2013

Senator Patrick Leahy
437 Russell Senate Bldg.
United States Senate
Washington, DC 20510

Senator Richard Durbin
711 Hart Senate Office Building
United States Senate
Washington, DC. 20510

President Obama
White House
Washington DC 20510

Dear Senator Leahy:

This is Ed Flint again and I need your help. I have enclosed 2 Petitions to the United States Supreme Court for your review. The courts in Kentucky won't give me a shot at justice because I sued judges and they know I will win my cases with a jury trial. They courts are after me big time.

I have told you before in letters how corrupt the court system, both the states and federal courts has become. As you know I have sued a number of judges for violating statutes and court rules, never for vindictive reasons.

The justice system as run by the judges are worse that the divide between the parties in Congress in Washington. I have never asked for nothing but a jury trial to prove my cases.

The 2 petitions that I have enclosed is 1) Flint v. Hewlett Packard It was just filled in the United States Supreme Court and the case No. is 12-1075. Hewlett Packard was producing junk printers and selling them to consumers. I filed the case in the Federal Court in Kentucky. The entire court is made up of Republican appointed judges. If a lawsuit is against a business, the complaint has no chance. The judge in my case dismissed the case by saying I filed the complaint in the wrong jurisdiction. I appealed to the sixth circuit Court of Appeals. The appeals court said the case was filed in the right court, but then they tried the case and said that I had no case. I ask that you or your staff read my petition. I need help from the 4 liberal judges on the Supreme Court if there is any way I can get it.

The second Petition is against a Condo Association in Louisville. I will be filing this Petition in about a month with the Supreme Court. A state Circuit Court granted summary judgment against me. I appeal to the Court of Appeals and they ruled against me. I asked the Kentucky Supreme Court for Discretionary Review and they denied review. I had submitted in my response to the other party's Motion for Summary Judgment, 26 Exhibits that showed I had the evidence to go to a jury with. All courts ignored my evidence and ruled against me. I know this may sound like a small case, but this shows what they are doing to me, because I sued judges. They will never let me win a case in Kentucky.

I ask that you or your staff read this petition and you will see how corrupt the justice system is.

They only shot I have and all I ask for, is the right to try each of my cases with a jury.

The only shot I ask for is the United States Supreme Court gives me that chance.

I believe that 90% of attorneys in America know how corrupt judges have become, however they can't say or do anything about it. Since I am pro, se and I don't have to depend on going in front of a judge to make a living, I can fight corruption like I have been fighting.

By the Senate holding hearing or by the Supreme Court sending my cases back for trial, is only way to start getting the justice system out of the conservatives' hands.

I am doing the will of God. God told me in 2007 through the Holy Spirit to file my complaints and I promise him I would, until he told me to stop. I believe that I am in involved in a fight between God and the Devil. I hope the Holy Spirit has talked with you about this and you will give me all of the help, possible.

I believe that if the 4 Supreme Court liberal judges would vote to send my cases back to the court for the right reasons, justice, it will be the start of correcting the corruption now taking place. I know you are thinking that it takes at least 5 judges to grant certiorari. I belief that there is a chance Judge Roberts might vote for certiorari. I believe that Judge Roberts has had enough of Judge Scalia controlling the votes on their court. I sent Judge Roberts a letter dated August 13, 2012 and have enclosed a copy for each of you to review.

Senator Leahy I only have one copy of the Flint v. Hewlett Packard Petition so if you read that enclosed petition will you please share them with the others, this letter is addressed to. I will send all addresses copy of the other Petition.

America needs to be the America out forefathers wanted.

Thanks
Ed Flint   I never heard from any of three

The Holy Spirit told me to give Judge Roberts a chance to change his ways, before writing any additions in the book. I gave Judge Roberts a chance to change and do the right thing. I wrote him this letter on August 13, 2012.

August 13, 2012

Attention: Chief Justice John Roberts
Supreme Court of the United States
1 First Street, N. E.
Washington, DC 20543

Chief Justice Roberts:

My name is Ed Flint. I am 82 years old and I am Pro, Se in a number of lawsuits. I understand how the law works.

I am writing a book, with the title **"Why Chief Judge Roberts switched his vote on Obamacare."**

Less than 10 people in America know why you switched your vote. I happen to be one of them. I am the only one outside of the Justice Branch or Congress.

The book is about 50% finished. I will finish the book soon, and then I will put it on hold before publishing it. You will find I am a man of my word.

In the years of 2010, 2011 and 2012 I filed with the Supreme Court fifteen (15) Petitions for Certiorari. I was denied certiorari in every case. I was right on every Petition I filed. I suspect that Judge Antonin Scalia was the vocal judge against my petitions. Judge Scalia is the most harmful person in America in my opinion. Judge Scalia believes that only his views counts and he intimidates the other conservatries judges. I know that you are a good person at heart and I know that you want to do the best for America. Don't let any person who wants to be the only one, bull you or sway you. Do what is right for America. Make the changes America needs and deserves.

I am going to try and bring back about 4 of my cases, that your court denied Certiorari. I have one more Federal case that may come up to your court, if I don't win it in the 6th Circuit and Kentucky. I also have about 4 Kentucky cases what might come up to your court, unless the Kentucky Supreme Court should rule in my favor, but for some reason all courts seem to protect judges, who write bad opinions.

If I lose another case in your court, that is when, I will publish my book.

I have asked the United States Senate for copies of the letters between you and Senator Leahy regarding the subject "Judicial Code of Conduct that governs the actions of judges." The Senate has refused up to this point, to give me copies of the letters regarding this subject. The letters between you and Senator Leahy were written between the end of 2011 and May of 2012.

I hope that you will see that I get justice on any Petition or Motion sent to the United States Supreme Court. I pray that the case that I have in 6th Circuit Appeals Court and the ones I have in the Supreme Court and Court of Appeals in Kentucky are ruled on properly and honestly.

I hope that you had a great vacation and are now ready, to get back to work. Thank you for your time to read this and I wish you good luck and much success. I know you are a good man at heart.

Thanks and I look forward to receiving the requested history of each case. If more information is needed please contact me.

Edward H. Flint
I never heard from him

The Holy Spirit told me to keep sending letters, he told me to send a letter to Judge Scalia. I had tried everything else trying to get fair and honest justice for America. So I wrote Judge Scalia a letter on January 27, 2013. Writing to Judge Scalia to is like butting your head against a wall. But the Holy Spirit told me to give him a chance. I would do anything to obtain fair and honest courts, so I wrote him a letter on January 27, 2013. The letter to Judge Scalia is as follows.

January 27, 2013

Attn. Justice Antonia Scalia
Supreme Court of the United States
1 First Street, N. E.
Washington, DC 20543

Dear Justice Scalia:

I have followed you career since you was appointed to the Supreme Court. I am 82 years old and I am concerned about the future of our country for our grandchildren. I know that you are a great believer in the constitution and in the protection of judges.

I have been involved pro, se, in a case that I believe has great conflicts in your two beliefs and I would like for you to shed some light on the two conflicting issues for me. The constitution gives each of us the right to file lawsuits and protect ourselves. Judges sometime see different and so rule.

I was sued in a state circuit court and the Plaintiff asked for a hearing regarding an0 injunction to stop me from suing the association that I had sued. The Plaintiff went first and presented his case. The judge refused to let me present any part my case and ruled and signed an order that prohibited me from suing anyone in the Jefferson County Kentucky Court System and granted them $11,000 attorney fees.

I sued the judge in Federal Court. The Defendant asked for a dismissal of the case base on, "Failure to state a claim." The federal judge dismissed the case for failure to state a claim and fined me for filing the lawsuit and further stated that I could not file any lawsuits against any judge, state or federal. I believe that the judge's actions are in direct conflict with the constitution.

I had enclosed for your review a CD video of the state judge's actions and rulings. I have also enclosed a copy of the complaint I filed in Federal Court and a copy of the judges Memorandum opinion and order.

I ask that you review the video and the judge's order and tell me which issue trumps as being the correct rulings. If the judge's order stands then the constitution means nothing.

As you know we have great judges and we have bad judges and if the judge's order stands, then soon judges could be limiting everyone in filing lawsuit.

I would appreciate your view on which of the two issues trumps the other.

I know that you believe in God and attend church. I struggle every day with Jesus' words that we will be judged on our thought and deeds on earth on judgment day. Life is becoming harder and more confusing each day trying to live by Jesus' teaching.

I thank you for your time to read this letter and I appreciate the long time you have served our country on the Supreme Court.

Ed Flint
I never heard from him.

Since I wrote the manuscript for this book and as it was being prepared for printing, another case has come to the forefront that shows how corrupt and vindictive Federal judges are. I have added that case to the book, so the public can see the truth. I had written about this case, in the letter above to Judge Scalia on January 27, 2013 on page 382-383 and to Senators Leahy and Durbin on January 24, 2013 which is on page 376-377.

In the Jefferson Circuit Court in Kentucky I had sued the condo association where I lived, for violating the association By-Laws, a number of times. The condo association hired a new attorney and he was very friendly with a lot of the local judges. They sued me, asking for an injunction to stop me from filing anymore lawsuits. The circuit court judge scheduled a hearing. At the hearing, the opposing counsel presented his side of why he wanted the injunction and why he asked for attorney fees. When it came time for me to present my side of the case, I stood up and the judges stopped me from talking and said, he didn't have to listen to any one who is not an attorney. He then signed the order the opposing attorney had submitted to him. The order stopped me from filing any more lawsuits without his prior approval, the order granted the other party $11,000.00 in attorney fees. The attorney for Coach House filed a garnishment against my bank account and took all of the money I had in the bank, and filed a lien against my condo.

I attempted to file another lawsuit and the Clerk of the Circuit Court refused to take my complaint and told me that I had to obtain the judge's permission. I refused to talk with a corrupt judge.

I file a complaint the Kentucky Judicial Conduct Commission. And I filed a complaint against the judge in Federal Court in Louisville.

The case in the Federal Court is Edward H. Flint v Martin McDonald case No. 3:12-CV-613-S. The case was assigned to Judge Charles Simpson. Judge Simpson is the judge that is Senator Mitch McConnell's friend, and who worked for Senator McConnell. After the complaint was sent to Judge Martin McDonald, Judge McDonald went to the Kentucky Attorney General to have him defend him. The Kentucky Attorney General was and still is Jack Conway. Jack Conway is a Democrat who ran against Senate Rand Paul for the senate seat. Jack Conway is now said to be running for Governor of Kentucky. Jack Conway answered the complaint for Judge Martin McDonald and asked that the case be dismissed.

I responded to Jack Conway's motion to dismiss and with my response I attached a copy of the video of Judge McDonald's action in the hearing where he denied me an opportunity to defend myself and wouldn't let me speak and denied me from filing lawsuits. I send a copy of the video to Judge Simpson attaching it to my response. I had sent Attorney General Jack Conway a copy of the video attached to a copy of my response.

I also filed a motion asking Judge Simpson to recuse himself from this case. This Judge Simpson is the same judge referred to throughout this book and who was judge in five (5) of the cases in this book. The same judge that refused to recuse himself even though Congress has passed a law that says they must. The law I have referred to throughout the book. He is the Judge that worked for Senator McConnell for seven years; he is the judge that Senator McConnell nominated to be a Federal judge He is the judge that practice law with Senator McConnell.

After I sent the video of the judge's action to Jack Conway, he filed a motion asking the court to sanctions. He asked for a $700.00 sanction, which I can't figure out, because the Attorney General is funded by the state of Kentucky and therefore he has no expense. Also the statutes of Kentucky says the Attorney General of Kentucky don't have to represent these type of corrupt people. Attorney General Jack Conway even submitted a memorandum in support of his motion for sanctions. In his memorandum he stated that I had a history of filing frivolous, repetitive and vexatious lawsuits and he listed every lawsuit I ever filed. No judge has ever ruled that I filed a frivolous, repetitive and vexatious lawsuits; Jack Conway lied, because he knew he had a friendly judge. Jack Conway wanted to be a United States Senator and the word is out he now wants to be Governor of Kentucky. He helped a corrupt judge, by telling lies on me. But some people will do anything for campaign contributions. He would make a poor governor.

Judge Simpson in the Federal case issued an order. His order contained six (6) different items. I will copy Judge Simpson's order for you to read yourself. It was dated January 17, 2013.

(1) The motion of the plaintiff, Edward H. Flint, to disqualify Judge Simpson (DN 6) is DENIED;

(2) The motion of the defendant, Judge Martin McDonald, to dismiss for failure to state a claim (DN 3) is GRANTED;

(3) The motion of the defendant, Judge Martin McDonald, for sanctions (DN 4) is GRANTED;

(4) The plaintiff, Edward H. Flint, is ordered to pay sanctions in the amount of seven hundred dollars ($700);

(5) The plaintiff, Edward H. Flint, is WARNED that if he files any additional lawsuits in this Court against federal or state judges on the grounds that he believes they were biased against him, made incorrect rulings, or otherwise improperly oversaw any of his cases, he will face further sanctions, which could include, but are not limited to, monetary sanctions of more than $700 or the imposition of filing restrictions; and

(5) This action is DISMISSED WITH PREJUDICE.

On June 7, 2013, the Louisville Courier-Journal on its front page had an article with the headlines, "PANEL SUSPENDS JUDGE MCDONALD." The article stated that the suspension is over two complaints. And the article stated, "In the first case, it said he refused to let a litigant who was representing himself last August present any argument because he was not a lawyer."

Judge Simpson let Judge McDonald off, setting him free and the State of Kentucky suspends him for the same action. There is something wrong with this picture. Judge Simpson is obviously corrupt and bias and should resign because he is not fit to be a judge. But he won't resign, because Senator McConnell needs him.

The Supreme Court of the United States has created monsters out of Federal judges. Senator McConnell feeds the monsters by his abuse use of power.

Judge Simpson's actions showed that even when he had proof of corruption in front of him against me, he was still going to rule against me.

This is just another example of what the Federal Court System has done to me and what they are doing to others, every day. The Supreme Court knows what is going on and refuses to do anything to stop it.

Because I won't do Hitler's goosestep to the Supreme Court's and Senator McConnell's tune, I have to suffer. I could get better treatment in a third world country.

My research has not revealed to me if other Republicans Senators were involved, regarding the issue of Judge Roberts switching his vote. The Holy Spirit tells me to keep searching. I personally believe there was others involved, but I have no proof.

The Holy Spirit told me that God was pleased that the Obamacare law became law; however, God still wants the Court System changed so all humans are treated equal. I was told to keep doing what I had been doing. The Holy Spirit also said Jesus is hoping there is some in Washington who believes in him, will help with this cause.

Both Senator Leahy and Judge Roberts lived up to their word in the deal they reached. However they failed to take into account one thing. They didn't take into consideration, what I had been trying to do, which was bring change to a corrupt court system. They forgot that I wanted my story told. I am 83 years old and don't have many years to live. Making the courts fair and honest for the future, is as important to me, as if I had 83 more years to live

We all have to face Jesus' judgment someday and I believe it is a sin not to help other people. Therefore the reason you are reading this book.

The courts documents that are inserted in this book prove the entire federal court system is corrupt; this includes the District Courts, the Sixth Circuit Court of Appeals and the Supreme Court. These are the only Federal courts I can speak about.

An old saying that is so true, "Power corrupt and absolute power corrupts absolutely." Supreme Court judges have been given absolute power, and for life. The Supreme Court judges say their fellow judges are not corrupt. But it's not what they say that counts, but what the judges do. Nowhere in the Constitution does it say that judges can have absolute immunity. But the Supreme Court took it as a right for them and when you take something from someone, you are stealing.

No country can exist as a free country, if their justice system is not fair and honest. For America to be the world's leader, it must have honest judges.

Our Court system is not only corrupt; it is more political than the Congress and to me that is not acceptable. We expect Congress to be political, because they have to be elected, but there is absolutely no reason for the Supreme Court judges to be political.

Corruption is like water; once it lands it keeps filtering down until everything becomes corrupt.

Because of a corrupt court system, that the Supreme Court created, America is crumbling.

America has no chance of surviving, unless people start living by God's Commandments. And the chance of that happening is so small that it must be zillions to one.

I ask each reader to think about this. The Supreme Court is the body we look to; to interpret our constitution and they don't adhere to the Constitution themselves. The Supreme Court is the body that we look to, to make sure that rules and laws are adhered to and the Supreme Court doesn't adhere to them, themselves. What chance does America have?

No entity of any type can give immunity and life time guarantees of employment, to members of that entity who are making decisions that affect people, without a member of that entity, taking advantage of their position.

<u>Nowhere</u> in our Constitution does it say that judges could be or should be given immunity. I believe that our forefathers rejected the thought of such thinking, for anyone. For any member of the Supreme Court to say and or vote for judges to have immunity is not a judge who believes in our constitution, but they are a judge who wants protection for themselves, for being corrupt. Any honest judge, who knows they are not going to be corrupt, doesn't need nor want immunity. Only corrupt judges want immunity.

In their 1978 decision in Stump v. Sparkman the Supreme Court created a monster by using their new found power, to protect themselves and their fellow judges.

The courts are using the Stump v. Sparkman and other similar past case rulings, to give ever judge in America absolute immunity. The courts are giving every judge, be state judges or federal judges, absolute immunity. Some courts are even using the ruling to give other official and or employees of the courts, immunity.

The Supreme Court in 1978 created the monster and they can kill that monster in one day, with a swipe of a pen. They can issue a rule that is designed after what our forefathers wanted. And that is equal justice for America as a whole and not just what judges want. But they must keep politics out of their thoughts. However the swipe of the pen must provide that judges when tried are to be tried by juries and not judges. Fair and honest justice for all has to be the only goal.

My guess is that this Supreme Court will never discuss this issue unless forced to. They have come to believe; they have the last say and can do as they please, on any subject. Apparently they answer to no one, including Congress. There is no oversight of the Federal court system, in America. They have no feelings for average people. They only care about their personal beliefs and desires. They have forgotten what our founding father desired in the Constitution.

It is my opinion that Judge Roberts is weak and Judge Scalia has him and the other conservatives' judges under his thumb and Judge Scalia is the puppet master of the court. This scenario creates a system that is harmful to America. Corruption is not a conservative or a liberal issue, it's the devils issue.

The court cases documents are true; the letters I wrote are originals, by me. There are some people who will never believe this book. Anyone who takes exceptions to other facts in the book should ask the Holy Spirit if they are true or not. Jesus said the Holy Spirit only brings truths.

Our Forefathers made it clear when the Constitution was written and approved; they demanded equal justice for all. Our Forefathers gave future Americans a process on how to change the Constitution if a change was needed. The Supreme Court refuses to live by the Constitution and they have not asked Congress to change the Constitution.

The Supreme Court in 1978, with a swipe of a pen became a dictatorial court and took away equal justice for all. This current Supreme Court had over 10 of my cases before them that they could have used to change the mistake, the 1978 Court made. In their mind, the Supreme Court is above the Constitution.

There are other issues that Congress needs to hold hearings on regarding equal justice for all. One being, Judge Roberts told the Senate during his confirmation hearing that a judge's duty was and I quote,

"Judges are like umpires. Umpires don't make the rules. They apply them. Their role of an umpire and a judge is critical. The make sure everybody plays by the rules. But it is a limited role. Nobody ever went to a ball game to see the umpires." His jurisprudence would be characterized by "modesty and humility."

The question is, did Judge Roberts lie to the Senate? If he lied he should be impeached. If he told the truth, then the entire Supreme Court is letting judges violate their duty, every day and all of them should be impeached. I inserted 14 lawsuits into this book and the Supreme Court in every case; let a judge or judges violate their duty. Every judge that was involved in my cases, failed to judge by their duty.

Supreme Court judges violate their duty, when they let other judges violate their duty. This has become the new America, justice for judges, but not the public.

Judge Roberts should resign from the Supreme Court for the way he has conducted himself and any Supreme Court judge that voted to deny me certiorari should resign from the Supreme Court. America must have judges that are fair and honest at all cost. I have reasons to believe Judge Roberts covered up for one and maybe two of Senator McConnell's corrupt judge friends.

I will continue writing letters regarding this nightmare, hoping the House and Senate will hold hearings. I hope others who read this book, from both parties, who want equal justice, will join me, by writing their Congressman and Senator and ask for hearings on a Code of Conduct for judges. God and I will welcome all of the help we can get.

If the Senate and House don't hold hearing after they read the details in this book, they will never hold hearings. Neither party Republican nor Democrat wants America to know the truth, about corrupt judges. Neither party has the guts to inform the public about the truth.

If Judge Roberts or Senator McConnell or Senator Leahy or anyone else denies the contents of this book, I beg both houses of Congress to hold public hearings and let all sides explain their side of the facts to the public.

I ask you to think about this; Every time a judge makes a decision, they adversely affect someone. Sometimes their decisions adversely affect a number of people and sometimes their decisions adversely affect the entire country. Every person who life's is being affected deserves at the very least, a fair and honest judge.

Any judge that is not fair and honest, is dishonest. And dishonesty is corruption. No Democracy can exist, if its courts are run by corrupt judges.

Our Constitution was drafted to stop abuse of power by any branch, but the Supreme Court abused their power and took away our right to have fair and honest justice and refuse to correct it. They did it intentional and the Congress of the United States has let them get by with abusing that power. There is something wrong with this picture.

It will be interesting to see if the Republicans and Democrats in Congress continue to fight each other or if they can come together to hold hearing in both the House and Senate on the issue of absolute immunity for judges and the overseeing of the Supreme Court. Every member of Congress that defends or agrees that absolute immunity for judges is a good thing and or the Supreme Court is doing a good job, should be voted out of office. This is not a Republican or Democrat issue; this is an issue about our county having a fair and honest and equal justice system, for every American.

In 1978 the United States Supreme Court by their ruling in Stump v. Sparkman that gave absolute immunity to judges, made all judges in America "God "over every person who files a lawsuit in America. Supreme Court judges thought more about using their power, than they cared for equal judgment for their fellow man. What a great country we have become. Most judges' motto is to hell with my fellow man.

God's first Commandment states, we should have no other God, except him. And we wonder why America is having so many problems. We keep offending our Heavenly Father. God is mad at the way the Supreme Court does as it pleases and doesn't do the duty it was meant to do. God was involved in establishing America and in the establishing the Supreme Court. He wants the courts to be equal for everyone.

Now you know the reason that God had me write this book through the Holy Spirit.

Now you know why Judge Roberts switched and voted for Obamacare.

www.ingramcontent.com/pod-product-compliance
Lightning Source LLC
Chambersburg PA
CBHW081430170526
45166CB00008B/2150